GAME SIX

Cincinnati, Boston, and the 1975 World Series:
The Triumph of America's Pastime

Mark Frost

HYPERION
NEW YORK

Library of Congress Cataloging-in-Publication Data

Frost, Mark
    Game six : Cincinnati, Boston, and the 1975 world series : the triumph of America's pastime / Mark Frost.
        p. cm.
    ISBN 978-1-4013-2310-3
    1. Cincinnati Reds (Baseball team)   2. Boston Red Sox (Baseball team)   3. World Series (Baseball)   4. Baseball—United States—Social aspects.   5. Baseball—United States—History.   I. Title.
    GV878.4.F76 2009
    796.357'646—dc22

                                                        2009023227

Hyperion books are available for special promotions and premiums. For details contact the HarperCollins Special Markets Department in the New York office at 212-207-7528, fax 212-207-7222, or email spsales@harpercollins.com.

Design by Karen Minster

FIRST EDITION

10   9   8   7   6   5   4   3   2   1

THIS LABEL APPLIES TO TEXT STOCK

We try to produce the most beautiful books possible, and we are also extremely concerned about the impact of our manufacturing process on the forests of the world and the environment as a whole. Accordingly, we've made sure that all of the paper we use has been certified as coming from forests that are managed to ensure the protection of the people and wildlife dependent upon them.

To Vin Scully

Baseball's master storyteller

GAME SIX

Georgie was always brave enough to do the right thing.

Rod Dedeaux

South Central Los Angeles, 1943

A NEW BASEBALL, SUBMITTED TO CARING AND REGULAR maintenance, might last an entire summer on the Rancho Playground, and there one lay in the dirt of a vacant lot, an unclaimed jewel, just outside the right field fence. The boys all jumped at it, but the smallest and quickest of them grabbed it fast, and to the others' shock withheld it.

Came from the ball field, said George Anderson, nine. *Ain't ours. We gotta give it back.*

Poor kids, toughened by poverty and the Depression, weren't used to forgoing found treasure for principle, but George, a year removed from Bridgewater, South Dakota, and outdoor plumbing, and tougher already than most, stood up to them. He walked back around the fences to the diamond, where the uniformed college boys were practicing on Bovard Field, picked out the older man who seemed to be in charge, and held up the ball.

This yours?

The coach stared at him with—what was that, shock or amusement?

Found it lying out past the fence.

Where you live, son?

Couple blocks, said George, and held it out again, thinking maybe this guy had forgotten the main point.

The coach, Rod Dedeaux, took the ball this time and studied the youngster for a moment.

What's your name, kid?

George Anderson.

George, how'd you like to be my batboy?

Diogenes, the eccentric Greek philosopher-cynic, who famously searched throughout Athens for a single honest man, claimed he never found one, but Rod Dedeaux just had. And so, for the next seven years, George Lee Anderson worked as the batboy for the University of Southern California's baseball team. The pay wasn't much; what little there was came from Dedeaux's pocket, although anything was a help to the hard-pressed Anderson family: George's father, Leroy, a painter and onetime semi-pro catcher back in South Dakota, had moved to Los Angeles to work the wartime shipyards and feed his four kids.

Raoul Martial "Rod" Dedeaux, like Leroy Anderson and most of the boys in the generation that came of age during the Babe's heyday, grew up on dreams of playing major-league baseball. Unlike most, Dedeaux had the goods: As the captain and star shortstop for USC, six months after his twenty-first birthday Dedeaux signed a contract with the Brooklyn Dodgers, played that summer for their minor-league affiliate in Dayton, Ohio, and earned a late-season call-up to the National League club.

A lot of promise, this Cajun kid, his longtime mentor and Dodgers manager, Casey Stengel, told the *Brooklyn Eagle. Exceptional glove, live bat; nothing but blue sky.*

Just starting his legendary career as a manager, Stengel had first scouted Dedeaux in high school and thought so much of the young prospect he paid Rod's $1,500 signing bonus out of his own pocket. On September 28, Stengel penciled Dedeaux in at shortstop against the Phillies, and he lived up to Stengel's hype in his first professional start, going 1–4 and driving in a run. The game itself, the back end of a meaningless doubleheader at Ebbets Field between two clubs long out of the pennant race, was played in front of exactly 124 paying customers and halted on account of darkness after eight innings, in a 4–4 tie.

The Dodgers never finished that game, and neither did their new shortstop; he never got the chance. After only his second professional game, Dedeaux's major-league career ended with terrible suddenness when he learned that a violent missed swing he'd taken had cracked a lumbar vertebra. He returned to Los Angeles and, using the last $500 of his bonus money, founded a trucking business with his father that succeeded so spectacularly he would never worry about a payday for the rest of his life. The college coach he'd played for at USC entered the navy in 1942 when the war began, and recommended Rod to take over his position with the team. Unfit for military service because of his injured back, Dedeaux took the job, but would accept only a token salary of $1 a year; and that spring, young George Anderson walked onto his diamond. During the off-season winter months of professional baseball, when he was back home in Southern California, Dedeaux's old mentor Casey Stengel became a constant presence on the USC practice field as well. The "Old Perfessor" managed Oakland in the Pacific Coast League after the war, before his glory years with the Yankees began in 1949, but for all the fun sportswriters made over the years of his famously fractured English, Stengel was as knowledgeable about the game as any man alive. (Dedeaux insisted he always understood everything Casey said, admitting, "which sometimes worried me.") For his batboy George Anderson, the chance to listen to the old fella talk baseball every day was, as Dedeaux years later described it, "like sitting at the feet of Socrates . . . if George had only known who Socrates was."

During his final season with the team, Anderson worked the game when the Trojans won their first College Baseball World Series for Rod Dedeaux in 1948. Before he retired thirty-eight years later, Rod Dedeaux would go on to capture ten more NCAA championships, winning 1,332 games along the way, more than any baseball coach in college history. He would also manage two American Olympic teams and train the actors in the movies *Field of Dreams* and *A League of Their Own* to look like major leaguers. Forever grateful for the early faith Casey Stengel had shown in him, Dedeaux later became the Old Perfessor's legal protector during his long and troubled dotage. Dedeaux never asked for or accepted more than that $1-a-year salary from USC, and became as beloved and celebrated a father figure inside his sport, if less well known outside of it, as John Wooden was in his, across town at UCLA. In the course of his joyful life's work, Rod Dedeaux recruited, taught, and nurtured dozens of remarkable young talents who would go on to play and star in the major leagues.

That scrappy little batboy Anderson never played a game for USC or any other college; higher education wasn't in the cards for Georgie. He had no taste for academics, but his years with Dedeaux gave him a tireless appetite for hard work, and the wisdom and enthusiasm of a great teacher soaked deep into his character. Using the skills and competitive fire he'd honed at Dedeaux's side, Anderson earned All-City honors twice playing shortstop for Dorsey High, a team that won forty-two games in a row on its way to consecutive championships, a record unmatched in Los Angeles to this day.

Harold "Lefty" Phillips, a former minor-league pitcher and then big-league scout who covered Southern California, took an early interest in George Anderson. Lefty befriended the boy, intrigued by his feral intensity on the field and, unheard of in a kid his age, his insatiable thirst for knowledge about the guts of the game. On Phillips's recommendation, the Brooklyn Dodgers signed Anderson to a minor-league contract less than an hour out of Dorsey High. He cashed his bonus check—a $3,000 windfall—and the Dodgers dispatched him to their developmental farm team just up the coast in Santa Barbara. George Anderson's dreams of playing professional baseball were right on track; given his lack of interest in all things academic, they needed to be.

A few years later, in 1955, the third season of George's wayward journey toward the big leagues, his team's radio announcer in Fort Worth commented on what had become a fairly common scene that summer: Anderson, hopping mad after a questionable call at second, going off on an umpire.

The sparks are flying again tonight.

Before he knew it, George "Sparky" Anderson had been stamped with what every bona fide major leaguer needed to make it to the top: a nickname.

Nicanor del Campo, Havana, Cuba, 1958

THE OLD MAN didn't want to see his son pitch. Why encourage him down this path where only disappointment and heartbreak waited? Let the boy finish his education, go to trade school, learn a craft or profession, something he could put his hands around besides a bat or ball.

Why did we take the trouble to send him to that private school, Isabel? Why did we teach him to speak English?

The first games his son played didn't even involve a real ball, but a stone wrapped in newspaper—or a cork freighted with nails—stuffed into a cigarette box, then smashed as close as possible to round and covered in Band-Aids. An old broom handle for a bat. When there was almost no money to eat, real equipment remained miles out of reach, but all the kids played just the same. Baseball had taken root on the island in the second half of the nineteenth century, not long after finding life in the United States, but it quickly permeated the bloodstream of Cuban culture, becoming the national sport and spreading from there throughout the Caribbean, then into Mexico and from there into Central and South America.

Baseball is no life for him. No life for any man.

El corcho, they called the street game. Cuban stickball. Young Luis still hit that makeshift *pelota* out of sight. And when he was pitching? No chance. Just take your cuts and pray he didn't drill you in the ribs.

Truth be told, everything Luis did, from cards to marbles, seemed exceptional, effortless, but he carried his talents so lightly, with such warmth and modest grace, that he inspired only affection in his many friends, not envy. And he always found a way to make you laugh, with that scratchy high-pitched voice, the joke you never saw coming, like that crazy curveball of his. You didn't mind losing to a boy like this—although you always did—but with his generosity of spirit you somehow only liked him more for it.

Once he reached the required age for Little League and took the mound as a pitcher, he dominated kids three and four years older; they could hardly even see his fastball. Officials refused to let him pitch in night games, for fear batters wouldn't pick up a pitch coming at their head under the insufficient lights. From the start, like so many other boys around the Americas, Luis Clemente Tiant began early to dream about the major leagues. But young Luis stood apart in more ways than just his talent: His Old Man had already lived the same dream.

Luis Eleuterio "Lefty" Tiant played professional baseball for twenty-two years, from 1926 to 1948, the last fourteen in the American Negro Leagues, where he won more than one hundred games, including two pennants and a championship, for the New York Cubans. Historians believe he may have been the best left-hander in the Negro Leagues' existence, a master of the art of pitching with impeccable control. A tall, elegant splinter of a man, they called him "Sir Skinny." His screwball—what he called his "drop" pitch—falling low and away from right-handed batters, was said to be even nastier than that of the New York Giants' acknowledged junk-ball genius, Carl Hubbell. Tiant developed such an extraordinary pickoff move to first base that he once nailed a runner there and so baffled the batter with his motion that the man swung at a phantom pitch, which started an argument about whether he'd struck out for a double play. Tiant faced most of the major leagues' Hall of Fame contemporaries at one time or another in exhibition games, and handled them all, including Babe Ruth and Mel Ott; Lefty held the Babe to a long single in six at bats, and Ott went hitless.

Consider the price he paid for that dream. Although they often played in Yankee Stadium and the Polo Grounds—when their white teams were away—the New York Cubans never had a home stadium, so they played their entire season on the road; a team of émigrés from the island, most of whom didn't speak English, the Cubans occupied an even lower social caste than the American blacks they usually competed against. Seven months a year away from his wife and only son, in the shadows of an unfamiliar culture, suffering the worst of Jim Crow apartheid in *los Estados Unidos*—third-class trains, broken-down buses, and segregated rooming houses—for his troubles, Sir Skinny never collected more than $1.50 a game. And by the time the Lords of Baseball decided to let Jackie Robinson take the field in a Brooklyn Dodgers uniform alongside Caucasian players, Luis Tiant Sr. was forty years old.

And at that age, in 1947, he put together one last extraordinary season: 10–0 with three shutouts and two victories in the Negro League World Series to lead his Cubans past the Cleveland Buckeyes. Then, his pitching arm beaten dead, the Old Man called it quits and went home to the island for good. He was widely recognized as the greatest pitcher—perhaps the greatest athlete—ever in Cuban history, and all he had to show for all those years was enough to buy half interest in a truck with his brother-in-law. The great *El Tiante* moved furniture for a living now, his wife, Isabel, worked as a cook, and they had scraped and saved and sent their only child to that private school where they taught him English so that he could one day build a better life.

Baseball couldn't give his son anything. The Old Man knew it every time he passed a mirror. He was only fifty-two, but with his mournful, deeply etched face and drugstore false teeth, he looked seventy.

Just watch him play, Isabel insisted. *Give him that much.*

You don't know about baseball, he told her. *I don't want him to be treated like I was, to be persecuted and spit on like I was in America. And for that he will have to give up his friends, his family, his country.*

But this is what he wants, she said. *Things are different now in America, even in baseball. He deserves a chance, we owe him at least that much.*

Their son, eighteen years old now, had pitched his way onto a Havana All-Star team, competing against the best players from the other three provinces of Cuba. So much excitement around the city and in the newspapers about this Second Coming of *El Tiante:* Could the son possibly be as good as, or even better than, his father? There would be scouts in the stands, from both Mexico and America. One of them, thirty-five-year-old Bobby Avila, had once been a batboy for Señor Tiant's old Negro League team. A generation younger, Avila had lived a different dream after Robinson broke the color barrier, and gone on to become one of major-league baseball's first great Latin players—an American League batting title in '54, three times an All-Star at second base for the Cleveland Indians. Now a national hero in his native Mexico, when he played winter ball in Cuba Bobby Avila had stayed in touch with the Old Man and followed with interest young Luis's development since he was a little boy.

From the bus stop behind the factory you could see the playing field in Cerro Stadium. Señor Tiant stepped off the bus just as the game started and watched from there, hoping he wouldn't be noticed. He saw his son throw an overpowering game.

He has so much to learn. That move to first base, it could be much better. The leg kick, if he just hesitated a little, yes, I could show him that. Maybe he comes a little too much sidearm, across his body, that could hurt him eventually. If he mixed up his delivery, changed the angle, came overhand with that curve, then sidearm with the fastball. He throws hard, yes, but throwing isn't pitching . . .

But, Madre de Dios, he's a pitcher.

Of course Luis knew he had been there from the start. Spotted him hiding near the bus stop on his first trip out from the bench. Not much escaped his deceptively sleepy eyes. But he didn't look that way again, wasn't going to let his father know he knew. Luis left behind his kind and gentle nature when he walked between the lines; he had work to do out here. These batters deserved no respect, they were only there to take money from his pocket.

Okay, chump, dig in all you like, that plate belongs to me. You like that? You see that one? How about this? Okay, sit down. Bye-bye. Next victim.

Luis had from almost his first game known he belonged on a pitching mound. Curiously calm and in command, he just didn't experience the position's crushing pressures as a stress, but seemed to welcome them as a form of pleasure. Genetics? Yes, no doubt; he was his father's son, and already had the presence, the *cojones,* of a matador, but Tiant Senior remained a lanky rapier of a man, whereas there was more than a little of the bull in Luis: solid legs, thick core, barrel chest, and burly shoulders.

And a few days later Bobby Avila came to call at their house to tell them of the offer from the general manager of the Mexico City Tigers:

One hundred and fifty dollars a month to start, but the American clubs keep their eyes on the Mexican League now; someone's going to bring him over into their system if all goes well, I'll make sure of that.

Luis watched his father anxiously—$150!—but didn't speak a word. He had always been a dutiful son, secure in his parents' love, always respectful of their wishes. He saw only sorrow in his father's big, expressive features as he heard the news; he could never hide his feelings. He didn't want his boy to go.

But he nodded yes.

Now we're back in the lion's den.
If they beat us here, they deserve it.

CARL YASTRZEMSKI

If a man put a gun to my head and said
I'm going to pull the trigger if you lose this game,
I'd want Luis Tiant to pitch that game.

RED SOX MANAGER DARRELL JOHNSON

THE SUN ROSE ON BOSTON, MASSACHUSETTS, AT 7:03 IN THE morning on Tuesday, October 21, 1975. This, in itself, was news. Local meteorologists, who had been under siege for the last four days, hastily issued dispatches of an optimistic forecast: partly sunny, high near seventy degrees, 10–15 mph winds from the west to southwest. Clearing throughout the day and cooler, with temperatures dropping into the high fifties by 8:30 P.M., the moment on the mind of every resident in the region, native or itinerant, as they stirred that morning.

Game time.

BASEBALL'S FIFTH COMMISSIONER, Bowie Kuhn, woke shortly after six in his presidential suite at the Ritz-Carlton, went straight to the window, and saw the early rays of light filtering across the Boston Common. He had held his job for nearly seven years now, presiding over one of the rockiest periods in the game's history, beset by labor unrest and falling attendance. But to date this tense, competitive World Series had shown signs of reviving interest in the game, until the New England weather intervened. The sturdy law-yer's Oxfords that Kuhn had worn the day before to walk the soggy field, before postponing the game at yet another elaborately staged press conference, still sat drying by the fireplace. When the rains first hit, Kuhn had moved Game Six of the World Series, originally scheduled for Saturday afternoon, to Sunday afternoon, and then pushed it back again, as the storm lingering over Boston persisted, to Monday night. Now, at last, after a third day's delay, sunshine on Tuesday morning.

The forty-eight-year-old Kuhn rang for coffee, sat down at his desk, and paged through his phone book. Even before he notified Red Sox owner Tom Yawkey, in his own suite down the hall at the Ritz, his first call would be to network executive Chet Simmons. The commissioner worked for baseball's twenty-four wealthy own-ers, but during World Series Week NBC paid the bills.

Chet, I am cautiously optimistic that we are back in business.

AT THE STATLER HILTON, half a mile closer to Fenway Park, Cin-cinnati Reds manager Sparky Anderson woke at first light—no alarm clock necessary for Sparky—and crept to the window. One look outside and the butterflies in his guts cranked their engines; his stomach was so jumpy he could have juggled three eggs on it. His nimble, restless mind leapt to the morning's systematic check-list as he popped his first stick of gum and headed for the shower. *Let's get it on.*

Two floors below, the Reds' All-Star catcher Johnny Lee Bench, still in the grip of a lingering, miserable virus, registered the sky outside, his weather eye delivering an instant calculation—*ball game today*—then rolled over and went back to sleep.

IN A SUITE at the Parker House, David Israel, a twenty-four-year-old sports reporter for the afternoon *Washington Star,* had stayed up long after midnight, dictating his game-day column to an inexperienced receptionist at the newspaper's switchboard. Only one year out of Northwestern's prestigious journalism school, Israel had brashly conned his way into his deluxe digs for the whole weekend when the rains washed out Saturday's Game Six. As the deluge lingered, his suite had become a crash pad for a number of other reporters, who had either checked out of their own rooms by the time the game was called or missed the day's last shuttle back to New York. When he woke up that morning, two of Israel's journalistic idols were sacked out in his living room: NBC's Dick Schaap and the *New York Times* baseball scholar George Vecsey. Schaap cracked open an eye as Israel called down for coffee; ever solicitous of his elders, Israel apologized profusely for waking Schaap up the night before during his lengthy, frustrating phone call to the newspaper. His regular dictationist—a sharp young cookie named Maureen Dowd— had been unavailable, and it seemed the woman he ended up with had never seen a baseball game before.

"I knew you were in trouble when you had to spell 'World Series,'" said Schaap.

IN SUBURBAN MILTON, ten miles to the south, Luis Tiant was the first one out of bed in his full and bustling household, padding to the kitchen before the kids woke up for school. Still trying to shake off his own nasty cold, he drank his first coffee and looked out at bleak autumn sunlight brushing the lush green wood in his backyard, just off the eleventh fairway of Wollaston Golf Club. His back and shoulder still felt tender from his last outing, a prodigious 163-pitch complete-game victory in Game Four at Cincinnati the previous Wednesday.

Okay. So we play. Doc says my back's okay, but this is late October in Boston and it's going to be fucking cold tonight.

He downed one of Doc Shapiro's miracle anti-inflammatories. Morning prayers to follow.

. . .

AT HIS FURNISHED APARTMENT a few miles to the east of Milton, in Quincy, Red Sox center fielder Fred Michael Lynn had stayed up well past midnight with his wife and some of his young teammates, watching O. J. Simpson's Buffalo Bills lose their first game of the year to the New York Giants on *Monday Night Football.* Like the Juice, Fred had been recruited to play football at USC, returning punts and backing up future Hall of Fame wide receiver Lynn Swann, before deciding to focus exclusively during his last two years on baseball for Rod Dedeaux. Hearing this unwelcome news, USC's imperious football coach John McKay had told Lynn he was making the biggest mistake of his life, and didn't speak to him again for twenty years. After starring on three consecutive NCAA championship teams for Coach Dedeaux and now, less than a year later, putting together what was beyond dispute the most sensational rookie season of any player in the history of pro baseball, no one else ever second-guessed Fred Lynn's decision again. Bigger postseason awards were in the offing, but Lynn was about to learn that morning he'd been the leading vote getter on the Associated Press Major-League All-Star team for 1975.

They hadn't played ball now in five days, since flying back to Boston from Cincinnati early Friday morning, the Red Sox's longest break between games since spring training began back in March. From the weather reports on the radio Lynn figured they'd finally get in Game Six that night, but he pondered the curious lack of excitement he felt about the prospect.

Like we're going to be playing any other regular season game.

He wasn't the only one who felt it that morning; players, coaches, journalists, and fans all over Boston agreed that this delay—tied now for the second longest in World Series history—had really taken the edge off the game.

Well, that'll probably change when we get to the park.

AT THE *BOSTON GLOBE* on Morrissey Boulevard, the sports department staff slowly rolled in around nine, more than a few of them the worse for wear. Editor Tom Winship called their morning meeting to order and began to divvy up the day's assignments on Game Six story lines. They had written themselves cross-eyed trying to wring angles and fill columns out of the three-day delay—a few had finally thrown up their hands and written about how little they had to write about—and with no small relief they welcomed the chance to process and package the meat of a real game again. Bob Ryan, Bud Collins, Cliff Keane, Will McDonough, Leigh Montville, Ray Fitzgerald, Peter Gammons—old-school newspapermen, self-styled sentimental cynics covering the most literate sports-mad town since Athens. While the Celtics and Bruins routinely won championships and their fans' dogged admiration, the Red Sox remained the region's more inconstant and elusive muse; a beautiful, terrible object of obsession, blind faith, and reliably unhappy endings.

Globe staffers would all pursue variations on the same themes that day: After a valiant, uplifting pennant-winning season and their first postseason series victory in fifty-seven years—a commanding three-game sweep over Oakland in the American League Championship—Boston's beloved, star-crossed Sox found themselves down three games to two in the World Series against Cincinnati's indomitable Big Red Machine. *Here we go again:* The bastards had raised their hopes all summer then delivered them once again to the brink of heartbreak, and for the past few days a damned nor'easter wouldn't even let them get it over with. Would the old funereal dirge play again at Fenway tonight, or could this unlikeliest collection of local heroes mount one last stand and extend the Series to a seventh and deciding game?

Lesley Visser, twenty-two, Quincy native, recent graduate of Boston College, former cheerleader—and every man on staff's favorite cub reporter—hovered on the margins and kept quiet whenever this formidable group gathered. Sportswriting had for a century been exclusively a male fraternity; Visser wasn't just a pioneer, she was nearly Jackie Robinson. Following the unlikely dream she'd had since the age of ten had brought her inside the doors of her favorite newspaper, but just by inches; only patience, sustained excellence, and quiet persistence would take her any further. When the meeting broke at ten, once again without a Series-related assignment sent her way, and the tribe's elders dispersed to begin tapping sources, Lesley walked back to patrol her bottom-rung beat, checking the schedule of high school football games she'd be covering that weekend.

Disappointment must have shown on her face—she hadn't even been able to finagle a ticket to any of the three Series games at Fenway yet—because Peter Gammons suddenly appeared over her desk, holding up a small green tag in his hand, saying he had called in a favor. She didn't initially realize what she was looking at, and then noticed the word "PRESS." And someone had scrawled across it with a felt-tip pen: "**Game Six.**"

A press pass.

Peter got a hug. The pass went into Lesley's purse.

ALONE ON THE DIAMOND at Fenway early that morning, Joe Mooney stood out near second base, waiting for the helicopters. If they'd held a contest for "grumpiest and most exhausted man in New England," Mooney would've won by acclamation. The park's head groundskeeper had manned his post for four straight days and nights like an army surgeon at Gettysburg. He had pulled and replaced the tarps over the field for the "Grand Pooh-bah" Kuhn a dozen times and dumped five tons of a moisture-absorbent substance called "Turface" onto the dirt and grass. The infield, against all odds, remained playable, while the rain had slowed to a drizzle that morning and finally stopped midday. Then Kuhn goes ahead at his Monday afternoon press conference yesterday and dumps the third day's delay on Joe Mooney.

"Although the weather is improving, the groundskeeper here doesn't feel there's any way the field can be ready for play by tonight."

The dough they pay that big stiff and all he does is parade around sticking his fancy Florsheims in puddles, sniffing the air like Punxsutawney Phil with eight hundred reporters and the players hanging on every word, and then he says the field's not playable. And besides, that *wasn't* what Mooney had told him when he'd first asked him about it at noon. He'd said: "Give me eight hours and we'll have the field ready."

What His Excellency didn't *say at his press conference was he didn't want his precious Game Six going up against* Monday Night Football.

This time of year moisture always seeped up in the outfield at night. The park was built on the fens—*That's a fancy word for swamp, okay?*—that chunk of the Old Back Bay they dredged out and land-filled when the city grew west a hundred years ago. Add three inches of rain on top of that and you're always gonna get water backing up out there, but it was nothing Joe Mooney and his crew couldn't handle.

So, whatever, it's done with, we'll play tonight.

Mooney could see his shadow in the dirt; that was a good sign. He had kept the lights on all night, calling on every little bit of heat to help dry out the turf. He heard the dull thwack of the rotor blades as the choppers reached earshot. Mooney thumbed his walkie-talkie to life and guided them gingerly in over the light stands fanning the rim of Fenway Park, until they leveled at twenty feet above left and right field, jacked up the rpm's, and went to work fanning the grass.

Maybe the commissioner would like us to send one over to his hotel after and dry his hair for him.

WALKING BRISKLY down Boylston Street on his way to Fenway Park, Chet Simmons decided he had a good kind of problem. Although Bowie Kuhn insisted they stage another walk-through on the field before making it official—as far as the media was concerned— the commissioner's phone call had woken him with the welcome news that Game Six was a "go" for tonight. As the executive in charge of NBC's exclusive radio and television coverage of the World Series, Simmons immediately pushed the button kick-starting the network's national machinery to prepare for the broadcast, while his bottom-line mind quickly sorted through a calculus of pluses and minuses. Although many of his corporate colleagues had yesterday relished the machismo prospect of the Series going head-to-head against ABC's *Monday Night Football*, Simmons knew that at best the likely outcome would have been a bloody draw—with CBS and its slate of established middle-brow sitcoms, anchored by *All in the Family*, being the main beneficiary. Now that they had Tuesday night to themselves, this third and last rain delay looked like a blessing in disguise.

But NBC's field accountant in Boston had called Chet soon after Kuhn's report with news that the rain delay was going to cost the network $150,000 in additional hotel and living expenses. And what was worse, the extended days of work for his technicians and engineers, who had remained on standby throughout the lost soggy weekend, meant they were now unavoidably in "golden time" for the one or two Series games that remained—triple the standard union wage.

Simmons then received a more welcome call from Carl Lindeman, president of NBC Sports, telling him that this World Series had averaged a robust 43 percent share of the viewing audience during its first five games, winning six out of seven nights and the week for NBC and lifting them into a narrow lead for the young season over CBS. The three midweek night games had performed surprisingly well, climaxing in a 48 percent share on Thursday's Game Five in Cincinnati. Night games, introduced into the World Series only in 1971 and still a subject of bitter debate for baseball purists, were clearly the wave of the future. The math was simple: A sixty-second spot during any prime time Series game cost advertisers $100,000. Only after any World Series moved beyond the four games of a dreaded sweep were the network's baseline investments covered, and every nickel banked after that was pure profit. Since NBC first broadcast it in 1947, the World Series had perennially retained its title as the biggest ratings event of the television year. This year's balance sheet looked rosy for NBC, and that was very good news for Chet Simmons.

But all was far from well in baseball. The previous three World Series had been won by Charles Finley's colorful, small-market Oakland Athletics. Great for Charles Finley, one of the game's last and most flamboyant showmen/owners, but not necessarily good for the sport; since the late sixties, for the first time in decades, both live attendance and television ratings had begun to deteriorate. Not coincidentally, the game's bellwether big-city franchise New York Yankees—winners of nearly half the World Series played in the last fifty years—had suffered through a decade of disappointment and decline. Hard to believe now, in a modern world that daily serves up hundreds of viewing choices—and the complete daily schedule in baseball, if you care to pay for it—but in 1975 the multiple channels offered by cable TV penetrated less than 10 percent of America's top media markets, so relatively few games outside of local broadcasts were ever seen. The three major networks still held an ironclad monopoly on the nation's viewing options, and NBC owned the baseball contract, and since the 1950s NBC had determined that during the regular season Americans should consume only one nationally televised game a week.

Trouble of a more ominous nature threatened from the heart of the game itself. Encouraged by the radical social turn much of the country had taken since the late 1960s, baseball players were becoming increasingly vocal about the gross inequity of baseball's reserve clause, a restrictive, almost medieval legal provision that allowed teams to retain their rights to any player they had under contract for a year after that contract expired. As a result, bargaining power for the player hardly existed; few used agents or lawyers to represent them, which in most cases meant accepting whatever salary their owners saw fit to hand them. These annual "negotiations," usually conducted face-to-face by the player himself with the team's legal hatchet man, amounted to little more than ritualized humiliations. Professional baseball players, from the lowliest scrub to those considered national treasures, had all the legal status of indentured servants.

The players union, led since 1966 by a former labor lawyer named

Marvin Miller, was determined to change this, and in 1970 the union had fought for and won the right to submit stalemated contract negotiations to independent arbitration. Then in 1974, when A's owner Charles Finley reneged on a contractual annuity he owed his star pitcher, Jim "Catfish" Hunter, Marvin Miller took the case to arbitration; baseball's arbiter Peter Seitz ruled that as a result of Finley's breach Hunter had the right to walk away from his contract and offer his services to any team of his choosing. Overnight he became baseball's first "free agent," and the New York Yankees immediately signed him to a five-year, $3.5 million contract. That number sent a blast wave through the game at every level—the average major-league salary in 1975 was $45,000 a year—but the game's plutocratic owners, secure that baseball's sacred antitrust exemption would continue to protect them from the evils of socialist labor practices, had long ago ostracized the A's owner as an oddball exhibitionist, and viewed the Hunter case as a onetime aberration brought on by Finley's hubris. They remained convinced, almost fanatically so, that the biggest challenge to baseball's continued supremacy came from another sport whose season overlapped baseball's by only a few weeks.

The National Football League was coming on fast as the favorite attraction of the American sports fan, riding a wave accelerated five years earlier by ABC's *Monday Night* gamble. The sport was ideally suited to television's rapidly evolving technology—multiple cameras, slow motion, zoom lenses, and instant replay broke down its brief bursts of choreographed violence into mesmerizing spectacle. The NFL's championship Super Bowl, only nine years old—Roman numerals had from the second year on amplified its self-mythologizing importance—now threatened to surpass the World Series as sports' biggest show, and television's biggest payday. Blaming their loss of audience shares on the decline of offense during the late sixties when the game was dominated by pitching, baseball's owners responded by rolling out reforms designed to put fireworks back on the field: lowering the pitcher's mound to even the odds for hitters, breaking the sport's long-established leagues into two divisions apiece to increase the number of postseason games, and, in the most radical and controversial rule change since the advent of the "live ball" in the 1920s, the American League had taken the bat out of the pitcher's hands by adding the designated hitter. The prospect that baseball might lose its almost century-long standing as America's Pastime—and what that implied for the increasingly complex, splintering demographics of the United States—had become a major obsession of both the chattering classes and the game's grandees. But, to date, as always in baseball, the numbers didn't lie: Less than 25 percent of Americans now listed baseball as their favorite sport, and most of those were over fifty, lower-income folks, a demographic that the television age had decided was headed for the sociological scrap heap.

Waking to the reality that a seismic shift in viewing habits was under way, NBC had recently—and for the first time since 1947—declined to renew its exclusive contract with Major League Baseball. Starting in 1976, for the next four years, NBC would now alternate covering the World Series with ABC. (So eager had ABC been to get into the baseball business that the perennial third-place network had ponied up considerably more than half of the $92,000,000 bill.) In the meantime, hedging its bets, NBC began quietly looking for ways to turn around the money it had saved on baseball into an increased commitment with the National Football League.

The bright lights of Fenway appeared in the distance and Chet's step quickened; the sight of any ballpark still put a charge in him. Simmons, New York–born and a lifelong Dodgers fan, lived for his favorite sport of baseball. He'd had more than a little to do with its past success as a televised sport, but on any other morning he would've gladly stopped to watch a bunch of kids play a sandlot game with a taped ball.

Seventy engineers at triple time versus $100,000 a minute in ad revenue. Yes, he could live with that.

In truth, this World Series so far had seemed heaven-sent. Easy to identify and follow story lines, a boatload of marquee names performing to the level of their All-Star reputations, three one-run games out of five played between clearly defined antagonists: New England's scrappy, scruffy, counterculture underdog Red Sox pitted against the Teutonic, clean-shaven Big Red Machine of the conservative heartland's Cincinnati Reds. Critics and fans agreed that to date this had been the most entertaining Series since the New York Mets' miraculous win over the Orioles in 1969. In the cutthroat, competitive world of network television, you couldn't have overpaid some Hollywood hack to concoct a more perfect scenario.

And if the percentages played out, the Red Sox would win Game Six tonight—Simmons was comforted by knowing that a Series hadn't *ended* in six games since 1959—and deliver the golden coin of sporting events, for both the executive and the fan in Chet Simmons: *a Game Seven.*

DICK STOCKTON needed a tie. Living out of a suitcase in the Lenox Hotel on Boylston for the last six months had wreaked havoc with his stylish wardrobe. The dapper and affable thirty-two-year-old had recently concluded his first effective season as the Red Sox television play-by-play announcer—alongside flamboyant former Red Sox outfielder Ken "The Hawk" Harrelson—and his clothes were hopelessly spread out between the hotel in Boston, his New York apartment, and two different dry cleaners. Only weeks earlier, during the final home stand of the regular season, just after the Red Sox clinched the American League's Eastern Division title, Stockton had received a telegram that delivered the biggest break of his young career:

> We are pleased to advise you of your nomination and approval to work with us during the 1975 World Series for the telecast of the first and sixth game. $500 a game. Please do not include the color blue in your wardrobe. Good luck. Chet Simmons, NBC Sports.

Bringing an announcer from each home team's broadcast unit into the booth with NBC's national two-man team, for both television and radio, had been just one of the network's many innovations for the 1975 Series. The idea behind it: that their familiarity with the club they'd covered all year would add an informed local perspective to the broadcast. Stockton and Marty Brennaman—the Reds' outstanding young play-by-play man, just finishing his second year with the team after replacing Al Michaels, who had moved on to the Giants—both immediately accepted Chet Simmons's offer. Ten days earlier, Stockton had worked Game One from Fenway with his idol, NBC's Curt Gowdy—a former Red Sox announcer himself, and for the last decade the network's number one baseball voice—and Tony Kubek, the ex–Yankee shortstop, widely acknowledged as the game's sharpest "color" commentator, and one of the most widely liked and admired human beings in the baseball universe. Both veterans did their gracious best to make Stockton feel at home, and the broadcast, by all accounts, had gone perfectly, with Stockton earning positive reviews. After traveling to Cincinnati to work Game Four for NBC Radio, Dick had flown home to New York and then back up to Boston for the scheduled broadcast of Game Six on Saturday. But after three days of rain he had burned through all the clothes he'd brought with him or had on hand.

Stockton had a deserved reputation to uphold as a clotheshorse and man about town and he rifled through the racks at Filene's Department Store that afternoon, searching for a tie to complement his orange plaid sport coat, the height of fashion in '75, improbable as it sounds today. He was slated to work tonight's Game Six alongside Kubek and Joe Garagiola, NBC's number two baseball play-by-play man, and was more than a little apprehensive about the prospect.

Joe Garagiola made it to the big leagues after World War II as a highly touted prospect, and in his rookie season helped lead his hometown St. Louis Cardinals to victory over the Red Sox in the 1946 World Series. That turned out to be his high-water mark as a player; he bounced around the league for the rest of his nine-year career as a journeyman backup catcher on three other teams. A few years after he retired, while working Cardinals games as a broadcaster, Garagiola turned a mostly ghostwritten, humorously self-deprecating collection of anecdotes about his mediocre playing years into a surprise best seller, which he then parlayed into one of network television's unlikeliest success stories. NBC signed him and brought him to New York, where he refined his folksy broadcast personality working as a game show host, moving up eventually to become cohost of the network's long-running early morning flagship, *The Today Show*. Recently replaced after nine years on *Today*— and less than happy about what he perceived correctly as a demotion—the forty-nine-year-old Garagiola had returned to baseball broadcasting in 1975 on the network's perennial Saturday *Game of the Week.*

Belying his on-screen image as an enthusiastic, slightly goofy Everyman—a personality he shared in part with, and perhaps slightly shaded toward, his colorful childhood friend and teammate Yogi Berra, who had gone on to much bigger things as a player— away from the cameras Garagiola was better known for his sharp elbows and insecure ego. Marty Brennaman, who had worked World Series Games Three and Four in Cincinnati while sharing the booth with Garagiola, had tipped Stockton off that, although Tony Kubek had graciously worked him in throughout their broadcast, Garagiola had been less than welcoming, reacting to the addition of a third voice in the booth as a challenge to his turf. Stockton felt fairly certain that another good outing during the game tonight might lead to a network job, but if Garagiola froze him out that could jeopardize his chances. Stockton's response, as it was to every adversity he faced, had been to double his intense preparation for Game Six.

After buying a tie—black, with pumpkin-orange and white stripes—Stockton hurried on to Fenway Park for the network's afternoon pregame meeting. Two long trailers tucked under the ancient right field bleachers near the players' parking lot served as NBC's broadcast and command center. Chet Simmons welcomed everyone back to work, then stepped aside to let his creative and technical producers Scotty Connell and Roy Hammerman run the meeting, and they walked their team through the night's featured story lines. Having already worked the first two games of the Series from Fenway, much of what they discussed was boilerplate stuff to the most experienced and professional baseball broadcast crew alive. Crew chief Harry Coyle, a laconic World War II bomber pilot, had directed every World Series broadcast for the network since 1947, and these were all his handpicked guys. He spoke only occasionally, chainsmoking brown cheroots, but he got a laugh when he reminded veteran cameraman Lou Gerard that he'd drawn the short straw again and would be working the lonely camera position behind a hole they'd found in the scoreboard on Fenway's signature left field wall, the Green Monster.

Stockton walked out onto the field after the meeting and caught up with Tony Kubek as the grounds crew rolled out the batting cage. The tall, striking, square-jawed former shortstop, only thirty-nine but ten years retired from the game, still looked fit enough to suit up and play. Stockton mentioned that for the last two days the mood around press headquarters at the downtown Statler Hilton had been spiraling toward indifference about this Series, and he wondered if the players would be similarly deflated by the layoff. Kubek looked out at the first players who were trickling onto the field for early stretching and warm-ups.

"In 1962, we flew back out to San Francisco for Game Six with a three-to-two lead, just like Cincinnati has here. Rained for three straight days out there. Ballplayers are creatures of habit; during the season every minute is scheduled and regulated. Something like that breaks up your routine, it's unnatural, makes you deeply uneasy. It got to the point where everybody just wanted to get it over with and go home."

Players trotted into the outfield, gingerly testing their footing in the rain-soaked turf. Others began tossing across the sidelines, stepping back to deeper range, warming up their arms.

"What was it like to play again?" asked Stockton.

"When we finally got back on the field, it was as tough as any Series I played in." Stockton reminded himself that Kubek had played in six—and won three of them—as part of one of the greatest everyday lineups in history. "All of a sudden we were back out there and it dawned on you exactly how much was at stake. And it got to some people."

The home team Giants held off the juggernaut Yankees to win that Game Six in 1962 and tie the Series, and Stockton suddenly remembered that Tony Kubek had the next day created the only run of the contest to win Game Seven and the World Series.

"The biggest advantage in sports is playing in your home park, and you can almost double that advantage here," said Kubek, who had played more than seventy games in Fenway. "But those guys over there . . ." He nodded toward where some of the Reds—Pete Rose, Bench, Joe Morgan—had gathered around the batting cage. "They know how to play the game." Tony paused and said it again, with emphasis.

"They know how to play the game."

As the first crisp cracks of ball on bat and leather filled the air— the relaxed, preliminary rituals of any ball game—Stockton began to feel an expectant buzz build again around the stadium.

Now we're ready.

LATE THAT AFTERNOON, from all around Boston and surrounding environs, lucky ticket holders for Game Six left home or work to make their way downtown and slowly converge on Fenway Park. Optimists arriving without tickets found scalpers outside offering grandstand tickets for as much as $60—face value of $7.50—while buck-fifty seats in the outfield bleachers were going for $35. Standing room along the top of the grandstands would set you back $25. When all those aftermarket transactions concluded that evening, a capacity crowd of 35,205 had flowed through the turnstiles at Fenway. Another eighty or so, mostly enterprising teenagers, found cheaper seats on the girders of a whiskey billboard atop the roof of a Lansdowne Street building, about five hundred feet from home plate.

In the years to come, the number of people who would later claim to have been at Game Six that night would increase twenty-fold.

If the Boston fans will bear with me, I think I'll eventually
give them the club they deserve, the finest in the country.
I don't intend to mess around with a loser.

TOM YAWKEY, 1932

Tom Yawkey has a heart the size of a watermelon.

TED WILLIAMS

B EFORE THEY MOVED DOWNSTAIRS FOR THE PREGAME
ceremonies, the two old men, friends for more than forty years,
watched the crowd file in from the owner's box on the roof of Fenway's grandstand above the first base line. George Edward "Duffy"
Lewis, eighty-seven, was the sole surviving member of the "Picket
Line," what had forever been thought of as the greatest outfield in
Red Sox history. Playing alongside future Hall of Famers Harry
Hooper in right and Tris Speaker in center, Lewis had patrolled left
field in Fenway Park from the day it opened in 1912 until he entered
the army in 1918 to serve in World War I. Those had been the glory
days of the Boston franchise, winning four of its five World Series
titles on the strength of that outfield and, during the last two in 1916
and 1918, the left arm of a phenomenal young pitcher named Babe
Ruth.

During the intervening fifty-seven years, the World Series had
only come back to Fenway Park twice.

Duffy Lewis looked out toward left field and the looming, iconic
Green Monster. In his day they hadn't painted it green yet, or dubbed
it a "monster," but an earlier incarnation of the wall had been there
from Opening Day, a quirky concession to the limits of Fenway's

original land rights. Baseball was never played at night in 1912, which meant home plate had to be anchored in the southwest corner of the park so batters in late innings wouldn't be staring directly into the western setting sun. That set the fixed line of Lansdowne Street just beyond left field, not much more than 320 feet from home, which meant no room for left field bleachers; no room for anything between the edge of the ballpark and Lansdowne Street but a sheer vertical wooden wall, built over thirty feet high at the insistence of the street's local business owners, who didn't want baseballs crashing through their fancy glass storefronts. Soon, plastered with advertising, the left field wall morphed into the biggest billboard in town, and ever since had developed its reputation as the most distinct architectural oddity of any American ballpark.

During Duffy Lewis's playing days the ground in deep left field sloped sharply up to meet the base of the wall—ten feet of grade in less than thirty feet of space—from the left field line all the way across to center. So adept had Lewis become in patrolling this perilous chunk of real estate, racing up the slope to pluck line drives off the wall with acrobatic abandon and fire the ball back in with his cannon arm, that fans called the area "Duffy's Cliff" for years after he left the game. Until, in its entirety, the quirky hillock was removed in 1934 by the man standing next to Duffy Lewis in the owner's box at Fenway before Game Six that night.

Thomas Austin Yawkey, seventy-two, had been the sole proprietor of the Boston Red Sox since 1933. He made a handshake deal to buy both the ball club and Fenway Park for $1.2 million only four days after his thirtieth birthday, the moment when the vast timber and mining fortune that had long been held in trust for him came legally under his control. The genesis of the Yawkey fortune reached back into the middle of the nineteenth century, a dynasty built on the paper mills and virgin pine forests of the American and Canadian west, and a story rife with enough family melodrama to fill a dozen potboilers. If Tom Yawkey's young life had been dreamt up by F. Scott Fitzgerald, that generation's most eloquent chronicler of the moral perils of American wealth and fame, no one would have believed it.

His mother, Augusta Yawkey, had married a straightlaced insurance executive named Thomas Austin, a match that pleased her conservative tycoon father, William Clyman Yawkey, the reigning patriarch of their clan. But Thomas Austin died suddenly during his son's first year, and when Augusta proved unable to subsequently cope with the trials of single motherhood, three-year-old Tom was delivered into the care of her brother, Bill Yawkey, a notorious New York bachelor playboy. Under the category of "What were they thinking?" young Tom grew up in his uncle Bill's Upper East Side penthouse, a madcap whirligig of dissolute socialites, degenerate gamblers, pliable showgirls, and professional wrestlers. Determined to help his wayward son find some semblance of a vocation, William Clyman Yawkey made a bid to buy the Detroit Tigers in 1903 for the baseball-obsessed Bill, but died suddenly before the deal went through. With his share of the family fortune now available to him, Bill Yawkey doubled back and made an even better deal for the Tigers, and quickly decided he had found the millionaire's ultimate toy train. Ballplayers, he discovered, shared all of Bill Yawkey's manly interests—hitting, pitching, hunting, drinking, and playing the field, not necessarily in that order—and with Bill writing the checks, the party never ended. A few years later, in 1907, his Tigers rewarded their owner's largesse by winning the American League pennant and playing in the World Series against the Chicago Cubs. Yawkey enjoyed that ride so much, even though they lost in five games, that he rewarded his Tigers with Series bonuses bigger than the shares received by the winners.

When Augusta Yawkey died during the influenza epidemic of 1918, Uncle Bill legally adopted his young ward, rearranging his name from Thomas Yawkey Austin to Thomas Austin Yawkey. But Bill Yawkey would follow his sister in death less than a year later, not long after he and Tom had set out on a motoring trip across the country to celebrate Tom's sixteenth birthday. They had just stopped

in Georgia to visit Bill's closest friend on the Tigers, legendary outfielder Ty Cobb, when Bill was stricken with a virulent pneumonia.
He died days later in his famous friend's arms, but not before ex-
tracting a promise from Cobb that he would help look after Tom after he was gone. Bill's stake in the Tigers was sold off by his estate's
conservators—for considerable profit—but Ty Cobb kept his word,
serving as a substitute foster father to young Tom. The fiercely aggressive, and probably sociopathic Cobb thus became the second of
Tom Yawkey's dubious male role models.

Now the presumptive heir to both his mother's and uncle's shares
of the Yawkey fortune, Tom moved on to Yale, and got down to seriously pursuing the around-the-clock cocktail-hour lifestyle he'd
learned from Uncle Bill; he came closest to applying himself aca-
demically when he played some second base for the Bulldogs baseball team. He also ended up in the vanguard of a tumultuous cultural
revolution: GIs returning from World War I tours of duty in Paris
and other European capitals had brought home with them an appetite for more sophisticated sin; tastemakers and advertisers capital-
ized, and young Americans following their lead threw aside the
lingering puritanical inhibitions of the nineteenth century with a
vengeance. The last gasp of the Victorian generation's crusade to
stamp out the evils of hedonism came in 1919: a misguided consti-
tutional amendment called the Volstead Act, better known as Prohibition, which outlawed the production and distribution of alcohol.
Free, filthy rich, and twenty-one, openly scoffing at Prohibition,
Tom Yawkey was frequently singled out in the press as a standard-
bearer for this "Roaring Twenties" generation. A few years later Tom
married a Jazz Age icon, a legendarily alluring dancer and beauty
queen named Elise Sparrow, who had once posed for a famous por-
trait as a "flapper," the era's signature party girl. During the rest of
the decade, their sybaritic life drifted hazily between a Park Avenue
penthouse, the old family manse in Michigan, and a sprawling rural
estate in South Carolina, stocked with game birds and deer for
Yawkey's frequent hunting trips. During one of the many stag retreats they spent together there, his mentor Ty Cobb planted the idea

in Yawkey's head that, just as his late uncle Bill had, Tom might find his calling—and prove to his disapproving trustees he could *make* money as well as spend it—in the ownership of a major-league baseball club. On another hunting trip the following year, Yawkey received something a lot less welcome from his old friend: a brutal alcohol-fueled one-sided beating—sudden acts of violence being just one of Cobb's misanthropic tendencies—that abruptly ended their relationship.

The Jazz Age ended just as suddenly not long afterward, but 1929's catastrophic stock market implosion hardly dented the Yawkey family's commodity-based businesses. As his thirtieth birthday approached, the age when the trust stipulated that control of his fortune would pass into his hands and instantly make him one of the fifty wealthiest men in America, Tom Yawkey remembered Cobb's advice. When he got word that Boston's American League franchise was in play, Yawkey swooped in and snapped up the Red Sox during the darkest hour of the Great Depression. Like much of the rest of the country, America's national pastime, and the Red Sox and Fenway Park in particular, had fallen on hard times. For the first time in his life, when many of baseball's owners were either scraping by or actively looking to get out from under their obligations, Tom Yawkey had bought himself a job—and set course on an obsessive quest for the prize that had eluded his uncle and, he declared, would give his life meaning: winning a World Series.

Yawkey landed in Boston as a complete stranger—worse yet, a lifelong New Yorker—with no connections to its cloistered, tight-knit community; New Englanders greeted him warily. To win them over and demonstrate the seriousness of his intent, Yawkey immediately began a badly needed renovation of twenty-year-old Fenway Park. The park was stripped down to its original steel frames, and out went the old wooden bleachers and the slope on Duffy's Cliff. Yawkey ordered up a new clubhouse and state-of-the-art amenities for his players, including a bar and a bowling alley in the basement. A new thirty-seven-foot-tall metal-and-steel wall, the exoskeleton of the Monster that stands to this day, went up over the newly level left field, sporting the game's first electric scoreboard. Pouring fifteen thousand cubic yards of concrete, Yawkey added over ten thousand new seats and an expansive press box, employing more Bostonians than any other construction project had since the Crash. Having spent well over a million dollars, he now had the far more difficult problem facing him of a complete renovation of the Red Sox roster, a team that had finished dead last in nine of the last eleven seasons.

At the first owners' meetings he attended that winter, Yawkey stunned his conservative old-school colleagues by jumping to his feet and bluntly announcing he was in the market for top-shelf players with which to stock his new ballpark and that money was no object. The other owners, quickly getting over their shock at this impropriety, proved only too happy to help; before the week was out, Yawkey had dropped another quarter of a million on a handful of has-beens and never-would-be's, who would contribute little to changing the Red Sox's losing ways. An informal competition developed around the league over the next few years to see who could get the Red Sox to overpay the most for marquee names like Lefty Grove and Joe Cronin, who were past their prime. Even bottom-of-the-roster players earned more than the league average under Yawkey, who proved to be a soft touch above and beyond salary for any of his men who came to him with a hard luck story; players on other teams began calling them the "Gold Sox." By introducing "checkbook" baseball, Tom Yawkey changed forever the way the game was played in the front office, and his hyperactive turnover of talent, perpetually chasing big names with big bucks without much regard for actual need or overall chemistry, set the mood for much of the team's next four decades.

Another destructive team dynamic was set up by Yawkey's spendthrift tendencies: A long line of competent field managers found themselves constantly at odds with their general manager—all three of the men who ran the team through 1960 were Yawkey cronies, who only sporadically delivered the sort of player the field manager felt he needed to win. When in 1935 he finally landed a future Hall of Famer still in his prime, burly slugger Jimmie Foxx, Yawkey went out almost every night after games pub-crawling with the hard-drinking first baseman. Yawkey began a tradition of taking batting practice with his boys before home games and working out with them in the field, casting himself a whole lot more as a pal than a boss. Borrowing another page from Uncle Bill's playbook, during spring training he arranged regular visits for his team to a local brothel; decades later a tenacious reporter from the *Boston Globe* uncovered evidence that Yawkey may have actually *owned* the brothel. For any manager trying to push, mold, or discipline the owner's grab-ass buddies, the job was virtually impossible; turnover at the position became a constant.

Although he anticipated the future of baseball by pursuing big-name stars without much regard for cost, Yawkey was slow to react to the most important changes the game would experience over the next twenty years. During the first four decades of professional baseball's existence, major-league teams had relied on the inexact science of scouting and a loosely defined "regional rights" system to find and sign young players. In the 1920s general manager Branch Rickey of the St. Louis Cardinals, lacking the funds to compete for expensive talent, decided to buy a series of minor-league teams all over the country—and the rights to all the players he then placed on their rosters—thereby controlling and streamlining the process of developing future major leaguers. When this revolutionary innovation produced a roster that resulted in five National League pennants between 1926 and 1934 for the Cardinals, every other team in the majors quickly adopted the same business model. With Tom Yawkey's mind fixed on chasing established major-league stars, the Red Sox were one of the last to assemble what Rickey had called an effective "farm system." They were the third to last team to add lights and schedule night games, the prevailing social trend as America's game transitioned from its pastoral daylight roots to a primary form of evening entertainment for industrialized inner city workers. Then Yawkey missed the game's next great sea change by a mile: After Jackie Robinson broke the color barrier in 1947, the Red Sox were the last major-league team to sign African-Americans—passing up players like the great Willie Mays and Robinson himself, who had been treated shabbily by team officials during a workout at Fenway and forever held a grudge against the Red Sox. As a result Yawkey's Red Sox became the last major-league franchise to field a black player in their everyday lineup—second baseman Elijah "Pumpsie" Green, twelve years later, in 1959, a hard-to-justify reluctance that raised enduring and legitimate questions about Yawkey's racial politics.

Off the field, as he entered middle age, Yawkey's personal life came untethered; he never showed much interest in his only child, an adopted daughter, and he periodically lost his running battle with alcohol. His marriage to Elise had quietly died years earlier, but it ended legally with a Nevada divorce in 1944; she remarried in less than a month, and a few weeks later, just before Christmas, Tom Yawkey married the woman whom he'd been quietly seeing for over three years, Jean Hiller, an attractive, younger model whose interests, in sports and the outdoors—and pleasing her wealthy husband—more closely matched his own. Unlike the independent, socially ambitious Elise, Jean Yawkey doted on her husband, and for the first time in his life he found some measure of domestic stability. But the World Series title he craved continued to elude him. The Red Sox didn't win their first American League pennant for Yawkey until 1946, then lost that World Series in seven games to the St. Louis Cardinals, the only time the first great star to emerge from Boston's farm system, Ted Williams, would ever play in the postseason. The team wouldn't deliver Yawkey a second pennant for twenty-one more turbulent years. During that long stretch, although he continued to profess that he wanted to win, it became increasingly difficult for New England's die-hard fans to believe their team represented more to its owner than a big, shiny plaything that only intermittently captured his interest.

By the early 1960s, as the Red Sox continued to tread water,

Yawkey had largely become an absentee owner. He had never bought a home in Boston, operating instead out of his suite at the Ritz-Carlton and preferring to base both his business and personal life in New York and on his forty-thousand-acre coastal estate in South Carolina. That left most of the chores of running the club to the Sox's fourth general manager, Dick O'Connell. A Massachusetts native and war veteran, the disciplined, dedicated O'Connell had been with the team since 1947, worked his way up through the organization, and inherited the job by default when Ted Williams turned it down after retiring in 1960. For the first time in thirty years, the Red Sox had a general manager in place who was an executive first, not just another featherbedding former player and Yawkey yes-man. By mid-decade O'Connell had revitalized the Red Sox farm system, producing the first steady stream of solid prospects the team had ever seen; and, not coincidentally, for the first time in franchise history many of them were Latin or African-American. When the first wave of these players was ready to step up to the majors, O'Connell tapped the man who'd been managing most of them at the team's Triple-A franchise in Toronto, hard-liner and future Hall of Famer Dick Williams, to take over what had devolved into an aging, overpaid, and complacent Red Sox squad that played to crowds occasionally numbering in the hundreds. Fans derisively referred to this bunch as the "country club Sox" and like the team itself, Fenway Park had also fallen into disrepair. Far from the cherished shrine of the game it is today, with its peeling paint and broken windows Fenway was dismissed by most as a rusted relic from a bygone age. In the course of lobbying for a new, modern park in downtown Boston, Yawkey used the now familiar refrain of blaming his team's woes on their antiquated stadium, and like owners everywhere he also wanted the city and taxpayers to underwrite it. His new manager was about to change all that.

Schooled in the disciplined Dodgers tradition, the thirty-seven-year-old Williams brought the hammer down, replacing what he correctly perceived to be deadwood on the Red Sox roster with many of his players from Toronto, and opened the 1967 season with the second-youngest lineup in either league. Everyone expected that a few seasons of rebuilding had to follow. Expectations were so low that fewer than ten thousand people turned out for Opening Day and oddsmakers calculated that the Sox were 100–1 to win the American League pennant. But with his marine drill instructor's mouth and sharp baseball mind, Dick Williams turned his team into a contender from day one; what was known as the "Summer of Love" across America became the "Impossible Dream" in Boston, as fans hung the theme of the hit Broadway musical *Man of La Mancha* on their improbably resurgent Red Sox. Young outfielder Tony Conigliaro slugged fifty-six home runs in his first two seasons and had already earned matinee idol status with Boston's female population. He was joined now by a fiery, hard-hitting shortstop from Brooklyn who quickly became another fan favorite, Rico Petrocelli. But these Sox were led on the field by the man who had replaced Ted Williams in left field in 1961 but in the minds of Boston's demanding fans never come close to equaling him, blue-collar workaholic Carl Yastrzemski. Solid but hardly a superstar to that point in his career, Yastrzemski came of age in response to Dick Williams's tough discipline and won the Triple Crown in 1967, leading the American League in batting average, home runs, and runs driven in; he was only the third man to pull off that trifecta since Ted Williams himself, who did it twice. Yastrzemski was named the American League's Most Valuable Player for his efforts, but it was his performance during the season's last two weeks that earned him a place in the hearts of Red Sox fans forever. With four teams still in the pennant race down to the wire, Yaz hit five home runs, drove in sixteen, and hit an astounding .523 as Boston won eight of their last twelve games and captured the American League pennant with a one-game lead. Tom Yawkey embraced Yaz in the clubhouse, calling it "the happiest day of my life." Despite Yastrzemski's continued heroics in the World Series, the Sox came up short once again, when the Cardinals' ferocious African-American star pitcher, Bob Gibson, beat them three times, and they lost in seven games.

But the memories and emotions stirred by that breathtaking pennant race had provided such a joyride it hardly seemed to matter; baseball fever had been born again in New England. The old fans who'd drifted away during the indifferent years came back to the fold, and a generation of baby boomers fell in love with this modern edition of their parents' and grandparents' Red Sox. During an era when clubs around both leagues tore down their charming old pre-war bandboxes, putting up soulless cookie-cutter concrete "multi-use" stadiums in their place, fans also renewed their affection for the quirky, angular ballpark where their Red Sox worked and played. The "Impossible Dream" also rekindled Tom Yawkey's ancient obsession, and between 1968 and 1975, the frayed civic image of both the ballpark and its owner underwent a complete and remarkable conversion. For all the money the Red Sox had cost him through their many lean years—by 1967 his total losses were calculated at close to $8 million—Yawkey never felt the pinch; he was worth hundreds of millions now, and against the weight of that fortune the team remained at best a minor item on his balance sheet. And as a result of their "Dream" season, from '67 on the franchise began doing something it had never done before: making more money every year. All talk of Tom Yawkey selling the Sox, a persistent rumor in Boston for the past decade, now vanished, as did any thoughts of tearing down Fenway Park. Yawkey showed up on most game days again, an old man now but still out there in spikes and sweats playing pepper with his bat boys—he often paid for the college education of his favorites—or taking a few grounders from longtime clubhouse attendant Vinnie Orlando before games. When he shuffled into the Red Sox clubhouse, a soft-spoken, retiring figure in baggy pants and a cheap windbreaker, newcomers occasionally mistook him for an attendant himself; during their first meeting in 1974 newly acquired outfielder Bernie Carbo asked Yawkey to run out and grab him some lunch.

Yawkey's forty-four years as the sole owner of a professional major-league franchise had now become the longest tenure of any owner in the history of his sport, and the futility of his quest for a World Series title remained equally unmatched. In his service as vice president (now emeritus) of the American League, a post he'd held for twenty years, Yawkey stood tall as a stabilizing figure in a sport evolving through uncertain times. Most of the men who played for him remained fiercely loyal to Yawkey because of his personal kindness and undying private generosity. Although no longer his contemporaries or partners in crime, the Red Sox players had always provided the nearest thing he would ever know to an extended family; those closest to him, like Ted Williams or Carl Yastrzemski, could accurately be described as his surrogate sons. By 1975 the people of New England had bestowed upon both Yawkey and his ballpark the respect and affection they had historically shown to any person or place that in their long memories had stood the test of time; they embraced them both as local monuments. All past sins and transgressions forgiven, the Sox's benevolent monarch had at last become beloved in his adopted town. His team hadn't suffered another losing season since their "Impossible Dream" year; they were a perennial front-line contender now, and winning a World Series was no longer just an achievement that Red Sox fans craved for themselves; they had embraced it as a sacred and sentimental responsibility: "Let's win one for good old Tom Yawkey."

AT EIGHT O'CLOCK, Yawkey escorted Duffy Lewis from his rooftop perch down through the stands to the playing field for the opening rituals of Game Six. Red Sox officials parted the crowd ahead of them, but as always, Yawkey stopped to offer a soft hand and exchange smiles or encouraging words with the admiring fans he greeted along the way. When they finally reached the field, the proceedings were called to order by Fenway's longtime PA announcer Sherm Feller, who greeted the crowd with his signature phrase, offered in his familiar gravelly baritone: "Attention please, ladies and gentlemen, boys and girls, welcome to Fenway Park." After "The Star-Spangled Banner" was played by veteran organist John Kiley on his Hammond X-66, Duffy Lewis hobbled toward the mound to

throw out the ceremonial first pitch for Game Six, and his introduction was greeted by a long and emotional ovation.

Lewis had thrown out the first pitch on Opening Day for the 1975
season back in April, when the Brewers came to Boston with Hank
Aaron, making his debut in the American League after breaking
Babe Ruth's home run record, in order to finish his career back
where it began in Milwaukee. After his own playing days ended,
Duffy had put in twenty-five years as traveling secretary for the Boston Braves, the city's longtime National League franchise—which
moved to Milwaukee in 1953—and he had known Aaron when they
were both with the Braves. Now, after the Red Sox's dramatic charge
to this World Series, Tom Yawkey had brought Duffy back as a good
luck talisman for the difficult task ahead in Game Six. Whispered
stories passed between the generations in the stands, revived memories of this half-forgotten ghost of greatness past—*See that old man
down there? He knew Babe Ruth, they were teammates together.
That's right, Babe Ruth played for the Red Sox back then, and Duffy
saw the Babe hit his first home run. Duffy could hit, too; he hit over
.400 in the Series in 1915.* The consensus seemed to be that surely
his presence augured well for the business at hand, and the crowd
cheered wildly as Duffy's throw reached Red Sox catcher Carlton
Fisk on the fly.

Tom Yawkey watched quietly, seated beside Commissioner Bowie
Kuhn in the front row, just to the left of home plate, before returning
to his private box upstairs. Every person in that crowd knew how
badly their team's owner wanted a World Series trophy, and seemed
ready and determined to will their Red Sox to victory that night.
Yawkey had traveled to Oakland for the one-game conclusion of
their surprising sweep of the A's in the League Championship, and
had also gone with the team on their recent trip to Cincinnati, but
he had been taken ill there and instead of braving the cool night air
in the stands at Riverfront Stadium had watched Games Three and
Four on television in a room off the visitors' clubhouse. He then flew
back to Boston early on the day of Game Five, which he watched

from his suite at the Ritz. It was explained to the press that Yawkey was suffering from the same heavy chest cold that had hit many of his players, including Luis Tiant and Red Sox right fielder Dwight Evans.

With the exception of his wife, Jean, and a few team executives, no one else in the stadium that night of Game Six knew that this year's quest for a championship had taken on an even starker urgency: The seventy-two-year-old Yawkey had recently been diagnosed with leukemia, was already undergoing chemotherapy at New England Baptist Hospital, and had less than nine months to live.

Baseball is a private game.

George Plimpton

For george "sparky" anderson, half of the job of managing a game was over by the time the ink was dry on his lineup card.

Hell, we played a hundred and sixty-five games already—and we won a hundred and eleven of 'em, by the way—you know what your fellas can do, just let 'em go out there and play!

It didn't hurt that four of the men in his everyday lineup would amass Hall of Fame–level credentials, and three of the other four, at one time or another in their careers, were or would be All-Star-caliber players. The Reds had been called the "Big Red Machine" since the phrase first appeared on their yearbook in 1970; Pete Rose always claimed he'd jokingly coined the name to distinguish the team from an antique Ford he had dubbed the "Little Red Machine." Whatever its genesis, the "Machine" tag stuck—and became a key to Cincinnati's extraordinary marketing of the team—but 1975 was the first year people began to refer to Sparky's starters out on the field as the "Great Eight."

Pitchers—now, they're a different category—their own *category, if you know what I'm saying*—and they were Shep's responsibility, Cincinnati Reds pitching coach Larry Shepard. If Sparky needed to know something about one of them during a game, Shep was always right there sitting on the bench to Sparky's right. Shep had been a pitcher himself; he spoke their language, knew all their peculiar mechanics and goofball tendencies, and he rode them hard, calling everyone "dumb ass" whenever they screwed up.

Pitchers—what are you gonna do?

From the men on Anderson's pitching staff's perspective, it seemed that at some level their manager didn't even think of them as *ballplayers,* not in the same way he did his everyday players. As far as they were concerned, Sparky was in the superstar business, taking care of Rose, Morgan, Bench, and Tony Perez, the team's glamour guys and poster boys. Unless they came to him first, practically the only time Sparky ever talked *directly* to a pitcher was when he called one into his office to tell him he was or wasn't starting—or he was being sent down or traded or released, not exactly pleasant prospects for either party—or when Sparky marched out to the mound to pull one of them out of a game.

Which Anderson had done in 1975 more frequently than any other manager in the history of baseball—277 times, to be exact. They'd started calling him "Captain Hook" a few years before for just that reason. At one point during the '75 season the Reds staff had set a major-league record by going forty-five straight starts without one of their pitchers throwing a complete game.

And that pitcher better not say word one once Sparky got out there to pull him.

I'm your boss, I'm not out here for your opinion—unless I ask you for it—and I sure as hell *ain't interested in your opinion about the soundness of my judgment.*

Sparky always kept his hands stuffed in his back pockets whenever he went out on the field; that way if he lost his temper during an argument with an umpire, he wouldn't end up strangling the man, which he'd nearly done once during his fiery minor-league days. Nor did he want to show up the pitcher he'd come to yank—if he protested—by means of an eloquent gesture. Sparky had strict rules about decorum for everything that took place, on or off the field—and he made doggone sure from the first day of spring training on that every last Red knew them.

Don't you hand me that damn ball until I reach out and ask you for it. We're professionals out here. We've got another man coming in

*to do this job now, and we'll all damn well stand here together like a
team and wait until he's on his way.*

As soon as the summoned reliever reached the edge of the infield, Sparky reached out, took the ball, slapped his departing pitcher
on the ass to start him toward the showers, then handed it to the
next guy once he got there, laid out the situation and what he expected of him, slapped *him* on the ass, and trotted back to his place
on the bench.

*What the hell am I gonna tell anybody about pitching? I played
one season in the majors and hit .218! That's what we're paying Shep
for, and if I need another opinion, hell, I got Johnny Bench behind the
plate. Think he don't know how a guy's throwing? You want to know
how good and smart Bench is? God reached down and touched his
mama when she was carrying him, that's the only way to explain it,
because he plays* his *position better than anybody else played* theirs
in the history of the game. Period.

Sparky, of course, knew a great deal more about pitching and his
pitchers than he let on, but he never second-guessed his catcher; a
glance, a gesture, a quiet word from Bench ("He's done") was all he
needed to reach for the hook. Sparky was a worrier, by nature; and
nothing provoked more of it than the mysterious souls of pitchers.

But the source of his torment that Tuesday afternoon, and during
the previous night's fitful sleep, the reason he'd fretted over this
lineup for an hour as he chain-smoked in his little rat-hole cubby off
the cramped visitors' clubhouse at Fenway, was right there near the
top of the card, just below the name he'd written in almost every day
for the last six years: "PETE ROSE."

*Who hits behind Peter Edward in the two spot tonight, Morgan or
Griffey?*

Second baseman Joe Morgan was about to be named the National
League's Most Valuable Player for the 1975 season; he was the en-
gine of Cincinnati's offense, the man whose acquisition by trade
from Houston in late 1971—a move Sparky requested and cam-
paigned hard for from the Reds' front office—had proved to be the

missing piece that kicked the Big Red Machine into overdrive. Sparky had slotted Morgan into that second spot in the order since the day he arrived, and the results had been stunning—they reached the Series in Morgan's first season with them, losing in seven games to Charles Finley's A's—but they'd fallen short the next two years. They lost to the Mets in a bare-knuckle National League Championship Series in 1973, and although they still won ninety-eight regular season games in 1974, an emerging Dodgers team had edged them out of the Western Division Championship by four games.

And in case anyone needed reminding, the Reds hadn't won *this* Series yet either, even if they did lead three games to two.

One radical lineup change Sparky made earlier in the 1975 season had propelled the Reds to the National League pennant and a club record 108 regular season wins, the most racked up by any National League team since the 1909 Pirates. The Reds had limped to a disappointing start that spring, stuck at .500 through the first five weeks, for a reason that Anderson readily identified but couldn't find the right player to solve. Third base had been the weak link in his formidable everyday lineup for three years, on both sides of the ball; the Reds were also flush with a group of promising young outfielders who needed a place to play and develop. In a flash of inspiration during infield practice before a game in early May, Sparky asked his perennial All-Star left fielder and team captain Pete Rose—he always called him "Peter Edward"—if he'd consider moving to third.

"I'm not telling," said Sparky. "I'm just asking."

Instead of laughing or scoffing or brushing off the suggestion— the prerogative of any star of his stature then, and the automatic response of almost any *player* today—Rose instantly grasped the big picture.

"When?" asked Rose.

"Tomorrow too soon?" asked Anderson, then adding what he knew would be the clincher. "We're on *Game of the Week*."

"Whatever you need, Skip," Rose said, and went looking for an infielder's glove to borrow.

Rose had come up through the Reds farm system as a second base-man, and began his big-league career there, but he hadn't played the infield in nine years, and only a handful of games ever at what he called "the coffin corner"—which he'd hated at the time—way back in 1966. Positioned as much as twenty-five feet closer to the batter, third base is a much more instinctive defensive position than second, making greater demands on a player's reflexes, hands, footwork, and arm. Pete characteristically charged straight at the challenge, pester-ing Reds first base coach George Scherger—and wearing him out in the process—into hitting him hundreds of grounders. Exhibiting a lot more enthusiasm than skill, Pete attacked the ball like a commando trying to throw himself on a hand grenade. (Reds announcer Marty Brennaman said that in his first game at third Rose "looked like a monkey playing with a football.") Black and blue from the pounding he'd taken—wearing a heavily padded jockstrap because of it—within a week Rose told Sparky he *loved* playing third because it put him right in the middle of the action. He took relentless ribbing from his teammates for his Cro-Magnon fielding style—that infield already included three smooth, perennial Gold Glovers in Bench, Morgan, and shortstop Dave Concepcion—but Rose was an all-world trash talker who always gave as good as he got, and all their provocation did was make him work even harder. Penciling Rose in at third solved Sparky's other problem by opening up left field for twenty-six-year-old George Foster, a prodigious bat and decent fielder with a powerful but erratic throwing arm who'd always seemed slightly out of his depth in right or center. Putting Foster in left allowed Sparky to install twenty-four-year-old second-year man Ken Griffey, a phenom-enal athlete and former football star who was still relatively new to baseball, as his everyday right fielder.

And with that, voilà: Particularly on the artificial turf of their home field, Riverfront Stadium, adding Griffey's speed near the top of the lineup, between Rose and Morgan—and Foster's power in the sixth spot, after Bench and first baseman Perez—revitalized the Reds' dormant offense, and the Big Red Machine kicked into over-drive. They won forty-one of their next fifty games; by the All-Star break Cincinnati led the National League's West Division by twelve and a half games. Winning 96 of their final 138 games, the Reds clinched their division by 20 during the first week of September, then marched right on to dust the powerful Pittsburgh Pirates in a three-game sweep of the National League Championship, to reach their third World Series in six years.

And Pete Rose, just as he'd predicted when he switched positions, made the 1975 National League All-Star team and would spend most of the rest of his career at third base.

All the experts in the national press had picked these rampaging Reds to walk all over the underdog Red Sox in this World Series, but with unexpected grit Boston had pushed them hard into this sixth game and shocked everyone in the sport, with the possible exception of George Anderson, who never took anything about his team's prospects, or anything in baseball for that matter, for granted.

After nearly seven years in the minors, Anderson saw his own baseball dreams crash and burn after a single mediocre season in 1959 playing second base for the bottom-dwelling Philadelphia Phillies. The only record he established was hardly one to brag about: most games ever played by a player who only spent one year in the major leagues. He hung around for four more years playing for Toronto in Triple-A, the top tier of the minors, hoping for another chance, but Sparky never made it back to the Show, picking up odd jobs to make ends meet in the off-season back home in California. Turning thirty and facing facts, but determined to stay in baseball, and without an education to provide for his young family in any other arena, Anderson decided that managing in the game he knew so thoroughly represented his best and only chance. He received crucial advice and encouragement from the last man he'd played for in the minors, Charlie Dressen, who'd managed the sensational Brooklyn Dodgers in the early 1950s. Once he was given the chance, Sparky's instincts, energy, and aptitude manifested with stunning immediacy; working his way up through the sport's rural backwaters, the minor-league teams he managed won four consecutive pennants in four different leagues, culminating in a championship for Cincinnati's Double-A affiliate in Asheville, North Carolina. That earned him his first ticket back to the bigs the following year, as a third base coach for the San Diego Padres in 1969, at which point thirty-five-year-old Sparky Anderson had begun to be talked about by baseball executives as major-league managerial timber, and sooner rather than later.

An opportunity to run Gene Autry's California Angels club appeared to be in the offing, when the Cincinnati Reds' general manager Bob Howsam, a fan from Anderson's winning year for them at Asheville, made a preemptive strike and offered him the Reds managerial job for the upcoming 1970 season. Sparky had seen how good the Reds looked up close during his season with the Padres and leapt at the chance, but his selection came as a shock; few people outside of baseball, and almost nobody in the Midwest, even knew who he was. And when the team introduced him that winter, Anderson rocked the conservative Cincinnati press by guaranteeing they'd reach the World Series that fall—and damn if he didn't then go on to deliver. He'd learned to temper his public enthusiasms, and regretted that early prediction as boasting or blabbing—*I talk too much when I'm nervous, and I'm almost always nervous*—ever since.

The 1970 Cincinnati Reds were a veteran squad, packed with a host of gifted players who had never quite gelled as a team, and having watched managers come and go over the years, they greeted this peppery little bush leaguer with open skepticism. After they stopped asking "Sparky who?" they called him "the minor-league motherfucker." Sparky saw it, heard it, sensed it—he could always read people—and told them straight off: *You don't have to like me. You don't have to respect me. I'm here to earn* your *respect.* He started by taking the time to get to know them and their families, comprehending who each of these men was inside and what they needed not just as players but as people. From day one of spring training in 1970, Sparky installed the same rigorous, regimented training program that had been a crucial component of the Dodgers' system in which he'd grown up. The Reds' veterans grumbled—catcher Johnny Bench called their camp that year "Stalag 17"—but the team emerged from Florida in tremendous physical shape. Anderson also recognized the corresponding values of imposing strict discipline while maintaining each man's self-respect, and had an unerring instinct for keeping that equation in balance. Managers in baseball then still held absolute authority; Sparky wielded his without lording it over you, although God help you if you pushed him too far. Whenever the Reds needed a shakeup, he'd call a team meeting, then single out and rip one of his superstars, who were tough enough to take it, and smart enough to realize that he was sending a message to the rest of the squad. By the end of their first season together Sparky had brought each of his men face-to-face with the mirror, and from then on they gave him everything they had. Anderson knew that he'd inherited a unique core of talent, and he was always first to acknowledge the part that luck had played in landing where he had when he had, but it took skill, toughness, psychology, street smarts, attention to detail, and bone-grinding hard work to keep adding the right pieces and then forge all that talent into a *team*. Sparky's philosophy as a manager of a team this deep and strong was simple: If the clubhouse was under control, the field would take care of itself, and the Reds' record since he'd taken over offered irrefutable evidence. The Big Red Machine had won more games during the 1970s than any other team in baseball.

Anderson would have been perfectly happy remaining their anonymous commander in the dugout, but during the Reds' ascent a fascinating transformation occurred in their manager as well: The modest, down-to-earth, formerly camera-shy George Anderson developed what amounted to a public alter ego, and this chatty, magnetic, approachable, and (now) white-haired character named "Sparky" had become one of the most liked and instantly recognizable characters in all of American sports, an ambassador for his sport and a star in his own right. By the end of his first season, when he'd led the Reds into a World Series that they lost in five games to Earl Weaver's fearsome Baltimore Orioles, Cincinnati's management insisted that their manager now sign all his autographs as "Sparky." Contemporary marketing experts call the process "building the brand," but his popularity came about in a much more organic way: Sparky simply liked every kind of people, and the impact he made on them was often profound. During the week they'd spent in Boston for this World Series, Sparky had already made a dozen friends for life, won over every tough Southie cabdriver he'd encountered, and had the notoriously cynical Boston sportswriting fraternity following him around like a pack of happy puppies. Sparky possessed the rare gifts of presence and poise, sincerity, good humor, and authenticity, and as his parents had taught him to do, he treated every human being he met as his equal. As much as Sparky always liked to downplay his contributions, there was a whole lot more to managing a big-league squad than writing out the lineup card. But you never heard him take credit for it—Rod Dedeaux and Casey Stengel had taught him that as well—another part of what made him such an exceptional leader of men.

The 1975 Cincinnati Reds had everything: power, speed, exceptional defense—at one point in 1975 they went fifteen straight games without committing an error, another major-league record—a strong and versatile bench, and a bulletproof committee bullpen that had led the National League in saves with fifty. No wonder their good starting pitchers never got the credit they deserved. But as great as the Reds were in 1975, and had been consistently for the six years since Anderson arrived, they hadn't yet won the World Series that would validate their vaunted reputation. Cincinnati's historical record in the Fall Classic, although not as operatic or lavishly lamented as that of the Red Sox, was every bit as dismal, and on the facts less than half as productive. After winning their first World Series championship in 1919, the Reds waited twenty years for their second and had captured just one more National League pennant since, in 1961, only to be steamrollered in a five-game Series by the powerhouse Yankees. Another decade of doldrums followed, but since Sparky had taken the helm, the Reds had climbed within reach of that elusive prize twice, only to come away both times empty-handed. So it hardly mattered now that they were only one game away from the championship again; Stengel had said it to him first decades ago and Dedeaux had repeated it ad infinitum, and Sparky kept saying it now in the same classically fractured baseball syntax until he was blue in the face: *They don't hand out no trophies for second place.*

If his Reds didn't close the deal this time, Sparky knew that the combustible mixture of talent, luck, and locker room chemistry that enabled any winning ball club to perform at its peak could blow apart on the first strong breeze. No one in Cincinnati's front office had said as much to him, and they didn't need to; he knew that his own job, the jobs of his coaching staff and almost every man on the roster, hung in the balance. Every championship team had to learn to win at this level, and by any fair measure the men of the Big Red Machine had all had more than enough postseason education. It was *expected* of them now. It was time.

One more win.

And so the question for tonight. He'd moved Morgan back up into the second spot for the first two games of the Series, on the heavy, wet grass of Fenway, dropping Griffey down to seventh. They'd split those games, an acceptable result. Back home on the turf at Riverfront for Games Three through Five, he'd slotted Griffey back in between Rose and Morgan. With their speed restored at the top of the lineup, the Reds had won two of those three games and seized the Series lead. Now, back at Fenway for Game Six, especially after the weekend's torrential rains had muddied the track, percentages dictated he should go back to Morgan batting behind Rose, and drop Griffey to the seven hole again. Griffey had come through with a timely ninth-inning hit to win Game Two but had been struggling at the plate since—Sparky thought his budding young star was feeling the pressure of his first Series—and even the rock-steady Morgan had been pressing a little, trying to make things happen, although he'd started to come around in Cincinnati. Anderson needed power more than speed on the damp field at Fenway tonight, and nobody set the table for the meat of his lineup like Little Joe. Morgan himself had been lobbying for the move since the playoffs began, and Sparky gave everything his best all-around player said a lot of weight.

But something ate at him. Every time he picked up the pen that afternoon to write in Joe's name under Pete's, he hesitated. Sparky lived and died with percentages, but he also trusted his gut, and right now it was burning a hole through him.

He knew it had something to do with that pitcher the Sox were throwing at them again tonight. The man this damn rain delay was letting them bring back a game earlier than they otherwise would have been able to, the one who'd single-handedly won the only two games the Red Sox had taken in this Series, the second one—Game Four, one that Sparky felt the Reds should have grabbed—on sheer guts and willpower alone. Their ace, the only man in a Boston uniform who really unnerved him, the wild card in this whole mysterious equation.

That damn Tiant.

FOUR

When we play, we play. Forget the excuses.

RED SOX SHORTSTOP RICK BURLESON

O N THEIR WAY UP TO THE BOOTH TO PREPARE FOR THE broadcast, Tony Kubek and Dick Stockton made a pass through Fenway's rooftop press box and grabbed a quick bite to eat at the buffet. *Boston Globe* beat writer Peter Gammons came over to say hello to Kubek, and introduced his colleague Lesley Visser, the comely, wide-eyed young woman at his side. Gammons explained that Lesley was the beneficiary of the press pass that Kubek had graciously procured for him that day. Trying not to gush, Lesley thanked Kubek profusely. Kubek, in turn, introduced her to Dick Stockton, whom Lesley knew from television as the Red Sox play-by-play man.

Stockton responded the way most red-blooded American males did upon meeting Lesley; he began figuring out how he was going to end up with her phone number by the end of the conversation. Not without cause, Dick had developed a bit of a reputation around town as a ladies' man—he was a high-profile bachelor and this was the mid-seventies—and pressed as he was for time, he threw caution to the wind and asked her out to dinner. Accustomed as any attractive young woman is to fielding male attention, Lesley might have demurred, but this was her first visit to the fabled Fenway press box, with scores of the nation's best sportswriters preparing to man rows of typewriters arrayed like a battery of guns toward the playing field. The room was flooded with lifelong heroes from her improbable chosen field, and this was the first time she'd ever laid eyes on most of them: Dick Young, the irascible dean of baseball beat writers, from New York's *Daily News;* the *Los Angeles Times*'s wry humanist Jim Murray; the *New Yorker*'s elegant essayist Roger Angell. The whole experience left her "feeling a little like Dorothy after crash landing in Oz." An unknown walking into the commissary at MGM wouldn't have felt more starstruck.

So she said yes to dinner. Stockton pocketed her phone number, excused himself, and hurried after Kubek to the NBC broadcast booth; so far, so good. Lesley stepped back out of the way, standing behind the top row of press box seats as game time approached, and prepared to drink it all in.

ON GAME DAY before his scheduled starts nobody talked to Luis Tiant. Before every other game, on any other day, Luis was the club-house clown, the prankster who kept the whole team loose. As his friend Tommy Harper liked to say about him, Luis "woke up funny," and his sly, corner-barbershop perspective punctured all pretension; take yourself too seriously around *El Tiante* at your own peril. His elaborate practical jokes had become the stuff of legend in Fenway, and there was no limit to the lengths to which he'd lie in wait to exact revenge for any retaliation. A major-league club's locker room chemistry is the submerged end of the iceberg the public seldom sees, but has as much to do with its success as what happens on the field. Every squad is hierarchical and naturally forms a pecking order, immediately apparent to everyone on the roster, that dictates deference and ritualizes daily routine—stars at the top, scrubs at the bottom—for better or worse. But Tiant had tweaked the Red Sox status quo from the day he first arrived in Boston in 1971—at that point a broken-down former star, buried in the bullpen, trying to resurrect his career after two lost, injured seasons—and his first target had been the team's dour veteran captain, Carl Yastrzemski.

By virtue of his talent, work ethic, and decade-long tenure, Yaz was the Red Sox's unquestioned leader, but although as intelligent and articulate about the game as any man playing it, he didn't tend to say much. Intimidated by Yaz's intensity and smoldering self-containment, the team's younger players went out of their way to avoid ruffling his feathers, which created an unintended air of tension around the captain and their locker room. Although deeply talented, the Red Sox of that moment hadn't come together as a team, and were succinctly described as "twenty-five players taking twenty-five cabs." Tiant immediately sensed that the driven, reticent Yastrzemski was also simply shy, and when he responded to the first prank Luis pulled on him with roars of laughter—and soon after retaliated with a prank of his own—the ice was broken. Tiant dubbed Yaz the "Great Polacko"—nobody else could get away with that—but he made even more fun of himself; everybody laughed at Luis. The squad had grown steadily closer off the field ever since, with the good-natured Tiant as its unifying center; his ability to accept the bad with the good—and laugh at both—had given these Red Sox a guiding philosophy.

And during that time, regaining arm strength and control after nearly losing his career, Luis Tiant had reclaimed his status on the field as one of the most respected starting pitchers in the game. He'd won seventy-nine games for the Red Sox since, winning twenty in three consecutive seasons, if you counted his recent postseason wins, a feat no Boston pitcher had accomplished since the dawn of the twentieth century. As Darrell Johnson had predicted when they signed him, Tiant was now the number one starter on the Red Sox staff, but his recent performance during their drive to the pennant in 1975 had elevated him to the revered status of a Boston folk hero.

Twice in the previous three seasons the Red Sox had squandered substantial late-season leads in the East Division and let a postseason berth slip from their grasp; in 1974, their epic collapse had been one of the most wrenching any team had suffered in twenty years. With that heartbreak fresh in their minds, the Red Sox reached September of 1975 with a six-game lead, and New England's fatalistic fans began glancing over their shoulders, certain that another specter of doom must be gaining on them. Misfortune seemed even more certain when later that month their power-hitting rookie left fielder

Jim Rice was lost for the year, his left hand fractured by an errant fastball. Earl Weaver's Orioles, who had overtaken them in '74, charged hard at the Sox again now, cutting the lead to four and a half games.

Their running battle climaxed in the most exciting game Fenway had seen since 1967, a tense pitchers' duel on September 16, between Oriole ace and future Hall of Famer Jim Palmer and Luis Tiant, who tossed a masterful 2–0 shutout in front of an ecstatic crowd, to extend Boston's lead. Tiant had defended the ramparts. From that point on the Red Sox held firm; the Orioles couldn't gain any more ground and, exhausted by the effort, faltered at the wire. Despite the loss of Rice, their offense never sputtered, and the Red Sox clinched the American League East in the final week of the season. Their subsequent sweep of the three-time defending World Series champion Oakland A's in the League Championship confounded the national pundits, who never placed much stock in Boston's chances, and worked their faithful into a frenzy. Much of their adoration settled on their number one starter, Luis Tiant, the foundation of their finishing kick and the player Tom Yawkey singled out as "the man who did it for us." His numbers cinch the argument: In the last three weeks of the season, and thus far into the League Championship and World Series, while throwing five complete-game victories at Fenway Park in a row, Luis Tiant had allowed *only one earned run* to cross home plate.

Out in right field, Luis finished his warm-ups in the bullpen, slipped on his jacket, strutted into the dugout, and sat by himself on the Red Sox bench—eyes hooded, brow furrowed, in a trance of concentration—until it was go time. When *El Tiante* stepped out on the field to take the mound for Game Six, the fans at Fenway rose as one, an extended standing ovation. No starting pitcher had won three games in a World Series since the Tigers' Mickey Lolich in 1968, and only once had a team *ever* lost a Series when a pitcher pulled off that rare feat. The crowd urged Tiant to his task, and the chant they'd adopted as their battle cry that summer filled the air: "Loo-eee, Loo-eee, Loo-eee!"

In the press box, the staccato clatter of keys from two hundred typewriters signaled the onset of hostilities. Young David Israel from the *Washington Star* had managed to secure a seat next to Red Smith, the seventy-year-old veteran baseball writer for the *New York Times,* poised over his blue portable Olympia. The chilly evening air in the open press box felt electric; Israel sensed a story was waiting out there on the field for him, the kind that could make careers. If half of catching a break was being in the right place at the right time, this might just be his night.

In the trailer under the right field stands, at precisely 8:30 P.M. Eastern standard time, director Harry Coyle called the broadcast's first shots, cued Joe Garagiola in the booth, and Game Six, the first World Series game ever played at night in Fenway Park, went out live to the nation and around the world on NBC. Garagiola made his opening remarks and then introduced the audience to Dick Stockton, who would handle play-by-play for the first half of the game, then turn it back over to Garagiola.

Boston Celtics forward John "Hondo" Havlicek drew a big hand from the crowd as he and his wife, Beth, took their seats near the field. The thirty-five-year-old forward, a week away from starting his fourteenth season with the club, was one of the last remaining links to the remarkable 1960s Celtics dynasty that had captured eleven NBA championships in thirteen years. After most of that group, led by center and coach Bill Russell, retired, Havlicek had captained the Celtics to their first title in five years, in 1974, and his presence seemed to encourage the crowd to believe that tonight anything was possible for their Red Sox. With its smaller rosters, basketball had been the first of the major sports to start lavishing star players with contracts that made more headlines than the games themselves; Havlicek was playing for $250,000 this year, more than the entire championship Celtics roster had cost just a decade earlier.

On the Cincinnati bench, Sparky Anderson jammed another stick of gum in his mouth and took his place on the bench beside coach Larry Shepard; he always had Shepard sit to his right, and when the Reds were in the field, third base coach Alex Grammas sat on his left. Superstition, the secret religion of baseball—and Sparky was a devout believer—demanded that they always assume this formation.

Home plate umpire Satch Davidson handed the game's first ball to Red Sox catcher Carlton Fisk, who threw it out to Tiant, and he completed his final warm-up tosses.

In his small area off the press box, Fenway's public address system announcer Sherm Feller slipped out his dentures—a small personal secret; that was how he created his distinctive speaking style—clicked on his microphone, and said: "Now batting for the Cincinnati Reds . . . Rose, third base, Rose."

A smattering of boos greeted the thirty-four-year-old Rose as he trotted over, dug in on the left side of the plate, and assumed his familiar coiled crouch, waving his bat in a tight circle, while he grinned out at Tiant, who glared back, his elaborate Fu Manchu mustache adding piratical menace to the glower. Bad blood had sprung up between Rose and Tiant over the course of the Series, on the heels of some sour grapes Pete had spilled to the press and recycled in his own ghostwritten column for the *Cincinnati Enquirer*—they titled it "Rose Prose"—in the aftermath of Tiant's 6–0 shutout victory in Game One, the first complete-game World Series win thrown by any pitcher in four years.

"His best pitch wasn't that curve, fastball, slider, knuckleball or blooper pitch. It was his 'at em' pitch. He threw a lot of 'at-ems'; pitches we hit 'at' somebody. We hit 'at-ems' all day long. I hit three line drives at people myself, I couldn't have hit the ball any harder. But I was due for a collar, I'd hit in seventeen straight games. Yeah, he shut us out, but I wouldn't mind facing him every day, I'd like to see him a hundred times, I might go 0 for 100 but I wouldn't mind hitting against him."

Tiant might still speak somewhat fractured English, and Rose was seldom accused of doing his native tongue many favors, but in any language this is called disrespecting your opponent, and is seldom expressed within the boundaries of the *mano a mano* battle between batter and pitcher. Giving your opponent bulletin board material at this point in a Series is also considered a strict, unwritten baseball taboo, but trying to get under an opponent's skin was not only a big part of what Peter Edward Rose saw as his job on the Reds, it was also an essential expression of his street fighter's personality. As he often did, even while serving up a dig, Rose had managed to slip in a self-regarding reference to his recent hitting streak.

More than any other man in baseball, "Charlie Hustle" cast himself as a self-conscious agitator. He wasn't just their captain and spark plug at the top of the lineup, but the guy you loved to hate—who wanted and dared you to hate him—unless you wore the same uniform. Everything Rose did on the field seemed designed, deliberately or not, to aggravate opponents; he ran everywhere, from the dugout to the field and back, and if he drew a walk, he sprinted down to first base like a man whose pants were on fire. During the Series, one of Boston's more colorful sportswriters repeatedly referred to him as "the Hun." A Cincinnati native, son of a former semi-pro football player who worked in the same bank for forty-two years, Pete Rose possessed a lot more skill as a player than he was often given credit for, because the way in which he'd made himself a star in the major leagues appeared to be such a sheer act of will. Although his background wasn't strictly as working class as he wanted people to believe, he had become a hero in his conservative home town by personifying the underappreciated lunch-bucket qualities in themselves they most admired—and often felt were disparaged or scorned by the country's coastal liberal elites. Richard Nixon had tapped into that same simmering middle-class resentment in what he branded the "Silent Majority" and ridden it into two terms in the White House.

Not unlike Nixon, who had been driven from office in disgrace only fourteen months earlier, qualities that most fans viewed as admirable and all-American during Rose's first decade in the game—his boundless energy, gap-toothed Huck Finn enthusiasm for the game, and ditch-digger work ethic—were at this point in his career beginning to uneasily coexist with suggestions that something darker might be coiled beneath the surface. Rose had hurled himself into Cleveland Indians catcher Roy Fosse in a horrific collision at home plate during the 1970 All-Star Game—where nothing but pride is supposed to be on the line—and injured him so badly it severely curtailed Fosse's promising career. In 1973, during their losing National League Championship Series against the Mets, Rose had gone in hard and high on a force play at second base and threw an elbow at Mets shortstop Bud Harrelson, triggering an ugly brawl and a near riot at Shea Stadium. Just the other night, in the first inning of Game Five, while sliding into a tag at home plate, Rose admitted to reporters that he had tried, and failed, to kick the ball out of Carlton Fisk's hand. None of these moves, considered case by case, crossed the line—to the contrary, they were offered as evidence of his passionate devotion to winning—but a body of evidence had begun to accrue.

"That's the only way I know how to play the game" became Pete's matter-of-fact defense, and he was always so open and available and engaging with the press that they had perpetually given him a pass. Although, in the wake of Watergate, the emerging ethics of "new journalism" now encouraged reporters to tread deeper into what had formerly been considered the private lives of public figures, sportswriters—particularly team "beat" writers whose livelihood then depended on close, often protective daily relationships with their subjects—were among the last in print to change their ways. Rumors of Rose's questionable off-field behavior and relationships with bookies abounded but remained strictly off-limits in the papers. But now that public opinion, prompted by journalistic digging, had finally returned a damning verdict on Nixon, Pete Rose had begun to represent a walking question for some observers: At what point does an unbridled competitive instinct cross over into pathology?

After flying out in his last at bat against Tiant in Game One at Fenway, Rose had crossed back to the dugout behind the mound and said to Tiant: "Bring your lucky charm with you to Cincinnati: You'll need it." Early on during Game Four, when he faced Tiant for the second time, Rose turned to Red Sox catcher Carlton Fisk after a few pitches, held his thumb and forefinger in a zero sign, and said: "Nothing. The guy has nothing. He wouldn't win five games in the National League."

When a Boston reporter showed a published account of that moment to Tiant in the clubhouse over the weekend during the long rain delay, hoping for the kind of incendiary response that beat writers can hammer into headlines, Tiant calmly read the piece, crumpled it up, and threw it in the trash.

"I don't have anything to say," he said quietly. "I just hope I get a chance to face them again."

The scorecard so far: Rose versus Tiant 1–7, with two walks, one run scored. Tiant versus the Reds 2–0.

Rose took Tiant's first pitch of the game, a fastball with some zip on it that moved slightly away from him and caught the outside right corner for a called strike.

How you like that *fastball, Pete?*

What Rose had been trying to get at about Tiant, in his own needling way, had an element of truth; in both Series games he'd pitched against the Reds, Tiant did not come at them with an overpowering fastball. The Reds were a dead fastball–hitting team, and for over a decade the National League had been thought of as offering a "purer" form of the game's reddest meat: power pitchers trying to throw it past power hitters. The American League, it was said, lived more on corners, curveballs, and finesse, an image that "innovations" like the designated hitter had done little to dispel. But during Tiant's first tour of duty in the bigs, a six-year stint for the mediocre Cleveland Indians in the mid-sixties, he'd been one of the most dominating fireballers in the game; in his best season, 1968, he'd gone 21–9, struck out 264 batters, and posted an otherworldly earned run average of 1.60, the lowest number posted by *any* pitcher in the American League since Hall of Famer Walter Johnson in 1919. Batters, for that entire season, hit only .168 against Tiant. He led the league with nine shutouts, at one point threw forty-one consecutive scoreless innings, and one night struck out nineteen in a ten-inning complete-game win; that's power pitching.

After struggling through the 1969 season, Tiant became the centerpiece of a multiplayer trade to the contending Minnesota Twins. He showed no signs of letting up after starting the season for the Twins 6–0, but then suffered the first serious injury of his career: a fractured right scapula damaged by the exceptional demands he'd been making on his arm for ten years. No team doctor had ever seen this injury in a pitcher before; it abruptly ended his ability to rely on strength and power alone, and should have ended his season. But eager to help his new team, he tried to come back from the injury too soon and pitched indifferently, losing three of four starts down the stretch of a pennant race. The Twins won the West Division, but the Orioles swept them in the American League Championship Series.

A few months later when Tiant didn't immediately bounce back, notoriously tightfisted Twins owner Calvin Griffith gave up on him at the end of spring training in 1971, handing him a shocking outright release. No time on the disabled list to heal, or minor-league assignment to work his way back into shape—he had been fired, his contract rendered null and void. The transaction sent a coded but unmistakable message across the wire to the rest of baseball: Luis Tiant is washed up. Griffith was then quoted as saying he could "get four or five young kids for the money I was gonna pay him": all of $65,000. The team left Luis at their Orlando hotel while they returned to Minneapolis for the start of the regular season. His shocked and outraged teammates filed past him in the lobby on their way to the bus, some of them near tears as they said good-bye to their most popular player. But taking Griffith at his word that Tiant was damaged goods, no other major-league team stepped up to take a chance on him.

At the age of thirty, just when he'd reached the point where a decade of excellence had resulted in a contract that might offer Tiant the first professional and financial security of his life, the cautionary warnings his father had made about the cutthroat practices of pro baseball appeared to have come to pass. Yes, the Old Man had let young Luis go to Mexico to pitch back in 1959, and three baseball seasons later his son had defied the odds when he signed a contract with the Cleveland Indians. Never shy of the spotlight, Tiant made a startling major-league debut, throwing a four-hit shutout against Whitey Ford and the mighty Yankees in their fabled home park, but despite the success he then went on to have with the Tribe, becoming by acclaim one of the best pitchers in baseball, Tiant had never been paid accordingly. Latin players in particular had a hard time negotiating with their teams during this era in the game. Struggling to establish themselves in a different country and culture and language, without effective representation, they were reluctant to be perceived as troublemakers and as a result often had to settle for less than their fair market value. He had been one of the few bright spots on a mediocre Cleveland team for six years, but rather than reward Tiant after he had earned a bigger contract, the Indians moved him to Minnesota. Understanding that this game was a business first, Luis had always been cautious with his money, and Tiant Sr.'s advice hadn't gone completely unheeded; Luis had never moved his wife, Maria, and their three young children to the United States from her native Mexico City.

But in the spring of 1971 he was out of a job, and perhaps out of chances.

One man refused to give up on him: fellow pitcher Stan Williams, who'd been his teammate in Cleveland and seen Luis in his prime, and who'd also gone to the Twins with him as part of that same trade in 1969.

"I thought what was happening to Luis was a tragedy," said Williams. "I knew Luis when he was sound, and I was so sure in my heart that he wasn't finished. He's the best friend I ever had in baseball; I respected him as an athlete and I loved him as a person. I also knew how much this game means to him, which has nothing to do with cheers and headlines."

Williams worked the phone, reaching out to every executive he knew, and convinced a scout in the Atlanta Braves organization to give Luis a thirty-day contract with their International League Triple-A franchise in Richmond, Virginia. Although Richmond only used him sporadically, Tiant had two particularly effective outings against the Louisville Colonels, the league's Boston Red Sox affiliate, that made Louisville's manager Darrell Johnson take notice. A former major-league catcher with a keen eye for pitching talent, Johnson alerted the Red Sox to take a look at Tiant. At the end of Tiant's contract, the Atlanta front office, which was committed to a youth movement and had signed Luis primarily as a favor, released him again, at which point Johnson quietly persuaded Boston's general manager Dick O'Connell to sign Tiant to a full year's contract with the Red Sox organization.

Darrell Johnson put Tiant to immediate work in his rotation at Louisville and saw his confidence, control, and command grow with every outing; in thirty-one innings, he struck out twenty-nine and posted a 2.61 ERA. Johnson called Dick O'Connell less than three weeks later to tell him that "whoever your best pitcher is up there right now, Tiant is going to be better."

O'Connell sent his director of player personnel Haywood Sullivan out to Rochester that night to confirm the opinion, and he watched Tiant throw a seemingly effortless shutout in the first half of a doubleheader. The next morning, Sullivan met Luis for breakfast.

"Are you ready to come back to the big leagues?" asked Sullivan.

"Just give me the ball," said Tiant, "and I will show you."

After being called up by the Red Sox in June of 1971, Tiant spent most of his time in the bullpen, pitching effectively but compiling only a 1–7 record. Regaining his form in 1972, Tiant worked his way into the starting rotation by mid-season, went 15–6, won his second ERA title (1.91), and ended up being named the American League's Comeback Player of the Year. He then followed that up with back-to-back twenty-win seasons. If he never did fully reclaim the monstrous fastball of his youth, by 1975 no one could dispute that he had reestablished himself as one of the game's marquee talents. That was the distinction Pete Rose had failed to recognize: Luis Tiant wasn't merely a *thrower* anymore; like his father before him, he had matured into a *pitcher.* A pitcher recognizes that he can and must use any means necessary to win his battle with hitters, and Tiant had developed one of the most varied and wicked arsenals of weapons that students of the game had ever seen. Recognizing that at its core the art of hitting is about timing—a batter has, at best, one fifth of a second to decide whether or not to swing at an average major-league pitch once the ball is released—Luis did everything in his power on the mound to confound and disrupt a hitter's perceptions. His windup, an elaborate, herky-jerky montage of gyrations, tics, and seemingly gratuitous embellishments—which included looking up at the sky, the lights, or fans in the upper deck, while completely turning his back to the plate—came toward the batter at four different tempos and from three different directions: overhand, three quarter, sidearm. He could throw five different pitches employing all those variations, with equal proficiency, and never look exactly the same way twice.

The casual observer might dismiss all his exertions as theatrical excess, but Tiant's methods had a purely practical purpose: They allowed him to disguise the ball for so long that it became nearly impossible to pick up the release point when it left his hand, the crucial moment in a batter's effort to then infer a pitch's direction and speed. Add to that Luis's pinpoint control—home plate is seventeen inches across; he worked primarily on the two inches of black rubber on its outside edges—his masterful knowledge of the strike zone, his ability to change speeds *without* altering his windup, and the comprehensive book he kept on the tendencies of every batter he faced, it was no wonder so many hitters walked back to the dugout shaking their heads. No, Tiant didn't throw as hard as he used to—although he could still top 90 mph on the speed gun when he reared back, like on that first pitch to Rose—but batters seldom seemed able to do anything about it. His teammate Carl Yastrzemski, who knew a little bit about hitting, had faced Tiant often when he pitched for the Indians earlier in their careers.

"Luis is the only guy I can think of who kept me guessing every minute," said Yaz.

During the 1975 season, when the Red Sox appeared often on NBC's *Game of the Week*, Tiant's contorted delivery had become the windup most imitated by young baseball players not just in Boston but across the country, and had led to his growing national popularity. He also recognized as few others did that an essential part of his job—the job of the game itself—was to entertain people, and a pitcher occupies center stage more obviously than any other athlete in team sports. Tiant made himself entirely available to fans before and after games, signing autographs, posing for photos, engaging in real conversations, impressing everyone he met with his gentle and genuine demeanor. When he'd played and lived in Cleveland, neighborhood kids knew they could always ride their bikes over, knock on his door, and spend some time with him; sometimes he'd even come outside and toss a ball around. Luis was at heart a showman, who embraced and relished his leading man's role, but he was also deeply devoted to the game for the skill, guts, and artistry it allowed him to express. That was an even bigger reason for the respect and affection he inspired in people; when the biggest stakes were on the table, he gave the game every last measure of himself.

Pete Rose labored every day of his life to grind out the maximum result from what by any measure was far from the game's biggest talent, and he had earned his reputation as the hardest-working man in baseball. Both he and Luis Tiant had by this time, for all these reasons, become the public faces of their respective franchises. Not surprisingly, off the field both men also liked to gamble, hooked on the adrenaline rush of being in the center of the action. But in Tiant, for maybe the first time in his life, Pete Rose had met his match as a competitor.

Rose lashed at Tiant's second pitch, a high, hanging breaking ball, and lined it crisply to left field. Carl Yastrzemski dashed forward at the crack of the bat, slipped slightly on his first step, recovered, slid onto his left knee in the moist turf, and snatched the sinking liner out of the air. Another hard hit "at-em" ball, with the same result: one out. Rose, batting .315 in the Series and leading his team in hits, was now 1–8 against Tiant.

Ken Griffey stepped into the box. Sparky had gone with his hunch that afternoon and kept Griffey in the second spot of his lineup. Mindful that Griffey had gotten a hit against Tiant in both his games so far, and hit the ball hard two other times for outs, Sparky hoped that his speed could help the Reds manufacture some early runs and take the crowd out of the game. Tiant fed off the energy in Fenway, Sparky could feel it, and tonight they'd turned the dial into the red; they needed to get to him fast. He also trusted that gut instinct of his: Griffey was going to do some business tonight.

Tiant came right at him with a fastball, taken, strike one.

At Sparky's urging, Cincinnati's hitting coach, fifty-one-year-old Ted Kluszewski—one of the greatest pure sluggers in Reds history, a sequoia of a man with Popeye biceps—had counseled Griffey that day to be more patient at the plate and wait for his pitch. Home run hitters didn't historically have a strong record as hitting instructors—power was still regarded then as more an instinct than a coachable skill—but Kluszewski, a sensitive, patient, and intelligent man, had worked wonders with the Reds lineup; one could argue that he had also been given an embarrassment of wonders with which to work. But Ken Griffey had been one of "Klu's" best projects.

Outside, fastball, ball one.

Griffey had been playing organized ball for only six years, and as a kid had hardly even been schooled in the game's fundamentals. He was a football and basketball star in his hometown of Donora, Pennsylvania, and he played baseball primarily to have something to do during the off-season. A Reds scout, there to check out another player at one of his high school games, put a stopwatch on Griffey and was astonished to realize he motored from home to first base faster than any player he'd ever timed. The Reds drafted Griffey in the twenty-ninth round in 1969 for that one reason: They had just made an organization-wide commitment that, because of the artificial carpet they were installing in their new home, Riverfront Stadium, their club would be built on speed. Although he had college football scholarships on the table, Griffey decided to accept the Reds' offer of immediate cash: $500 a month to join their team in the rookie league. Their long-shot bet on Griffey's potential paid off quickly; by 1973 he'd earned a late-season call-up to the big club and hit .384. By 1975, his rapid development had made possible Sparky's shuffle of Rose to third base, and Griffey responded to his promotion by hitting .305, stealing sixteen bases, and most important, getting on base enough to be driven in ninety-five times by the big guns batting behind him.

Screwball, breaking away from the left-handed Griffey, outside and low, 2–1.

He had also, at Kluszewski's insistence, started to learn patience at the plate. Drawing sixty-seven walks in 1975, Griffey's on-base percentage nearly reached .400, the most reliable indicator that he had arrived as a major-league talent.

Griffey swung at a high off-speed curve, fouling it back near the broadcast booth, where Tony Kubek almost caught it barehanded. Griffey chopped the next sidearm breaking ball foul off first base.

Kubek mentioned on the air that Luis Tiant often reminded him of Juan Marichal, the star of the San Francisco Giants' pitching staff in the 1960s. Marichal, one of the first players to reach the major leagues from the baseball-crazed Dominican Republic, had been known for his high leg kick, which had a similarly distracting effect on hitters. He also possessed extraordinary control and the ability to adapt his pitching style to whatever the circumstances of a game required, all qualities he shared with Tiant. Only a few years apart in age, Marichal and Tiant had briefly crossed paths as teammates in Boston the previous season; after one last stint with the Dodgers, Marichal had recently announced his retirement, and eight years later he would become the first Latin-born pitcher to enter the Hall of Fame.

Tiant's next pitch, another screwball that Griffey resisted, just missed the outside corner to run the count to full. Griffey's patience paid off when the payoff pitch missed inside, the first time Tiant had come inside to him during the entire at bat. Griffey trotted to first with a walk.

Second baseman Joe Morgan came to the plate. Standing a trim, compact five foot seven, he looked like a school kid beside the imposing, battle-geared Carlton Fisk, but Morgan was only weeks away from being named the National League's Most Valuable Player for the 1975 season. Born in Bonham, Texas, Morgan had come of age in Oakland, California, where despite his small stature he'd made himself into one of the toughest players to ever come out of an extremely tough neighborhood. Signing after high school as a low-level prospect with the National League's new Houston Colt .45s franchise, Morgan shocked everyone in that organization by making it all the way to the big-league club by the end of his first full season in professional ball. Within two years, at the age of twenty-one, he had established himself as the team's everyday second baseman, the same year they changed their name to the Houston Astros. A pattern had been established that would persist for much of his career, and indeed his life: Joe Morgan striving to overcome the limits imposed on him by other people's inaccurate perceptions. Morgan's size played a considerable part in those prejudicial opinions and in those days, in baseball and the South, so did his race. His confidence in himself then had a lot to make up for—and in the opinion of many often turned to arrogance—but it never wavered. And this season, in 1975, as he played for Sparky and the Reds, that great talent had come to full fruition.

Morgan dug in, took his stance, oversized bat held high, and snapped his left elbow up and down like an airplane flap, one of the most imitated batter's box tics in baseball. Tiant made a couple of tosses over to first base, trying to keep Griffey close to the bag. Tiant's stretch windup was every bit as eccentric as his full one; bringing his hand and glove together at chest level as he straddled the rubber, he brought them down to his waist in a series of small bounces, as if they were being lowered by a ratchet. The routine never looked the same way twice, and at any point in the process he might whirl and fire to first; the Old Man had indeed helped teach him a superb pickoff move, one of the best for a right hander in either league.

THE "BALK"

Before the Series, Sparky Anderson, who'd never managed against Luis Tiant—and only seen him throw in a game once in person, briefly, during the 1974 All-Star Game— had watched film on Boston's ace and thought he'd spotted something he could exploit. To Sparky's eye, it appeared that Tiant never brought the ball to a complete stop during that stretch windup and often released his pickoff throws to first base before planting his left foot; the baseball rule book states the pitcher must land that step before throwing or it should be considered an attempt to "deceive the runner" and be ruled a balk, awarding the runner free passage to the next base. Sparky brought these points up to the umpiring crew ahead of Game One—there were later rumors that he'd sent videotape of Tiant to their office ahead of time, which he denied—and he talked it up extensively to the press, a form of psychological warfare to try to gain an advantage for his runners against the crafty Tiant. The Reds had led the National League with 168 stolen bases, and were successful 82 percent of the time they ran; Sparky knew that getting a balk called early, possibly breaking Tiant's confidence and concentration in the process, could be a key to beating him. National and American League umpires were still administered by two separate organizations, the World Series and All-Star Game being the only two occasions when they actually worked together. The composite umpire crew chosen for the Series had consequently spent extensive time reviewing the balk rule before Game One, which put the issue in the forefront of their minds.

In the fourth inning of Game One, Sparky's tactic paid off. After Tiant retired the first ten batters he faced, Joe Morgan singled to become the Reds' first base runner. Tiant made two routine throws to first, then caught Morgan leaning toward second and nearly picked him off on the third; the crowd and Sox first baseman Cecil Cooper thought he was out. After Tiant's fourth pickoff throw, first base umpire Nick Colosi called a balk and waved Morgan to second. Red Sox manager Darrell Johnson ran out to argue the call, and Tiant rushed over from the mound, both of them shouting at Colosi. Tiant was outraged and for good reason; he hadn't had a balk called on him in the American League for the last six years. On tape, in NBC's slow-motion replay, Tiant's left foot clearly lands before he makes the throw, but at least one of the umpires—from the Reds' National League, it should be noted—appeared to have been influenced by Sparky's lobbying; Nick Colosi had swallowed the bait. Morgan later admitted that he wasn't sure an American League umpire would have made the same call, but insisted it was still his job to try to make Tiant balk. Sparky's mind game had worked to perfection, landing his best runner on second with only one out and a still visibly upset Tiant facing the Reds' dangerous cleanup man Johnny Bench: advantage Reds. A furious Darrell Johnson and the rest of the Red Sox bench continued to give Colosi an earful from the dugout, stirring up the crowd against him. Colosi—a onetime waiter at New York's famed Copacabana nightclub, and notorious for his imperial air on the field—came over to stab a finger in the air at Johnson and threaten him with ejection.

"I realized while I was arguing that this was just what Cincinnati wanted me to do," said Tiant. "I just told myself not to get mad and get back to thinking about pitching."

Red Sox second baseman Denny Doyle trotted over to Tiant on the mound and reminded him to forget about it;

Tiant patted him reassuringly on the cheek, and it was clear he already had. While the hubbub roiled on around him, Tiant regained his composure, bearing down and battling Johnny Bench for ten pitches before finally getting him to foul out to Fisk. As the chant of "Loo-eee, Loo-eee!" broke out in Fenway, Tiant then struck out first baseman Tony Perez to end the inning and the threat created by the phantom balk. The Reds would advance only three runners as far as second base during the rest of the game, and the unflappable Tiant cruised to a five-hit, 6–0 shutout victory in Game One.

Morgan had managed only two hits off Tiant while facing him nine times during the Series, but he'd also worked him for two walks. No one had to remind Morgan to be patient at the plate—with his small strike zone and good eye, he led the majors in bases on balls with 132—and he worked the count full against Tiant now. Morgan not only led the Reds in steals with 67, with Sparky's blessing he'd become their de facto base running coach, with Ken Griffey, the runner at first, his number one disciple. Morgan ran clinics during their practice sessions, showing his teammates how to measure and hold a precise lead, how to read a pitcher's motion for tells on when best to break for second, and how to use the *threat* of stealing to disrupt his concentration. But oddly, for most of the season, with Griffey batting ahead of him, Morgan had forbidden the fleet young outfielder to attempt to steal or even *feint* toward second while he was at the plate, claiming it distracted him while he was trying to hit, a large part of why, despite Morgan's tutelage, a man with Griffey's extraordinary motor had stolen only sixteen bases that season. Although Joe had supposedly "given Sparky the green light" to send runners ahead of him during the Series—more on their unusual relationship to come—Griffey never made a move toward second during Morgan's first at bat, which ended when he popped a high foul up above the screen that drifted on the wind blowing steadily toward center and died quietly in Fisk's mitt.

Reds catcher Johnny Bench stepped in. Although more circumspect in his public comments about it than Pete Rose, Bench had been similarly frustrated by the steady diet of off-speed stuff he'd seen from Tiant during the Series. One of the greatest fastball hitters the game had ever known, he felt he was seeing Tiant's ball well but just couldn't get his bat on it; he'd had no more success against him to date than Pete Rose, going 1–8 with only one RBI. Still bothered by his cold, his injured left shoulder aching in the cool New England air, Bench took a fastball for a strike, fouled the next one off, and then missed a low slider that broke out of the zone for Tiant's first strikeout.

The crowd rose to their feet again, Tiant trotted to the dugout, and the Red Sox came in for their first turn at bat.

Luis doesn't want to impress them.

He only wants to beat them.

RED SOX PITCHING COACH STAN WILLIAMS

It's just a stay of execution for Boston.

JOE MORGAN

F OR ALL THEIR SUCCESS IN 1975, WINNING ONE HUNDRED games to this point, the Red Sox had reached Game Six of the World Series without the presence or benefit all season of a single "traditional leadoff" man. Since the advent of the personal computer in the 1980s, a new breed of baseball statisticians has revolutionized the way players are viewed and evaluated. Although these analysts were initially amateurs working outside the professional structure of the game, most teams have embraced their findings and many now employ at least one full-time "sabermatrician," after the Society for American Baseball Research, or SABR, founded by Bill James, who is currently a consultant for the Red Sox. Baseball is a game exquisitely suited to measurement by numbers, with a vast trove of available—and, before these passionate wonks came along, previously underutilized—historical records. As they sifted through this remarkable database, breaking down every aspect of the game into new arcane definitions of value—like True Defensive Range, or the number of actual Runs Created—their formulas for the first time provided a solid scientific understanding for many of the game's traditions, and called into question most of its conventional wisdoms.

One of the most stubbornly enduring ideas in baseball had been that you stick your speediest player at the top of the lineup, turn him loose, and hope that a lot of stolen bases translate into runs, a notion that for a number of reasons the game's new statistics had largely discredited. (The last man to fit that profile for the Red Sox, outfielder Tommy Harper—who'd set a team record for steals with fifty-four in 1973—had been traded after the '74 season to make way for promising rookies Jim Rice and Fred Lynn.) A more refined philosophy had begun to emerge that you should send the man with the best on base percentage (hits plus walks plus hit-by-pitches, divided by at bats plus walks plus HBP plus sacrifices) to the plate first in the hopes of then bringing him around, as Sparky Anderson was able to consistently do with Pete Rose, who stole not a *single* base in 1975, but reached first more than 40 percent of the time.

In 1975 Boston's manager Darrell Johnson didn't possess that luxury; the highest OBPs among his regulars belonged to Fred Lynn and Carlton Fisk, men he wanted and needed deeper in his lineup because of their ability to drive in runs. His Red Sox had stolen only sixty-six bases all season, and the co-leaders on Johnson's squad were Lynn and the disabled Jim Rice, both with ten; Sparky's Reds had *six* regulars with as many as or more steals than that, including catcher Johnny Bench. Johnson's best option was probably reserve outfielder Bernie Carbo, who'd drawn a lot of walks and performed well in the leadoff spot earlier in the season, but he had been injured and gone cold down the stretch; Johnson decided to hold Carbo in reserve as his number one left-handed pinch hitter in the Series. The fastest man on the Red Sox was Juan Beniquez, a onetime shortstop, utility outfielder, and sometime designated hitter whom they had recently tried to convert to third base, with little success. But baseball had decreed that the American League's new and still controversial designated hitter rule would not be used in this Series. (In response to charges that this was unfair to teams that had depended on it during their regular season, starting in 1976 the DH was allowed in the Series during even-numbered years, until 1986, when the current rule of using it only during home games in

American League parks in *every* Series went into effect.) With the DH position unavailable to him, Johnson preferred to use the right-handed Beniquez in platoon duty against left-handers, and had penciled him in as his leadoff man in Games Four and Five, against Reds southpaw starters Freddie Norman and Don Gullett. In Game One, also against their ace Gullett, Johnson had somewhat randomly used his power-hitting right fielder, Dwight Evans, as the leadoff man. In Games Two and Three, against Reds right-handers Jack Billingham and Gary Nolan, left-handed first baseman Cecil Cooper went into the top slot. None had proved markedly successful. For Game Six, Johnson decided to go back to Cooper again.

The twenty-five-year-old Cooper, a tall, rangy line-drive hitter, had batted a solid .311 for the season, with respectable power numbers in 305 at bats. A quiet, unassuming, and intelligent team player from the Houston area, he was the youngest of thirteen children and had been taught the game by his father and two uncles, who had all played in the Negro Leagues. Drafted by the Red Sox in 1968, Cooper finally earned a spot with the parent club in 1974, but found himself struggling for playing time after the splashy emergence in '75 of Fred Lynn and Jim Rice. Rice's big bat won the left field job early in the year, which allowed Johnson to permanently install Carl Yastrzemski at first base—a transition for their gracefully aging captain that had been gradually under way for two years—which pushed Cecil Cooper out of his everyday position. A streaky hitter, Cooper had gotten hot and stayed that way throughout the summer, fighting for and finally earning his spot as the team's regular DH against right-handed pitching. He had appeared in only thirty-five games at first, a solid if unspectacular defender whenever Yaz needed a day off, but when Rice's hand was broken by a pitch in late September, Cooper saw a lot more action at first when Yastrzemski shifted back to left. Cooper had had his own brush with danger in the batter's box on September 7, when he was hit in the face by an inside fastball and had to be carried off the field on a stretcher. He returned to the lineup a few games after the beaning, but his productivity at the plate tailed off dramatically for the rest of the season. In the ruthless arena of the batter's box, pitchers quickly discovered that they could pitch Cooper inside, where the human instinct for self-preservation hindered his ability to make a committed swing just enough to throw off his superb professional hitter's timing.

That trend had continued into the World Series; Cooper stepped in as Boston's first batter in Game Six with only one hit in thirteen at bats.

Opposing Cooper on the mound was Reds starting pitcher Gary Nolan. In its broad outlines, the twenty-seven-year-old Nolan's career bore a more than passing resemblance to that of Luis Tiant. He had arrived in the major leagues in 1967 as a highly touted eighteen-year-old prospect, after less than one full season of minor-league ball, and won fourteen games as a rookie while striking out more than two hundred batters. By 1970, when Sparky took over and the early edition of the Big Red Machine made its first trip to the World Series, Nolan had established himself as the staff's ace and one of the premier power pitchers in the National League. He continued to enhance that reputation through 1972, when the Reds returned to the Series against the A's; Nolan turned in his finest performance to date that year, going 15–5 with a 1.99 earned run average. But a minor flaw in his mechanics finally caught up with him late in that season; after coming down with a sore shoulder, he discovered that years of throwing slightly across his body had seriously frayed his right rotator cuff. At a time when the soundness of pitchers' arms was under much less scrutiny—one of the most frequent prescriptions for arm trouble then was still to "throw through it"—Nolan was encouraged by the team to gut it out for the remainder of the season. When the injury persisted into 1973, he went to see Dr. Frank Jobe in Los Angeles, just then establishing his reputation as the country's first orthopedic surgeon with an enlightened understanding of—and operating table solutions for—damaged throwing arms. Jobe recommended immediate surgery; once again the Reds counseled Nolan to hold off and see if he could rehab the injury with a regimen of physical therapy. He complied but was able to throw only ten innings in '73 before shutting it down for the season, and finally went under the knife in the spring of 1974 to remove what turned out to be a large calcium deposit that had been ripping a hole in his shoulder muscle.

After almost two years on the sidelines, Nolan had returned to the Reds rotation in 1975, and gone 15–9 in his thirty-two starts, but he was a less dominant pitcher now, and in his absence twenty-four-year-old Don Gullett, a flame-throwing left-hander, had stepped in to replace him as the Reds' number one starter. Nolan no longer threw anything like the same blazing fastball, but he could still spot the one he had, as well as a sharply breaking curve, for strikes, and he retained command of his best "out" pitch, an exceptionally well-disguised changeup. Like Luis Tiant—even more so—he now relied on control, guile, and skill instead of sheer speed. Both men had confronted the fate that awaits almost every professional pitcher: when the unnatural strain of repeatedly throwing a five-ounce sphere as hard as you can for sixty feet, six inches causes the sinew and bones of your arm, shoulder, or elbow to break down. These two, unlike most, had worked their way back from devastating injury to the winner's circle, but unlike Tiant, Nolan had never lost the support of his team. A highly intelligent student of the game, family man, stand-up guy, and committed team player, Gary Nolan embodied more than any other man on their roster the straight-arrow values that the Reds prized and projected as an organization. He never griped to the press about his injury or bemoaned the bad luck that had befallen him, soldiering on to do whatever Sparky and the team asked of him, but since the injury, all through the '75 season, and for the rest of what remained of his career, he pitched in constant and considerable pain.

Nolan had been the Reds' starter in Game Three back in Cincinnati—his fifth career World Series start—throwing four strong innings while allowing only a single run on a Carlton Fisk home run. When his neck and shoulder tightened up, Nolan left the game with a lead the Reds would eventually yield and then reclaim for the win in the bottom of the tenth inning, after one of the most controversial plays, also involving Fisk, in Series history. It had appeared as if that would be Nolan's only action in the Series—the nature of his arm trouble made it impractical for him to be used out of the bull-pen, where he might have to warm up more than once—when Sparky named Jack Billingham as his starter for Game Six and, if necessary, Don Gullett in Game Seven. The extended rain delay over the week-end changed all that.

Nolan snuck an inside fastball past Cooper for a called first strike, then came right back at him with another down and away that Cooper swung on and missed.

When Commissioner Bowie Kuhn called off Game Six on Sun-day for the second day in a row both Sparky and Darrell Johnson had taken the opportunity to reassess their starting pitching assign-ments. Given his commanding performance in the Series to date, moving a rested Luis Tiant up from Game Seven to a must-win Game Six was a no-brainer for Johnson, although it prompted an entertaining eruption in the press from voluble Sox left-hander Bill Lee, who was pushed back to a possible Game Seven. The choice Sparky made with Larry Shepard—dropping Jack Billingham for Nolan, but keeping Gullett slated for a Game Seven—appeared to be a riskier call. Billingham had been the winningest pitcher on the Reds staff over the last three years, a tall, seasoned, rubber-armed sinker-baller who on the face of it seemed a better fit for the chal-lenges any pitcher faced in Fenway Park: keeping the ball on the ground, to use the slow infield track to his advantage and minimize the hazards of the Monster in short left. Billingham had demon-strated he could do exactly that during his only start of the Series, in Game Two, holding the Red Sox to a single earned run through six innings, a game the Reds then went on to win with two runs in the top of the ninth.

In explaining the rearrangement of his rotation to the press on Sunday, Sparky reasoned that the rain delay had allowed Nolan's tender arm to recover from his last start, and since he couldn't throw out of the bullpen, giving him the ball to start Game Six was the only way to utilize one of his best men. Sparky was also privately con-cerned that his celebrated relief corps had begun to tire after he'd worked them so hard throughout the year, and keeping Billingham in reserve in the bullpen should Nolan falter early seemed his best insurance policy. Having already lost two World Series, Sparky had also decided to shorten his notorious hook another notch on this night and throw every arm he had except Gullett at the Red Sox to win Game Six, anything to avoid another final, deciding contest. And Gary Nolan felt good as he took the mound; he'd warmed up without any pain or stiffness despite the cool weather, and his fastball had some visible pop in it.

Nolan came back with a change of pace perfectly set up by the first two fastballs; Cooper tried to adjust to it mid-swing, but the ball lofted off his bat for an easy fly out to center fielder Cesar Geronimo.

Red Sox second baseman Denny Doyle came to the plate. Perhaps more than any other man on the field that night, Denny Doyle was just happy to be there. A classic old-school middle infielder—he stood only five-nine and weighed 175—the thirty-one-year-old small-town Kentucky native had spent five years in the majors toiling on mediocre teams in Philadelphia and Anaheim before coming over to the Red Sox in a trade on June 13. He'd never hit much—his career average was .242—acknowledging he'd only made it this far in the game because of his glove and hustle, and that spring for the Angels he'd abruptly lost his starting job to a talented rookie from Massachusetts named Jerry Remy. Riding the pine for a last-place team, Doyle had started to worry his major-league career might be over— he had a wife and three young daughters to support, with no formal training in any other field to fall back on—when the Red Sox, desperate for a second baseman to lighten the workload of their oft-injured longtime starter Doug Griffin, pulled the trigger on the deal, obtaining Denny Doyle for cash and the proverbial "player to be named later."

Given scant attention in the press at the time, this turned out to be general manager Dick O'Connell's most important transaction of the season. Energized by his new opportunity, the left-hand-hitting Doyle joined the team in Kansas City and made an immediate impact, with a defensive play that preserved a win in his first start, and a crucial home run in his second. The Red Sox went on to win their first six games in a row with Doyle at second base. Doyle's sound fundamental abilities to bunt, execute the hit-and-run, and advance runners proved to be a perfect fit in the number two spot of their lineup, which helped compensate for the lack of an ideal leadoff man. He continued to play sound defense, turned the double play to perfection, and hit over his head all season; in his eighty-nine games with the Red Sox Doyle averaged over .300 for the first, and only, time in his career. When hard-luck Doug Griffin was seriously beaned for the second time in the season at the end of August, Doyle had the second base job to himself for most of September's stretch run, and throughout the American League Championship against the A's. Griffin had made only one pinch-hit appearance in the Series through five games, while the dependable Denny Doyle had hit safely in every game so far, the only man on either team to do so.

Nolan started him with a fastball that Doyle fouled straight back.

Because their surge to the American League title had coincided with his arrival, the slightly elfin Doyle had been adopted by the Red Sox and their fans as a kind of good luck charm during the '75 season; seldom, either, does it hurt to be named Doyle in Boston. He was a steadying veteran presence in the locker room, and another hardworking grinder on the field, so he fit right in with the tone set by Yastrzemski, Fisk, and Rico Petrocelli, the team's acknowledged leaders. The other Red Sox often kidded him that, despite his size, he was far from the fleetest foot on the team, and he walked with a sprightly, splayfooted gait, so naturally they nicknamed him "Ducky."

With his quick bat, Doyle turned on Nolan's next pitch, a fastball up in the zone that Doyle chopped sharply on one hop a step to the right of Reds first baseman Tony Perez. The swing imparted considerable backspin to the ball, and it kicked up and caromed off the heel of Perez's glove, but he had just enough time to pick it up and toss it to Nolan covering first for the out, a step ahead of Doyle.

Carl Yastrzemski stepped into the left side of the box, twice carefully measuring the outside corner of the plate with a single tap of his bat, then stood erect and lofted it straight and high, and stared down his hawkish beak toward Nolan. With his raptor's eye, Yaz took the first pitch, a slow curve low and away, for a ball, then laid off a high fastball for ball two. The thirty-six-year-old Yastrzemski was still at any time one of the most dangerous hitters alive; ahead in the count, he was an assassin. Nolan kicked around the mound for a beat, gathering himself, frustrated that he'd missed with both those pitches. He'd gotten Yastrzemski out twice in Game Three by keeping the ball low and inducing grounders to the right side. That's the signal Bench gave Nolan again now—they'd been battery mates since the Instructional League, had come up to the Reds as rookies, become close friends and then major-league stars together; by now they could almost read each other's mind on the field—but Nolan missed again with a fastball, just outside, behind to Yaz 3–0 now.

On a signal from Darrell Johnson in the dugout, the Red Sox third base coach Don Zimmer flashed the take sign, something of a surprise; Yastrzemski had led the team in walks, wasn't ever inclined to chase bad pitches, and Johnson usually gave Yaz the green light under any circumstances, but not here, not in this game; this early in the contest he wanted base runners any way he could get them. Taking all the way, Yaz watched a hittable fastball sail across the meat of the plate for strike one.

Now the payoff: Forced to come back into the zone, Nolan threw a moving fastball that drifted up and over the inside corner, an effective pitch to most batters; Yaz unleashed a full-bodied hack and lashed it past Perez into right field for the game's first hit. The ball skidded on the damp grass, losing most of its steam by the time Ken Griffey picked it up and tossed it back to Morgan covering second.

Cleanup hitter and catcher Carlton Fisk stood in, the first right-handed bat in the Red Sox lineup. With his broad-boned frame, Fisk looked even larger than his six-two, 225 pounds; he was in fact one of the biggest men to ever play his position. He was raised on his family's New Hampshire cattle farm, and both of Fisk's parents had been superb athletes; all six of their children inherited the talent.

Carlton had been the slowest of the Fisks' four boys to grow into his body; the early nickname his brothers hung on him, "Pudge," certainly no longer applied, but would stick throughout his life. Harsh New England winters limited Fisk's early baseball career; basketball was his best and favorite sport early on, and playing center for his small high school against much taller players helped forge his pronounced mental and physical toughness. Those skills earned Fisk a basketball scholarship to the University of New Hampshire, where his older brother Calvin was captain of the soccer team, and as an undersized power forward he led their freshman team to an undefeated season. Despite playing less than a hundred baseball games in his amateur career—many of them as a pitcher; he ended up behind the plate almost by accident, when he replaced his injured older brother in a game—Pudge attracted enough attention from the Red Sox to be selected as a catcher in the first round of the 1967 draft. (His brothers Calvin and Conrad were also drafted by the Orioles and Montreal Expos respectively, but Uncle Sam's draft took priority. Calvin ended up in Vietnam, and the Orioles had lost interest by the time he returned; Conrad blew out his arm before he ever pitched a professional inning.) Facing the reality that having reached his full height he'd never play for the Celtics, and eager to make a living and reduce the financial burden on his family, Fisk left college after one year to accept an offer from the Red Sox, the team he'd loved since childhood, the only one, Fisk had insisted to all the pro scouts who took an interest in him, that he would ever play for.

Pitching from the stretch, Nolan's first fastball to Fisk missed high and over the middle of the plate, not the outside corner where Bench had set up.

A much harder thing for Carlton Fisk to accept about baseball was losing; he had never done much of it, ever, in any sport. The passion and fiery will to win that would become the hallmarks of his Hall of Fame career took a beating in the lower ranks of the minor leagues. He occasionally struggled at the plate, but continued to hit for power and play solid defense wherever they sent him, and within three seasons Fisk ended up in Triple-A at Louisville, where manager Darrell Johnson, the onetime major-league catcher, made a project of teaching him the finer points of baseball's most complex position. Under Johnson's tutelage, Fisk earned a September call-up to the Red Sox in '71 and made an immediate impact on both sides of the plate. During the spring of 1972, when starting catcher Duane Josephson was badly hurt in only the third game of the season, Fisk walked on stage and grabbed the job in his Bunyonesque fists. For Boston fans he seemed almost too good to be true; a towering, ruggedly handsome New Englander with phenomenal power, the strength of an ox, catlike reflexes, fearsome competitive drive, and the balls to call out any pitcher—rookie or veteran—during a game who didn't measure up to his high standards. Carlton Fisk's 1972 season played out like a dream; he was named to the All-Star team, hit .293 with twenty-two home runs, earned a Gold Glove, and became the first player in the American League ever named Rookie of the Year by unanimous vote. Comparisons to the Reds' Johnny Bench, already his generation's and perhaps history's gold standard at the position, inevitably followed. The Red Sox, who hadn't been able to develop a standout catcher in a generation—they hadn't landed a starting catcher on the American League All-Star team since 1953—appeared to have found a new field general. But in spite of his remarkable debut season, the bitterness of losing the East Division by a half game to Detroit lingered even longer for the driven Fisk than all the postseason accolades. He was nearly inconsolable in the locker room after their final loss, as Tom Yawkey tried in vain to comfort him, stricken more by Fisk's suffering than his own.

Fisk came back to earth the following year in 1973; although his home run and RBI totals increased, and he made his second All-Star team, his batting average dropped fifty points during the second half of the season. Refusing to take days off, he lost twenty pounds from the heavy workload, visibly tiring down the stretch as pitchers fed him a steady diet of curveballs. He also became something of a lightning rod for opposing teams—not unlike Pete Rose, in this one respect—irritating them with his relentless will to win and assertive presence on the field. Prickly Yankee catcher Thurman Munson, an established star considered the best backstop in the American League before Fisk arrived, resented Fisk being selected ahead of him to that year's All-Star team and took repeated public exception to Fisk's haughty manner. In early August, with the two teams in a tight East Division race, and deadlocked in the ninth inning of a tense game at Fenway, Fisk blocked home plate after batter Gene Michael missed a suicide squeeze attempt and Munson stormed down the line straight at him. Fisk didn't yield when Munson crashed into him, tagging him hard for the out. When Munson tried to keep his weight on top of Fisk, in an effort to allow the base runner behind him to advance, Fisk kicked him off and the two ended up in a fistfight that cleared the benches. Unlike Pete Rose, none of what Fisk did in pursuit of winning was consciously or deliberately provocative; it appeared to be simply an expression of who he was and the way he'd been brought up.

Pure Connecticut River granite, as teammate Bill Lee described him. *Pudge wouldn't ask out of a game if he had both legs cut off.*

Despite winning four more games during the season, the Red Sox finished second in the division in 1973, this time *eight* games behind the Orioles; popular manager Eddie Kasko lost his job, and Fisk's former tutor Darrell Johnson was brought up from Pawtucket to replace him. Johnson cleaned house in 1974, releasing on the same day three future Hall of Famers who were near the end of their careers: pitcher Juan Marichal, designated hitter Orlando Cepeda, and shortstop Luis Aparicio. This opened up opportunities for many of the youngsters Johnson had managed at Triple-A, and they responded by seizing the East Division lead through the end of June. Both their star catcher and, as it turned out, the Red Sox postseason prospects, ended on June 28 in Cleveland, when in the ninth inning of a tie game Fisk extended his leg to protect the plate on a play at home. The throw came in high, and Cleveland outfielder Leron Lee barreled into him, shredding Fisk's vulnerable and exposed left knee in a brutal collision. After extensive surgery to repair two torn ligaments, he was placed in an ankle-to-thigh cast and the prognosis was dire; doctors warned Fisk that not only might his career be over, but he could be left limping for the rest of his life.

Working harder than Stallone in a *Rocky* training montage, Fisk rehabbed the knee throughout a long, cold, lonely winter in New Hampshire. Two hundred and fifty-six days after the injury, he made a cautious return to action in a March spring training game in 1975, catching five innings, feeling gimpy and sore afterward, and conceding that the knee wasn't fully healed yet. But the next day, a determined Pudge told Darrell Johnson that he was ready to go again. In his first at bat, the second pitch sailed inside, and when he checked his swing, the ball nailed him two inches above the right wrist and cracked the head of his forearm bone. Backups Bob Montgomery, Tim Blackwell, and veteran Tim McCarver filled in admirably, but this second injury turned out to be a blessing in disguise, allowing Fisk's knee to completely recover by the time Pudge was ready to return to action in late June, two weeks after the energizing arrival of "Ducky" Doyle. When he finally suited up, the Carlton Fisk of 1972 appeared again; he hit .331 with ten home runs in less than half a season, and his commanding presence behind the plate, and in the locker room, steadied the entire Red Sox squad. He had hammered Oakland's pitches during the League Championship, hitting .417, but with only four hits in eighteen at bats so far against the Reds, Fisk felt he was due for a breakout game.

The Reds defense put on a power shift, playing shortstop Dave Concepcion a step shy of the outfield grass, moving second baseman Joe Morgan nearly even with the bag, and Rose shallow at third, expecting Fisk to put the ball in play on the left side in his home park. Bench set up outside and low again, but when Nolan delivered his second straight fastball up and into the strike zone, Fisk spanked it through the hole between Rose and Concepcion for a single to left. Yastrzemski advanced to second as George Foster tossed the ball back in to Concepcion.

Two on, two out.

In the Reds dugout, Sparky nudged pitching coach Larry Shepard, who moved immediately to the phone on the wall by the tunnel to the visitors' clubhouse. Reds backup catcher Bill Plummer answered the call in the Cincinnati bullpen beyond right field; moments later, Jack Billingham and left-hander Freddie Norman shed their jackets and began to loosen up. Only thirteen pitches into the game, true to his word, Captain Hook was already prepared to call in the cavalry. Sparky stared down at the floor of the dugout from his seat on the bench, hands stuffed in his jacket, swinging his feet anxiously.

Alarmed at the ominous way his old friend's fastball was rising up in the zone—and, much worse, over the plate—Johnny Bench trotted out to settle Nolan down and refresh him on their book for the next Sox hitter, Fred Lynn: low and away, up and in. Unspoken, always, although they both knew it, Bench was also out there to buy a little more time for the men in the Reds bullpen to get ready.

Fred Lynn, the fourth left-handed bat to step to the plate in the inning, was playing in his 154th game of the year, not including more than thirty spring training games, in a season that began back in March at the Red Sox complex in Winter Haven, Florida. This was only Lynn's second full year of professional baseball; he had played fifty-three games in Double-A after being drafted, then less than five months in Triple-A at Pawtucket in 1974, before arriving on the scene in the American League like a comet. When he'd hit .419 in two weeks for Boston at the end of their 1974 collapse, a bright future was cautiously anticipated for him—Red Sox watchers were habitually wary, for sound historical reasons—but no one in their right mind would have dared predict what Lynn would go on to do for them in 1975. His fellow rookie outfielder, the now injured Jim Rice, had been in the team's farm system a few years longer and posted much flashier numbers than Lynn during the time they played together; most scouts and pundits expected Rice to develop and produce sooner. No one appeared to realize that four years in Rod Dedeaux's baseball academy at USC—winning three straight NCAA titles in the process, and playing in a number of international exhibitions as a result—had turned Fred Lynn into a complete and polished star. At this point not many players had ever made the move from the collegiate ranks straight to the major leagues—a slow slog through the minors after being drafted out of high school remained the beaten path—and not one of them had ever made the leap to stardom with the swift suddenness of Fred Lynn.

The Yankees had drafted him out of high school, as the sixtieth player chosen, but Lynn turned them down flat; he had a football scholarship in hand from USC, and hadn't yet decided which sport to favor. He was also determined to become the first person from his family to go to college. Growing up in Southern California, he had dreamt of one day playing for the Dodgers, but they failed to select him in the first round of the 1973 draft, and the Red Sox grabbed him in the second—the twenty-eighth pick overall—one slot ahead of Los Angeles. Lynn's stock had fallen when a few pro scouts somewhat mysteriously returned mixed reviews after his stellar USC career, centered on unfounded projections that he wouldn't be able to hit left-handed pitching at the major-league level. All of which only made him more eager to prove them wrong, and that he had done, with prejudice; feeling uncannily at home in Fenway Park, Lynn tore up major-league pitching from day one, and when he ran out onto the diamond on Opening Day he was already the swiftest, surest center fielder the American League had seen in many years. He defended his turf with the fearlessness of the sturdy football player he'd been, hurling his body after every ball hit his way, making one game-saving highlight-reel play after another. Fred Lynn checked all the boxes: He hit for average, he hit for power, he played lights-out defense, he could run like a gazelle, and he had a strong and accurate throwing arm. He was also unfailingly polite, keenly intelligent, thoughtful, and cooperative with the press and public, and modest almost to a fault. "Lynn mania" hit critical mass one amazing June night in Detroit when he belted three home runs, a triple, and a single, while driving in ten; from that point on the whole country started paying attention, and by the end of his rookie season, writers had run out of superlatives. The only apt comparisons they could find were with baseball's immortal trinity of center fielders, Joe DiMaggio, Mickey Mantle, and Willie Mays, and when you lined up the numbers, only DiMaggio's rookie record stood up to what Fred Lynn had accomplished in his first full year, at the age of twenty-three. After hitting .364 in the Sox's League Championship Series sweep over Oakland, Lynn had skipped the champagne—he didn't like the taste—preferring to celebrate with a glass of milk. It was as if Joe Hardy from *Damn Yankees* had suddenly materialized wearing a Red Sox uniform. No wonder they adored him in Boston.

But the six-month-long season, the endless travel, dealing with all the extra attention he'd attracted with his remarkable performance, had slowly worn Freddy down. He was having trouble maintaining his weight, and for the first time in years had dropped below 180 pounds. Although he'd continued to hit for average, ending the season at .331, his power numbers had dropped precipitously during the second half of the season. He'd launched only five home runs since the All-Star break, and when he came to the plate in Game Six on October 21, Lynn hadn't hit a home run at Fenway Park in more than a month. The recent rain delay, the subject of more gripes over the lost weekend than the I.R.S., had actually done Fred Lynn a world of good. Four solid days of rest, at home in his own apartment twenty minutes from the ballpark, away from the insistent spotlight of the media, had restored the sharpness to his eye and the jump in his bat. He'd noticed the difference just the day before, when he took an extended batting practice session in the cage under the stands, and today before the game. His bat felt quick and lively again, but as was his habit, the private, self-possessed Lynn hadn't mentioned it to anyone, and as he dug in and stared out at Nolan an extra surge of adrenaline fired through him.

Up in the NBC broadcast booth, Dick Stockton made the play-by-play call as Gary Nolan missed with his first pitch to Lynn, up and away. Just as Stockton outlined how drastically Lynn's home run production had fallen off over the season's final days, Nolan made his first mistake of the game, a grooved fastball that moved slightly to the right, belt-high, dead over the heart of the plate. Lynn jumped on it, a smooth, flawless swing, and the crowd rose to its feet as the ball sailed up, over, and past the Boston bullpen, toward the stands in right field. The Red Sox pitchers in the pen leapt from their seats, jumping up and down, waving their caps wildly as Lynn's towering shot passed over their heads and landed ten rows back. Yaz crossed the plate with the game's first run, clapping as he waited for Fisk to join him; the two of them together greeted Lynn as he glided around the bases and touched home, and then they escorted him to the dugout, where his teammates mobbed him and Darrell Johnson clapped him heartily on the back.

Jack Billingham, warming up in the Reds bullpen, turned to Freddie Norman on the other mound to his left.

"Well, shit," said Billingham.

Ignoring the crowd, they went back to work with more urgency.

As the Red Sox swarmed over him, Fred Lynn stalked around the dugout, fired up, the adrenaline still coursing through him; he hadn't hit a ball that far in two months, not even in batting practice.

The crowd continued to buzz as Red Sox third baseman Rico Petrocelli followed Lynn to the plate. Furious at himself for his mistake, Gary Nolan labored at a noticeably fast pace and moved back to the corners, working Rico to a 1–1 count. One of the team's last remaining veterans of the "Impossible Dream" campaign, after suffering through a frustrating, injury-plagued season, Petrocelli had swung a hot bat through the first five games of the Series, leading the Red Sox in hitting at .368. After Nolan missed outside with a slow roundhouse curve, Petrocelli hammered a low outside fastball to the warning track in the deepest part of center field, where Cesar Geronimo gathered it in at the base of the wall for the final out of the inning.

To Geronimo's right, the number had just gone up on the manually operated scoreboard at the base of the Monster: Red Sox 3, Reds 0.

For the fifth time in six games, Boston had drawn first blood.

SIX

You don't really belong up here if you worry about
losing your job. You're gonna wake up the next morning.
The sun's gonna shine again.

SPARKY ANDERSON

BEFORE THE WORLD SERIES BEGAN IN 1975, THE CINCIN-nati Reds and Boston Red Sox had never faced each other in competition, outside of spring training games, but they shared some common roots in the tangled, untidy origins of nineteenth-century professional baseball. Like most enduring forms of life, the modern game would undergo a long evolutionary process, full of fits and starts, misfires and dead ends, before assuming the shape we recognize today. Emerging as a variant of a number of more primitive games—including most prominently the old English country game of "rounders"—"base ball" first sprang up as a casual, amateur sport throughout many regions of the country, played according to widely varying local rules, in the early 1800s. The game's first codified set of rules appeared in print in 1845, published by an amateur club called the New York Knickerbockers, and over the next twenty years their prevailing vision of the game slowly incorporated and standardized many of the fundamental concepts we would recognize in its modern incarnation. In the aftermath of the Civil War in the 1860s, as hundreds of thousands of young men returned home, traumatized and determined to establish more peaceful lives, base ball took firm hold as their favorite form of local recreation. Played in parks or open fields, with its emphasis on healthy outdoor exercise and the pleasures of participation as opposed to winning, the game helped knit back together the ravaged social fabric of the country, weaving its way into the summer daylight rhythms of both small town and big city American life. Players in communities began organizing into social "clubs" that scheduled regular games between their members, then with other nearby clubs, and eventually against teams from neighboring areas. These games attracted spectators, offering a free form of lighthearted, open-air entertainment in a bleak era when there wasn't much to be found. One of those amateur clubs, founded in 1866 as the Cincinnati Red Stockings, three years later declared itself base ball's first "professional" team and began paying its players a modest wage. Barnstorming around the country on an exhibition tour, charging a token admission to their contests and taking on all challengers, these highly skilled Red Stockings won well over one hundred games over the next two seasons, and changed the national perception of what a "ball club" could be. The team inspired admiration but also a flood of criticism: These players were nothing more than mercenaries, brought in from the outside with no connection to the community they were paid to represent—make that *over*paid—and all they cared about was "winning." This was the first time these charges had been brought against what was by now widely known as the "National Pastime," and it wouldn't be the last. But once enterprising capitalists began to smell money in "baseball"—its popularity resulted in the contraction of the name of the game to a single word—there would be no going back to its more innocent, pastoral roots.

The Cincinnati Red Stockings' guiding force was player/manager Harry Wright, the immigrant son of a professional English sportsman, who had moved to America in 1838 to work as the resident pro for a New York City cricket club. Wright thus grew up playing both cricket and base ball—not entirely disparate disciplines—and turned out to be gifted at both. Although by the time the Civil War ended Wright was past his own athletic prime, he was also a gifted executive with a sharp eye for talent; and in guiding the team he had assembled to their notable success, Harry Wright ended up becoming the origin figure for the modern sport's field manager. When Cincinnati's traveling but homesick pros voted to revert to their amateur status after the 1870 season, Wright put down stakes in Boston, where he became the manager of that city's first professional team, formed in order to join the sport's first professional *league,* which called itself the National Association and sounds a lot more organized than it actually was, featuring "franchises" in cities throughout the Eastern Seaboard. Unwilling to mess with a winning formula, Wright named his new team the *Boston* Red Stockings (both teams' nicknames referred to the bright crimson leggings worn by their players). Although they shared elements of the same family tree, neither of these teams evolved directly into the teams that would meet in the 1975 World Series.

Built on a nucleus of players from his Cincinnati road club, Harry Wright's Boston franchise dominated the early years of the National Association. In 1876 that organization was supplanted by the National League, the oldest of baseball's governing organizations, which survives to this day, the reason why it's still often referred to as the "Senior Circuit." At that juncture, a *second* Cincinnati Red Stockings team—with no formal connection to the first beyond the name—was invited to join the National League as a charter member. Four up and down seasons later, that ill-fated Cincinnati franchise was kicked out of the league for violating a number of rules, the most serious among them selling beer to its predominantly immigrant German fan base in order to cover expenses. A *third* Cincinnati Red Stockings team then sprang to life two years later to join a new rival professional league called the "American Association," known informally as "the beer and whiskey league" for its more alcohol-friendly attitude. Ten years later, after the 1891 season, the American Association went bust—which hastily thrown together "leagues" had a regular habit of doing then—and the Cincinnati Red Stockings (along with the Brooklyn Superbas—later Trolley Dodgers, and then Dodgers—and two other teams) accepted an invitation to jump over and join the National League. Soon afterward they shortened their name to the Cincinnati Reds. Eighty-three years later—some team histories occasionally and incorrectly claim a direct lineage back to the earlier Red Stockings incarnations—these same Reds earned their way into their seventh World Series with what most believed was the strongest team they'd ever fielded; Bob Howsam and Sparky Anderson's Big Red Machine.

From the start Harry Wright set the tone for another enduring aspect of the professional baseball manager's life: never holding on to the same job for long. Wright moved on to yet another team in 1882, but the Boston Red Stockings he'd founded remained the powerhouse franchise of the National League, winning eight pennants during the next quarter century, and in the process giving life to a demanding and discriminating baseball culture in Boston that would persist into two following centuries. These Red Stockings picked up the name Beaneaters in 1882, and in 1906, they were dubbed the Doves—after their new owners, the Dovey brothers—and then later, under new management each time, the Rustlers and then the Pilgrims, until a fifth set of owners finally settled on calling them the Boston Braves in 1912. That name stuck, and that National League club lived on in Boston—winning only one World Series, in 1914—until 1953, when after falling on hard times they moved to Milwaukee, and then once again to Atlanta in 1966, where the Braves remain to this day.

The American League—baseball's "Junior Circuit"—was cobbled together from the bones of a second-tier organization called the "Western League" in 1900, when its president, Byron Bancroft "Ban" Johnson, decided to step up and compete with the established National League, at that point the pro game's eight-hundred-pound gorilla. The National League had withstood numerous challenges to its preeminence from rival leagues during its first quarter century, and beaten back all comers; despite this, or perhaps because its owners had grown complacent and corrupt from a lack of competition, trouble had long been stirring in the National. The central issue then was the same one that haunts the game to this day: Who in fact represents the "game of baseball," the players on the field or the owners behind the cash register? National League owners had imposed a punitive salary cap on their field hands; players were limited to a maximum salary of $2,000 a year with no say in improvement of their working conditions, and on many teams they were compelled to pay for their own equipment and uniforms. A mutinous, hastily organized "Players' League" had sprung up in protest for one season in 1890, but died penniless, and within five years most of its humbled players were out of the professional game. Those that stayed were now bound to their teams for life, by the implementation of a questionable legal doctrine that owners insisted they needed to survive, the infamous "reserve clause."

The reserve clause was originally intended to serve as a self-policing defense against rival teams and leagues raiding an owner's roster. After it was formally drawn up in 1879, as a secret pact between the original National League teams, each owner was allowed to list five players who would remain off-limits to his competitors; you "reserved" the right to retain that player for one year beyond the life of his current signed contract, and then reserved the right to *renew* that right on a yearly basis, in perpetuity. Owners expanded the scope of the list to eleven men a few years later, then to fourteen, and by the turn of the century the reserve clause covered all twenty-five players on major-league rosters.

Labor relations were not the National League's only problem. Operating with the unregulated freedom that only a monopoly can provide, owners often owned percentages of their fellow competitors' teams—they called their league a "syndicate"—and brazenly manipulated rosters and schedules for one another's benefit, raising justified questions from fans about their loyalty and integrity. Not only had the National League's owners appeared to have lost their moral center, the game on the field had turned violent, rebellious players were almost unmanageable, and urban ballparks had devolved into dens of iniquity dominated by drunkenness and open gambling, unfit for families, the subject of many scolding editorials and Sunday sermons across the country. In this sea of troubles, Ban Johnson, a tough-minded, upright former Cincinnati sportswriter who had been running the smaller Western League for six years, saw an opportunity. He had from the start imposed a strict code of conduct on both his owners and players, banning liquor, fighting, and gambling from games, drawing fans back to his parks by offering a family-friendly atmosphere, and he had quickly made the Western League the most solvent and successful of the country's many "minor" leagues. When four financially crippled National League franchises collapsed after the 1899 season, reducing its number to eight, Johnson declared war.

Johnson first changed the Western League's name to the more patriotic-sounding "American League," and then organized eight solid teams, all of them based either in cities where the National League had already failed, or where he now endeavored to challenge them head-to-head. He secured additional financing from an independently wealthy investor, giving him the security he knew he'd need to survive the red ink his teams would bleed while the American League established itself. When, as expected, the National League brushed aside his initial entreaties to recognize the American League as an equal, Johnson let their players know he was willing to ignore both the reserve clause and their established salary limits and began hiring away the National's strongest talent. At the start of the American League's second season in 1901, Johnson planted his flag in the territory of the National League's strongest team; he decided to bring the franchise he'd been on the verge of establishing in Buffalo into Boston, assembled the strongest roster he could field, and announced he would soon build a new state-of-the-art ballpark to house them. Boston's fans, the most passionate and informed in the country, long accustomed to excellence, had come close to open revolt about the declining state of their once great National League team, and they embraced Johnson's fresh new product wholeheartedly.

Two seasons later these Boston "Americans"—named after the league itself, as were a few of Johnson's other new teams, to distinguish them in those cities with established National League franchises—won their first American League pennant in their brand-new South End ballpark, the Huntington Avenue Grounds. The cornerstone of the franchise had become thirty-four-year-old pitcher Cy Young, whom Johnson signed away from the National League's team in St. Louis—which would later become the Cardinals—two years after it had merged rosters with the same owners' failing Cleveland Spiders. An Ohio native, Young had spent the first nine years of his career close to home in Cleveland, averaging twenty-six wins a season, but he hadn't taken to St. Louis, and chaffed at the National League's punitive salary cap. Johnson offered Young $3,000 a year to jump leagues and pitch for his flagship Boston franchise. Young was an imposing, dignified master of control on the mound, but most insiders had assumed his best years were behind him; he promptly averaged thirty-one wins a year for the Americans during their first three seasons and became a legend in Boston. Young had more than a little of Abe Lincoln in him—a frontier farm-boy philosopher, he would publish two books of his baseball musings, full of pithy aphorisms steeped in common sense—and had become a bona fide role model dedicated to clean living and the beneficial tonic of hard physical labor. The fledgling team rallied around the estimable Young, and their early success encouraged Boston's rabid fans, led by a fanatical social club called the "Rooters," to tilt their loyalties away from the old National League franchise toward the city's new American League entry. Johnson's gamble had paid off.

Although the warring leagues had ostensibly signed a "peace treaty" at the onset of the 1903 season, a cloud of anger and resentment over Ban Johnson's hardball tactics still hung over the field. At the behest of their fellow owners, when the 1903 season ended, the then three-time-straight National League champion Pittsburgh Pirates issued a challenge to these upstart Americans—or Bostons, Pilgrims, or Puritans, as they were alternately known; team names continued to be fluid and casual for another decade—to play in a "best of nine games" postseason exhibition. Ban Johnson had raided the deep Pirates roster during the previous off-season, luring three of their biggest stars over to his American League. The Pirates had screamed foul, raising a hue and cry in the national press at this outrage; a perfect case of the pot calling the kettle black, since the Pirates had earned *their* name a few years earlier for brazenly stealing players from other National League teams. (Before which they had previously been known, without a hint of irony, as the Pittsburgh Innocents.) Now the Pirates had asked for and obtained this high-profile showdown, privately planning to expose and humiliate the American League, in front of a baseball-loving nation, as a grossly inferior product.

The owners decided to call this blood-feud exhibition the "World Series."

WHILE THE FANS in Fenway continued to chatter with excitement over Fred Lynn's home run, Luis Tiant returned to the mound and Cincinnati's first batter of their second inning, first baseman Atanasio "Tony" Rigal Perez, came to the plate.

Perez and Tiant were fellow countrymen and near contemporaries—at thirty-three, Perez was less than two years younger—and both had traveled a similar path out of the *beisbol*-rich environs of Cuba. Also like Tiant, Perez had been a precocious talent, earning his way onto a traveling Cuban All-Star team at the age of fourteen. He was a skinny kid then with a big friendly grin, tall for his age— almost six-two—grown powerfully strong from the summers he'd spent working beside his father and grandfather in a sugar mill. But their paths never crossed in their homeland; Tiant grew up in suburban Havana on the northwest coast, while Perez lived in the region of Camaguey in central Cuba's rural countryside. Luis Tiant Sr.'s professional baseball career had inspired not only his son but a whole generation of young Cuban pitchers. For hitters like Tony Perez—he played shortstop in his early days—who came of age in Cuba during the 1950s, their inspiration was a man named Saturnino Orestes Armas Minoso Arrieta. Baseball fans around the Americas would come to know him, in a pleasing, almost cartoonlike contraction, as Minnie Minoso.

Tiant started Perez with a sidearm slider that missed low and inside for ball one.

Since banishing black players from its leagues in 1884, organized baseball had long made a fine distinction that allowed a few light-skinned (or "Caucasian") Latins to play in the majors, occasionally even letting a few darker-skinned Latins into the minors as long as they could be verified as "Cuban" and not African-American. After playing for almost ten years in Mexico and the Negro Leagues, Minoso wasn't allowed to play an inning in the American major leagues until Jackie Robinson broke the color barrier in 1947; Minoso was nearly twenty-eight by the time he appeared in a few games for the Cleveland Indians in 1949. Never appreciating what they had, in 1951 the Indians traded him to the Chicago White Sox—where he became the first black player to wear a White Sox uniform, and instantly established himself as one of game's most flamboyant and colorful figures. Displaying speed, power, defense, and an exuberant personality, Minoso made seven All-Star Games during the fifties, and gave hope to every kid in Cuba with a bat that their dreams might be within reach.

Tiant's second pitch to Perez was a slow, arcing overhand curve that dropped in for a strike to even the count, a touch of showmanship that stirred up the crowd. Perez had struck out waving at that same weightless changeup from Luis in Game One. *El Tiante* was rolling out his full repertoire for the Reds' dangerous RBI machine.

"Tani" Perez, as everyone called him then, knew that the only future Cuba could give him was the same backbreaking factory life his father and grandfather had endured, and that following in the footsteps of the great Minoso offered the only avenue of escape. Similarly inspired by Minoso's success, American big-league teams had for the past few years dispatched a brigade of scouts to scour the Cuban countryside looking for hidden gems. One of those scouts, Tony Pacheco, director of scouting for the Havana Sugar Kings—at that time the Cincinnati Reds' Triple-A farm team in the International League—spotted Perez when he was sixteen, saw a glimmer of potential in his raw skills, and got him the instructional help he thought he needed to develop. When Perez turned seventeen, Pacheco was sufficiently encouraged by Tani's progress to sign him as a Reds farmhand; the deal he proposed would only cost the Reds a one-way plane ticket to Tampa, and a grand total of $2.50, the price of Perez's visa. There wasn't much to recommend the offer, but other pressures had come into play that weighed heavily on Perez's decision.

In the early hours of New Year's Day in 1959, revolutionary forces led by a thirty-two-year-old lawyer named Fidel Castro had overthrown the corrupt regime of Cuba's longtime military dictator Fulgencio Batista, promising new elections and a swift return to democracy. Those elections never materialized, and Cuba's long relationship with Batista's patron United States swiftly deteriorated once Castro established his government. Amid a wave of murderous reprisals against former Batista supporters, Castro balked at attempts by the American government to paternalistically influence the direction of his country the way it had grown accustomed to doing so routinely throughout the twentieth century. When President Eisenhower imposed a punitive quota on Cuban sugar imports, Castro retaliated by seizing and nationalizing American-owned industries throughout his country. He also made a series of alarming moves toward the threatening embrace of the Soviet Union, all the while publicly denying any interest in establishing a socialist government. Rumors spread that every available young man would be conscripted into compulsory military service and that all emigration off the island would soon be curtailed. Luis Tiant, now pitching in his second professional season in Mexico, had never shown an interest in politics, but he was alarmed by the changes afoot in Havana that his father told him about whenever they spoke by phone. Life, as the Tiant and Perez families had known it in Cuba, had reached a treacherous crossroads. Although Castro himself spoke often of his love for the great sport of *beisbol*—he had pitched for his college team and made a show of appearing on the mound in games after he took office, bragging that he had once been offered a contract by a scout from the New York Giants—if he broke off relations with America, the bridge for Cuban players to the major leagues that had been built by the success of Minnie Minoso might instantly collapse.

Tiant went back to the sidearm slider, laying more heat on it this time, and it broke inside off the corner of the plate toward Perez's hands. Perez took his first swing at a hittable ball and whacked it hard and foul down the first base line. One and two, advantage Tiant.

So Tani Perez accepted the Reds' paltry offer. He spoke only two words of English when he arrived at their spring camp in Florida—"yes" and "no"—and didn't know a living soul on the continent. The Reds dispatched him to their rookie club in Geneva, New York, where the frigid weather of the early northeastern spring shocked his system. He was still rail thin, and the Reds tried him initially at second base, then moved him to third, where he would remain until his body filled out. But everywhere they sent him, Tony—during the acclimation process his nickname had quickly been Americanized—Perez ripped the cover off the ball. In his third year, with the Reds' farm team in Rocky Mount, North Carolina, he hit .292, with 18 home runs and 74 RBIs. He also experienced his first taste of Southern segregation when he was grouped with the team's African-American players and denied access to white restaurants and hotels. Luis Tiant went through the same shocking introduction to American apartheid in 1963, playing for Burlington in the Carolina League. Perez's performance earned him a promotion late that season to the Reds' Triple-A franchise in the Pacific Coast League, the San Diego Padres. He tore up PCL pitching in 1964, hitting .309 with 34 home runs and 109 RBIs. Tiant made it to Cleveland's Portland franchise in the PCL that same spring, their number two starter behind the Indians' best prospect, fireballer "Sudden" Sam Mc-Dowell.

Tony Perez shared another crucial quality with Luis Tiant: As a person off the field, and at the plate in even the most pressurized situations, he possessed an almost unearthly calm, and with extraordinary consistency he delivered hits when runners were in scoring position; by now it was clear that it was only a matter of time until Perez would get the call to the major leagues. To go with his great natural talent, he owned the perfect temperament for baseball's long, trying seasons, a relaxed, generous, easygoing, good-humored confidence that never called attention to itself and, like Tiant's, defused the tension in every locker room he entered. Johnny Bench said that with his engaging attitude, booming baritone, and wide, contagious smile, Perez "cast a net" over the entire team and wouldn't let them wander. His teammates had already tagged him with the nickname he'd carry throughout his career: "Doggie," the "Big Dog," or "Big Doggie," the man you could always count on to come through when the game was on the line.

After Perez stepped out of the box to gather himself, Tiant nodded at the sign from Fisk and reared back into the same overhand motion he'd used for that tantalizing slow curve, but instead fired a high, hard fastball an inch beyond the outside corner, exactly where he'd wanted to put it; that was an "out" pitch and a less disciplined hitter would've ripped at it and missed. Perez kept the bat on his shoulder. The count went even, two balls, two strikes.

The parallel paths of Tony Perez and Luis Tiant would come close to crossing again in July of that 1964 season. After Sam McDowell was called up by the Indians, Tiant had stepped in to become the unquestioned ace of the Pacific Coast League Portland Beavers, compiling a commanding 15–1 record only halfway through the season. The Beavers traveled to San Diego for a weekend mid-July showdown with the Padres, with Tiant scheduled to start the first game on Friday night, and the local paper splashed this impending showdown, between their local Cuban slugger and the visiting Cuban hurler, all over the front page of their sports section.

Home plate umpire Satch Davidson put a new ball in play, and Tiant slipped off his glove for a moment to give it a brief rub before he looked in to Fisk for the sign.

But that first showdown in 1964 between the two rising Latin stars never materialized; when Tiant arrived with the team at their San Diego hotel that afternoon, he was immediately summoned to the room of his manager, Johnny Lipon, who broke the news he had just received from Cleveland Indians general manager Gabe Paul; they wanted Tiant to join the Indians on the road in New York City immediately. The moment Tiant had been waiting for since coming to America had arrived, but his initial instinct was to refuse the call-up; the way the Indians had left him off their roster at the beginning of the year after an exceptional spring camp had wounded his considerable pride. He felt that no matter what he did he would never get the same respect as their fair-haired favorite, Sam Mc-Dowell. Lipon had to gently convince his best pitcher that that was exactly why he had to seize this moment and prove to the Indians how wrong they'd been about him. Luis never unpacked his bags; when the Portland Beavers took the field against the Padres that night in San Diego, Tiant was already on the red-eye to New York, where the next morning he signed his first big-league contract, for $5,000—$1,000 below the league minimum. The following day, twenty-three-year-old Luis Tiant won his first big-league start in memorable fashion, besting the first-place Yankees and their ace Whitey Ford with a four-hit shutout. Tiant never looked back; he ended his season for the Tribe at 10–4 with a 2.83 ERA. Tony Perez received his own call-up to the Reds just one week later, and spent the next two years working his way into Cincinnati's regular lineup, finally winning the third base job outright at the start of the 1967 season. Over the following years, in their respective leagues, the two men had gone on to stardom; in Tiant's case twice, with an interruption, while Perez established himself as the steadiest, most unshakeable component of the Big Red Machine. But they had still never faced each other in regular or postseason competition until Game One of the 1975 World Series.

Before the Series Darrell Johnson had identified Perez as the man they needed to stop to shut down the Big Red Machine. Perez had simply slaughtered Pittsburgh's pitching during their three-game sweep of the Pirates in the National League Championship, hitting over .400 and driving in four runs. But Tiant had hung the collar on Tony during his Game One shutout, striking him out twice and baffling the canny veteran with his whirling dervish delivery and offbeat timing. "Doggie" had been slow to regain his footing; Perez remained hitless in the Series through Game Four, when Tiant shut him down again, 0–4 with a strikeout. The next night, before Game Five, Sparky dropped his star first baseman a spot in the order behind Bench and calmly reminded him of what might be within his reach: "Tony, if we let this go seven games and you don't get a hit, your children can tell their children that their grandfather had an all-time World Series record: most at bats without a hit." Taking their cue from Sparky, the rest of the Reds' superstars gave him the business about it as well, which turned out to be the only prescription he needed; Perez broke out of his funk that night in spectacular fashion as he won Game Five single-handedly with two towering shots that rocketed out of Riverfront Park, driving in four of the team's six runs and giving the Reds their first Series lead. "You can't keep the Big Doggie down," said Sparky afterward. As the Series moved back to Boston, Tony Perez coming to life did not augur well for the Red Sox's prospects.

Tiant went into his windup. This time, at the top, weight perched precariously on his right leg, his back turned completely to home plate, Luis tossed in a little extra head feint, a peek up toward the left field lights, and after that extra embellishment he dropped down and let go of a nasty three-quarter sidearm curve that broke low and a foot away from the outside corner. The crowd oohed in appreciation at his flourish before the ball had even left Luis's hand, and then jumped to their feet and cheered when Perez futilely leaned forward from the waist and lunged across the plate at it, almost a gesture of surrender. Tony Kubek remarked on the air that he wasn't even sure Perez had seen the ball leave Tiant's hand. For the ninth time in a row during this World Series—and for the fourth time on strikes—Luis Tiant had won the battle with Tony Perez.

Left fielder George Foster came up for the first time with one out. If Tiant's byzantine deliveries had baffled Perez and most of the other Reds to date, Foster had proved the most immune to them; he had registered four of his five hits in the Series—all singles—during Tiant's first two outings. Wary of Foster's power, Tiant started him with a fastball that missed outside.

Foster was twenty-six, tall, lean, and muscular, a quiet country kid from Alabama who had been drafted out of high school by the San Francisco Giants. He had no sooner made the parent club in 1971, playing left field beside Willie Mays—the fellow Alabaman he'd grown up worshipping—than the Giants appeared suddenly to give up on him, trading him to the Reds for backup shortstop Frank Duffy, who had been edged out by the unexpected emergence of Davey Concepcion. That trade had been engineered by the Reds' advance scout, Ray Shore, a former player and brilliant evaluator of talent, who had been with the club for a decade and was never shy about stating his strong opinions to general manager Bob Howsam. In 1968 the Reds and Shore had in essence invented his job, becoming the first major-league team to send a seasoned eye ahead of the team to scout the squad they were scheduled to play next. Shore's nickname "Snacks"—and his ample midsection— testified to the dietary perils of living almost the entire season on the road. He compiled a detailed notebook for every team in the National League, with a page devoted to each of their players' specific situational tendencies—at bat, on the bases, in the field, or on the mound. Copies of Shore's reports were distributed throughout the organization before every series, and when Sparky Anderson took over in 1970, he embraced this innovation and relied heavily on Shore's findings; Sparky believed this extra intelligence gave him an edge in games that translated into five to fifteen additional wins during a season. By 1975 the Reds' success had persuaded most of the other teams in baseball, after the initial skepticism they had expressed at the expense involved, to employ an "advance scout."

The Reds also used Ray Shore to size up talent they were interested in acquiring, and when the Giants had mentioned that Foster might be available for Frank Duffy, Shore urged the front office to take him. The deal didn't pay immediate dividends; Foster's fragile confidence had been severely shaken by the trade, and he failed to make the club out of spring training in 1972. After two seasons split between the majors and minors and winter ball in the Dominican

Republic—where they changed Foster's stance, encouraging him to stand more upright, which seemed to awaken his bat—he stuck with the Reds through the 1974 season, showing flashes of the prodigious power they believed he possessed. When Sparky moved Pete Rose to third in May of '75 and awarded Foster the regular left field job, their investment paid off: Foster responded with twenty-three home runs, drove in seventy-eight, and hit an even .300. That kind of bat in their lineup behind Bench and Perez added a whole new level of threat to the Big Red Machine, and the Reds felt George Foster had only just begun to realize his potential.

Foster was a fastidious, deliberate hitter at the plate, almost painfully so, and he stepped in and out of the box twice now—tugging at his belt, digging in his back foot before getting set—a tactic designed to upset a pitcher's rhythms. The crowd booed but Tiant showed no signs of irritation, patiently waiting on the rubber and then uncorking that lazy, slow dropping curve on the outside corner for a called strike, 1–1.

On his second throw Tiant challenged Foster, turning his back completely to the plate, giving him the extra head tip, then turning and launching a fastball toward the outside corner. Foster took a fierce cut at it and missed for strike two; that was the pitch he'd been waiting for, and he looked mad that he'd missed it. Tiant didn't usually give anyone more than one hittable pitch in an at bat, and he had just blown one by Foster to go ahead in the count.

Foster stepped out again, grabbed some dirt, and rubbed his hands together, and the Boston crowd let him hear their displeasure again. Luis let fly a stream of tobacco juice from the thick wad he kept stuffed in his cheek during games; he was a dedicated cigar man—Cubans from home, naturally, obtained by a lawyer friend who knew ways around the American embargo—and the kick of the nicotine helped sharpen his focus on the mound. It also kept him from drinking water, which he didn't like to do during games and had never been encouraged to do at any level when he pitched; the concept of "hydration" was still a decade away in baseball's conservative culture. This contributed to the extreme weight loss Tiant often experienced during a complete game, sometimes as much as ten or twelve pounds.

Foster made a defensive swing at the next pitch, a low outside curve that he fouled back to the right. Tiant and Fisk sensed an opening and they fed him a high off-speed change that Foster failed to adjust on; catching just a piece of the ball, he lofted it foul down the right field line, where Cecil Cooper retreated to make the catch for the second out.

Shortstop Davey Concepcion stepped in. He had managed one hit against Tiant in eight at bats so far, a double that drove in a run in Game Four. A tall, gangly kid from Venezuela, Concepcion had arrived ahead of schedule with the Reds after only two years in the minors, in 1970, the year Sparky took over. He played spectacular defense from day one, displaying remarkable range, speed, and a surprisingly strong arm for a six-two string bean who weighed one-fifty soaking wet. The first time he saw him, Gary Nolan said Concepcion looked like he could take a shower in a shotgun barrel. With their powerful lineup, the Reds could afford the luxury of a purely defensive shortstop, but Sparky thought Concepcion could give them more. He possessed a good eye and decent bat speed, and hitting instructor Ted Kluszewski—in his remedial English, Concepcion called him "Klooski"—gradually taught him to be more aggressive at the plate. After sharing duties with shortstop Darrel Chaney for two seasons, Concepcion won the job outright after a strong performance in the 1972 World Series. He was on his way to a breakout year in 1973, and he had just been named to his first All-Star team, when he caught his spikes in the dirt trying to go from first to third on an infield out, broke his left leg, and dislocated his ankle, a nasty injury that ended his season. He bounced back solidly in 1974 and, after finally packing another fifteen pounds on his slender frame, began to show some power, hitting fourteen home runs; Davey wasn't just out there for his defense anymore. In 1975, the twenty-seven-year-old Concepcion won his second straight Gold Glove award, made the All-Star team as a starter for the first time, and had begun to earn respect around the league as one of the best all-around shortstops in the game.

Everywhere, that is, but in the Reds clubhouse. In a locker room dominated by the outsized presence of the Reds' four superstars, ever since Concepcion had joined the team as a twenty-one-year-old rookie, he had seemed—and been treated by his fellow infielders— like a goofy kid brother who was always a half step behind and never realized the joke was on him. He longed to be taken seriously and be accorded the same reverential treatment that he saw Rose, Morgan, Bench, and Perez receive; a tough task when their nickname for you is "Bozo," a jab at his colorful and occasionally mismatched wardrobe. During the recent off-seasons Davey had been greeted as a huge star back home in Venezuela, the biggest his country had produced since fellow shortstop and future Hall of Famer Luis Aparicio, and he couldn't comprehend why the same level of appreciation hadn't come his way in America as well. But what almost amounted to a generation gap still divided him from the Reds' Big Four, who were all mature men, all over thirty with the exception of Bench—who was twenty-seven but had seemed years older than his age since the day he arrived. Although Tony Perez had taken Concepcion under his wing as a mentor off the field, whenever the team gathered, Davey became the frequent target of the star players' jokes and wicked one-liners, and when he tried to respond with zingers of his own—in often comically fractured syntax; his English was still shaky—it often backfired into even bigger laughs at his expense. None of their ribbing was entirely malicious, but it never seemed to end, and within the confines of the team's culture his search for commensurate status with that formidable quartet remained a steep hill for Davey Concepcion to climb.

Nor did he seem to have earned much respect from the man facing him on the mound. Tiant nicked the outside corner with a low, moving fastball for strike one, then challenged him with a hard, high fastball that Concepcion fouled back, quickly behind in the count 0–2. Sniffing blood, the crowd began their chant "Loo-ee, Loo-ee, Loo-ee." Tiant stared in for the sign, still and composed as a statue, turned his back to Concepcion, and sidearmed a curve over the outside corner. Concepcion lifted a lazy fly ball to center field, almost to the spot where Fred Lynn was stationed; he hauled it in for the third out of the inning and cantered toward the dugout.

All felt right with the world in Fenway and for fans glued to their TVs and radios throughout New England: The Red Sox had the early lead, and it seemed clear that for the third time in this Series their hero, *El Tiante,* had his mojo working.

SEVEN

Baseball is a wholesome game, which should instill
and encourage the highest moral values.

AMERICAN LEAGUE PRESIDENT BAN JOHNSON

T HAT FIRST "WORLD SERIES" IN 1903, BETWEEN THE BOSTON
Americans and Pittsburgh Pirates, almost failed to take place
because of a labor dispute. Pittsburgh's players were under contract
through the middle of October and obligated to play, but Boston's
season had ended on September 28. Before they agreed to take the
field against the National League champion Pirates on October 1, the
Americans insisted on two additional weeks of guaranteed pay and
a 75 percent cut of the gate. Their heated negotiations with Boston's
owner Henry Killilea stalled—public sentiment tilted heavily toward the players—and Pittsburgh threatened to withdraw unless
Boston's players would commit. At the last minute the Americans
grudgingly settled on their regular salary for the length of the Series, and a fifty-fifty split of Killilea's profits.

The World Series began with three games in Boston, and an
unprecedented level of local interest prompted the creation of the
first separate "sporting sections" in the city's six daily newspapers.
The other phenomenon sparked by this Series sounds unsavory if
not downright illegal by today's standards but, in that rough-and-
tumble era, was considered as integral to the game as peanut vendors: Big-time gamblers from all over the East Coast had descended
on Beantown to make book on the Series; a feverish wave of wager-
ing gripped the city's hotel lobbies and saloons, and the contagion
apparently spread to more than a few of the players.

Regular season ticket prices doubled for the Series: fifty cents for standing room, a dollar for grandstand seats, a buck fifty for a field box. More than fifteen thousand spectators crowded Huntington Avenue Grounds for Game One, overwhelming capacity in the stands. The surplus crowd flowed onto the playing field itself, where police made liberal use of their nightsticks to herd spectators behind ropes strung in front of the bleachers. Each league had supplied one umpire for the Series, and they hastily decided that any ball rolling into the crowd beyond those ropes would be ruled a ground-rule triple. With their reliable ace Cy Young taking the mound in Game One, Boston had emerged as a prohibitive favorite in the betting line, which brought heavy action on the Pittsburgh side and set the stage for shenanigans. Suspicions began immediately as the peerless Young, entirely out of character, piped pitch after pitch straight over the plate; Pittsburgh hit him hard. Three of Boston's fielders, among the finest defensive players in the American League, committed *four* errors between them through the opening innings, most of them obvious boots. At the plate the Americans' early at bats smelled equally fishy; Pittsburgh's starter Deacon Phillippe, a junk artist whose fastball you could time with a calendar, struck out ten of them. The score was 5–0 Pittsburgh by the end of the third inning, and the Pirates stretched it to 7–0 in the seventh, at which point Young shut them down, and the Americans finally plated a few runs to make the final result—7–3—take on the appearance, if not the actual character, of respectability.

There didn't seem to be much dispute that the Americans had thrown Game One, but curiously, neither was any outrage in evidence, or much beyond mild protest voiced in Boston's customarily volatile press. Baseball and gambling had become so connected in many people's minds at this point—and, after all, this was just an "exhibition," with nothing but bragging rights at stake—that the whole unseemly spectacle was treated as little more than business as usual. Whether Boston's players were in on the fix, expressing their displeasure at the hard deal they'd cut with their owner, or dogging it to ensure that the Series would go the distance so they'd collect their full salaries remains unknown; Cy Young, the most celebrated of the players involved, never commented on the issue. Perhaps discouraged by their team's halfhearted charade, a much smaller and more manageable crowd showed up for Game Two; the Americans' players showed up for it as well and won handily 3–0. That convincing victory revived the city's interest in the Series, and an unruly mob once again swarmed over Huntington Grounds Park the next day for Game Three, requiring the efforts of the city's riot squad and, at one point, both teams' players armed with bats to clear them off the field. Nearly nineteen thousand people had squeezed into a park built to hold fewer than half that number, jamming in alongside the length of the foul lines and shortening the outfield's dimensions to less than 250 feet. This time the umpires ruled that any ball landing or bouncing into that crowd would be a ground-rule double. In the midst of that teeming sea of humanity, and some questionable plays by Boston's fielders that once again raised the specter of fixing, the Pirates won Game Three by a score of 4–2.

The World Series, along with trainloads of Boston's fanatic Rooters—and their spiritual leader, saloon owner Michael T. "Nuf Ced" McGreevey—now shifted to Pittsburgh.

GARY NOLAN took the mound in the bottom of the second inning in Game Six, still seething at himself for the gopher ball he'd served up to Fred Lynn. Feeling he'd let his teammates down, and with Jack Billingham and Fred Norman continuing to throw in the Reds' bullpen, Nolan knew that Sparky wouldn't hesitate to pull him now at the first sign of trouble.

Nolan opened the frame with his best fastball of the game and caught the outside corner for a strike against Red Sox right fielder Dwight "Dewey" Evans.

The tall, powerful twenty-three-year-old Evans had just finished his third season as the Red Sox right fielder, but amid all the hype and excitement created by the startling debuts of rookies Fred Lynn and Jim Rice he had become something of a forgotten man in 1975, which the modest and personable Evans hadn't seemed to mind one bit. He was a consummate team player, who demonstrated remarkably little hunger or fondness for the spotlight. Born, like Lynn, in Southern California, Evans had spent some of his early childhood in Hawaii—and drew some of the island's hang-loose ways into his soul—until his family moved back to the San Fernando Valley when he was nine and his baseball obsession began in earnest. He had been drafted by the Red Sox in 1969 after an outstanding high school career as a third baseman, but on the strength of his remarkable throwing arm they converted him to the outfield. After steadily advancing through the minors, Evans jumped a step to Triple-A Louisville under manager Darrell Johnson in 1972. (The Red Sox relocated this franchise to Pawtucket, Massachusetts, after the 1972 season.) Although he had progressed rapidly through their system, Evans struggled against the better pitching at this higher level, taking too many pitches and swinging defensively instead of attacking the ball. He was on the verge of being sent back down when Johnson intervened, arguing that Evans should be given one more week to find himself; DJ saw more potential in the quiet Evans than any of his previous managers. He suggested that Dewey slightly shorten his stride as he stepped into pitches, which quickened his bat and helped immediately. Boosted by DJ's confidence in him, Evans broke through that week and then went on a tear, leading the International League in RBIs and winning its Most Valuable Player award by season's end, which earned him a September call-up to Boston in the middle of a pennant race. By June of the following season, Evans had laid claim to the Red Sox right field job, then held on to it with his remarkable defense while his power and patience at the plate steadily improved.

Nolan missed way outside with a wayward curve to even the count at 1–1.

When Rice and Lynn joined Evans in the Red Sox outfield at the start of the 1975 season, Boston reporters and fans woke to the idea this might be the best trio their team had fielded since the old glory days of Duffy Lewis, Tris Speaker, and Harry Hooper. Much is always made of the defensive challenges posed in Fenway's left field by the Green Monster, but in truth that amounts largely to learning how to effectively play caroms off the wall, as the area one has to cover is greatly reduced by the shortened dimensions. The park's vast right field, which with its own odd shapes and angles is equally if not obviously as quirky, demands much greater range and a far stronger throwing arm to properly defend. Evans had demonstrated superb range from the moment he arrived, and a sniper's rifle for an arm. When Evans's best friend on the team, Rico Petrocelli, missed a stretch of games early in the season, there had been some foolish talk about moving Evans back to his original position at third base. After Evans finished second in the American League in outfield assists in 1975, initiating eight double plays, that notion was laid to rest for good.

Evans looked down to Don Zimmer for a sign, then dug in and chopped at a good Nolan changeup, fouling it into the dirt at his feet.

Evans had struggled at the plate during the Division Series against the A's, but during the first five games of his first World Series, despite suffering from the flu that had waylaid many of the Red Sox, Evans had broken through and emphatically answered the only question about him that remained: Could he produce under pressure in the postseason? His two-run homer in the top of the ninth in Game Three at Cincinnati had sent that one into extra innings, and his triple in Game Four had proved to be the decisive blow in a five-run fourth inning that sparked Tiant's and the Red Sox's second victory. Dwight Evans had hit .353 through the first five games of the Series, and his four RBIs led the team; he had virtually carried them at Riverfront Park, and this performance didn't go unnoticed by the opposition. Pete Rose paid Evans his version of the ultimate compliment by comparing him to his favorite player: "He reminds me a lot of myself." No slouch as a judge of talent himself, Sparky Anderson had remarked at Sunday's press conference that he'd known about all the big-name talent on the Boston roster from Ray Shore's extensive scouting reports, but from what he'd seen so far, Dwight Evans might be the Red Sox's best all-around player. "This guy is a surprise package," said Sparky. "He's as good a young outfielder as there is in baseball and he's just starting to touch his ability. He's a future superstar."

Out in the Reds bullpen, Jack Billingham took a seat, as left-hander Freddie Norman continued to throw. Sparky had made up his mind about who he'd go to next, and once again, it wasn't Billingham.

When a reporter pointed out Sparky's comments about him to Evans before Game Six, he responded in the way that would always endear him to Boston's baseball purist fans: "It's very nice of him to say such things, but let's face it: I'm not the Fred Lynn, natural ability type. I don't want to be a star, I just want to be a winner."

Johnny Bench, liking the way Evans had flailed at that last pitch, signaled for another changeup, and again Evans hacked the off-speed offering into the dirt, dribbling foul down the third base line to Rose. Evans dug in and guessed a fastball must be in the offing, but Bench won the chess match when he called for a third off-speed pitch in a row, a big curve that Satch Davidson thought nicked the outside corner, and he called Evans out on strikes. Evans put a hand on his hip, silently protesting Davidson's call, then stalked back to the dugout.

Evans was followed to the plate by his former minor-league teammate, shortstop Rick Burleson. Like Lynn and Evans another Southern California native and prospect, Burleson had initially been the most highly touted of the three, the Red Sox's first-round—and fifth overall—pick of the 1970 draft. He had also played for manager Darrell Johnson in the minors, and won his confidence just as Lynn and Evans had, but that's where Burleson's similarity to the two laid-back outfielders ended; the slight, taut, fiery infielder burned with an arclight intensity on and off the field that should have reminded Pete Rose even more of his favorite player. After three grinding seasons in the minors, Burleson battled his way onto the Boston roster in 1974 as a utility infielder, then made the most of an opportunity created when second baseman Doug Griffin went down with another in a series of serious injuries. Burleson hit over .300 in his absence and played such solid defense that when Griffin returned, the team couldn't afford to take Burleson out of the lineup, so they installed him as their starter at short, where he showed consistent toughness and determination, and one of the strongest throwing arms in the league. He finished the season batting .284 and ended up second in the voting behind the Yankees' Bucky Dent as the best rookie shortstop in baseball. Reservations about his range at the more demanding defensive position persisted through the off-season, however, so Burleson had to battle for the starting job all over again in spring training of 1975, when he not only won the starting nod but the blessings of fifty-six-year-old Johnny Pesky.

Born John Michael Paveskovich, former manager and broadcaster for the team, Pesky, now a member of Boston's coaching staff, was one of Red Sox Nation's sage tribal elders. A hustling overachiever who by the end of his career had become the most celebrated shortstop in Red Sox history, he had been a mainstay of the squad during Ted Williams's prime years in the 1940s. The short right field foul pole in Fenway, only 302 feet from home plate, had for years been unofficially called "Pesky's Pole," supposedly for a walk-off, game-winning home run he hit there in support of Sox left-hander Mel Parnell in 1948. Although the record shows Pesky hit only one of his six career home runs in Fenway when Parnell was pitching—and it came in the first inning—the story had passed into legend during the 1960s, when both Pesky and Parnell worked on the Red Sox broadcast team. Pesky was also remembered for something less celebratory. With two outs in the eighth inning of Game Seven in the 1946 World Series against St. Louis, Cardinals outfielder Enos Slaughter scored all the way from first with what turned out to be the Series' winning run on a double by Harry "The Hat" Walker. After catching the throw-in from Red Sox center fielder Leon Culberson, Johnny Pesky made the relay from short left field to home but not in time to catch the speedy Slaughter, who never broke stride all the way around the bases. Pesky, unfairly as film of the moment confirms, was accused in some accounts of "holding the ball" in a moment of indecision before throwing to the plate. The real culprit was probably Culberson, who wasn't expecting Slaughter to keep running and half-lobbed the ball in to his shortstop, but the goat horns ended up on Johnny Pesky, blamed for the first of what would become a lavishly documented Red Sox tradition of blown World Series chances.

"Burleson comes to the ballpark mad, and he goes home mad," said Pesky. "I always played as if somebody better might come along, and that's the way Burleson plays. He's never satisfied, and I don't think that's a bad thing."

Burleson watched a Nolan fastball catch the inside corner for a called first strike.

During fielding practice before a game in 1974, Pesky's fellow Red Sox coach Don Zimmer—another former major-league infielder known for his short fuse—hit a succession of tough grounders at Burleson that he had trouble handling. The hotter the shot, the more he struggled, and the angrier he got at himself, until Zimmer noticed that Burleson's neck had turned a radioactive red, and when he ripped off his cap and tossed it to the ground in disgust at himself his hair stood straight up in a comblike tuft.

"Look at that little bugger out there," said Zimmer, admiringly. "He looks like a bantam rooster."

That's how nicknames are born in the big leagues. The "Rooster" had hit .252 and led the Red Sox in thrown bats, umpire confrontations, and slammed doors in 1975, bringing a street fighter's scrappiness to the team that it had been missing for years and sorely needed. Johnny Pesky had offered the ultimate compliment to their new shortstop before the Series: "We wouldn't be here without him." Burleson had more than backed up those words during the World Series, playing errorless ball in the field, and leading the team in hitting at .389, another performance that had earned the praise of the Reds.

Burleson fouled Nolan's next pitch—a roundhouse curve—wide of third, into the face of the left field grandstand that jutted out sharply to meet the third base line about halfway between third base and the Monster. He resisted the next one, a fastball that missed just outside, and the count was 1–2.

Burleson's gritty performance in the Series against the Reds had also drawn frequent comparisons to Billy Martin, the blustery, troubled manager—who had recently been hired by their new owner George Steinbrenner to manage the Yankees; the first of Martin's five tempestuous tenures with the team—who had played mid-infield with similar intensity for the great 1950s Yankees teams. A career .257 hitter, Martin had capped his playing career with three outstanding World Series performances, winning the Series' MVP award in 1953. Burleson possessed the same kind of red-hot nuclear core, but, unlike the tragic Martin, confined it to the field, living quietly with his wife in suburban Boston.

Burleson went into his crouch and lined another outside fastball pitch sharply toward first base, where Tony Perez deftly picked it up and trotted over to touch the bag. Out by twenty feet, Burleson continued digging down the line, hitting the bag at full speed even after Perez had begun to toss the ball around the infield.

The crowd rose to its feet again as Luis Tiant came to the plate; Kubek remarked that Luis was leading the World Series in standing ovations, and nobody was going to catch him. Since the American League's adoption of the designated hitter rule in 1973, Tiant had recorded only one official at bat in a game until this World Series, but prior to that, since his sandlot days, he had always prided himself on his hitting. Blessed with exceptional hand-eye coordination, he had hit five home runs in the bigs while knocking in forty runs, and during his season with the Twins in 1969, albeit in only thirty-two at bats, had hit for an amazing .406 average. He had also surprised the Reds in this Series, going 2–6 while drawing a couple of walks, for an on-base percentage of .500. Tiant had singled and come around to record the first, and what turned out to be the game-winning, run of a tense, scoreless Game One, when the Red Sox exploded for six runs in the seventh inning, then went back out to finish nailing down the complete-game shutout.

Eager to get the inning over with, Nolan threw a fastball down the middle that Tiant watched for a strike. Nolan came back with a big bender that started inside and gave Tiant a serious case of jelly leg; he stepped halfway out of the box and waved at it for a second strike.

After recording another single in the fourth inning of Game Four, Tiant again scored what turned out to be the game-winning run of that game. Given Tiant's success at the plate so far, Bench had decided not to show him too many fastballs, and he took Nolan's next bender low and outside for a ball, as NBC cut to the field-level view from their camera inside the left field scoreboard. Bench signaled curveball again, and Nolan whisked the outside corner for a called third strike, his second punch-out of a sharp and effective 1-2-3 inning. Tiant turned and trotted back to the dugout, to another big hand from the crowd.

Gary Nolan had started six World Series games for Sparky Anderson and the Reds since 1970, but had yet to win one. He had bounced back effectively after a shaky first inning, but wouldn't win this one either; Nolan had just thrown his last pitch of Game Six.

1. Fenway Park, 1917

2. Fenway Park from the air, 1975

3. Tom Yawkey, Red Sox owner, circa 1948

4. Red Sox owner Tom Yawkey, 1975

5. Commissioner Bowie Kuhn

6. Cincinnati Reds president Bob Howsam

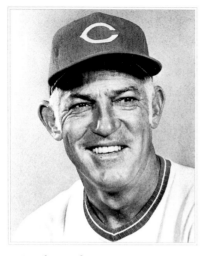

7. Sparky Anderson

8. Darrell Johnson

9. Sparky Anderson and Darrell Johnson, press day at Fenway Park before the 1975 World Series

10. Luis Tiant

11. Gary Nolan

12. Tiant and Rose, the first pitch

13. Tony Kubek
and Joe Garagiola

14. Dick Stockton
and Curt Gowdy
at Fenway Park
before Game One

15. Police escorting
school buses, Boston,
October 1975

16. NBC executive
Chet Simmons

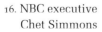

17. Sparky Anderson
and Peter Edward Rose

18. Sparky Anderson
and Johnny Bench

19. Sparky Anderson
and Joe Morgan

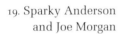

20. Pete Rose

21. Fred Lynn and Jim Rice; "The Gold Dust Twins," 1975

22. Carl Yastrzemski

23. Carl Yastrzemski

24. Umpire
Larry Barnett,
Carlton Fisk,
Ed Armbrister;
"The Armbrister
Incident,"
Game Three

25. Red Sox second baseman
Denny Doyle

26. Cecil Cooper

27. Tony Perez

28. Davey Concepcion

EIGHT

When the chips are on the line, he's the greatest
competitor I've ever seen. Luis Tiant is "The Man."

HALL OF FAME PITCHER JIM PALMER

AFTER EACH OF THE FIRST TWO SEASONS HE PITCHED FOR the Mexico City Tigers, Luis Tiant returned home to Cuba for the off-season. He had established himself as a rising star during his second year, in 1960, going 17–7 and leading the Tigers to the Mexican League championship. That summer at a coed softball game he also met Maria del Refugio Navarro, a young beauty who worked for the Social Security office and was playing left field that night, the start of a traditional yearlong courtship that would lead to their marriage. During the winter of 1960–61, as young Tony Perez prepared to spend his first season on a Reds farm team in upstate New York, Luis pitched in the Cuban League. One of the oldest and most storied baseball organizations in the Western Hemisphere, the Cuban League had developed dozens of players who went on to play in either the majors or the Negro Leagues. Since 1900, the Cuban League had also been baseball's only fully integrated league, where white American players were regularly sent by their major-league owners for seasoning against top competition from around the Caribbean. But the anti-American policies of Cuba's newly installed leader Fidel Castro ended that arrangement before the 1960–61 season; when President Eisenhower broke off diplomatic relations, major-league baseball was told that players from the United States were no longer welcome. Luis Tiant went 10–8 for "Habana" that year, a famous franchise that had been founded during the league's first year, in 1878, and the same team his father had starred on more than twenty years earlier. "Lefty" Tiant watched all of his son's starts with pride, and Luis was named the Cuban League's Rookie of the Year.

Luis returned to Mexico City for his third season with the Tigers in May of 1961, just as Castro put into place the rigid anti-emigration policy many Cubans had feared was coming. More than a million people—10 percent of the country's population, many from the middle and upper classes—had fled the country since Castro took power, and he now imposed a three-year waiting period for anyone else who wished to leave; during the wait they would have to forfeit their jobs and all personal property, and would be treated as enemies of the state. Whether anyone would actually be allowed to leave at the end of that purgatorial ordeal remained to be seen. The policy had the desired effect: The flood of people legally leaving Cuba came to a sudden halt. Castro also announced that there would be no more "professional" baseball in their country; the ninety-year-old Cuban League had played its last game. Cuban-born players would now enjoy the privilege of playing baseball only for the glory of the state, in a new league that Castro organized personally.

Luis Tiant's third straight winning season for the Mexico City Tigers in 1961 led directly to his first minor-league deal with the Cleveland Indians, who purchased his contract outright and told Tiant they planned to bring him to spring training the following year. Luis and Maria married that summer, but put off their honeymoon until after the season ended in September. To celebrate both their marriage and his new opportunity in baseball, he had planned to introduce Maria to his parents and spend a week together with them at an island resort off Cuba's southern coast. When he called his father to finalize the arrangements, Luis received the shock of his life.

The Old Man told him not to come home. The United States' newly elected president, John F. Kennedy, had taken office in January, and an ill-fated, CIA-backed invasion at the Bay of Pigs by Cuban exiles had failed miserably in April; hundreds died and thousands of suspected sympathizers had been thrown into Cuban prisons, pushing Castro ever closer to socialism. Life in Havana had grown more oppressive ever since, and under no circumstances was Luis to return now, not if he had any hope of ever leaving again and fulfilling his dreams.

Stay in Mexico, his father said. *Make a good life for your family now.*

But when will I see you again? Luis asked.

The Old Man hesitated. *I will let you know.*

Less than three months later, Fidel Castro officially announced to the world that he was an avowed Marxist-Leninist and that Cuba would become a client state of the Soviet Union and a communist country.

Luis Tiant would not see his father again, and the Old Man wouldn't set eyes on his three grandchildren, for the next fourteen years.

REDS CENTER FIELDER Cesar Geronimo faced Tiant to begin the top of the third inning. The twenty-seven-year-old native of the Dominican Republic had enjoyed the most success of any Reds regular against Tiant in his first two outings, going 3–5 with two walks. The left-hand-hitting Geronimo had come over to the Reds from the Houston Astros before the 1972 season, as part of the blockbuster Joe Morgan trade. The Reds had lost their starting center fielder Bobby Tolan the season before to a torn Achilles tendon; Sparky had been forced to use seven different men in center after Tolan went down, and the team desperately needed a long-term replacement. Geronimo's last-minute inclusion in the Morgan deal, which seemed like an afterthought to Houston at the time, was actually a key component for the Reds, and a tribute to the due diligence of their GM, Bob Howsam, and his super-scout Ray Shore, and manager Sparky Anderson's ongoing commitment to speed and defense.

Tiant started him with a hard fastball on the outside corner for a called strike.

Cesar Francisco Geronimo hadn't played a lot of formal baseball growing up, but he discovered while playing softball for his high school seminary that he'd been blessed with a freakishly strong throwing arm. On the strength of that alone he'd been scouted and signed in 1967 by the Yankees, who tried and failed to make a pitcher out of him. They moved him to the outfield, but when he didn't show much promise at the plate, the Yankees let him go to the Astros, who were impressed by his speed and that spectacular arm, qualities they desperately needed in the cavernous, artificial-turf outfield of the Astrodome.

Tiant came right back with another fastball down the middle for another called strike, challenging Geronimo now, ahead in the count 0–2.

Starting in 1969 Geronimo had played three part-time seasons for the Astros, primarily as a defensive replacement, getting to the plate only 138 times. He still hadn't hit much and showed almost no power, but he'd caught the Reds' attention with his nine-foot stride and howitzer arm. Sparky had been preaching the importance of defense ever since he arrived, particularly up the middle; he considered the catcher, the two middle infielders, and the center fielder to be the heart of any defense. With Bench and Concepcion already in place, Sparky figured that Morgan and Geronimo—who wouldn't have to hit much if he patrolled center like they thought he could on the carpet in Riverfront—would give him the strongest defensive quartet in the league. Not only did the Reds' bet pay off on Geronimo's defense—he had just won his second straight Gold Glove as one of the National League's best defensive outfielders; all four of the Reds' defenders up the middle took home that award in 1975—under coach Ted Kluszewski's sound tutelage he'd grown into a much better and more patient hitter than they'd ever anticipated, giving them bonus production out of the eighth spot in the lineup.

Tiant came back in with a live fastball inside that just missed for a ball, then another that Geronimo just caught a piece of with a late, defensive swing, fouling it back to the screen.

The Reds' most effective pinch hitter, Terry Crowley, had moved out to the on-deck circle, to bat in the pitcher's spot, officially indicating that Gary Nolan was done for the night. Sparky hadn't said a word to Nolan when he came in, and didn't have to; even though he'd shown much better stuff in his second inning, Nolan knew they couldn't afford to fall any further behind. Although he felt dejected about being pulled from the game so early, Nolan didn't hang his head, and instead of staying in the clubhouse after his shower, he put on a fresh uniform, walked back down the tunnel to the dugout, and grabbed a seat on the bench, hoping to see his team come back.

Having set the table with a steady diet of fastballs, Tiant gave Geronimo the full-throttle windup and then pulled the string on a slow outside curve that Geronimo swung at and missed by a foot for Luis's third strikeout of the game.

Without a runner on base, Sparky called Crowley back to the dugout, saving him for later in the game, and sent up Darrel Chaney in his place. The twenty-seven-year-old Chaney was a Reds lifer, a slick-fielding switch-hitting infielder who had shared the starting shortstop job with Davey Concepcion until he won the job outright in 1972. Chaney had become one of the leaders of the Reds' second stringers who occasionally cracked the lineup of the "Great Eight" during the regular season, but who disappeared almost completely in postseason play. This self-deprecating group of scrubs banded together off the field and played an important role in the Reds' positive team chemistry, keeping one another loose, never complaining about their limited roles, good soldiers in Sparky's reserve corps. They prepared for their sporadic appearances with diligent professionalism and took an almost perverse pride in the degree to which the press and anyone outside of the most fanatic Reds boosters completely ignored them. They decided to call themselves, not for public consumption, the "Big Red Turds," and even had T-shirts made bearing the phrase, which they wore under their uniforms. Chaney had made one previous pinch-hit appearance against Tiant, in Game Four, striking out with a runner on base.

Chaney's appearance here in Game Six was even briefer, as he lifted a first-pitch fastball into the prevailing wind in deep left field, where Yastrzemski hurried back to the base of the Monster and snagged the ball over his head for the second out of the inning.

Both Larry Shepard and Ted Kluszewski had noticed something in the team's chart of Tiant's pitches and pointed it out to Sparky just before Chaney's at bat. Instead of the dizzying array of off-speed offerings they'd seen from Tiant during his first two games—which had caused most of the Reds to lay off his first pitch—they'd noticed that tonight he was starting almost every batter he faced with a fastball around the plate, trying to sneak in a strike and get ahead in the count. Armed with that information, Sparky had warned Chaney to be looking for a first-pitch fastball, and sure enough Tiant had thrown him one in the zone; Chaney, with a grand total of seven home runs in his seven major-league seasons, had hacked at it and driven the ball to the warning track.

Word spread quietly through the Reds dugout. Back to the top of the order, Pete Rose came to the plate for the second time, looking fastball, and when Tiant came at him with one, Pete nodded and watched it land outside for a ball. Now expecting him to come with something off-speed, Rose sat back, and Tiant served him one on a platter, a soft change that broke down over the heart of the plate; Rose whacked it into center field for the Reds' first hit of the game.

Sparky got up on his feet, clapped his hands, and climbed the first step of the dugout, as Rose rounded first; no one else in Fenway might have agreed at that moment, but Sparky felt the stirrings of a shift in momentum.

Ken Griffey came up for his second at bat, as Rose took a short lead; no threat to steal in this situation—Sparky was more interested in continuing to field-test his new theory about Tiant.

And there it was, another first-pitch fastball; Griffey swung and stung it back up the middle of the box. Tiant reached down low to his left, the direction his follow-through was already carrying him, and the ball just ticked off the webbing of his glove. That redirected it right to where Denny Doyle was drifting to his left off second, and he scooped it up and fired to Cooper at first, beating the swift Griffey by a step for the third out, to end the inning.

The Reds were still down three runs, had only one hit through the first third of the game, and Darrel Chaney's at bat wouldn't amount to much in the game's final box score, but in the eternal chess match between pitcher and batter, Sparky had found his first exploitable edge against the baffling Tiant.

NINE

I thought I had to show all my stuff and almost
tore the boards off the grandstand. One of the fellas
called me "Cyclone," but finally shorted it to "Cy"
and it's been that way ever since.

CY YOUNG

SUGGESTIONS THAT THE FIRST GAME OF THE FIRST "World Series" in 1903 might have been fixed weren't helped when one of Boston's regulars was approached by an infamous gambler in the lobby of their hotel before the fourth game in Pittsburgh and offered $12,000 if he'd lie down and let the Pirates win. That same player, catcher Lou Criger, had been the most obvious suspect in the Americans' shameful performance during Game One—he committed two errors in the first inning alone—but this time, either stricken with remorse or insulted by the size of the offer, Criger immediately reported the incident to American League president Ban Johnson. Aware that public opinion already harbored suspicions of monkey business on the part of his league's best and most representative team, Johnson suppressed information about the offer—it wouldn't reach print for twenty years—and the Americans still went on to lose Game Four, although not before mounting a spirited and genuine ninth-inning comeback, by a final score of 5–4. Boston now trailed in the best of nine Series three games to one; the success of Pittsburgh's mission to crush their upstart rivals from the junior league appeared inevitable.

Game Five changed everything. Throughout the game Boston's fanatical Royal Rooters—many of them newspapermen, led by saloon owner "Nuf Ced" McGreevey and his brass band—staked out a position on top of the Americans' dugout, belting out improvised lyrics to the popular song "Tessie" that called out and individually savaged members of the Pirates' lineup. In the sixth inning of a tense, scoreless contest—with Cy Young back on form for Boston—two of Pittsburgh's outfielders, unable over the Rooters' racket to hear each other calling for a routine fly ball, ran into each other and the ball dropped. With the team unnerved by the play, a slew of errors by Pittsburgh followed, Cy Young drove in two runs with the key hit, and Boston broke the game open, going on to win in a rout 11–2. They came back the following day to win again, 6–3, and even the Series at three games apiece. Both Pittsburgh's players and their fans appeared stunned, while McGreevey and his Rooters went marching triumphantly around the city after the game. The Pirates' owner tried to steal his tired pitching staff some rest the next day by claiming it was too cold to play Game Seven—it was sixty degrees— but the plan backfired when Boston was then able to come back at them with an equally refreshed Cy Young. Young handled the Pirates easily again for his second victory, winning 7–3, and seized the lead for the Americans in the Series, which now headed back to Boston.

In front of their devoted fans, who had hoisted Cy Young on their shoulders when the team arrived home on the train at the South Station, the Americans shut out the depleted and dispirited Pirates 3–0 in Game Eight, to cap their improbable comeback in the first World Series, five games to three. Not unlike the way Joe Namath and the New York Jets would sixty-six years later shock the world by beating the heavily favored Baltimore Colts in Super Bowl III, and thereby establish the legitimacy of the rival AFL, Ban Johnson's brash American League had proved it belonged on the same playing field as the older National League. The Senior Circuit's monopoly of America's pastime had been broken, but the equality of the two leagues—now established as fact on the diamond—had yet to be formalized on paper.

When Boston repeated as American League champions in 1904, the National League's pennant-winning New York Giants—led by their legendary hard-ass manager John McGraw, who according to Ban Johnson had been behind that offer in Pittsburgh to Lou Criger to fix the first Series—refused Johnson's challenge to meet again in any postseason exhibition. Although McGraw and the Giants' owner, John Brush, claimed the National was still the only "major league" without equal, their refusal had more to do with the fact that at the time it was made—while the regular season was still going on—the American League was being led by the Giants' new cross-town rival, the New York Highlanders. One of Ban Johnson's original eight American League franchises in 1901, the Highlanders had begun life as the Baltimore Orioles, but Johnson changed their name and moved them to New York in 1903, as a direct territorial challenge to the arrogant Giants. A problem franchise for the first two decades of their existence, the Highlanders wouldn't enjoy much success—and become considerably better known—until a few years after they changed their name in 1913 to the "Yankees." They faltered in 1904 as well, but Boston would not pass them to clinch the American League pennant until almost the final game of the season, and by then it was too late for the Giants to change their mind about another World Series; and what would have been a matchup for the ages between Boston's Cy Young—who that season threw the first perfect game in major-league baseball history—and the Giants' great young star pitcher, Christy Mathewson, never materialized.

The following year, in 1905, the two baseball leagues buried the last hatchet and agreed to end each baseball season with a mutually sanctioned showdown between their champion teams, who would "meet in a series of games for the Professional Base Ball Championship of the World." They decided to scale their World Series back from nine to seven games—although it would briefly revert to nine from 1919 to 1921—and the New York Giants won that first official title in 1905, four games to one, over the American League's Philadelphia Athletics.

In the remarkable twenty-two-year career of Denton True "Cy" Young, the Ohio farmboy's greatness spanned and connected the ancient and modern eras of his sport. When he began playing pro "base ball" in 1890, the mound was still just fifty feet from home plate—it was moved back to its current distance of sixty feet, six inches three years later—and pitchers had only been allowed to throw overhand to batters for the previous six years. Young went on to win 511 baseball games, the most by a mile in baseball history, and along the way established a host of other records that will never be broken. He had always been great, but he became an immortal in his sport while earning 192 of those wins in a Boston uniform, until the team's new owner traded him to Cleveland in 1909 at the age of forty-one. Two years later Young finally retired back to the same Ohio farm, where he would spend the rest of his life, becoming one of the first grand old men of the pro game. He was the third pitcher inducted into baseball's Hall of Fame, in 1937, and the year after he died in 1955, at the age of eighty-eight, major-league baseball honored his pioneering contributions by establishing the Cy Young Award, initially given to the single most outstanding pitcher of the season in both of baseball's two leagues. (Eleven years later, the award was expanded to honor the best pitcher from *each* league, which is how it's been awarded ever since.)

But after his timeless performance during Boston's first championship season of 1903, Cy Young would never pitch another inning of a game in the World Series.

ONCE DARREL CHANEY had batted for Gary Nolan, Cincinnati Reds left-hander Fred Norman walked in from the right field bullpen to the dugout and then out to take the mound, as the Red Sox came to bat in the bottom of the third inning. With three left-handed batters due up, and four of the first five in the Boston order, Sparky had played percentages and called in his own southpaw. Norman was a tough, scrappy thirty-three-year-old Texan from San Antonio, who stood only five-eight—the shortest starting pitcher in baseball— and weighed in at a hundred and sixty pounds. After being signed by Kansas City and bouncing back and forth between the minors and majors for nine years, he'd finally played most of a full season for the Dodgers in 1970 as a situational reliever, before St. Louis claimed him off waivers. The Cardinals dealt him again in '71, to the woeful San Diego Padres, a 1969 expansion team that was struggling to survive financially. Nearing thirty, Norman earned a spot in the Padres' starting rotation and pitched decently over the next two years, but with a cellar-dwelling team behind him he could manage only a 12–23 record. The fortunes of the Padres then went from bad to worse, and Norman's record was 1–7 nearly halfway through the 1973 season, but the only win he'd notched had been against the Reds, where Bob Howsam and Sparky both saw some grit in his gutty performance that caught their eye. Short of starting pitchers at the time, when they learned the cash-strapped Padres had put Norman on the trading block, the Reds offered them a promising young outfielder and a substantial check. (A few months later, McDonald's tycoon Ray Kroc bought the Padres; their finances improved dramatically—saving the franchise—and eventually so did the team on the field.)

Few stood up and cheered the acquisition in Cincinnati, but skeptics were won over when Norman promptly went 12–6 during the rest of the year and won another thirteen games the following season. He'd turned in his best campaign yet in 1975, with a 12–4 record in thirty-four games and a 3.73 ERA, and even more important had been at his best late in the year, going 5–1 after the middle of August, filling the gap when the usually steady Jack Billingham faltered. Freddie Norman fit the profile of a Cincinnati Reds starter perfectly: a quiet, deeply competitive team guy who did whatever Sparky asked of him, and seldom overpowered batters but got them to put the ball in play, where the superb defense behind him could go to work. He kept the team in games, earned the respect and friendship of his catcher, Johnny Bench, gave way to the team's superb bullpen in the sixth or seventh inning, and the Reds offense did the rest.

Red Sox first baseman Cecil Cooper stepped in, leading off the inning for his second at bat of the game. Norman started him with a slider that missed outside for a ball.

Because he didn't possess a blazing fastball, Norman depended on changes of speed and location. From a hitter's perspective, the speed of any pitch is not an absolute value, but matters only in relation to the other pitches he sees within the confines of any at bat; the ability to take ten miles an hour off a curve or slider, as Fred Norman could do at any time, made selective use of his modest fastball much more effective. He also never liked to use the fastball on a fastball count; his best pitch in those situations was a screwball, a reverse curve that broke sharply in on left-handers, often jamming them for outs; that remained his meal ticket as a major leaguer.

Norman caught the low, outside corner with a slider for a called strike to even the count.

After his clutch performance down the home stretch of the season, Norman had earned a start in the League Championship Series against Pittsburgh, and won the second game of their sweep with six strong innings that neutralized the powerful Pirates lineup. He had come out of the game with a slightly stiff arm, and a sore knuckle on the index finger of his left hand, neither of which appeared to be serious, and Norman fully expected a spot in the World Series rotation as well.

Bench called for the same pitch again, slider low and away. Cooper swung late, and lofted a high pop fly to short left field, where Concepcion backpedaled under it for the first out. Cooper's slump continued. Second baseman Denny Doyle dug into the box, and Norman started him with a breaking ball that missed outside.

When Sparky announced his starters for the first three games of the World Series, Norman discovered he'd been left out. Don Gullett, the Reds' ace, was the obvious choice for Game One, as was their number two man, Gary Nolan, whose turn in the rotation after starting the clincher in Pittsburgh put him into Game Three. Fred Norman then appeared to be the perfect fit for Game Two.

Norman missed outside with a fastball, continuing to keep the ball away from Boston's left-handers, to fall behind in the count 2–0.

In his most surprising managerial move of the Series, Sparky had elected to go with Jack Billingham to start Game Two at Fenway

Park. After two years as the Reds' most dependable starter, Billingham's 1975 season had turned sour in September. Although he still won fifteen games against ten losses, only one of those victories had come in the last month, and his ERA had ballooned to 4.11. He'd been relegated to the bullpen during the League Championship Series against Pittsburgh and never made it into a game.

Bench kept his target on that low, outside corner, and Norman hit it with a slider for a called strike, 2–1 to Doyle.

Pete Rose edged onto the infield grass in front of the bag at third, to protect against a surprise bunt, a threat from Doyle's skilled bat at any time. Between pitches he chattered back and forth with the Red Sox third base coach, Don Zimmer; the two men had gone to the same high school in Cincinnati and been close friends for years. Like Rose, the fiercely competitive Zimmer was a baseball lifer, who'd never cashed a paycheck from outside of the game. After his playing days ended in 1966, Zimmer had spent a few years as a manager in the Reds system, worked with many of their current players in winter ball, then briefly managed the Padres before joining the Red Sox coaching staff in 1974.

Norman's next pitch, a low slider in the dirt, bounced away from Bench, running the count to 3–1.

Sparky's reasoning had been simple enough: He liked his chances in Fenway with Billingham's dependable sinker, hoping to keep the ball out of the air and away from the Green Monster, and the hunch paid off with a win in Game Two, when Billingham threw his best game since mid-season. Sparky also wanted a second left-hander in the bullpen to complement his rookie flame-thrower Will McEnaney, insurance against the Red Sox's dangerous left-handed hitters. Absorbing a hit to his pride, and even issuing a mild, out-of character grumble to the press—"I believe I'm one of the guys that got us here"—Norman had watched the first two games at Fenway from a seat in the right field bullpen, without ever throwing a pitch.

Johnny Bench signaled first baseman Tony Perez to position himself back a few steps, then moved his glove high and inside, setting up for the screwball, but when Norman came inside for the first time in the inning, Doyle turned on the ball, slapping it into right field over the head of Perez. Ken Griffey sprinted toward it quickly, but the ball slowed and sliced to the right after two bounces and hit the face of the grandstand that angled out toward the foul line beyond the dugout. It caromed back onto the field just out of the reach of Griffey, which allowed Doyle, never breaking stride, to round first and cruise into second with a stand-up double. Doyle had now hit safely in all six games of the Series, and the quirky dimensions of Fenway had just handed him an extra base.

Sparky had decided to hand the ball to Fred Norman to start Game Four against *El Tiante* back in Cincinnati, but it turned out to be the little left-hander's least effective outing in two months; the Red Sox hit him hard, and touched him for four of their five runs in an explosive fourth inning, which turned out to be all Tiant would need to eventually secure the win. Norman went only three and a third innings, giving up seven hits; that subpar performance remained fresh in Sparky's mind, and Doyle had hardly reached second before the call was made from the dugout to the Reds' bullpen; Jack Billingham immediately got up and began to throw again to catcher Bill Plummer.

Carl Yastrzemski came to the plate with one out and a runner in scoring position, worked through his deliberate routine, then waved his bat high in the air in small, tight circles as he waited, staring out at Norman. Even at thirty-six, Yaz exerted a palpable gravity at the plate, but then for him playing baseball had always been a matter of asserting his implacable will on what many feel is the most difficult physical act in all of sports: hitting a round ball moving at over ninety miles an hour, seldom in a straight line, with a spherical hunk of wood. The demands placed on visual perception, hand-eye coordination, and fast-twitch muscle response are extraordinary. The more daunting part of the challenge most often forgotten by everyday fans, who've never stood in the box and felt a major-league fastball sizzle by them like a bullet, is that every batter in the game has to deal with the persistent, nagging fear that the next pitch could maim or even kill them, as an inside fastball had done to Cleveland Indian shortstop Ray Chapman in 1920.

Norman's first pitch to Yaz, a curve, missed high and outside.

Carl Yastrzemski had grown up in Bridgehampton, Long Island, on his father's seventy-acre potato farm. A big, clannish family of second-generation Polish Catholic immigrants, the Yastrzemskis worked hard at the farming skills they'd brought over from the old country, and played hard at the game they'd learned in their new country, a game that soon became their consuming passion. For many years Carl's father, Carl Senior, had starred for and managed a local semi-pro hardball team—the Bridgehampton White Eagles— that played doubleheaders every Sunday after Mass, its roster filled almost exclusively with his brothers, in-laws, and cousins. Carl Senior was skilled enough to have given pro ball a chance if the Depression hadn't prevented his leaving the security of the farm; the demand for the family's humble product only increased when times were hard. Carl Junior had chores to do on the farm from the time he was old enough to walk—an early instillation of the tireless work ethic that later became his hallmark as a player—and he also seemed predestined to inherit his father's love of baseball.

Bench set up inside, Norman came in with a curve, and Yaz took a home run cut and fouled it back for strike one.

Carl Junior became the Eagles' batboy at the age of seven, and was good enough to join his dad on the field by the time he was fourteen. At forty-one, Carl Senior could still play shortstop and hit .400, but he kept suiting up primarily so that his son could learn by example how the game was supposed to be played. They were teammates on a couple of semi-pro teams during the next three years. Along with the genetic gifts and disciplined values Carl Senior had given to his boy, nothing would be more important to Yaz's future greatness than watching his father's resolute denial of the aging process, which never dimmed his intense dedication to excellence.

Norman came back with his best pitch of the inning, a wicked slider that caught the outside corner for a called strike; he was ahead of Yaz now, 1–2.

When it became clear early on in his high school career that Carl had the talent to play the game for a living, Carl Senior took his son's future firmly in hand, guiding him through every important decision. Carl yearned to play in the major leagues, but just in case baseball didn't work out—stranger things had happened—his father made him promise that he'd also finish his college degree. He played the infield then, like his dad, but also showed exceptional promise as a pitcher, and pro scouts were willing to sign him as one, but Carl Senior felt he'd grow up into an even better hitter. He was right; by his senior year, when he hit nearly .500, Carl had become one of the hottest prospects on the East Coast. They lived in Yankee territory, and Carl put on a batting clinic for team management during a spectacular tryout at Yankee Stadium; that upped the ante as far as Carl Senior was concerned, and he threw the Yankees' player development rep out of his kitchen for refusing to raise the team's signing bonus offer above $45,000. The unschooled but shrewd Carl Senior, who had never made more than $10,000 a year in his life, made it clear to every scout who came calling that his son wouldn't sign for a penny less than $100,000, plus the cost of his college education, an unheard of sum at the time. The Braves offered $60,000; no dice. The Phillies raised the bar to $80,000, and threw in the tuition; Carl Senior wouldn't budge. The Reds were the first to reach $100,000, but choked on the college fees. Carl Senior wavered momentarily, but their parish priest and family confidant, Father Joe Ratkowski, encouraged the Yastrzemskis to stick to their guns. So instead of accepting less than his price—which he now raised to $125,000—Carl Senior secured a full athletic scholarship to Notre Dame that fall, for Carl to play both baseball and basketball, his second best sport, at the nation's number one Catholic university. He then drove him out to South Bend for the start of his collegiate career. His classmates elected Carl their president during freshman year, and by the time he went home for Thanksgiving, the Red Sox, who had shown the most persistent interest in him for years, finally agreed to Carl

Senior's price—at which point he promptly retired from playing himself—and the following spring Carl Michael Yastrzemski's storied career as a professional ballplayer for the franchise in Boston began. He made the Red Sox roster as a full-time player two years later, in 1961, and five years after that, already an established star in the major leagues, Carl finally fulfilled the promise he'd made to his father and completed his college education.

Norman made another effective pitch, a slider low and away from Yaz's strength but in the zone, that he had to defend against; the ball floated harmlessly high up into the air near second, where Joe Morgan snagged it for the second out.

Up in the booth, Tony Kubek talked through the circumstances on the field, putting himself into Sparky's decision-making process for the broadcast audience: two outs, runner on second, first base open, left-handed pitcher on the mound, right-handed hitter Carlton Fisk coming up, left-handed Fred Lynn on deck.

"I might put Carlton Fisk on in this situation," said Kubek.

Joe Garagiola began to offer a slightly different opinion, until he saw Johnny Bench standing up behind the plate, holding his right hand out to the side, signaling for the intentional walk. Kubek had read Sparky's mind perfectly.

"You like to see that in managers," Joe added hastily. "They put him on, and that's the way it should be."

"It's a percentage play all the way," said Dick Stockton.

Home crowds traditionally greet intentional walks with half-mocking boos, expressing disdain for the opposing manager's cowardice at avoiding confrontation, and they did again here, forgetting that Sparky's strategic decision to put Fisk on first recreated the very circumstance that had given them the lead: two runners on, two outs, and Fred Lynn at the plate. Pitchers have been known to miss the catcher entirely and allow runners on base to advance—there have even been a few instances in baseball history where managers elected to walk a slugger with the bases loaded in order to avoid even more damage—but intentional walks still continually provoke the same question: If it is the team in the field's clear intention to give the batter an uncontested pass to first, why are pitchers and catchers then compelled to go through the charade of throwing four unhittable balls to home plate? Engaged in the receiving end of this apparently empty exercise behind home plate, Johnny Bench could answer that question better than anyone in Fenway. During the eighth inning of Game Three in the 1972 World Series in Oakland, the Reds held a 1–0 lead with runners on first and third and one out, when Bench came to the plate against the A's ace reliever Rollie Fingers. Fingers pitched Bench carefully to a full count, at which point manager Dick Williams came out for a conference on the mound with Fingers and the entire A's infield. The outcome clearly appeared to be that they now intended to intentionally walk Bench to load the bases; Williams returned to the dugout and catcher Gene Tenace stood up behind the plate with his arm held out to the right, signaling for the outside balloon ball to float in and complete the walk.

Instead, Fingers fired a hard slider over the outside corner, Tenace dropped back down into his crouch in time to catch it, and a red-faced Johnny Bench was called out on strikes. With a little help from their bullpen, the Reds' Jack Billingham held on to complete their shutout in that game for the win, but Johnny Bench never forgot the humiliating burn of that moment; his needling teammates wouldn't let him.

The Reds attempted no similar trickery here, but Norman did spin and threaten a pickoff throw before the final toss to keep Denny Doyle close to second. After the fourth ball, Fisk moved into his curiously refined trot down the line to first, dropping his bat along the way.

The crowd stood to greet Fred Lynn with an ovation as he came to the plate, and he discreetly tipped his cap to acknowledge their appreciation. Two on, two out; Fred Norman knew that in all likelihood unless he got him out, the left-handed Lynn would be the last hitter he'd now face in Game Six.

Bench set up outside, but Norman missed the target badly, a fastball high and inside, and Lynn took a wicked home run cut. He had guessed fastball, correctly, but the ball sailed half a foot out of the strike zone and he missed it entirely.

Not about to let this kid put the game out of reach with a second three-run jack, Bench set up even farther outside, and Norman threw a curveball that almost hit the dirt, for ball one. Then he creased the outside corner with a fastball on a pitch that Lynn resisted; Bench held his glove in place waiting for the strike call, but Satch Davidson didn't give it to him. Bench dropped his head and mitt with visible disappointment, pegged it back to Norman, and turned to Davidson to try a little gentle lobbying. Diplomacy was only one of the many skills Bench had mastered behind the plate; combined with his supreme knowledge of the strike zone, it bought him universal goodwill from umpires—who, despite traditional epithets to the contrary, are only human—and who knows how many benefit-of-the-doubt calls when games hung in the balance. Umps never changed their minds in the moment, but they might think twice about it the next time.

It didn't take long to reap the benefits on this occasion, when Norman's next pitch, a sweeping curve that Lynn leaned in and looked hard at before laying off, landed in Bench's mitt at least six inches to the right of the previous pitch: Davidson signaled strike two to even the count. Now Lynn rolled his eyes. Bench wanted that same pitch again, trying to get Lynn to chase for the strikeout, but Norman came in even wider with it, and the count went full.

Two on, two out, full count. The crowd stood up in anticipation. Bench dropped into his authoritative crouch. Doyle and Fisk took off with Norman's pitch, another broad sweeper that missed low and outside for ball four to load the bases.

A wall of noise filled Fenway now as the tension tightened. Norman went back to pick up the rosin bag but soon knew his night was over; here came Sparky up the steps, walking out to meet Bench at the mound. He might trot out occasionally to have a word with his battery, but whenever he walked, that was it. Carefully avoiding the first base chalk—another of his superstitions—Sparky stepped over the line and gave a little right-handed toss signal toward the bull-pen: with the right-handed Rico Petrocelli coming up, he wanted Billingham.

They exchanged a few words, then Norman handed Sparky the ball and headed for the dugout. Slipping on his warm-up, Jack Billingham left the bullpen and stepped into the waiting golf cart, which was dressed up like a baseball wearing a big Red Sox cap—another cutesy 1970s innovation that had invaded many parks—to cover the two-hundred-foot drive to the infield.

Billingham offered a stark contrast to Norman as he took the mound; the laconic, six-four, 215-pound right-hander looked like he'd just ridden into town on horseback. Some of his teammates called him "John Wayne"; during his years in Houston they'd nick-named him "Cactus Jack." Billingham was a Florida native who'd initially been signed out of high school by the Dodgers, and he went 3–0 when he finally made their roster in 1968, but because of their stacked pitching staff he was left unprotected in the expansion draft, where he was picked up by the Montreal Expos. They dealt him six months later to the Houston Astros, a perennially mediocre team, where he earned a spot in the starting rotation, before coming over to the Reds as the second most important piece of the big Joe Morgan trade in 1971. Billingham had more than justified the Reds' faith in him ever since, winning sixty-five games over the next four seasons and becoming the steady anchor of their starting rotation.

Sparky handed Jack the ball, offering his usual words of encour-agement, but during the last few days there had been genuine hard feelings between them that remained unresolved. On Sunday, the morning after the first rain delay, when it became clear the rain wouldn't let up that day either, the Reds scheduled a workout at the indoor field house at Tufts University in suburban Medford, outside Boston. That resulted in a comical bus ride from the hotel, when their driver got lost, and Sparky, in full uniform, had to jump out at a gas station and ask directions from an astonished attendant. Once they got to Tufts, Sparky called Billingham into a small cubicle off the field house with Gary Nolan and pitching coach Larry Shepard, to explain why he was pulling him from his scheduled start in Game Six and giving it to Nolan instead.

"If I don't start Gary, I can't use him, Jack," said Sparky. "If he gets in trouble now, you can be ready in seven minutes."

"That explanation is not satisfactory to me," said Billingham.

Larry Shepard tried to take the heat off his manager by explaining that it had all been his idea, but the trouble really started when Sparky characteristically tried to coat the bitter medicine with a little sugar.

"Now, I know your wife's going to be mad at me," said Sparky.

"No, I'm mad at you," said Jack. "Why are you bringing my wife into it?"

Billingham was a straight shooter; he expected the same from people around him, and usually got it. His relaxed demeanor—he often napped in the clubhouse before starts—disguised a fiercely competitive spirit; he despised being taken out of games. Much as Billingham liked him personally, he felt that Sparky saw his principal responsibility to be the care and maintenance of his regulars, particularly the team's four superstars, and so he didn't seem to understand the key component of a pitcher's psyche: Pitchers were creatures of confidence. During the last two months of the '75 season Billingham had gone through the worst stretch of his remarkably consistent career; he had been one of the most dependable starters in the National League for seven years—an "inning eater" is the mistakenly derisive phrase sometimes applied to his kind of workhorse talent—and he was an equally solid presence in the clubhouse. Jack was also a distant cousin of Hall of Famer Christy Mathewson, one of the greatest pitchers in baseball history, and that same competitive spirit was in his blood. But by late September, a lot of Cincinnati sportswriters had written Billingham off; when he didn't make an appearance in the Pittsburgh series, it only confirmed their opinion that, at thirty-two, Cactus Jack might have seen his last roundup. He hadn't started a game since September 22, when Sparky upset everyone's expectations and handed Jack the ball in Game Two. In response he'd reached down past all the frustration and disappointment and delivered one of the clutch performances of his life; they had to win that game to get the split they needed in Boston, and Billingham had given it to them. But when Sparky announced the change in starters for Game Six, that confidence he had shown him appeared to have vanished; Jack's effort in Game Two seemed to have bought him no credit at all. Baseball still operated under the old school rule that players never asked a manager "Why?" Although Sparky had given Jack his reasons at their meeting, he didn't invite any further discussion, and Billingham went away steaming mad. He stormed out of the team's workout at Tufts that day and took his wife sightseeing up the coast outside Boston in the rain. But before they left the hotel, in an uncharacteristic display of anger, Billingham let off steam to Cincinnati beat writer Bob Hertzel.

"I'm supposed to be the guy who can keep the ball on the ground in Fenway," said Billingham. "I pitched well here before and we won. I finally get my shit together, pitch a good game, and they hit me in the side of the head with something like this. They seem to think, 'Good ol' Jack, he won't get mad.' Well, I'm tired of being pushed around."

Billingham was able to cool off after his day away—and at no time had he wished any ill will to Gary Nolan, who was one of his closest friends on the team—but his outburst to Hertzel, as he must have known it would, showed up in the *Cincinnati Enquirer* on Monday. When Sparky was then asked about Jack's outburst by Hertzel, he calmly refused to take the bait.

"There's nothing wrong with him being upset and saying so in print," said Sparky evenly. "During the season a player shouldn't open his mouth, but I can understand something like this in a World Series. If he wasn't mad I figured he wouldn't have wanted to pitch in the game."

On Tuesday afternoon, when they got to the park before Game Six, Larry Shepard had taken Jack aside to say, "I know you're upset, but I know you're gonna be a pro about it."

Billingham had been hopping mad, and when he took the mound in the third inning of Game Six that night he was still simmering. But for a guy who never said much and whose game had recently come into question because he seldom showed much emotion whether he won or lost—they didn't call him Cactus Jack because of his chatty mood swings—maybe, Sparky had calculated, a little fire in the belly might do him some good.

With the Reds behind by three runs with the bases loaded, and the dangerous Rico Petrocelli at the plate, as Sparky walked back to the dugout he hoped to hell he was right.

Americo Peter Petrocelli—inevitably "Rico"—a twelve-year veteran and one of the most popular players in Red Sox history, came to the plate and the crowd greeted him with a big cheer. At thirty-two, the same age as Jack Billingham, Rico had also faced his own recent crises of confidence. A fierce competitor who led by word and deed, and earned a reputation as one of the toughest guys in baseball, he'd grown up in Sheepshead Bay, Brooklyn, the youngest of seven kids in a big working-class Italian-American family, during the golden years of 1950s New York baseball, when Mays, Mantle, and Duke Snider patrolled center field for the city's three franchises. When he blossomed into an outstanding high school student and athlete, Rico's four older brothers pitched in with extra money so he could concentrate on sports instead of helping after school in the family's garment industry business. He was offered a basketball scholarship to North Carolina State, but the same Red Sox scout who'd signed Carl Yastrzemski brought Rico to the team's attention, and the game he'd always loved the most won out when he signed with Boston. Like Yaz, he'd also been an excellent high school pitcher, but they would both end up making a living with their bats. After only three years in the team's farm system, Petrocelli earned a spot on the Red Sox roster, where Carl Yastrzemski became his closest friend on and off the field.

Rico won the starting shortstop job out of spring training in 1965, but the team's manager at the time, an old-fashioned autocrat named Billy Herman, rode the shy, insecure rookie mercilessly, and nearly drove him out of baseball; Rico credited Yaz's steadying support during that time as the only thing that sustained him. When Dick Williams took over the team two years later, he tried a gentler tack with his gifted young shortstop by giving him more responsibility; Rico responded with his first All-Star season and became an integral part of the "Impossible Dream" team. Many credited a midseason fight that broke out on the field between Rico and his childhood friend, Yankee first baseman Joe Pepitone, as the spark that ignited the Red Sox season, and he came through under pressure at the plate time and again, most famously hitting two home runs in Game Six of the Series against St. Louis. Petrocelli went on to become one of the most feared power hitters in the game, setting an American League record for home runs by a shortstop, with forty in 1969, and proved equally adept in the field, establishing new defensive standards for the Red Sox at his position. When the team had a chance to acquire the great veteran shortstop Luis Aparicio in 1971, which would necessitate moving Petrocelli to third, they told Rico the deal wouldn't go through unless he approved; the consummate teammate, Rico agreed to make the switch. He continued to steadily produce with his bat and, even more remarkably, set a major-league defensive record at a position he'd never played before, going seventy-seven games in one stretch at third without an error. A series of nagging injuries dampened his offensive production over the next two seasons, but Rico seldom failed to come through in the clutch, which, along with his heart-on-the-sleeve style, forever endeared him to Red Sox fans. He was one of their acknowledged team leaders now, and Boston had appeared to be well on their way to their first Eastern Division title in 1974.

Then on September 15, in a day game at Fenway against Milwaukee, blinded by the glare of the midday sun on the center field bleachers, Rico was unable to see a fastball from Brewers pitcher Jim Slaton that nailed him flush behind the left ear, below the protective edge of his batting helmet. Tied for the team lead in home runs at the time, and their best RBI man, Petrocelli was unable to play for the rest of the season, which accelerated their shocking collapse at the wire, when they lost the division title to Baltimore.

Jack Billingham, pitching from his regular delivery with the bases loaded, for his first pitch came in with a hard sinker that Petrocelli hammered foul for strike one.

When Rico tried to come back during spring training of 1975, he continued his usual excellent play in the field, but the effects of the beaning persisted at the plate; he suffered from vertigo, disabling migraines, and occasional severe bouts of dizziness, and had trouble focusing his eyes, which left him unable to pick up the ball out of the pitcher's hands. A chronic worrier to begin with, as his average and power numbers plummeted, he developed an ulcer that would torment him all season. He tried glasses in June to correct his vision, but abandoned them three weeks later when they didn't help, and frequently had to take himself out of games when the vertigo or headaches came on. As his condition worsened, Petrocelli left the team during a road trip in mid-August and for the first time in his life began to seriously contemplate retirement. Finally, after days of exams and consultation, doctors at Massachusetts Eye and Ear Hospital hit on a mix and dosage of medication that helped allay his symptoms. He returned to action in early September and quickly regained his hitting stroke; with Baltimore creeping up from behind on the Sox's division lead again, Rico hit the climactic home run on September 16 that secured Luis Tiant's 2–0 showdown with Jim Palmer and effectively ended the Orioles' charge.

Billingham missed outside with a slider to even the count at 1–1.

Petrocelli continued to deliver through the League Championship Series against the A's, hitting a key home run off their ace reliever Rollie Fingers to nail down the win in Game Two. When he'd continued to swing a hot bat through the first five games of the World Series as well, leading the team in hitting, fans and writers in Boston assumed that their old, dependable Rico had come back for good. They didn't know that the heavy medication he was on had begun to cause some deleterious side effects, and that in the last few days even some haunting whispers of his balance and vision problems were starting to recur.

Billingham had struck Petrocelli out the first time he faced him in Game Two, and he challenged him again now with a low, running fastball that Rico took a big cut at and missed. Behind in the count now, 1–2.

Rico didn't have to look far to witness the fearful damage a pitched baseball to the head could do to any hitter. He had seen his good friend and former Red Sox teammate Tony Conigliaro's stellar career destroyed by a hideous beaning in 1967. The popular young outfielder nearly lost his life on that terrible night, and although he gamely attempted to come back twice from the injuries, he hadn't been close to the same ballplayer, and the vision in his damaged left retina never completely recovered. Conigliaro's second comeback finally ended with his retirement, at the age of thirty, earlier in the 1975 season; he was at Fenway for Game Six that night, covering the game as a regional television reporter. The team's former starting second baseman Doug Griffin still hadn't recovered from a 1974 beaning he'd taken from feared fastballer Nolan Ryan, necessitating the trade for Denny Doyle. Red Sox third base coach Don Zimmer still carried four steel screws in his head from a couple of terrible beanings that had curtailed his major-league career in the early 1960s. Despite dozens of these crippling, career-ending injuries throughout the decades, major-league baseball had only instituted the mandatory use of the batting helmet in 1971.

Trailing three games to two in the Series, Rico had privately admitted to himself as he took the field that night for Game Six that this might well be the last ball game he would ever play. But he wasn't through yet; he'd faced Billingham in Game Two, and after that early strikeout, he'd singled off him in the sixth inning, driving in the second Red Sox run of that game. A hit now with the bases loaded, two outs, and runners moving could blow Game Six wide open.

Billingham would come back with that fastball again now, Rico figured, and he set up for it. But Bench called for the curve, low and outside, disguised brilliantly by Billingham's easy, rocking sidearm motion, which never varied from pitch to pitch. Already committed to the swing, Petrocelli realized what was coming a hair too late, but with his timing disrupted, he could only wave at it helplessly as the ball broke sharply down and away, well out of the strike zone, and he went down swinging for the third and final out.

"Cactus" Jack had ridden in and put out the fire.

TEN

My specific interest in writing to you is to seek
your assistance on a matter of deep concern to myself
and one of my constituents, Mr. Luis Tiant.

SENATOR EDWARD BROOKE

L UIS TIANT AND HIS WIFE, MARIA, HAD DECIDED DURING
the early years of their marriage to keep their home in her native Mexico City, where all three of their children would be born.
After making the Cleveland Indians' roster in 1964, Luis left his
family every spring, often not returning for longer than a few days,
over the All-Star break, until the season ended in October, just as
his father had done during his career in the Negro Leagues. Not
until he went through his fall and rise, reestablishing himself as
a star in Boston, did Luis even consider buying a home and moving his family to the United States. Once he had gained that sense
of security, after ten years of seasonal separation, the Tiant family
was finally reunited in August of 1974 when they bought a house
next to the eleventh fairway of Wollaston Golf Club in suburban
Milton.

The following February, while working out with his friend Judge
Robert Schreiber at a local YMCA, Luis confided in him the greatest
longing of his life: Now that he had realized his version of the
American dream, the one thing missing was to be reunited with his
mother and father and introduce them to their grandchildren. His
parents were aging and struggling in Cuba, where life was hard and
money remained scarce. Luis's father, past seventy and ailing, had
to pump gas at a service station to put food on their table, while his
mother, Isabel, still worked as a housekeeper. Although Luis was

now a celebrity in Boston, and recognized throughout the country, the iron curtain surrounding his homeland left him powerless to help. He spoke to his parents occasionally by phone, but never free from worry that their calls might be monitored by the Cuban state apparatus. Isabel had been able to make one brief visit to see Luis and meet her daughter-in-law and grandchildren in Mexico City in 1968; Luis Senior had been forced to spend that week in a Havana jail to ensure her return. Aside from seeing him pitch a game or two on television when the Red Sox made *Game of the Week*—the broadcast of Miami's NBC affiliate, officially forbidden by the Castro government, just barely reached across the ninety miles separating Cuba and Florida—the Old Man hadn't laid eyes on his son in nearly fifteen years. For the fortunate, lighthearted Luis Tiant, the likelihood that he would never see his parents again before they died had become a private and consuming sadness. He was haunted by the thought that if he lost them now, he wouldn't even be allowed to attend their funerals.

Ten years earlier, before he became a judge, Robert "Buddy" Schreiber had worked as an assistant district attorney under Edward Brooke, then the attorney general of Massachusetts, who in 1966 had become the first African-American to be elected to the United States Senate. A moderate Republican, Brooke was serving his second term now, and Schreiber offered to make contact with the senator on Luis's behalf, to see if there was anything he might be able to do about his family situation. As protection against even deeper disappointment, Luis never allowed himself the luxury of hope with regard to his parents' predicament, but he agreed to let Schreiber inquire on his behalf.

Edward Brooke, as it happened—not surprisingly for a senator from Massachusetts—was a Red Sox fan in general, and a fan of *El Tiante* in particular, and he took an immediate, personal interest in Schreiber's request to help the Tiants. Tom Yawkey and Dick O'Connell then weighed in on Tiant's behalf as well. When he learned shortly thereafter that his colleague Senator George McGovern was planning an unofficial visit to Cuba during the first week of

May, Brooke asked McGovern if he could deliver a letter from him to Fidel Castro and speak to him personally about the Tiants. McGovern, also a baseball fan, instantly agreed.

As the Democratic nominee for president in 1972, fifty-three-year-old George McGovern had suffered one of the worst defeats in American electoral history at the hands of President Richard Nixon. A decorated World War II bomber pilot and an unapologetic liberal from South Dakota, McGovern's principled opposition to the Vietnam War that had divided the country for a decade failed to win wide support, and the infamous "dirty tricks" waged against him by Nixon's White House operatives undermined his campaign throughout. An unfortunate decision to pick as his running mate Senator Thomas Eagleton from Missouri, who failed to reveal that he'd regularly undergone shock treatment for depression and emotional illness, doomed McGovern's candidacy and returned Nixon to office in a landslide. The shocking revelations of the Watergate investigation had since sent Nixon into exile and disgrace, while McGovern bounced back in 1974 to win reelection for his third term in the Senate, where he continued to champion progressive causes. One of those causes, most notably, was his ongoing attempt to repair the United States' relationship with Fidel Castro and Cuba. Since shortly after his first election in 1962, not long after the Cuban Missile Crisis ended with the Soviet withdrawal of nuclear weapons, Senator McGovern had spoken out about the futility of continuing to embargo and isolate Cuba, and the dangers those policies posed to rising anti-American sentiments in Central and South America. In 1975, after years of failed back-channel attempts to arrange their meeting, Castro had finally agreed to sit down with George McGovern, the first elected official from the United States to visit Cuba in fifteen years.

The day after McGovern arrived in Havana, on May 6, as a late private dinner with Cuba's vice president was winding down, Fidel Castro showed up unexpectedly, a day ahead of their scheduled appointment. He had come directly from a championship baseball game between two of his country's powerhouse state teams, and the two men began their conversation by talking at length about the game. Preferring to hold back his larger agenda for their more formal meeting the next day, and pour the footing of their relationship firmly in an area of mutual human interest, toward the end of the hour they spent together McGovern decided the time was right to bring up the matter of Luis Tiant.

Castro knew all about *El Tiante*—and his father before him—and as a former pitcher himself obviously looked on Luis's achievements as a Cuban-born player in the major leagues with evident pride.

Without hesitating, McGovern took Senator Brooke's letter out of his pocket and handed it to Castro.

JOE MORGAN came to the plate to begin the top of the fourth inning for the Reds, and Tiant started him with a curveball, high, for ball one. Morgan had been looking fastball; Sparky scratched and shook his head in the dugout: *That damn Tiant.*

Coming to the plate to lead off an inning and behind in the game, Morgan slightly changed his approach to an at bat, doing anything necessary to get himself on base for the power hitters behind him to drive in. Morgan tensed, chewing gum and flapping his left arm as if jacking himself up, still looking for the fastball early in the count. Tiant came inside with a changeup that fooled him and caught the corner for a strike to even the count.

Now thirty-two, Morgan had been a good player for the Houston Astros from the moment he broke into their starting lineup in 1965, and he'd gotten steadily better, improving every aspect of his game, but the team failed to advance with him. Morgan ended up marooned in a fractured, hostile environment, exacerbated by the Astros manager, Harry "The Hat" Walker, a former batting champion and eleven-year veteran of the National League from Pascagoula, Mississippi. (He'd earned that nickname for constantly fiddling with his cap—Walker played before batting helmets—between pitches during at bats.) Walker was an old-school martinet at a time when young people in the game—and throughout the culture in general—were demanding a larger say in how they were used and treated by their elders. Walker wouldn't give them an inch. Morgan and many of the other black and Latin players on the team also felt that Walker was one of baseball's most overt racists, and a sadist who took perverse pleasure in testing and breaking the spirit of his minority players. The proud and dignified Morgan was one of the last men on the team to snap back at Walker's constant provocations, but once he did, his relationship with the entire organization quickly soured. A toxic environment festered in the Astros clubhouse, and Joe Morgan—one of the most talented and intelligent players in all of baseball—ended up with a tarnished reputation as a troublemaker among the good old boys network around the league.

Tiant knew he had Morgan thinking—*Would he come back with the fastball now?*—and upset his expectations again, painting the outside corner with a slow curve for a called second strike.

Among the many innovations that Cincinnati general manager Bob Howsam had brought to the Reds when he took over in 1967 was a highly disciplined approach to trades. Howsam had served his apprenticeship in the 1950s under Branch Rickey, the onetime Cardinals and Dodgers GM, who had moved on late in life to run the Pittsburgh Pirates. One of the keenest baseball minds of all time, Branch Rickey had invented the farm system for the Cardinals and went on to break the color barrier with Jackie Robinson and the Dodgers, creating the modern prototype for a first-class national baseball organization. Bob Howsam had learned the game at Rickey's elbow, while running the Pirates' Single-A franchise in his native Denver, and it was Rickey's recommendation to the August Busch family that resulted in Howsam's first major-league job, as a GM for the St. Louis Cardinals in 1964. (In the interim, Howsam had founded the Denver Broncos, one of the charter franchises in the upstart American Football League.) The team that Howsam inherited in St. Louis won a World Series that very fall, and would repeat as champions three years later, but when Howsam's mentor Branch Rickey passed away in 1965, the Busch family chose to replace him with one of their beer executives, who constantly meddled with Howsam's decision-making. When the opportunity presented itself two years later, Howsam accepted the chance to make a fresh start in Cincinnati. As part of their established off-season routine, Howsam and his staff assembled a detailed annual survey of every team around the majors, identifying and rating players who would fit the speed, power, and defense profile of their ball club. Sparky Anderson came on board in 1970, and having spent most of his minor-league years in the Branch Rickey–designed Dodger system, he immediately grasped the scope and ambition of what Howsam was attempting to build in Cincinnati. They had both learned that there was a right way to find, mold, and shape major-league ballplayers, creating a disciplined and principled organization from top to bottom; by 1972 the Reds were indeed a "machine," in the best sense of the word. Howsam—who was given the additional title of team president in 1973—had also learned that the system wouldn't produce all the pieces they needed to succeed, that trades were a crucial tool for refining and finishing their roster; sometimes one player can turn a good team into a great one. When they fell short in their first trip to the World Series in 1970, Cincinnati put Houston Astros second baseman Joe Morgan at the top of their wish list. Once Morgan joined the squad, Pete Rose, the Reds' dominant locker room personality—who if he'd been anyone else might have resented the arrival of such an equally outsized presence—made it a point to become Little Joe's best friend on the team. Sparky made a conscious decision to put their lockers side by side, and the sharp, nonstop, needling, back-and-forth vaudeville routine that these two high-voltage characters began running with each other—masking the mutual respect and affection they soon came to develop—set the tone for the rest of the room. The message was clear: Not even the Reds' superstars could get away with giving anything less than a total commitment to excellence. Their entertaining corner of the clubhouse quickly became known as the "Circus."

Now Tiant finally came with the fastball, low and over the plate, and Morgan made solid contact but hit it straight to Denny Doyle at second base, who made the easy toss to first for the out.

That brought up catcher Johnny Bench. Bench had been so re-markable since the moment he stepped into the Reds' starting lineup that it was something of a shock to remember he was only twenty-seven. He not only owned the kind of outsized, folk-tale talent that had already redefined how people thought of the catcher's position, he possessed the intelligence and temperament to handle the non-sensical insanity that the world heaps on your doorstep when you achieve sudden stardom in the U.S. of A. Equally remarkable, Johnny had grown up light-years away from that spotlight, in the tiny coun-try town of Binger, Oklahoma. Blessed with a solid, upright working-class family, and a father, uncle, and two older brothers who were baseball crazy, he found an early home behind the plate on the local Little League team coached by his dad, and he came of age during the golden years of Mickey Mantle, Oklahoma's greatest homegrown export since crude oil; the Mick offered living proof that there was at least one way out of Binger. Before he turned ten, Johnny Bench saw that path ahead of him lit up like a runway. He grew strong from picking cotton and peanuts in the field, and by the time he graduated as valedictorian of his high school class in 1965—although he'd want you to know there were only twenty-one seniors in the school—he was a man among boys.

Tiant came in sidearm with a curveball that Bench chopped foul down the third base line. Johnny looked a tad frustrated; he'd been looking for a fastball.

During Bench's senior year, the bus carrying his high school baseball team lost its brakes coming down a hill on their way back from a road game, flipped over, and rolled down a ravine. After he extracted himself, unhurt, and helped pull injured kids from the wreckage, Bench realized that two of his lifelong friends and team-mates had been thrown from the bus and killed instantly. The emo-tional toll of the tragedy echoed throughout his last months in Binger; Johnny felt himself changing in response, a hardening he felt powerless to stop even as he watched it happening. As long as he could remember, he'd possessed the ability to stand outside himself, coolly observe the world around him, and take whatever comes. His extraordinary talent and athleticism had already set him apart from his peers, and he clearly seemed destined for bigger things; the accident rendered him even more distant and self-contained, harder to know. It also, strangely, prepared him for the transient, itinerant life of professional baseball, where men you've worked and played alongside for years can vanish from your life in a flash.

Tiant missed outside with a slider to even the count at 1–1.

The Reds drafted Johnny Bench in the second round of the 1965 draft—a young outfielder from Detroit named Bernie Carbo became their first pick—for a grand total of $14,000. Eight thousand of that bonus was set aside as insurance for tuition if baseball didn't pan out and Johnny decided to go to college, which never became an issue. After his first season away from home with Cincinnati's rookie and instructional league clubs, he earned an invite to the Reds' spring training in 1966. He had barely turned eighteen, and knew from the moment he arrived at camp in Tampa, just from looking at the players around him, that he belonged there. The Reds thought so, too; out of dozens of prospects throughout the organization, they had already made it clear that Johnny Bench was going to be their next big-league catcher.

Now Tiant challenged him, with the best fastball he'd thrown all night; looking dead-red ready for it, Bench swung mightily but missed for strike two.

Although there had been talk of putting Bench on the Reds' roster as their third catcher that first year, the consensus was that a little seasoning would do him more good. A season of Class-A ball for the Peninsula Grays in the Carolina League followed; Bench hit twenty-two home runs and drove in sixty-eight in ninety-eight games. Behind the plate he already showed a veteran's grasp of baseball's most demanding position; how to call a game, defend the plate, handle pitchers, position his fielders. His throwing arm immediately became the stuff of legend; he threw out three runners in one *inning* in the Carolina League All-Star Game. The Grays retired his number after the season, an almost unheard of honor in the minors, which the club had never conferred on anyone before.

Near the end of the season, after breaking his thumb in a game a few days after losing his virginity—not hard for a born-and-raised Baptist to connect the dots between those events—he was driving home to Oklahoma late at night when a drunk driver broadsided his car. A seat belt saved his life, but he spent two days in the hospital and they had to shave his head to close the gash in his skull. Just eighteen, he'd already had two close looks at the valley of the shadow, and those barricades he'd already put up to protect himself from the unknown drew in a little closer. Pitcher and fellow top prospect Gary Nolan never forgot their meeting a few weeks later back in Florida, when he pulled into the team's motel and laid eyes on Johnny Bench for the first time, sitting poolside, his shaved head stitched like a baseball and still painted orange from the Mercurochrome, singing "If I Were a Carpenter" in full voice. *Wow,* thought Nolan, *that's my new catcher. He's nuts.* Six months older, Nolan made the big club that spring and won fourteen games for the Reds, finishing third in the National League's Rookie of the Year voting behind the Mets' sensational Tom Seaver. Bench made the leap from A-ball to the Reds' Triple-A team in Buffalo, where his equally impressive performance changed nobody's mind that he'd soon become a fixture behind home plate in Cincinnati.

Instead of coming back with the fastball, Tiant threw a dazzling slow curve that nicked the outside corner. Bench didn't swing, and didn't protest—a real man knows when he's been beaten—but simply turned and walked briskly back to the dugout without a backward glance.

Luis Tiant appeared in complete command of himself, his pitches, and the game; he'd thrown four different pitches to Bench with four different deliveries, like a jazz artist riffing an inspired solo. Just as the Reds had spotted his tendency to start hitters with fastballs, Tiant hadn't thrown one to the first two men he'd faced in the inning. So far the best hitters on the best hitting team in baseball looked almost helpless against him. Stan Williams, Luis's former teammate with Cleveland and Minnesota, the man who helped salvage his career after the injury, had become the pitching coach for the Red Sox before the 1975 season. Williams had lasted four-teen years in the majors, a tall, menacing power pitcher, with a rep-utation for throwing hard and inside. Only recently retired, he stayed sharp by throwing batting practice for the Red Sox. He watched Tiant now from the dugout steps, marveling once again at the range and control of his repertoire; Luis was cruising now, and the Fenway crowd relished every pitch.

Tony Perez followed Bench to the plate for his second at bat, with two outs in the inning and nobody on. Doggie set his bat and stared out at Tiant, determined, all business, looking for that fastball. Luis started him with his oddest pitch of the night, a slow hesitation pitch that wouldn't have cracked a pane of glass, fluttered almost like a knuckleball, and just missed the outside corner for a ball.

Tony Perez's approach to hitting had become so thorough and professional it was almost impossible to fool him with the same pitch twice. Tiant didn't try to, coming back with a fastball that caught the outside corner for a called strike.

After he originally cracked their starting lineup as a first base-man in 1965, the Reds moved Perez to third two years later when another big young slugger named Lee May came along whose only position was first base. The two men grew into their prime power together, hitting more than 250 home runs between 1968 and 1971; add Johnny Bench's 113 to that number over the same period and you had the most dangerous murderer's row in contemporary base-ball. But when the Reds fell short to Baltimore in the 1970 World Series, and failed to make the playoffs the following year, Howsam and Anderson pulled the trigger on the deal with Houston for Joe Morgan. The deal would grow more complicated, but from the start Houston demanded a power-hitting first baseman in return. Knowing they could shift Perez over to his old spot, Lee May was moved on to the Astros in the Morgan trade and Tony Perez moved back to first.

Another glance to the heavens, and a sidearm fastball missed outside for ball two. Tiant had thrown forty-five pitches in the game to date, and not one of them had come inside on a batter; for the most part he was pitching to and hitting that two inches of black on the outside corner of the plate.

During Cincinnati's subsequent rise to dominance, while Rose, Morgan, and Bench garnered most of the headlines, Tony Perez had quietly become the most indispensable part of the Big Red Machine. For nine seasons in a row he had driven in more than ninety runs; his steadiness and consistency weren't flashy qualities, but they served as the bedrock of the Reds' offense. He also remained their most even-keeled leader on and off the field, where his serene sense of self, generosity of spirit, complete lack of insecurity, and built-in bullshit detector somehow kept all the other big egos in the Cincinnati clubhouse in line.

Tiant threw a wicked, tempting curve that broke outside and nearly provoked Perez to lean forward and attack, but he checked his swing and the count went to 3–1. He looked down to third base coach Alex Grammas for the sign and got the green light. Tiant went after the outside corner with a slider, a hittable pitch, and Perez fouled it back to fill up the count, 3–2. When Tiant came back with a fastball, Perez fought it off again.

Tiant didn't like the next ball umpire Satch Davidson threw him and tossed it back. When Davidson nearly threw the next one over Tiant's head—he had to leap for it—the crowd let Davidson hear it.

Tiant's next pitch hit the outside corner, but it was up in the zone, and Perez, his timing locked in as he saw his third fast pitch in a row, got the meat of the bat on it and lined a shot toward right that glanced off a diving Denny Doyle's glove after one hop and skittered all the way out to Dwight Evans. After a patient at bat, Tony Perez finally had his first hit of the Series off Tiant, and the Reds had their second hit of the game.

Left fielder George Foster stepped into the box, decided his right shoe was untied, signaled for time, stepped out, and, while he was at it, retied both shoes. In response, Tiant played catch with Davidson again, trying out a new ball, eager to get the one that Perez had spanked out of the game.

"A little gamesmanship," said Garagiola, amused, watching the two men try to out-stall each other. "Nothing wrong with it."

Luis went into his stretch and now came in with his first first-pitch fastball of the inning, up in the zone. Foster, waiting for it, took a big cut and fouled it straight back. After another delay as Foster stepped out of the box and rubbed dirt on his hands, Tiant threw a big overhand curve. Foster took only a half swing at it below his knees, but with his immense strength he hit it hard on the ground into the hole to shortstop Rick Burleson's right. Burleson took three quick steps to his right, scooped it up, and fired it to Doyle covering second for the force-out on Perez, but the ball hooked left on him and pulled Doyle off the bag. Doyle lunged out and got a glove on it, slowing it down and probably saving a run. Perez hopped up out of his slide and ran to third, but had to hold there when Doyle tracked the ball down as it trickled onto the outfield grass. Foster held up at first.

Error, Burleson—his first, and the fourth Red Sox gaffe of the Series. Reds at first and third, two out.

Looking at the replay from the left field camera, former infielder Tony Kubek thought that Doyle might have made the throw look worse than it was by coming straight across the bag, cheating toward first instead of circling slightly to his right. Whatever the reason for the error, aflame with self-disgust, "Rooster" Burleson kicked at the dirt and returned to his position.

Shortstop Davey Concepcion crossed himself and stepped into the box, for the first Reds' at bat in the game with a runner in scoring position. Tiant, calm and cool, pitching from the stretch, missed the outside corner with a low fastball for ball one. He came back with his tantalizing slow curve, which dove down and missed in the same spot for ball two.

Thinking a move ahead, in case they kept the inning alive and he needed someone to pinch-hit for Billingham in the pitcher's spot two batters later, Sparky told his best pinch hitter, Terry Crowley, to get loose again and put Larry Shepard on the phone with the bull-pen, where Clay Carroll took off his jacket and began to throw.

Ahead in the count, Concepcion saw Grammas flash him the sign to swing away; they expected a fastball here. The crowd broke into their "Loo-ee, Loo-ee" chant. Tiant came with the fastball, and Concepcion fouled it straight back for a strike. Still ahead 2–1, Concepcion got the swing sign from Grammas again. Tiant fooled him with the next pitch, a live fastball that would have made his father proud, darting to the right and catching the inside corner, the first pitch he'd thrown there all night. Concepcion stepped out to collect himself, rubbed some pine tar on his bat in the on-deck circle, and looked into the dugout, where Sparky shouted some words of encouragement. The count was even now, 2–2.

Fisk called for the same pitch again; he liked the way that last one had seemed to trouble Concepcion. Tiant threw the exact same pitch, running right in on the fist. Protecting the plate, Concepcion tried to swing inside-out at the ball and drive it to the right, but he caught just a sliver of it and popped it into the air, foul, wide of first, where Cecil Cooper collected it for the third out of the inning.

Tiant, as he'd done all Series against the Reds, had pitched out of another jam. As Rick Burleson trotted in toward the dugout past Luis, he apologized for his error. Tiant smiled at him, radiating confidence, as if he didn't have a care in the word.

"Don't worry about it, man," said Tiant, patting the Rooster's shoulder. "We still got 'em."

Luis Tiant had just completed his fortieth consecutive scoreless inning at Fenway Park. But his extraordinary streak was about to come to an end.

ELEVEN

Luis's parents, Luis Eleuterio Tiant and Isabel Rovina Vega Tiant, reside at Calle 30, Apartment 9, Mariano, Havana, Cuba. He has not had a chance to spend any time with them for many years. Naturally, he has a great desire to do so.

Luis's career as a major leaguer is in its latter years. It is impossible to predict how much longer he will be able to pitch. Therefore, he is hopeful that his parents will be able to visit him in Boston during this current baseball season to see their son perform. I am sure we both agree that this is a reasonable desire.

I have contacted the State Department and have been assured that the granting of visas to enter the United States will be no problem. Therefore, with your help, I am confident that a reunion of Luis and his parents is possible this summer. Such a reunion would be a significant indication that better understanding between our peoples is achievable.

I look forward to receiving your response.

Sincerely,

Edward W. Brooke

WHEN FIDEL CASTRO FINISHED READING SENATOR Brooke's letter about Luis Tiant and his parents at the dinner party, he didn't speak for a while. George McGovern thought he seemed intrigued and engaged, while quietly calculating all the implications of the issue against his larger agenda.

"Let me check on this," he said. "I will give you an answer when we meet tomorrow."

Their meeting the next day began at four-thirty in the afternoon and, with the vast number of subjects they had to cover, would last until hours after midnight. But when they first sat down, the encounter began with Cuba's prime minister responding to Senator Brooke's letter.

"I've checked on your request about Mr. Tiant's parents," said Castro. "They have been advised that they can go to Boston and stay as long as they wish."

Senator McGovern conveyed the welcome news back to Edward Brooke, who then passed it on to Judge Schreiber and Luis Tiant. The wheels of statecraft and diplomacy moved a little slower; it took almost four months to smooth out all the details of the visit, while Brooke's office arranged for Luis to send his parents money and the plane tickets. After finally flying from Havana to Mexico City on August 15, the Tiants had to wait for nearly a week before their complex visas were finalized at the U.S. Embassy; on a road trip with the Red Sox in Chicago and Kansas City, Luis spoke to them by phone daily. Although the family had tried to keep details about their arrival private, word leaked to the press, and Luis was deluged with requests for interviews. Luis, Maria, and their three children drove to Logan International Airport on Thursday evening, the 21st of August, along with a number of close family friends. When they walked into the arrivals terminal, they found a pack of nearly one hundred reporters and photographers waiting for them. Doing his best to accommodate their interest, Luis patiently answered questions while struggling to maintain his composure. When they announced the arrival of their connecting flight from Mexico City, the press stepped back from around the family, uncharacteristically giving them space; many of them were sportswriters who had known Tiant for years and knew what this meant to him. A hush fell over the room.

When his father stepped off the plane into the terminal, Luis put a hand over his eyes and wept. Fifteen years; Luis had tried to prepare himself for the moment but to no avail. His father saw him and smiled and waved; Luis rushed to him, into his embrace.

"Don't cry, son," his father whispered softly in Spanish. "The cameras will see you."

"I don't care," said Luis.

The Old Man closed his eyes and held him tight and smiled. Then Isabel appeared at his side, and Luis bear-hugged his mother, while Luis Senior held out his arms to Maria and his three grandchildren, twelve-year-old Luis, seven-year-old Isabel, and one-year-old Danny, and they all crowded into his arms.

Few pictures were taken. Almost everyone else in the room, reporters and photographers included, was in tears.

As the family walked slowly away, a Spanish reporter asked Luis's mother who was the better pitcher, her husband or her son. Luis and his father, arm in arm, overheard the question and answered for her.

"She doesn't know anything about baseball," explained Luis Senior.

"My father was better than me," said Luis.

"No, my son is better," said Luis Senior, in his halting English. "I watch him pitch on television in Havana."

"My father brought the screwball to Mexico. He was a great pitcher."

"I've been in training," said Luis Senior, smiling again at the reporter. "You tell the Red Sox, if they need me, I'm ready."

When they got back to the family home in Milton, the welcoming party went on for hours, and for the first time since 1961 the entire Tiant family slept under the same roof. Luis and his father stayed up later than the rest, over drinks and Cuban cigars; life, baseball, all the missing years. The next morning, a photograph of the Tiant family reunion at the airport made the front page of every newspaper in Boston.

Luis had thrown the last game of the road trip in Kansas City; his next scheduled start at Fenway came the following Tuesday against the visiting California Angels, when his parents would see their son pitch a major-league game for the first time. Red Sox owner Tom Yawkey met them beforehand and asked if Luis Senior would like to throw out the first pitch that night. When Luis translated the offer for his father, he seemed initially reluctant—he didn't want to embarrass his son, or himself—but when the moment came and his name was announced to the crowd, Luis Senior popped up out of the dugout with a Red Sox cap on and energetically jogged to the mound, where his son was waiting for him. The ovation grew louder as the Old Man slid off his coat, traded it with his son for the baseball, straddled the rubber, made a full windup, and fired a screwball to reserve catcher Tim Blackwell behind the plate; he threw it back to Luis as the crowd cheered.

That was supposed to be the end of the ceremony, but Luis Senior asked for the ball back.

"What's wrong, Papa?" asked Luis.

"It wasn't a strike," he said. "Give me the ball."

Luis handed it to him. He signaled for Blackwell to get back into his crouch, and this time the slender and elegant "Señor Skinny" whistled a fastball right down the heart of the plate. The crowd, predictably, went nuts. This perfect evening didn't end perfectly, only because his parents didn't see Luis pitch the Red Sox to a win; they lost to the Angels 8–2 on the night of August 26. Still troubled by a sore lower back at the time, Tiant didn't have his usual velocity, and may have been pressing with his parents watching him play for the first time. But from that point on in the season, they hadn't seen him lose at home; five complete-game victories in a row, including the opening games of the team's playoff series against Oakland and Cincinnati.

The night after Luis's 6–0 gem in Game One of the 1975 World Series, the Tiants hosted an impromptu gathering for family and friends at their home in Milton. At around two that morning, as the joyful celebration was winding down, Luis came through a door and saw his father looking up at him from a nearby easy chair, the sweetest, proud, sad smile on his face. He held out his arms, and Luis sat down beside him and they held on to each other, without saying a word, both of them crying silently. The dream, passed down from father to son, had come all the way home.

. . .

JACK BILLINGHAM strode out to the mound in the bottom of the fourth to face his second batter of the game, right fielder Dwight Evans. He missed with his first pitch, low and away, then came back inside with a live fastball that rode in on Evans's hands, which he fouled off to even the count at 1–1.

Bringing in Norman and Billingham as early as he had, both of them starters by trade, Sparky hadn't actually called on the rank and file of his relief corps yet; they were still six deep out there, and if he had to, Anderson wouldn't hesitate to use every last one of them.

Billingham's third pitch, a slow curve, missed outside, 2–1.

The first member of that cadre, Clay Carroll, continued to throw in the Cincinnati bullpen; with Billingham due up second in the top of the fifth, Sparky prepared to use a pinch hitter in that spot and throw another arm at the Red Sox.

Bench set up outside and Evans swung and missed at a prototype Billingham sinker that dropped out of the zone, just below his bat, to even the count at 2–2. He barely fought off the next one, another sinker, swinging late, fouling it straight back; Billingham appeared to have the advantage.

Dwight Evans had played 115 games in right field for the Red Sox in 1975, hitting .274, with thirteen homers and fifty-six runs batted in. His performance at the plate had markedly improved throughout the year, as had manager Darrell Johnson's confidence in him. Only twenty-three, he was the oldest of Boston's three young star outfielders—Evans, Lynn, and Rice—and the way Evans had blossomed in this Series, the Red Sox appeared to have the makings of one of the greatest outfields of all time.

When Billingham came back with his third straight sinker, Evans was waiting on it, and caught it solidly on the meat of the wood, going with the pitch and driving it hard to right field. Ken Griffey took off at the crack of the bat, but the ball angled away from him, bounced once on the warning track about twenty feet inside the foul line, and bounced almost straight sideways over the short wall into the seats just past the Pesky Pole for a ground rule double.

The crowd sprang to life again as Rick Burleson walked to the plate. Billingham missed low and away for a ball.

At the corners of the infield Pete Rose and Tony Perez crept forward onto the edge of the infield grass, anticipating a sacrifice bunt. Burleson's task was to move Evans over to third any way he could, where with one out a fly ball to the outfield would bring him in; a bunt, deep fly ball, or ground ball out to the right side would all do the job. But with pitcher Luis Tiant due up next, the quickest path to manufacture a run here was through the considerable gap that had opened up between Perez and Joe Morgan, where a single could score Evans from second.

Billingham missed again, a fastball, low and just outside, 2–0.

Darrell Johnson never flashed the bunt sign out to Don Zimmer; he trusted that Burleson, with his sound bat control, could put the ball into play on the right side, as he'd been able to do consistently throughout the season.

But not unless Billingham gave him a pitch to hit; his next, a sinker, came in low for ball three, 3–0. Sparky had flashed a sign of his own to Bench: *Don't give him anything near the plate.* More signs from Johnson to Zimmer to Burleson; taking all the way. Another sign from Sparky: *Put him on.* The pitch missed low, nowhere near the zone, for all intents and purposes an intentional walk.

Burleson trotted down to first. Red Sox runners at first and second, nobody out.

Luis Tiant shed his jacket and walked to the plate. Third base coach Don Zimmer walked all the way down the line to Tiant, and they talked for half a minute, Zimmer making sure that Tiant understood exactly what they needed: a bunt, down the third base line, to prevent the force play at third and advance both runners.

But Sparky put his own play on: He was willing to gamble to prevent another run, and so Tony Perez charged in hard from first with the pitch, while Rose hung back near the bag at third; Billingham would field any ball hit to the left and either he or Perez would try to nail Evans at third for the force-out.

Tiant squared to bunt with the pitch, and as Billingham's high fastball broke in on him, he poked his bat out at it and popped it weakly into the air down the first base line. Luis hesitated, thinking the ball would easily be caught for an out—and possible double play—but with Perez charging in, the ball gently arced just over his head and dropped fair. When he saw it land, Tiant, surprised, tossed his bat and ran. Perez turned and chased the ball down as it rolled near the foul line, picked it up, and flipped it underhand to Joe Morgan covering first for the out.

Luis Tiant's luck was still holding; his little oops blooper had worked to perfection in the face of the Reds' aggressive defense, advancing Burleson and Evans to second and third with one out.

First baseman Cecil Cooper came to the plate. Playing the percentages, Sparky pulled the Reds' entire infield onto the grass, hoping for a ground ball from a Billingham sinker that would allow them to either hold Evans at third for an out at first or make a play at the plate if Evans ran on contact. The risk: As good as they all were, drawing his infielders closer to home reduced their effective range by nearly 40 percent; a sharply hit ball that found a gap would score two runs and break the game open. Sparky accepted the risk; although his powerful offense had come from behind to win forty-four times during the '75 season and four times in the playoffs—half of those in their final at bat—on this night he didn't feel that his Reds could afford to fall any deeper in the hole.

Billingham's first pitch missed outside for ball one.

Cooper was now 1–15 in the Series; if he was ever going to find a moment to break out of his slump, this was the time.

Billingham's sinker missed low for ball two. Clay Carroll continued to throw in the Reds bullpen. The crowd revved up, on their feet again.

When Billingham came back with a sinker, Cooper swung and missed, looking awkward and uneasy. Joe Morgan trotted in and shouted some encouragement to Billingham: *That was the pitch, that was the one we need.*

Bench called for the sinker again, Cooper swung late, and topped it into the dirt in front of home plate, where it squirted weakly down to the drawn-in Tony Perez. Perez looked Evans back to third, then ran over to touch first and retire Cooper, unassisted, for the second out. Cooper's slump continued.

The scoring threat diminished, Sparky returned his infield to their normal depth for Red Sox second baseman Denny Doyle; only Rose stayed close to the bag at third in case Doyle tried to drop in a sneak bunt.

The first pitch missed just low, Bench and Billingham staying with the sinker. Billingham came back with it again and caught the inside corner for a strike to even the count. His third sinker in a row to Doyle then produced the desired result: Doyle chopped it down into the dirt directly out toward where Joe Morgan had him played. Morgan charged in to confidently field it, and took his time tossing to first to get Doyle by two steps for the final out of the fourth.

Billingham's sinker ball had done the job again at Fenway. Due up second in the top of the fifth, Jack already knew as he walked off the mound that he was done for the night. He also couldn't help but think that if only he'd been out there from the start, Fred Lynn wouldn't have hit one out of the park to give the Red Sox the early lead.

If only.

For his career, Jack Billingham had now pitched twenty-two and two-thirds innings in two World Series and given up exactly one earned run. He would never be given another World Series start, and appeared in only one more Series game before he finished his long and successful pitching career; but to this day Jack Billingham, cousin to Christy Mathewson, still holds the record for the lowest career ERA in the World Series in all of baseball history.

TWELVE

We never have any pressure. We just go out and
play as hard as we can, and if we win, we win.

SPARKY ANDERSON

AMAZING AS LUIS TIANT'S COMEBACK FOR THE RED SOX
had been, capped by his commanding performances down
the stretch of the pennant drive and throughout the playoffs, viewed
in the context of what was happening in Boston during the summer
of 1975 it becomes even more remarkable. A place with a long memory, built on a tradition of clearly defined class lines, Boston had
evolved from a confederation of succinct and separate neighborhoods into a city that has been described, accurately, as the biggest
small town in America; closely knit but cloistered and partitioned.
Never as robust and vibrant a melting pot as New York, throughout
its history racial and ethnic boundaries in Boston had tended to
be drawn in more indelible ink. When the northward migration of
African-Americans fleeing Reconstruction and the Jim Crow South
in the late nineteenth and early twentieth centuries brought thousands to eastern Massachusetts seeking factory and manufacturing jobs, those segregated neighborhood lines became even more
sharply carved in the earth. By the 1960s, as the Civil Rights Movement advanced the cause of fuller social equality, atavistic racial
attitudes, often provoked by incidents of prejudicial police brutal-
ity, erupted into violence throughout the inner cities of the United
States. The black neighborhood of Roxbury, where tensions had
simmered near boiling for years, experienced three nights of riot-
ing and violence in June of 1967, the summer of the Red Sox's "Impossible Dream." Seven years later, the flash point in Boston for

these ancient, lingering antipathies became implementation of the Supreme Court's 1971 ruling that segregated public schools should now be integrated by forced busing of students.

The first phase of that policy in Boston had been mandated by Federal District Judge Arthur Garrity prior to the school year of 1974, and brought chaos throughout the city, particularly in Roxbury and the nearby working-class-white South Boston, known as "Southie." Not only were disadvantaged African-American kids bused into predominantly Caucasian schools, white kids were compelled to move the other way, into crumbling, underfunded, and understaffed inner city schools. When Garrity ordered that the busing program expand into what he called Phase 2 during the fall of 1975, a move that brought some of the city's largely white suburbs into the plan and affected another fifteen thousand students, the outcry dominated headlines in Boston and elevated tensions to dangerous levels all summer. City officials, Garrity in particular, seemed to have forgotten that Boston's nostalgic national image as America's historical "cradle of liberty"—the basis of its lucrative tourist trade—was actually predicated on the hardheaded, violent resistance of its citizens to "outside" government interference. That same independent and willful Yankee temperament of the region's first patriots still hummed in the DNA of their contemporary blue-collar descendants—some at protest rallies even echoed the cries of Paul Revere by shouting: "The buses are coming, the buses are coming!"

Working- and middle-class white resistance to what they perceived as unwanted federal meddling led to an ugly, reactionary grassroots political movement led by a former Massachusetts congresswoman named Louise Day Hicks. This accelerated the city's rampant "white flight" to the suburbs, but disapproval of Garrity's busing plan wasn't confined to just one side; more than 80 percent of all Boston's residents hated the idea. Although the program's goals of racial equity remained admirable, at the heart of forced busing was a paternalistic and perhaps inherently racist notion that African-American children could only become better students when seated next to whites. Some progressive proponents of the plan openly admitted that, regardless of the negative stress it put on the kids involved, busing needed to be enforced simply to open people's eyes to the massive problems facing inner city schools, and that the only way to change and improve those schools was by forcing the white community to suffer the same injustices. Judging by the results, which showed no overall improvement in student performance on either side, cost the taxpayers millions, threatened to shatter the culture of many long-standing communities, and severely disrupted thousands of families, forced busing appears in retrospect to be the classic big-government blunder that made no one's life better. Within twenty years the entire program would be abandoned and openly acknowledged as a misguided failure, not only in Boston but around the country, but as the 1975 school year neared, with the prospect of what citizens perceived as a direct threat to their children's education and social existence, incidents of racially motivated violence traumatized all the affected neighborhoods. As both sides increasingly demonized the other, the number of murders that summer in Boston shot up dramatically, many attributable to this lamentable rise in tensions. Trouble even spilled over to the safe haven of sports, when a racially motivated stabbing in the stands marred a Red Sox game at Fenway. The start of the school year in September had brought continued unrest, regular student walkouts, and a teachers' strike. With hundreds of local and state police brought in to patrol troubled neighborhoods and campuses, the net result was a city on edge, left even more racially polarized and increasingly segregated. In trying to light the lamp of freedom, Arthur Garrity had instead lit a fuse in a room full of gunpowder. All of this turmoil took place during the highly publicized run-up to the country's upcoming bicentennial celebration in 1976, in which Boston, because of its prominent place in America's revolutionary past, was slated to play a starring role.

In the middle of this pressure cooker, almost desperate for diversion from its pervasive problems, Boston had rallied around a burly, balding black Latin-American pitcher who seemed to rise above it all, standing alone on a mound in the most public of places, radiating cool and style and grace under fire, as he led his adopted city's team toward the redemptive prospect of a long-sought-after World Championship. Those cries of "Loo-ee, Loo-ee" that filled the summer and autumn nights at Fenway contained more than the usual fervor of sports fans' casual idolatry; they carried the hopes and dreams of a community looking for relief from its intractable racial dilemma. Luis Tiant would be the first to tell you that he was not a political man—in most ways he was the classic first-generation citizen-immigrant, grateful for the life his new country had afforded him, eager for assimilation—and the recent storybook deliverance of his beloved parents to America had confirmed his faith in the benevolence of democratic life. He was also a realist, who knew that out of uniform and away from Fenway, unrecognized, he was still a black man who had trouble hailing a cab in downtown Boston. Racial prejudice was a part of life, and so be it; he didn't hold any of those beliefs himself, that wasn't how his parents raised him, and on balance he saw the bright side. If strangers perceived him as a hero, it never for a moment affected how he perceived himself, but he remained grateful for their attention and believed wholeheartedly in the golden rule. The burden he carried was more personal, and more profound.

Ever since his early days in Cuba, when he struggled to win acceptance from his father for his own desire to pitch and to get people to see him as more than just his famous father's son, to his years in Mexico City, establishing himself as an outsider in a foreign country, to his early seasons with the Indians, in an era when Latin players were constantly undervalued, underappreciated, and underpaid, to when he was so casually and cruelly discarded by the Twins and fought his way back to the major leagues, Luis Tiant had been battling for respect. As a consummate competitor and professional, he had earned it from teammates and fans wherever he played, but that didn't diminish his need; it remained central to who he was as a man—a man, if he works hard and his intentions are honorable, *must* be respected—because that respect wasn't ultimately just for himself, it was for all the Latin players who had suffered during those decades when the highest levels of baseball remained closed to them, and for one of them in particular, the man who was sitting with his wife in the stands at Fenway watching him pitch Game Six that night, Luis Tiant Sr., who had given everything he had to this game and received nothing in return, spending the next thirty years of his life in poverty. To survive his own struggles, Luis Tiant had always lived by the code he'd learned from his father: Do your best and try your damnedest, that's how you honor your God, your family, and the talent you were born with; the first step to earning respect from others is to respect yourself.

CENTER FIELDER Cesar Geronimo led off the top of the fifth inning for the Reds. Tiant started him with an off-speed curve, fat and up in the zone, and Geronimo hit it on the button, driving it to right field, where Dwight Evans moved two steps to his left and hauled it in for the out.

The pitcher's spot was next; the Reds' top pinch hitter, Terry Crowley, had for the second time come out to loosen up in the on-deck circle—Jack Billingham had already made his way back to the clubhouse, cracked open a beer, and hit the showers—but when Geronimo failed to get on base, Sparky once again called Crowley back to the dugout, saving his best left-handed bench player for a later situation when he could possibly drive in a run, and sent out reserve outfielder Ed Armbrister in his place.

Edison Rosanda Armbrister was twenty-seven, the last and least important piece of the Joe Morgan trade with Houston three years earlier. He hailed from Nassau in the Bahamas, just the fifth man from his country ever to make it to the major leagues—cricket was still king in the former British colony, which had only gained its independence in 1973—and he benefited from that island's characteristically sunny disposition. A mid-level minor-league prospect at best, Armbrister had never played an inning for the Astros, but he fit the Reds' need for speed, so Bob Howsam asked for him to be included, and he had spent parts of the last three seasons on the Reds' roster as a reserve outfielder. The happy-go-lucky Armbrister could run and field any outfield position, but while appearing in fifty-nine games he'd barely hit his weight in 1975—and he only weighed 170—and driven in just two runs.

But Ed Armbrister had already earned a spot in World Series history—and Red Sox infamy—during the turning point of Game Three of the Series back in Cincinnati. After Dwight Evans tied the game at five runs apiece with a clutch home run for the Red Sox in the top of the ninth, which sent the game into extra innings, Armbrister came up to pinch hit for Reds reliever Rawly Eastwick in the bottom of the tenth, when Cesar Geronimo singled to open the inning. One of the few things the offensively challenged Armbrister could do exceedingly well was bunt, and everyone in Riverfront Stadium that night knew that he was at the plate to sacrifice Geronimo to second, in the hope that the top of the Reds' lineup could then bring him home for the win. But Boston reliever Jim Willoughby had pitched three strong innings to shut down the Reds and keep his team in Game Three; Geronimo's hit was only the second he'd allowed.

Tiant started Armbrister with a sidearm fastball, outside for ball one.

During his pinch-hit appearance in Game Three, Armbrister squared around to bunt on the second pitch, got his bat on the ball, and drove it straight down into the dirt right in front of home plate. As it hopped almost straight back up, Armbrister took a step toward first and froze directly in the path of catcher Carlton Fisk, charging forward out of his crouch to grab the ball in midair with his bare hand in fair territory. Fisk appeared to push Armbrister out of his way, but when he fired to second to try to get the force on Geronimo, slightly off balance from their collision, the ball sailed high and right off the glove of Red Sox shortstop Rick Burleson into center field as Geronimo slid into the base below him. Geronimo hopped to his feet and kept on running, sliding into third base safely, just ahead of the alert and accurate throw from Red Sox center fielder Fred Lynn, while Armbrister advanced to second on the play. Then the fun started. Red Sox manager Darrell Johnson sprinted out of the dugout, and he and Fisk cornered home plate umpire Larry Barnett, arguing furiously that Armbrister had interfered with Fisk's ability to field the ball, and since it had happened in fair territory, the rule book stated that Armbrister should be called out for interference, and Geronimo, who represented the winning run, should be returned to first base with one out.

Tiant's second pitch to Armbrister also missed outside and low, two balls, no strikes.

Home plate umpire Larry Barnett stuttered defensively, but stood his ground, explaining repeatedly that in his judgment Armbrister had done nothing to "intentionally" interfere with Fisk, therefore absolving him of guilt. Darrell Johnson, a former big-league catcher who knew the rule on this backward and forward, reminded him that the rule book never mentioned "intent," and in fact stated that the batter should be called out "whether the contact was intentional or not." Barnett did not agree; in his opinion, the collision had not interfered with Fisk's ability to make the throw, and his throw to second only "went wild because he threw it wildly." Johnson pleaded with Barnett to consult with other members of his crew for help. Barnett refused, and Johnson realized he was banging his head against a wall, so he walked down the line to try to enlist the support of first base umpire Dick Stello.

Tiant's third pitch, a sidearm fastball, just missed high, to put Armbrister ahead in the count 3–0.

While Johnson argued with Stello, NBC's broadcasters Curt Gowdy, Tony Kubek, and full-time Reds announcer Marty Brennaman scrutinized the incident repeatedly on slow-motion replay and all agreed that Armbrister, by stepping into Fisk's path, appeared to interfere with his ability to make a play. Darrell Johnson went back to home plate to give Larry Barnett one last earful before departing for the Red Sox dugout, defeated and angry, but Barnett's original no-call would stand, and Fisk was officially charged with an error on his throw. Fisk, still simmering, then got into a shouting match with Dick Stello—who, as a matter of random interest, was married to a notorious exotic dancer named Chesty Morgan—and had to be separated from him by Denny Doyle and, of all people, Larry Barnett. Fisk stalked back behind the plate, kicking dirt around, picked up his mask, and went back to work in front of the home plate umpire, the two of them avoiding eye contact like a couple after a fight at a dinner party.

Tiant's fourth pitch to Armbrister finally caught the outside corner for a strike, 3–1.

Red Sox manager Darrell Johnson came back out of the dugout to pull his pitcher Jim Willoughby from the game and bring in left-hander Rogelio "Roger" Moret to face Pete Rose, while Curt Gowdy, who had been handed the baseball rule book by his producer Jay Scott—who was himself a part-time Triple-A umpire—read the relevant rule 7.09 in its entirety on the air. After hearing the rule out loud, Tony Kubek reiterated his opinion that Armbrister had clearly interfered with and/or impeded Fisk's ability to field the ball. While Rose waited as Moret warmed up, he heard Fisk and Barnett continuing to jaw at each other, and later said, "Fisk was the maddest I'd seen anyone in a long time—and he had a right to be—so for once in my life I decided to keep my mouth shut." Once Rose stepped into the box, Fisk got his head back in the game and remembered they had decided to put Rose on first with an intentional walk to load the bases with nobody out. After Moret's four throws, Rose sprinted down to first, tossing his bat to the bat boy, and Sparky sent up his best right-handed pinch hitter, Merv Rettenmund, to bat for right fielder Ken Griffey. After Moret struck out Rettenmund for the inning's first out, Darrell Johnson moved the Red Sox infield back to double-play depth and waved in his outfielders toward the edge of the grass, giving them a chance to double-up Geronimo at home on any ball hit in the air to the shallow outfield. Joe Morgan came to the plate, worked the count to 2–1, then drove an outside fastball into the gap in left center field, where it landed well past the drawn-in

Fred Lynn. Geronimo trotted home with the winning run, and just like that the Reds had won Game Three, 6–5, and taken the lead in the Series.

Tiant's fifth pitch missed high again, and Ed Armbrister trotted down to first without ever having taken the bat off his shoulder, the second man Tiant had walked in the game.

The incident that ended Game Three in Cincinnati's favor generated enormous controversy, and divided opinions along strict party lines: Boston's players and fans saw only injustice; Reds supporters said Barnett's decision was by its very nature a judgment call and couldn't be questioned. Passions ran hot in the Red Sox dressing room afterward; a furious Carlton Fisk repeatedly slammed his mask into a wall, while many of his teammates stomped around screaming and shouting. In the postgame press conference, Fisk and Darrell Johnson continued to rip Barnett, with Fisk saying it was time to look around for better umpires while Johnson ill-advisedly suggested that Barnett might want to buy a "personal insurance policy." Sparky Anderson admitted in the press conference that had the same call gone against him he "probably would have gone insane, but it's over and the issue is closed." Larry Barnett and his umpiring crew, who reviewed the play on video for an hour after the game, continued to defend his call. The next day Ed Armbrister continued to maintain his innocence, after repeatedly viewing the replay on television. Red Sox pitcher Bill Lee, always good for a pithy quote, said bitterly that "the Series is now even: one for us, one for the Reds, and one for the umps." Editorials around the country used the incident as exhibit A for the argument that baseball should employ a policy of instant video replay. Sparky's last wry word on the rhubarb put it all in perspective: "The fact that guys all winter in bars will be arguing over this play is good for baseball."

The Armbrister-Fisk collision had overnight become the most scrutinized six seconds of footage since the Zapruder film—the case was reviewed the next day in criminal law classes at Harvard and Yale—but the fact remained that for the second time in a row the

Red Sox had let a World Series game slip away from them in the final inning, and the outrage all the Boston players voiced afterward
had as much to do with their frustration at themselves as it did with
Larry Barnett. The more uncomfortable truth was that Fisk didn't
have to make that aggressive throw to second, a low-percentage play
at best with the speedy Geronimo running from first on contact, and
he also could have easily tagged Armbrister right there out in front
of the plate or thrown him out at first. The probability remained that
Fisk had tagged Armbrister in any case while trying to move him
out of the way—and that Barnett missed that part of the play as
well—but this was hardly even mentioned in the post-mortems. If
Barnett had made that call and Fisk had held on to the ball, Geronimo would have stopped at second with one out; that would have
allowed the Red Sox to walk Rose, create a double-play situation,
and pitch more aggressively to Griffey. They might still have gone
on to lose the game, we'll never know; as it happened, all that bile
and anger stirred up about Barnett's actions would soon have a very
real and regrettable consequence.

Pete Rose came to the plate for his third at bat against Tiant in
Game Six. It's an old baseball adage that a pitcher holds an edge over
hitters the first time through the lineup, while the second time
through the odds even up as hitters adjust to the pitcher's speed and
style, and by the third time through, the advantage shifts to the batter. Rose's at bat marked the start of the Reds' third look at Tiant in
Game Six, in their third game against him in the last eleven days;
the question now was could Luis Tiant continue to outfox a lineup
stacked with the most professional hitters in the world, or would
this be the moment they figured him out and momentum shifted
back to the Reds?

On Tiant's first pitch, Rose tried to drop a surprise drag bunt
down toward third, but fouled the low-and-away fastball into the
stands above the Reds' dugout.

Umpires for the World Series used to be selected on merit by their
respective leagues, but after a one-day walkout staged by the then

two-year-old umpires union nearly upended the 1970 postseason, the men in blue had since bargained hard for better wages and working conditions. In 1974 their union pushed through a ruling that the World Series would henceforth be staffed by a crew drawn in random rotation from the pool of all umpires with at least six years of major-league experience, which in the minds of many players and managers simply ensured and rewarded mediocrity. By some strange luck of the draw, all six umpires for the 1975 World Series were working in their first Fall Classic. (Hearing that fact before the Series, Carl Yastrzemski had snorted contemptuously: "Then why don't they just rotate the teams?") Thirty-year-old Larry Barnett had been an American League umpire for seven years, garnering average reviews for his work, but by the time the World Series shifted back to Boston for Game Six, he had received a sack full of hideous hate mail for his controversial call in Game Three. An anonymous telegram had also been sent directly to his home in Prospect, Ohio, that threatened not only his life but that of his wife and two-year-old daughter. Local police immediately placed a twenty-four-hour guard on the Barnett house and family, and the FBI quickly came in to investigate at the behest of Commissioner Bowie Kuhn. Since arriving back in Boston on Friday, throughout the rain delay over the weekend, and that afternoon when he arrived at Fenway—even tonight, from in the stands, by agents stationed near where he was working the game at third base—Larry Barnett, scared half to death, had been under the watchful eyes of an FBI protective detail larger than the one that had protected former secretary of state Henry Kissinger at a game earlier in the Series.

Rose stepped back into the box and watched Tiant's second pitch sail high and away for a ball. Tiant asked for another ball, stared in for the sign, and delivered an excellent low fastball that appeared to catch the outside corner, but Davidson called it a ball, 2–1. Rose and Fisk, who had been carrying on a casual, needling back-and-forth with each other throughout the Series, debated the merits of that pitch, while Fisk set up for the next one.

The FBI agents guarding Larry Barnett weren't the only federal officers in attendance that night at Fenway. A Secret Service squad was also in the stands guarding the oldest son of President Gerald Ford, twenty-five-year-old Michael Ford, who was there watching the game. A longtime respected congressman from Michigan and the former minority leader of the House of Representatives, Gerald Ford had been elevated to the office of vice president in 1973 by President Richard Nixon, after Nixon's disgraced VP, Spiro Agnew, under investigation for charges of bribery, conspiracy, and extortion committed during his prior tenure as the governor of Maryland, had been allowed to plead no contest to a single charge of tax evasion as long as he resigned. Less than a year later, when President Nixon himself was forced to abdicate his office under even darker clouds of criminality and misconduct, Gerald Ford became the thirty-eighth President of the United States, the only man in American history to reach the White House without ever winning election to either executive position. Although he had already made it clear he intended to run as the incumbent in the upcoming 1976 election, Ford's formerly spotless reputation had suffered a serious blow a month after taking office, when he issued a general pardon for Richard Nixon, indemnifying him against the threat of any future prosecution.

Tiant came back with the same pitch, a sizzling fastball that nailed Fisk's target on the outside corner; Davidson called it a strike to even the count at 2–2.

Although an inaccurate public image of Ford as a clumsy bumbler had already taken root—he had a bad knee that occasionally buckled and resulted in awkward spills—he was actually the most accomplished athlete ever to hold the nation's highest office; playing both linebacker and center, he had anchored the University of Michigan's football team during back-to-back national championships in the early 1930s, and retained a lifelong fan's interest in every major American sport. There had been talk about President Ford attending a World Series game in Boston, but his chief of staff—an ambitious young political operative from Wyoming named Dick Cheney—had discouraged the idea. Security around the entire Ford family had been tightened severely during the previous month, after two bizarre and inept assassination attempts had been made on the President within weeks of each other in California. On September 5, a deranged former Charles Manson acolyte named Lynette "Squeaky" Fromme, while dressed in a blood red nun's habit, had pointed a loaded .45 automatic at President Ford during his appearance at a public park in Sacramento but was subdued before she could pull the trigger. Seventeen days later, on a crowded street outside the President's hotel in downtown San Francisco, a frumpy middle-aged housewife, five-time divorcee, and professional accountant named Sarah Jane Moore fired a single shot at Ford with a .38 revolver and missed before being tackled by an alert bystander.

Tiant waited until he saw the sign from Fisk he wanted—another fastball, low and away—and Rose fought it off, fouling it out of play into the stands near third base, still 2–2.

Prior to her assassination attempt, Sarah Jane Moore had been peripherally connected to a bizarre story that had competed with the downfall of Richard Nixon as a principal obsession of American culture over the previous two years: the kidnapping in 1974 of newspaper heiress Patricia Hearst. The nineteen-year-old granddaughter of publishing magnate William Randolph Hearst, Patty Hearst had been taken at gunpoint from her Berkeley, California, apartment by a scruffy, heavily armed left-wing group of urban anarchists who called themselves the Symbionese Liberation Army, better known in months to come as the SLA. After trying and failing to negotiate Hearst's return for the release of some of their jailed comrades, the SLA demanded that her old-money family—guilty of countless but unspecified "crimes against the people"—establish an organization to provide food to poor Californians in exchange for Patty's release. Her father complied by immediately creating People In Need (P.I.N.) and giving away more than $6 million worth of food to the poor and indigent in the San Francisco area. Sarah Jane Moore, reportedly obsessed with all aspects of the Hearst case, intersected the story here when she was hired as a bookkeeper for P.I.N. and quickly asserted herself into the organization's daily operations. Instead of holding up their end of the bargain, the SLA responded by claiming that the food hadn't been good enough, and Patty Hearst would remain their prisoner.

Tiant came back with a fastball again, falling off to the left of the mound and missing high and away, a full count now to Rose, 3–2. Rose immediately thought that the location and Tiant's off-balance follow-through might be an indication that the pitcher was beginning to tire.

The real shocker came a month later, when Patricia Hearst, after enduring what was later revealed to be weeks of unrelenting isolation, brainwashing, and sexual abuse, announced in a tape recording sent to the press that she had joined the SLA and would henceforth be known by her revolutionary name of "Tania"; she was soon afterward photographed carrying an M1 automatic rifle during a San Francisco bank robbery committed by the group. "Tania" and the rest of the criminal SLA gang remained on the loose, considered armed and dangerous, and Patty Hearst joined them on the FBI's ten most wanted list.

With Armbrister running on the pitch, Tiant threw another high fastball that Rose fouled straight back—it ended up in the hands of Dick Stockton up in the open-air broadcast booth, just to the third base side of home; Garagiola and Kubek wisely ducked—having confirmed Rose's opinion that Tiant was losing his edge and might finally be ripe for the plucking.

After six of the SLA's leaders were killed during a bloody shootout with a Los Angeles SWAT team in May of 1974, Patricia Hearst continued to elude authorities for more than fifteen months, until she was finally arrested without resistance in a San Francisco apartment on September 18, 1975. During those intervening months, the increasingly unstable Sarah Jane Moore had been forced out of her job at P.I.N., fallen in with some ex-con radicals connected to the SLA, become a part-time informant for the FBI against them, and claimed the Bureau then assigned her to go undercover into another Bay Area Marxist revolutionary cell. That group had no sooner converted the malleable Moore to their wacko radical manifesto when her FBI connection became public knowledge, both sides dropped her like a leper, and she spiraled into a delusional state that spawned a welter of violent fantasies. Some of those apparently involved "rescuing" the recently collared Patty Hearst from federal captivity, and four days after Patty Hearst's arrest—connecting dots that only a disintegrating mind could perceive—Moore took her shot at President Ford.

With the count full, Armbrister took off as the next pitch left Tiant's hand, a fastball low but in the zone, and Rose was ready: He lined it sharply into straightaway center field. Armbrister rounded second, hesitated, and then accelerated toward third as he saw the ball reach Fred Lynn on the first hop, but as Lynn tried to transfer the ball to his throwing hand it caught momentarily in the webbing of his glove. Armbrister safely reached third, and instead of rushing a throw to third, Lynn wisely threw behind him to Doyle covering second, holding Rose to a single, his second in a row and second of the game against Tiant. Pete Rose now led the World Series in hits, and the Reds had runners on first and third with only one out, their most serious threat of the game.

Ken Griffey came up for the Reds' biggest at bat of the game. Sparky and the Reds' entire bench crept forward toward the rail on the edge of the field.

Tiant started Griffey with a fastball, again up in the zone, but a little late on the swing, Griffey fouled it high into the stands down the third base line.

The crowd grew restive, sensing trouble. Griffey had produced under similar pressure in Game Two, driving in what turned out to be the game-winning run in the ninth inning. Then, in the bottom of the ninth in Game Four in Cincinnati, against Luis Tiant—with one out, men on first and second, and the Reds trailing by a run—Griffey had hit a screaming line drive toward left center; Fred Lynn turned around, tracked the ball down at full speed, and snagged it over his shoulder at the base of Riverfront's deep center field wall, the kind of defensive gem Lynn had been making all season. This one saved Game Four and the win for Tiant.

Tiant missed outside with a fastball, 1–1.

Pete Rose took an exaggerated lead off first base, trying to draw a throw and induce Tiant into an error that would score Armbrister from third. Tiant looked Rose back toward the bag but didn't take the bait. He came in again to Griffey, using the same windup and toward the same outside location, but pulled the string on a slow curve. Griffey resisted and the pitch missed low, 2–1.

Behind in the count, Luis needed a good pitch now, and he reared back and threw his best fastball of the game, which clipped the outside corner for a strike, evening the count at 2–2.

"Boy, that was a good pitch, Tony," said Garagiola.

"He needs another one," said Kubek. "Right now."

Fisk called for a curve, and set up low and away. The pitch arced toward the plate but floated and hung up, waist-high over the outside edge. Griffey had time to measure and adjust to the speed and then belted it, a majestic, deep drive toward left center field. The runners, Armbrister and Rose, held up halfway down the line, turning to watch the flight of the ball. Just as he had on the ball Griffey hit at Riverfront in Game Four, Fred Lynn immediately turned and with the briefest of glances sprinted back toward where his superb tracking skills told him the ball would come back to ground. His path took him straight toward the 379 sign in the corner formed by the left field wall angling sharply into the joint of the center field section. Ten feet from the wall, on the edge of the generous warning track, his back completely turned to home plate, Lynn glanced again over his shoulder, drew a bead on the ball, took one quick look at the wall, and then leapt up desperately to make the grab, knowing he was dangerously near the concrete and about to collide with it, turning his body counterclockwise back toward the infield.

His glove missed the ball by less than a foot; it smacked the left field edge of the wall almost on the numbers and caromed wildly back toward right center. Completing his awkward turn, Lynn's back slammed straight into the concrete just on the center field side of the angle, his limbs splayed out, his hat came flying off, and he immediately slumped to the ground.

Seeing the ball bounce free, Ed Armbrister trotted home for the Reds' first run. By the time Dwight Evans could reach the ball and throw it back in to Rick Burleson, Pete Rose had motored all the way around from first and scored the Reds' second run. Griffey was already gliding into third with a stand-up triple, and Burleson ran the ball in to hold him there. Carl Yastrzemski had joined Evans in right center, having chased the ricocheting ball all the way over from left, and then they both turned; NBC cut to a zoom shot of center field, the umpire at second called an urgent time-out, and Fenway went instantly silent as everyone realized that Fred Lynn was still lying motionless at the base of the wall. His bent legs turned to the right, his upper back still wedged against the concrete, his glove lying on the ground beside him, utterly motionless—he looked dead, a battlefield casualty frozen in time.

Yaz got to him first, leaning down, relieved to hear Lynn respond to his first question; his young teammate had never lost consciousness but was afraid to move. He'd hit the concrete at full speed, taking the impact into his lower back, and as he lay there crumpled on the track he'd lost all feeling in his legs, totally numb from the waist down. Dwight Evans reached them moments later and knelt down beside him.

Red Sox trainer Charlie Moss and manager Darrell Johnson sprinted out from the dugout, Moss reaching Lynn first. The entire crowd remained on their feet, straining to get a view. Fenway had gone as quiet as a tomb. The fans had seen Lynn make dozens of spectacular, headlong plays throughout his first season, and he'd never been hurt or injured on any of them; now it looked as if their Golden Boy's miraculous rookie year—and the Red Sox's prospects for both present and future as well—had met a tragic end. Charlie Moss gently helped Lynn extend his legs, easing him out of the awkward posture and trying to relieve any strain. Pitching coach Stan Williams then joined them from the bullpen as Lynn planted both hands on the ground behind him and crabbed forward slightly, going all pins and needles as the first feeling returned to his legs.

The anxious crowd clapped their hands and blew horns as Lynn began to stir, and when the other men helped him rise gingerly to his feet, they cheered. Lynn bent over from the waist, carefully assessing the damage. He'd taken worse hits on crossing patterns in the middle of the field as a receiver in football, but his legs and lower back felt stiff and bruised. He picked up his glove, took a few deep breaths, and walked back onto the outfield grass, Charlie Moss and Darrell Johnson at his side. Lynn stretched from side to side, moving a little easier, and told Johnson he wanted to keep playing. As Moss and Johnson started back toward the dugout, and the crowd realized Lynn was not only all right but staying in the game, the cheer became a sustained ovation.

With one out, the Red Sox lead reduced to one, and the potential tying run in Ken Griffey at third, Joe Morgan walked to the plate. Darrell Johnson drew his infielders in to the edge of the grass, unwilling to give up that run on a groundout. Tiant, looking slightly unsettled, missed high once again with a first-pitch fastball, then low and away with a hard curve, quickly behind in the count to Morgan, 2–0. Knowing he only needed a medium-deep fly out to bring home the swift Griffey, Morgan looked and waited for a pitch he could lift into the air. Going back to the same misdirection that had just failed with Griffey, Tiant threw the changeup again; Morgan adjusted, but slightly overanxious, he swung hard and missed the center of the bat by a fraction of an inch. The ball skied straight up in the air, a high pop fly to third base, where Rico Petrocelli barely moved and settled under it for the second out.

Two outs, and with the sacrifice fly no longer in play, Johnny Bench stepped into the box. Bench had been given the same tip in the Cincinnati dugout, that Tiant was tending to start batters with first-pitch fastballs for strikes. He hadn't needed to be told; from his extraordinary expertise behind the plate he knew more about most pitchers' patterns than they did themselves. He'd already hit 240 home runs in his career, more than any other catcher in baseball history besides Hall of Famer Yogi Berra, and done it on a steady diet of fastballs, for breakfast, lunch, and dinner. But for all the hoopla that had been made in the press about how the Reds' relent-less right-handed bats were going to dine out on Fenway's short left field, they hadn't yet hit a single ball off the Green Monster in two and a half games of the World Series.

That streak ended moments later when Tiant threw his next first-pitch fastball to Bench. It came in low, but Johnny reached out for it and hit a rope that rocketed toward left field and smacked into the wall about twenty-five feet up. The old master of the Monster, Yas-trzemski, retreated back exactly to where he knew the ball would rebound, caught it on the bounce as it came down, then whirled and fired to second, holding Bench to a 310-foot single.

But not before Ken Griffey trotted across home plate with the Reds' third run of the inning, to tie the game. Bench had come through again. The Red Sox's early lead had become a memory.

Now Tony Perez stepped in for his third trip to the plate in the game, the seventh Red to bat in the fifth, with the go-ahead run in Bench on first. The Cubans faced off; Perez lunged at Tiant's first of-fering, a slow curve, and whacked it foul down the first base line. Tiant came back at Perez with a fastball, but again missed up and away, certain evidence his legs were beginning to tire.

For the first time in the game, pitchers stood up and began throw-ing in the Red Sox bullpen—right-hander Jim Willoughby, their long reliever, and rookie left-hander Jim Burton.

Tiant challenged the dangerous Perez with another fastball that buzzed in on his hands, and Perez fouled it straight back, 1–2. He then tried to induce him to chase a low slider, but Perez held up and the count evened at 2–2. Tiant missed with yet another high fastball and the count went to full. Luis was obviously laboring; anxiety in Fenway deepened.

Manager Darrell Johnson moved to the top step of the Red Sox dugout, watching Tiant closely. He was always reluctant to remove his best pitcher from any game, but if Luis lost Perez here, he might have to make a move. These were the moments when Tiant reached down into a reserve few other players possessed; he blew a waist-high fastball by the swinging Perez to strike him out and end the Reds threat.

Sparky clapped his hands, walking the length of the dugout, exhorting his men as they grabbed their gloves and headed out onto the field for the bottom of the fifth. It was a new game again, and the Big Red Machine was alive and kicking in Boston.

THIRTEEN

Darrell Johnson has been falling out
of trees all season and landing on his feet.

RED SOX PITCHER BILL LEE

U P IN THE NBC BROADCAST BOOTH, APPEARING ON CAM-
era for the first time at the midpoint of the game, Dick Stockton turned over the play-by-play duties for the second half to Joe
Garagiola. Eager to be back in charge of the evening's narrative, Garagiola turned away from Stockton and went to work.

Sparky Anderson sent out his fourth Reds pitcher of the game to
start the bottom of the fifth inning as thirty-four-year-old Clay
Palmer Carroll took the mound. After a few years of knocking
around the National League and languishing in middle relief for
the underachieving Atlanta Braves, Carroll had caught the eye of
Reds super-scout Ray Shore. Shore thought the unheralded Carroll
had outstanding command and control, and the ideal psychological
makeup for a position that was just then being defined in the major
leagues: the dedicated closer in the bullpen. Shore's report put Carroll on the radar of GM Bob Howsam, and the Reds acquired him
mid-season in 1968, as part of a trade for starting pitcher Tony Cloninger. Cloninger never panned out, but "Hawk" Carroll—nicknamed
for his prominent beak—immediately won the job as the Reds'
closer. When Sparky Anderson joined the team and brought along
his emphasis on a strong bullpen, Clay Carroll became one of the
dominant closers in the National League, twice making the All-Star
team, averaging sixty-one appearances a season, and saving eighty-
nine games for the Reds during their resurgent half decade. In the
last year, as two younger closers emerged from the Cincinnati farm

system—right-hander Rawly Eastwick and lefty Will McEnaney—
the aging Carroll had been eased back into setup and middle relief
work. Hawk never complained—off the field he was the pitching
staff's court jester, a good ol' country boy from Alabama who kept
everybody loose—but whenever Sparky put the ball in his hand, he
still snarled like a Rottweiler.

His first assignment: left fielder Carl Yastrzemski. Fenway Park
and the Red Sox dugout remained quiet for the first time in the
game, as if the Reds' three-run outburst and the threat of serious
injury to Fred Lynn had knocked the wind out of them. Yaz stepped
in, looking to breathe some life back into his team and the home
crowd. The Red Sox leader was carrying another burden this night
that he seldom talked about: His beloved mother, Hattie, who had
been a fixture in the stands at Fenway throughout his two decades
in Boston, was undergoing chemotherapy, gravely ill since late
summer.

Hawk Carroll was as big and sturdy as a plow horse. His easy
throwing motion looked quite a bit like Jack Billingham's, and he
was equally durable, but he had a larger repertoire, four quality
pitches he could throw for strikes: a good running fastball, a sweeping slider, a nasty curve, and an outstanding changeup. He started
Yaz with a curve that caught the outside corner for a strike.

Hearing the footsteps of the youngsters coming up behind him,
Carroll had won seven games for the Reds in 1975, and saved seven
more, his ERA still an outstanding 2.62. This was the fourth time
Sparky had called on him in the World Series, but to this point
Hawk hadn't been particularly effective, giving up three hits, a
walk, and a couple of runs in less than three innings pitched.

Hawk tried the same pitch again on Yaz, but missed the outside
corner to even the count. He then missed high and outside with a
fastball; Yaz had the advantage now, 2–1, and looked for a pitch to
hit. Carroll fooled him with a changeup that caught the inside corner and evened the count again at 2–2.

Yastrzemski tightened his grip as Carroll came inside with a
hard curve, and then made a superb inside-out swing, lining the

ball to left field for his second single of the game. The Boston crowd came back to life as Carlton Fisk strode to the plate.

Clay Carroll had never finished high school, jumping to the minor leagues as soon as he was drafted at eighteen, and the evidence suggested he hadn't been paying much attention during the years he did attend. The funniest clubhouse moment of the Series for Cincinnati had come during the Reds' weekend workout at the Tufts University field house, when Sparky told the team upon their arrival that at long last they'd figured out a way to get Hawk to go to college.

Johnny Bench set up outside and Carroll nailed his target with a fastball for a called first strike. The Reds' infielders put a shift on for the pull-hitting Fisk, as Joe Morgan moved almost directly behind second base; with Perez holding Yaz on first, an enormous hole opened up between them, daring Fisk to punch the ball to the right side.

Carroll missed outside with a curve to even the count. In the on-deck circle, Fred Lynn swung the bat easily as he loosened up, demonstrating no lingering effects as yet from his collision with the wall.

Carroll came inside with a running fastball, and Fisk hit it on the screws, a screaming two-hopper pulled toward third. Playing in, Pete Rose snagged it as he stutter-stepped to his left, a tailor-made double-play ball, but then as he turned, he caught his spikes in the dirt and stumbled, and as he continued to stagger, he whipped the ball to Morgan at second for the force-out on Yastrzemski, while Fisk made it safely to first on the fielder's choice. Rose ended up on his hands and knees, all his strengths and weaknesses as an infielder on display during his first defensive chance of the game; the result was neither pretty nor perfect, but the Reds still had their first out of the inning.

"Rose did everything but bite that one," said Garagiola.

Fred Lynn came to the plate and impatiently swung at Carroll's first pitch, a low fastball running away from him. He caught it off the end of the bat, lofting it to short left field, where George Foster pulled it in for the second out. Lynn's swing had appeared fluid but considerably less powerful, as if he might have been protecting his back, and Tony Kubek speculated that the extent of the damage Lynn had suffered in his collision might not yet be known.

Rico Petrocelli came up next, with two outs and Fisk on first. Carroll crossed him up with the first pitch he threw, a fastball motion resulting in a beautifully camouflaged slow curve, and Rico hit it almost accidentally with a checked swing, straight out to Davey Concepcion at short, who made the short toss to Morgan for the force on Fisk at second, and just like that the Red Sox's fifth inning was over.

As he walked to the dugout, feeling pretty pleased about his best outing in the Series to date, Carroll looked toward the bullpen and saw that Captain Hook already had his next pitcher warming up. After just getting into the flow of the game, Hawk Carroll was done for the night.

RED SOX MANAGER Darrell Johnson now faced his toughest dilemma of the game. His eyes had told him that Luis Tiant was beginning to tire, and the Reds lineup no longer seemed fooled or bewildered by his diminishing stuff. Johnson's emotions urged him to stick with Tiant as long as he could; they were still tied with the Reds, and with his battler's heart, Luis might find a way to keep them in the game. Johnson had gone through the same argument with himself during Game Four in Cincinnati; when he'd gone out to start that night, Tiant had discovered that the mound in Cincinnati was higher than any he'd pitched from all year, and it adversely affected his balance and delivery in the early frames. Pitching with only a one-run lead in a hostile park after four innings, refusing to yield, Tiant had adjusted his windup to the higher mound and willed his way out of trouble in nearly every subsequent inning. When Darrell Johnson finally walked out to the mound after the Reds' Cesar Geronimo reached first with a lead-off single in the bottom of the ninth—fully intending to take Luis out and hand the ball over to his closer Dick Drago—Tiant had read him the riot act.

"What the fuck you doing out here, man?" said an indignant Tiant. "This is my ball game, I'm gonna finish this fucker. Get the fuck out of here."

Johnson, almost laughing at his man's sheer audacity and perhaps more than a little intimidated, walked back to the dugout and let Tiant go back to work. Reds pinch hitter Ed Armbrister bunted Geronimo to second for the first out, then Tiant walked Pete Rose, putting the winning run at first. After Ken Griffey lined one to deep left center, where Fred Lynn made his game-saving over-the-shoulder catch for the second out, Tiant got Joe Morgan to pop out to first, and the Red Sox had won Game Four to even the Series at two games apiece.

Obsessively charted pitch counts dominate the regulated lines of starting pitchers in the twenty-first century, each with their own rigidly established limits, almost no one allowed to throw more than 100–120 in a game. On this night in Cincinnati, when he had far from his best stuff, Luis Tiant had thrown *163 pitches* for his second complete-game win of the 1975 Series, one of the gutsiest performances in World Series history, but at what cost? Although the rain delay had given him an extra day of rest from his usual turn in the rotation, how much could *El Tiante* have left this late in the season, at his age, after 292 innings of work?

With the pitcher's spot due up third in the home half of the sixth, Johnson decided he had to give the man who'd brought them this far the benefit of every doubt, and so Luis Tiant went out to start the sixth inning.

GEORGE FOSTER led off the sixth for the Reds, and for once he stepped immediately into the box, ready to go to work. Tiant went right after him with a fastball that tailed up and in; fooled by the pitch, Foster made an almost protective check swing and accidentally put a slow grounder in play to the left of the pitcher's mound. Quick as a cat, before the hard-charging Rico Petrocelli could even reach it, Tiant darted to his left and snared the ball, ran a couple more steps before he could stop, then turned and fired a fastball to Cecil Cooper at first base to beat Foster by two steps. A superb defensive play, executed with flair, the best by a Red Sox player in the game so far.

The next man, Davey Concepcion, watched a Tiant changeup float by him for a ball, then took a home run rip at a fastball and missed for a strike. Tiant missed outside with another fastball, then came inside with a sidearm slider that Concepcion hit off the hands toward right field. Dwight Evans drifted back a few steps to his right and easily made the catch for the second out of the inning. Fred Lynn backed up the play, but as he walked back to center moved with a visible hitch in his stride; Tony Kubek kept a close eye on Lynn, sensing a developing story.

Darrell Johnson now felt a little better about his decision to leave Tiant in the game, but still kept his two relievers, Burton and Willoughby, throwing in the Boston pen.

Reds' center fielder Cesar Geronimo leaned back from a first-pitch fastball that missed inside, then watched a second one crack into Fisk's mitt for a called strike on the outside corner. When Tiant came back inside with his third straight fastball, low and inside, Geronimo made a terrific inside-out swing and whacked a low screaming liner past a diving Rico Petrocelli at third. As it flew over the base, umpire Larry Barnett immediately signaled fair ball, then had to jump out of the way as it shot past him and hit the face of the grandstand, where it cut sharply back to hug the foul line and bounce at a nearly ninety-degree angle into shallow left field. World Series umpire crews always carry two extra men to patrol the foul lines, and left field line umpire Dick Stello ran out onto the grass to follow the ball. Before Carl Yastrzemski could run in and reach it, shortstop Rick Burleson sprinted out to grab the dying ball and fired to Denny Doyle covering second. Reds first base coach George Scherger screamed at Geronimo, almost halfway to second, to put on the brakes; he did, just in time, and retreated to first with a single. At any other park in baseball, Geronimo's ball would have run all the way down the line to the outfield wall for a double; once again, the architectural quirkiness of Fenway Park, and a typical hustling effort by the Rooster, had saved its home team a base.

But Cincinnati now had six hits off Tiant, tying the Red Sox in that department as well, and putting the go-ahead run at first.

For the third time in the game, Sparky had sent his best pinch hitter, Terry Crowley, to the on-deck circle to bat for a pitcher. This time, with Geronimo reaching first, the left-handed Crowley finally made it into the batter's box. In his second season with the Reds, Crowley had come over from the Orioles in another of Bob Howsam's smaller, clever acquisitions for the Big Red Machine.

Tiant came in with a fastball, low for ball one; Fisk held his glove in place and Tiant stared in at Satch Davidson, both of them unhappy with the call.

Crowley had made only one other appearance in the Series so far, striking out against Tiant in Game Four when batting, as he was here, for reliever Clay Carroll. But Sparky had saved him for another reason: During his five years with Baltimore in the American League Crowley had seen Tiant pitch frequently, and had faced him more than any other Reds hitter; he was more than familiar with Luis's bag of tricks.

Tiant made a casual throw to first, sending Geronimo back to the bag, then tossed his soft marshmallow curve to Crowley, catching the outside corner for a strike to even the count.

Crowley, a Staten Island native, could play any position on the field except catcher, which made him an unusually valuable bench player, but he had spent most of the postseason riding the pine. Given the time he had on his hands, during this World Series he was also moonlighting for his hometown newspaper, dictating a "you are there" column for the *Staten Island Advance* after every game.

Another throw to first by Tiant, his "A" move this time—the one that Sparky still thought was a balk, but there would be no more of those calls from any ump at a time like this—sent Geronimo diving back to first. His next pitch to Crowley hit Fisk's target to the millimeter, a fastball that nicked the outside corner to put Tiant ahead in the count 1–2. Crowley fought off the next one as well, another good fastball in the same location, to stay alive.

Terry Crowley had become one of the Orioles' first designated hitters when the American League implemented the rule in 1972, but since coming to the Reds and the National League, he had made his living almost exclusively as a pinch hitter. Despite his defensive versatility, he had appeared on the field in only eight games in 1975. Good pinch hitters are a rare breed in baseball; the best can make a living for a very long time, and Crowley was one of them. He would stick around in the big leagues for fifteen years, and he was about to demonstrate why.

Tiant went back to the slow curve on the outside corner. Crowley swung and blooped a soft liner off the handle that appeared to move in slow motion toward Burleson at short. The ball bounced once, Burleson fielded it cleanly, and then he turned to make the throw for the force-out at second on Geronimo.

But Denny Doyle wasn't on the base. With the left-handed Crowley at bat, Doyle had been playing deep in the hole, shaded toward first, and he didn't have time to get to second ahead of the speedy Geronimo, who had left for second with the crack of the bat. When he realized Doyle wasn't there, Burleson held up his throw, and by then it was too late to catch Crowley at first.

Runners on first and second now, with two outs, for the Reds.

Since no obvious error had been committed on the play—although Burleson could have been held accountable for not recognizing that Doyle was out of position and making a throw immediately to first— the game's official scorer up in the press box awarded Crowley with a single, the Reds' seventh hit of the game.

"Talk about a wholesale base hit," said Garagiola. "That's one of those eighty-nine-cent jobs."

A recognizable shade of red flared up around the Rooster's neck; he was angry with himself again as he tossed the ball back to Tiant. But Tiant appeared calm and unflappable, even with Pete Rose—now 2–3 against him, seeing the ball well out of Tiant's hand and hitting it hard—coming to the plate.

The air taut with tension in Fenway, Darrell Johnson stepped up to the edge of the Red Sox dugout again; had he made the right call? Tiant missed with his first pitch, a fastball, inside and low. Rose, alert and focused, now looked for a pitch to hit; when Tiant threw him the slow curve—the same pitch he'd abused for a single in the fifth—it came in a little high and Rose fouled it into the left field stands.

Tiant tried another fastball, again up in the zone; Rose was ready and spanked it hard up the middle just to the left of the mound, but Burleson, stationed close to second to hold Geronimo close to the bag, glided to his left, scooped it up one-handed, and stepped on second, cleaning up his own mess for the force on Crowley to end the inning.

El Tiante had dodged another bullet.

IN THE BOTTOM of the sixth inning the Cincinnati Reds' fifth pitcher of the game took the mound: twenty-eight-year-old Pedro Rodriguez Borbon. Another discovery of super-scout Ray Shore, the young Borbon had been managed by him during a season in his native Dominican Republic's Winter League in 1967. Signed initially by the Cardinals before being claimed by the Angels, Borbon appeared in a few games for California late in the 1969 season, but the Angels didn't hold him in high regard; Shore had Borbon targeted as one of the twenty American League pitchers he liked the most, and Bob Howsam acquired him in a trade after the '69 season. When Sparky Anderson took over in 1970, he realized that Borbon, as he put it admiringly, was "an absolute animal": He had the arm to pitch every day, he was fearless on the mound, strong as an ox, and he could literally—as his Reds bullpen mates once discovered on a bet; Borbon took peculiar pride in the strength of his teeth—bite the cover off a baseball. Teammates never needed a bottle opener in the clubhouse; they just handed their bottles to Pedro. In the first inning of his first major-league start, the back half of a doubleheader against the Padres in 1970, Borbon gave up a three-run home run, then on his first pitch to the next batter tattooed fearsome slugger Nate Colbert with a fastball in the ribs. When Colbert took a few steps toward the mound, Borbon dropped his glove and walked right at him, ready to rumble and God knows what else, before teammates separated them. Sparky just shook his head in wonder; he hadn't given Borbon the order to throw at Colbert, and rookies just didn't behave that way in baseball, but Pedro Borbon was an altogether different breed of cat.

Dwight Evans stepped in to open the inning against Borbon, who had only pitched an inning in two appearances in the Series so far. A perfect reflection of his personality, Borbon was a power pitcher who didn't mess around, going right after hitters with fastball, sinker, slider—all of them thrown hard, all of them moving, most of them in or near the strike zone: He dared you to hit him. Evans watched Borbon's first fastball, a called strike that appeared to land below his knees; Evans turned and stared at Satch Davidson in disbelief at the call, but said nothing. He watched the next two come in low and outside to take the count to 2–1.

Dwight Evans talked to himself quietly and constantly when he was at the plate, small encouragements—*Come on, let's go*—and he swung hard at Borbon's next pitch, a fastball down the middle that he fouled straight back, evening the count at 2–2.

In the 1973 postseason, after establishing himself alongside Clay Carroll as one of the anchors in Sparky's bullpen, Pedro Borbon achieved a different kind of respect from his teammates during the infamous Pete Rose–Bud Harrelson dustup in Game Three of the National League Championship Series. They already knew he wasn't afraid of anything or anybody. When he saw the bench-clearing brawl break out after Rose's hard slide into Harrelson, Borbon immediately tried to rush in from the bullpen, but in his haste couldn't get the gate to open, so he simply ripped it off its hinges and tossed it to the ground. Borbon ran to the infield and charged into the melee like a berserk marauder—in the middle of the resulting scrum he allegedly bit one of the Mets on the leg—and by the time four teammates could pull him away, his jersey had nearly been torn off. He put on the cap he'd picked up in the scramble, thinking it was his, and when his teammates pointed out to him that he was wearing a *Mets* cap, Borbon took it off, ferociously ripped it apart with his teeth, spit it out on the field, and for good measure stomped on it. Ever since that incident his teammates had called Borbon "Vampire."

Borbon came back with the hard slider on the outside corner. Evans leaned in, went with the pitch, and smacked it hard to the right side. Morgan moved to his left to deftly grab the hot shot and throw Evans out at first. One out. Shortstop Rick Burleson stepped in next, and Luis Tiant, wearing his warm-up jacket, moved into the on-deck circle. Bench waved Ken Griffey in a few steps in right field, then called for a sinker, which bounced in the dirt and nicked off of Bench's right hand for a ball. Although he stood six-one and weighed in at a solid 210 pounds, Johnny Bench had the biggest hands most people had ever seen on a human being, freakishly outsized, almost as if he had an extra knuckle on each finger. He had been photographed a number of times demonstrating one of his favorite stunts: holding *seven* baseballs in each hand. On at least two occasions during his early career—once when his glove got snagged on his shin protector, another time when he was trying to show up a pitcher who wasn't throwing as hard as Bench thought he should be— Bench had simply reached out and caught major-league fastballs with his massive bare right hand.

Reflecting his hyper-charged metabolism, Pedro Borbon worked fast, hitting the outside corner for a called strike, then missing the same corner low twice in a row to fall behind in the count to Burleson, 3–1. When he missed again high and outside, Burleson trotted down to first with a free pass.

Sparky Anderson immediately popped out of the Reds dugout and walked toward the mound, as always stepping gingerly over the third base foul line. Bench met him at the mound as Sparky reviewed the situation with Borbon—one out, one on—but he was really there to stall for time as he waited to see who Darrell Johnson was going to send up to pinch-hit for Luis Tiant. Assuming Johnson would bring up a left-handed bat to face Borbon, Sparky had already told Larry Shepard to call the bullpen, where left-hander Will McEnaney was on his feet throwing to backup catcher Bill Plummer. To Sparky's surprise, he glanced back at home plate over Bench's shoulder—and did a double-take when he saw Tiant stepping into the batter's box.

Okay, that makes it easy.

Sparky immediately ended their "conference" on the mound and headed back to the dugout. One out, with a runner on first in the bottom of the sixth, tie game, his entire bench available to him, and his pitcher obviously running out of steam, and Darrell Johnson had decided to let his pitcher bat and, clearly, intended to send him out to start the seventh inning. A few of the Red Sox quietly shook their heads at the decision, questioning their manager's judgment.

Even while leading them to the World Series, Darrell Johnson had been through a rocky season, only his second as a big-league manager. The forty-seven-year-old Nebraska native had knocked around the minor leagues for most of the 1950s, finally sticking with the Yankees in 1957. He was on their roster, although he didn't see any action, for both of the back-to-back seven-game World Series that Casey Stengel's famed pin-striped squad split with Hank Aaron's Milwaukee Braves. After falling back into the minors, and beginning his career as a manager with a St. Louis Cardinals farm team, Johnson began the 1961 season as a bullpen coach for the Cardinals but was fired along with their manager in early July. He was immediately signed as a player by the Phillies, who then traded him a month later to Cincinnati, who were still in the pennant race and in need of an experienced backstop. Johnson played well in twenty games for Cincinnati, and when the Reds clinched their first pennant in twenty-one years, he reached the World Series for the third time, this time *against* the Yankees, and started two games facing Yanks lefty Whitey Ford, going 2–4 against him. The following spring the Reds released him, and he signed with Baltimore, where Johnson's playing career soon ended and he began working as a full-time coach. His peripatetic journey as a baseball lifer continued until he caught on as a coach with the Red Sox in 1968. Three years later he landed the managing job on Boston's Triple-A franchise, where he worked with and developed many future Red Sox stars: Fisk, Evans, Burleson, and Rice. After leading that team to consecutive playoff appearances, Johnson was finally tapped to succeed the popular Eddie Kasko as the organization's major-league skipper prior to the 1974 season.

Although most of the younger players he'd gotten to know in the minors remained loyal to him, Johnson had a harder time convincing the veteran Red Sox corps he'd inherited that he was up to the job. He was a stoic, conservative man to begin with, who didn't like to make a lot of moves on the field, and many of the team's older players felt he managed less to win than he did not to lose. Johnson also battled a drinking problem, a not uncommon fate for men who'd spent most of their adult lives knocking around the minor leagues. Red Sox players cited at least two occasions during the first half of the 1975 season when Johnson showed up at the stadium for a road game stone drunk—once, with a black eye, at seven in the morning— and they'd had to plant him in a corner of the dugout. He often quarreled with longtime Red Sox radio voice Ned Martin, who seldom liked what he saw from Johnson on the field and wasn't shy about saying so on the air. Even Carlton Fisk, who'd benefited more than any other current player from Johnson's tutelage in the minors, felt he wasn't the same manager he'd known in Louisville. Left-handed starter Bill Lee, who had a particularly contentious relationship with the old-school Johnson, felt that their bullpen coach Don "Bear" Bryant, a player-coach under Johnson during his tenure in Louisville, was in Boston largely to help wrangle the manager after hours and between bars. Tensions over strained communications had come to a head between Johnson and his team early on in the 1975 season, when an angry clubhouse meeting nearly resulted in an open player revolt. Johnson was able to smooth things over with them by promising to pay more attention to his veterans' point of view, and when the Red Sox went on a mid-season tear to seize the East Division lead that they never relinquished, winning, as it usually does, rendered most of those fractious disputes a memory. But many still felt they'd won the pennant in spite of their manager, not because of him, and after the Red Sox swept the A's in the Division Series, Johnson had taken no part in their clubhouse celebration in Oakland, remaining in his office, drinking alone with his off-season hunting buddy, A's outfielder Joe Rudi.

Once they reached the World Series, the contrast between the cautious, stone-faced Darrell Johnson and the gregarious, masterful managing style of Sparky Anderson could not have been starker. Firmly in command, acting always with conviction, but the first to admit mistakes if his proactive moves didn't pan out, Sparky handled his team during games like a maestro at the philharmonic. Aware that he'd be facing a notoriously tough and cynical Boston sportswriting corps, Sparky invited them all into his office at Fenway before the Series, and when the *Globe*'s Cliff Keane greeted him as "Busher"—a derisive baseball term used to describe lifers in the minors—Sparky smiled, worked his way through the crowd, and kissed the top of Keane's bald head.

"I just want you guys to know," said Sparky, "that's the way we National Leaguers treat you guys in the American League."

He'd had the press eating out of his hand ever since. With his rapid-fire wit, accessible emotions, aphoristic insights, and cheerfully fractured way with words, Sparky made their jobs so easy they clamored around him like trained seals. Darrell Johnson always showed up dutifully for their scheduled joint press conferences, but appeared to enjoy them about as much as a root canal, and reporters extracted sentences from him with something near the same ease; his lack of eloquence had become something of an inside joke among the working press. For the first time in a World Series, both managers had also agreed—Johnson reluctantly—to wear wireless microphones during the games and to allow their commentary to be used in the highlight film that would be assembled afterward by Major League Baseball. Sparky, predictably, gave them an avalanche of material and insights to work with. Johnson hardly spoke, and as the Series advanced, some of the Red Sox players made a joke out of going up to their manager and periodically cursing into the mic that had been duct-taped to the front of his jacket.

Darrell Johnson often defended his minimalist style of managing—another direct contrast to Sparky—as one that reflected his philosophy about the game itself: When you had players as talented as he did, the best thing a manager could do was set the lineup and get out of their way. Both men's methods had demonstrably worked; here their two teams were, after all, in the World Series. But to the degree that Johnson's reticence also reflected a deeper insecurity in his character, for the first time in Game Six, with his stubborn insistence on sticking with Luis Tiant, this tendency threatened to impact events on the field. Johnson had been Luis's manager when he began his extraordinary comeback in Louisville, benefited enormously from his greatness in Boston during the last two seasons, and had every reason to think the world of his talent, passion, and tenacity. When Johnson had defied the conventional odds and kept Tiant on the mound throughout his struggles in Game Four, Tiant had delivered magnificently for the win that had kept the Red Sox in this Series. But the thought now nagged at the minds of some of Boston's players, most of the press, and many of the fans at Fenway as Luis stepped up to bat in the bottom of the sixth: Had Darrell Johnson allowed his faith in Tiant to lead the Red Sox into danger?

Rose and Perez crept in again from the corners, and before Borbon went into his windup, Tiant squared to bunt, making it clear he was only there for a second straight at bat to sacrifice Burleson to second, where Cecil Cooper might drive him in. But Luis let the first pitch go by, and Davidson called it a strike on the outside corner. Tiant squared again, but watched the next one sail high for a ball, 1–1, and then another came in low, 2–1. Tiant bunted the next pitch foul down the first base line, taking the count to 2–2, then looked down to third base coach Don Zimmer for the sign: A foul ball off a bunt now meant a strikeout, but Zimmer flashed the bunt sign again, Rose and Perez charged in, and Tiant offered on a hard sinker from

Borbon that flanked off his bat, bounced down onto the plate, and kicked directly back over Bench's head.

Foul ball, out on strikes. Two outs now, their runner still at first—Darrell Johnson's gamble, as far as his pitcher's at bat was concerned, had failed.

First baseman Cecil Cooper followed Tiant to the plate. Working briskly, Borbon started him with a sinking fastball, low for ball one. He followed with a fastball that tailed wide outside, then another outside fastball that Cooper fouled off, taking the count to 2–1. Bench moved inside, called for a slider, and Borbon hurled a beauty that cut toward Cooper and nearly sawed off the bat in his hand. He swung defensively and chopped it down into the dirt, resulting in a harmless soft grounder to Morgan at second, who flipped to Perez for the easy out at first to end Boston's sixth inning.

After leading all American League designated hitters for average in 1975, Cecil Cooper had now gone 1–17, still mired in his horrendous World Series slump. Momentum, often invisible to the eye but apparent to any alert baseball sensibility, had firmly shifted to the Cincinnati Reds.

FOURTEEN

If Boston wins tonight, you would have to give the
favoritism in this Series to Boston. But even if they do, don't
bet your car or your house against us. Be very careful.

SPARKY ANDERSON

AFTER THEIR VICTORY IN THE FIRST WORLD SERIES IN 1903, and their second straight American League pennant the following year when the National League's New York Giants refused to play them for a championship, the Boston Americans fell into a brief but steep period of decline. In 1904, after nearly being sold to a popular Irish politician, newspaper mogul and future maternal grandfather of John F. Kennedy, the colorful John "Honey Fitz" Fitzgerald, the Americans were bought by the patrician WASP publisher of the *Boston Globe,* a Civil War veteran named General Charles Taylor. Hopes for improvement were soon dashed when it was revealed the general had purchased the team as an expensive plaything for his ne'er-do-well son John. General Taylor then put the dreamy wastrel in charge of the Americans' day-to-day operations in the hope these new responsibilities would give the boy some purpose in life. (As demonstrated by the Yawkey clan's early ownership of the Detroit Tigers, plutocratic nepotism has always played a major role in the history of professional sports.) No sooner had young John taken over than the 1906 season was marred by a gruesome tragedy: The troubled man Taylor had just named as his manager, Chick Stahl—a newlywed who, one theory suggests, was being aggressively blackmailed by a chippie he'd impregnated the year before—committed suicide during spring training. Undeterred, John

Taylor persisted in establishing his credentials as a clueless, med-dlesome young dilettante with a disastrous eye for talent.

After the Chick Stahl public relations debacle, Taylor decided he should manage the team himself, an idea that league president Ban Johnson immediately nixed; then Taylor ripped through two more bad choices in less than three weeks—the athletic director at the University of Illinois, who sensibly quit once he realized what he'd gotten himself into, and then the team's twenty-five-year-old first baseman, who'd never managed a game in his life—before Ban Johnson "suggested" he hire a more qualified veteran from New York named Jim "Deacon" McGuire. At the conclusion of the next two dispiriting seasons, during which he traded away most of the good players he'd inherited for dead wood, John Taylor decided that what his team needed most was a new look and name to rehabilitate its deteriorating image. Both of Boston's baseball teams bought their uniforms from Wright & Ditson Sporting Goods, the city's preemi-nent sports retailer. The store had become a resounding success for founder George Wright, younger brother and former teammate to Harry Wright, the player-manager who had founded both the origi-nal Cincinnati Red Stockings and, shortly thereafter, the Boston Red Stockings; George Wright had been the star shortstop on both those teams, and would later become an early inductee into base-ball's Hall of Fame. Wright & Ditson was also the store where a short time later a gifted young amateur golfer named Francis Ouimet would begin his professional life, as a stock clerk.

During a visit with George Wright before the 1908 season John Taylor learned that the city's older baseball franchise, the National League's Boston Nationals—the team that had begun life as the Red Stockings in 1871 but was now under new ownership and another name—had decided to give up their traditional red stockings for navy blue. In what is now remembered as the only good decision he ever made during his tenure, Taylor decided on the spot to co-opt the iconic crimson socks for his Americans and change their name to the Boston Red Sox for the 1908 season. Young John then promptly made the worst in his impressive string of bad executive decisions and traded pitcher Cy Young—coming off yet another twenty-win season at the age of forty—to Cleveland for a couple of nobodies and $12,500. In 1911, after his son had gutted the team's once peerless roster, John Taylor's father stepped back into the picture, took the reins from his knucklehead offspring, and the deeper nature of his initial interest in baseball finally came into focus: General Taylor had in the interim become a major shareholder in the Fenway Realty Company, which had bought up most of the usable land reclaimed by the city's massive expansion and engineering project in the Back Bay's boggy "fens" district. Taylor then sold half his interest in the Red Sox, through a shell company built to disguise his participation, to American League owner Ban Johnson. General Taylor then used the cash from that deal to "buy" a prime building site for a new ballpark from Fenway Realty Company, in essence, as one of that company's principal investors, funneling the funds back to himself after a thorough laundering. Taylor then leaned on his friends downtown to issue citywide bonds that paid for construction, and he became the principal owner of the place he decided to call Fenway Park, where the Boston Red Sox began playing ball in the spring of 1912. The new trolley lines to Fenway that the city then compliantly installed brought hundreds of thousands of fans to the attractive new ballpark that season—an exposure that ensured the rapid sale and development of the surrounding reclaimed neighborhoods—which, not coincidentally, also largely belonged to General Taylor and the Fenway Realty Company.

And that, for those interested in the ways of the world, is how the game was, still is, and has forever been played at the grown-ups' table.

THE BOSTON CROWD remained tense and subdued as Luis Tiant trudged out to the mound to begin the seventh inning, and Reds right fielder Ken Griffey dug in to face him. Doubts about whether Darrell Johnson had left his star in too long were raised anew on

Tiant's first pitch, another fastball on the outside corner, that Griffey turned on and whacked past the outstretched glove of Cecil Cooper into right field. Sparky's decision to move Griffey back up in his lineup had paid dividends all night, as he reached base for the third time in four at bats.

As Joe Morgan stepped to the plate, a quick pickoff move from Tiant nearly caught Griffey leaning toward second, but he slid back in safely just ahead of Cooper's tag. Turning his back completely to home on the windup, Tiant fell off to the right side of the mound again with his follow-through, and his first-pitch fastball to Morgan sailed high and away for ball one; his velocity had visibly diminished now as well.

Morgan looked sharp and hypervigilant as he read the signs from third base coach Alex Grammas; in a key at bat in the game, he lived for moments like this. Griffey would not be running now, nor would any other play be put on; Sparky's supreme confidence in Morgan's talent and judgment canceled all other strategies. Since arriving in Cincinnati, Morgan had been given an unprecedented degree of freedom by his skipper, and each year he'd rewarded Sparky's faith with improvement in every facet of his game. Morgan usually called his own plays at the plate, and whenever he was on base he had the green light from Sparky to run at his discretion. In Sparky's mind he'd earned that right.

Tiant threw another fastball, low and over the plate, challenging Morgan. He fouled it back for a strike. The Red Sox closer Dick Drago began to loosen up in the Boston bullpen.

During his career in Houston Morgan had been called selfish, cocky, and a lot worse, but under Sparky Anderson on the Reds he had turned into the most complete second baseman not just of his era but in the history of American baseball. He had just concluded what was arguably the most complete individual *season* ever by a man at his position—Rogers Hornsby in 1922 provided the only compelling competition—and he was about to be rewarded with his first Most Valuable Player award. Since baseball writers began handing out MVPs in 1931, only five had ever been won by a second baseman, the fewest by any position, and the proud Morgan didn't need to be told that no man in the National League had done it since Jackie Robinson in 1949.

Working more deliberately than he had all game, Tiant came at Morgan again with a fastball, one that just missed high for ball two, 2–1.

Anxiety permeated the air in Fenway, eerily silent; over the decades since Tom Yawkey had owned the team, disappointment had become such a central part of rooting for the Red Sox that after the Reds had fought their way back into the game, you could feel the crowd expecting a crushing blow to land.

Tiant took his time again, chasing Griffey back to first with a throw before coming back to the plate—fastball again, all he'd shown Morgan in this at bat—for a called strike on the low outside corner, 2–2.

Now Morgan backed away from the box, agitated—disappointed either with himself for letting that hittable pitch go by or with Davidson's call—glancing down at Alex Grammas for the sign. Morgan missed it the first time, then gestured with irritation at Grammas: *Run through them again.* Morgan read them this time, then stepped back in: With two strikes, would Griffey be going with the pitch?

For Morgan the question was: Would Tiant come back with a fastball again? Morgan seemed to think so. Fisk set up low and outside, and when Tiant's fifth straight fastball came at him, cutting away to the right, Morgan went with the pitch and lined it hard into left field. Yastrzemski made a long run to cut the ball off, but with nobody out, Griffey, who had *not* been running with the pitch, made no move toward third as he rounded second base. Yaz made a hustling play to field the ball quickly and throw it back in to Petrocelli. The Reds had runners at first and second with nobody out.

And Johnny Bench coming to the plate. Ask yourself, how often in the heat of a pivotal World Series game had a pitcher ever had to confront this dilemma? After failing to retire the best second baseman in baseball history, Tiant now had to face the greatest *catcher* who'd ever played the game.

Darrell Johnson headed out of the Red Sox dugout toward the mound, and Fisk moved out to join him. The silence grew more pronounced as the crowd waited to see if Johnson was finally coming with the hook, but it was almost immediately clear that no, Johnson was just out there to talk—review the situation, remind Tiant how to pitch to Bench, maybe buy more time for Drago to get loose. Tiant didn't say a word, just nodded repeatedly, then Johnson patted Luis on the butt and headed back to the dugout. The crowd responded with a smattering of applause that indicated little conviction; they wanted to believe leaving Tiant in was the right move but seemed to have a hard time persuading themselves.

What the hell is he thinking? Sparky said to himself, professionally irritated at Johnson's disregard for the obvious move. *The man's done, get him out of there.*

Tiant went into his windup and threw his first off-speed pitch of the inning, the same sidearm curve he'd used to strike Bench out in the fourth. Bench offered at it then pulled back, just breaking his wrists for a called first strike. Bench immediately turned to ask Satch Davidson if the pitch had actually been in the zone: *Yes,* said Davidson.

That had been Darrell Johnson's message to his pitcher: No fastballs for Mr. Bench. Tiant threw another slow curve, overhand this time, breaking down and away. Bench reached out for it, just as he had in the fifth when he slammed Tiant's first pitch off the Monster, but his right hand came off the bat and he caught a smaller piece of it this time, and the ball floated lazily out toward left, where Yastrzemski backed up and gathered it in on the edge of the warning track for the inning's first out. Griffey, halfway to third, hustled back to second, just ahead of Yaz's quick throw to Burleson covering the bag.

Relief flowed through the crowd; one out now, with the possibility of the inning-saving double play on any ground ball, as Tony Perez came to the plate.

Perez looked to Grammas for the sign, but he and everyone else in the park knew that with the Reds' two fastest men on base, he was there for one purpose: Drive Griffey and Morgan home with power. The Big Dog could put Red Sox fans out of their lingering misery with one swing.

So Perez looked for that first-pitch fastball from Tiant and got one, out over the plate, but he missed the center of the barrel by a fraction of an inch, slicing a catchable ball toward right field. Griffey retreated to second, preparing to tag up as Dwight Evans positioned himself under the dying fly ball, setting up for a throw to third. Once he had it in his glove, the man with the most powerful arm in the business reached back and uncoiled a rifle shot on the fly to the left side of the infield, where Burleson cut it off; Griffey reached third standing up, but Morgan remained at first.

First and third, two outs, still threatening, but Tiant had defused the imminent danger of Bench and Perez with only three pitches. The Fenway crowd stirred back to life; maybe Darrell Johnson's faith in him was justified and Luis's magic could deliver one more out.

George Foster came to the plate, the last of the Reds' big guns. Burleson walked in to consult with Tiant about how to play him, then Fisk trotted out to join them: Morgan was an obvious threat to run at first in this situation, and if he took off for second and Fisk tried to nail him Griffey might break for home on a double steal. Burleson's positioning depended on how they pitched Foster; if he played Foster to pull as they normally did, Burleson couldn't cover second on a throw from Fisk if Morgan made a move. That meant the weaker-armed Denny Doyle would have to cover second and then try to throw home if Griffey ran as well. Their other option was to give Morgan second unopposed and take their chances with Foster and two men in scoring position. In the meantime, Alex Grammas trotted to the dugout to counsel with Sparky: Sparky gave Grammas his orders, and he came back out to whisper them to Griffey and then flash the sign to Morgan.

The Red Sox set up in their normal defensive shift for Foster, shaded to pull. Tiant came in with a fastball in the zone, believing Foster probably had the take sign to facilitate the steal and he could sneak in a strike, and Morgan broke for second with the pitch. The

Red Sox made no move to stop him, but Foster had the green light, swung hard at a hittable pitch, and fouled it straight back to the screen for strike one.

Morgan retreated to first, clear now that the Red Sox would concede second, and as Tiant straddled the rubber, he took an ever bigger lead. Taut with tension, Foster stepped out again, prolonging the moment. When he resumed his stance, Tiant came back with a slow overhand curve that dropped toward the outside corner; but not far enough, maybe his worst pitch of the night. Foster appeared to be ready for something off-speed, because without having to adjust, he reached out and clobbered the ball, a high, towering shot toward deep straightaway center field. Fred Lynn turned and ran, immediately realized it was over his head, then pulled up short and watched it glance high off the center field wall, just below NBC's camera position, about ten feet short of a home run. Lynn fielded the ball cleanly on the first hop off the wall, turned, and fired back to Rick Burleson on the edge of the outfield just as Foster pulled into second base with a stand-up double. Ken Griffey, stationed behind home after he'd scored from third with the Reds' go-ahead run, signaled Joe Morgan to stay on his feet, and the speeding Morgan, who had broken for second again with the pitch, scored easily all the way from first before Burleson had the ball in his glove. Morgan ran right through home plate, didn't slow or turn until he'd reached the foul area behind home, and, pumping his right fist repeatedly, took a little victory lap back to the Cincinnati dugout, where his teammates swarmed around him.

Reds 5, Red Sox 3. George Foster, the only man on Cincinnati's roster who had figured out Luis Tiant in each of his previous starts, had delivered again with the Reds' biggest hit of the game.

The life sluiced out of the crowd in Fenway; that old familiar feeling of delayed but inevitable doom that had first appeared when Fred Lynn crashed into the wall in the fifth inning crept further into their collective spirit. Luis Tiant had given up ten hits and five earned runs now. Watching stone-faced from the silent Red Sox dugout, Darrell Johnson made no move; a second trip out to the mound would make Tiant's removal mandatory under the rules. Dick Drago was more than ready, but Johnson didn't want to bring his closer in now with his team behind. He told Don Bryant to call the bullpen and get left-hander Roger Moret up and throwing.

Davey Concepcion came to the plate with Foster standing on second. The Red Sox on the field appeared almost as stunned as the crowd. Foster took a huge lead off second with no one covering the bag, and when Tiant threw a sidearm fastball outside for ball one, Foster nearly broke for third, more than halfway down the line. Fisk held on to the ball and looked him back to second.

Tiant came back with a slow sidearm curve to Concepcion that missed high for ball two, ahead in the count. Dead silence in the park continued. Concepcion fouled Tiant's next pitch, an outside fastball, straight back for a strike, 2–1.

The only sounds issuing from the fans now were the lonely cries of Fenway's vendors, hawking their wares to a frozen congregation. One of Sparky's early prime objectives had at last been achieved: The Reds had taken Boston's boisterous home crowd completely out of the game.

Tiant came inside with a slider to Concepcion, and he pulled it hard, deep into the hole at short. Rick Burleson, playing Concepcion that way, fielded the ball cleanly, wound up with two short skipping steps, and threw it as hard as he could on a line to Cecil Cooper, beating Concepcion to the bag by less than half a step.

The inning ended, but the damage was done. At the seventh-inning stretch the home team was two runs down and the Cincinnati Reds were nine outs away from winning the World Series.

How would the Red Sox respond?

FIFTEEN

In the seventh inning, fans get up and sing
"Take Me Out to the Ball Game." Most of them
don't seem to realize they're already there.

RED SOX PITCHER BILL LEE

HALFWAY THROUGH THE SEVENTH INNING OF GAME SIX, the contrasting cultures of the two teams in the 1975 World Series, rooted in their histories, had begun to reveal their deepest natures. After the disastrous tenure of owner John Taylor had resulted in a new uniform and nickname and the construction of Fenway Park, in 1912 the Boston Red Sox embarked on the most glorious era in their history, winning four World Series in the next seven years, all in dominating fashion. They did it on the strength of their stalwart Hooper-Lewis-Speaker outfield and the singular presence of a young star pitcher who was about to dominate American sports with a personality as outsized and childlike as a folk hero: George Herman "Babe" Ruth. When recruiting for World War I thinned the ranks of their better hitters, the Red Sox experimentally stuck Ruth in the outfield as an everyday player. Ruth was and always would be a mess off the field, a big, sloppy maladjusted kid with unquenchable appetites, but with a bat in his hand on a regular basis he revolutionized baseball as the game's first home run hitting machine; he whacked twenty-nine of them in his first full season as an outfielder in 1919, an unheard-of total during the dead ball era, when single digits usually led both leagues. At the age of nineteen, fresh out of a Catholic reform school, Ruth had been signed as a pitcher by a middle-aged minor-league owner named Jack Dunn. Because he signed his prospects so young, seasoned baseball men used to call them "Dunn's babes." Like most southpaw pitchers, Ruth arrived as "Lefty," but during his first training camp the "Babe" nickname stuck as a better fit; in time the Italian immigrants from Boston's North Side who grew to worship him would translate that into *Bambino*. In mid-season of 1914 Jack Dunn's team—the Baltimore Orioles of the International League—nearly went bankrupt, and he was forced to sell off his best players to stay afloat; Ruth and two others went to the Red Sox for $25,000 and a legend was soon born in Boston. With Ruth going 18–8—and hitting four titanic home runs; the league's leader, an everyday player, hit only seven—the Red Sox won the pennant and the 1915 World Series. Four years later, just as the "Babe" had joined the outfield and established himself as the coming wonder of the age, he was packaged and sold again, when his immense, emerging talent was matched by the biggest blunder in baseball executive history.

The Red Sox's latest owner, New York theatrical producer Harry Frazee—a name that still lives in New England infamy—found himself strapped for cash after a series of flops and sold Babe Ruth in 1919, after the last of Boston's five World Series wins, to the—until this fateful moment—hapless New York Yankees. At which point the two teams' fortunes reversed directions and never took a backward glance: The Yankees went on to win twenty of the next fifty-six World Series played. In 1975, appearing in just their third World Series since losing Ruth, Boston was still looking for their sixth World Championship. Red Sox fans, once the proudest in early baseball history, by this time suffered from a collective form of post-traumatic stress disorder. Psychologists are just now beginning to study and understand the long-term hazards of emotional involvement with woeful sports franchises and the real deleterious effects that such perceived "social defeat" can have on a community's emotional equilibrium and self-image. By 1975, Boston, it's fair to say, was the first American city to have its case history so thoroughly identified and diagnosed; the city's discerning, intelligent fans had already suffered and exhibited the symptoms for three generations. As the Reds roared back to take the lead in Game Six, and now threatened to abruptly end the 1975 World Series with one of their patented late charges, the fatalistic, internal bargaining that was such an established part of rooting for the Red Sox had already begun throughout Fenway Park.

Fenway's organist John Kiley, who had begun his career accompanying silent pictures in the ornate movie palaces of the 1920s and knew a little bit about how to establish or change a mood, tried to bolster their spirits with his seventh-inning-stretch rendition of "Take Me Out to the Ball Game." The "stretch"—one of baseball's oldest traditions, dating back at least a hundred years—probably began in Cincinnati as a spontaneous gesture inspired by nothing more complex than the physiological necessity to move after two hours of sitting. The song came out of vaudeville in the early 1900s, written by lyricist Jack Norworth and composer Albert Von Tilzer— neither of whom at that point in their lives had actually *seen* a ball game—but was not wedded to the "stretch" until the 1940s, and wouldn't become an annoying, compulsory sing-along until the Chicago White Sox's announcer Harry Caray (by this point in the game often pixilated) began leading fans at Comiskey Park in 1976— a routine quickly standardized at the insistence of the Sox's maverick owner Bill Veeck that then spread throughout baseball. Not many New Englanders in Fenway felt like singing at this point of the night; emotionally leveled, their minds began drifting to the mundane realities of how to beat traffic home at the end of another crushing season-ending defeat. They could walk away from this latest disappointment carrying at least some residue of hope for the team's future, with all those rising young stars on their roster, and once Jim Rice was healthy—well, if only he *had* been healthy, why, we could've beaten *these* guys for sure—and so on, and so on; the tragic inner life of a Red Sox Fan.

In the Cincinnati dugout, attention—already keen—cranked up another notch as the Reds took the field, all their movements sharp, organized, and purposeful. The contrast between the two organizations could not have been more apparent. Cincinnati's systemic obsession with playing the game the right way, with instilling discipline off the field—the short haircuts, the strictly enforced uniform code, the suits and ties on road trips, the insistence on polite public relations—had created a remorseless and efficient killer on the field. No one ever strayed very far off the line in Cincinnati, not even the superstars. During their mediocre start to the 1975 campaign, after Johnny Bench and Reds broadcaster Marty Brennaman had burned the candle at both ends during a night in Montreal—and Bench showed up for the day game that followed the worse for wear—Brennaman had made the mistake of telling Sparky about their eventful evening. Sparky ripped both of them a new one in front of the team; Bench homered in that game and the Reds responded with their longest winning streak of the season, going 41–9 and running away with the West Division. Boys will be boys, but Brennaman learned never to confide in Sparky about their nocturnal adventures again. Bench had always kept a vivid memory of walking through the teams' hotel during their Series matchup with the Oakland A's in 1972 and catching a whiff of marijuana outside the room of one of the biggest A's stars. "I guess we're not in Kansas—or Cincinnati—anymore," said Johnny.

The fractious Red Sox, who had nearly risen in revolt against their manager earlier in the season, seemed almost adolescent by comparison; richly talented but emotionally undisciplined, not truly unified in the regimented, shoulder-to-shoulder way of the Big Red Machine. No player on Boston's roster exemplified this more than their gifted starting pitcher Bill Lee, who had won seventeen games for them now three years in a row, an unheard-of achievement for a left-hander in Fenway Park. Witty, well educated, supremely self-possessed and intelligent, Lee was a USC graduate who had played for and adored the great Rod Dedeaux, becoming the winningest pitcher in school history. Lee was also one of the first committed members of America's baby boomer counterculture to reach stardom in the major leagues. He was descended from two generations of outstanding baseball talent, including his aunt Annabelle Lee, perhaps the greatest pitcher of the women's professional baseball league that briefly flourished during World War II.

A confirmed Southern California kid, Lee enjoyed the intellectual stimulation Boston offered but spent his off-seasons hanging out in Malibu with rock stars like Warron Zevon and the Eagles, dating Hollywood starlets, living the high lifestyle. Very much a product of his time—but way ahead of it in pro sports—Lee was by nature an inquisitive searcher, a committed anti-establishmentarian with articulate socialist leanings. Like most other young red-blooded American athletes he also liked to party, but whenever you handed him the ball he was as fiercely competitive on the mound as any pitcher in the game. No less an authority than teammate Carl Yastrzemski thought that at this point Lee was the best left-handed pitcher in the American League. Lee remained single-mindedly devoted to the game of baseball and its history, particularly the art of pitching; he could, and gladly would, expound on any aspect of his craft for hours. And most of the hidebound, conservative men who had grown up in and now administered or reported on the old school world of baseball—which included most of the people long connected with the Red Sox—thought he was completely out of his mind.

His younger Red Sox teammates gave him a pass—like fellow USC alum Fred Lynn, who greatly benefited from Bill's generosity to him as a rookie, and thought Lee's stream-of-consciousness style with the press was actually good for team morale—and no one appreciated him more than fellow ace Luis Tiant, who recognized and respected any man who played his heart out on the field. Lee did it in a much more vocal and excitable style than the contained and elegant fire of *El Tiante,* but the bond between them as committed warriors who loved the game for its own sake was genuine and strong. Lee just didn't have much of an editing mechanism in place between his nimble mind and mouth, and although Boston beat reporters continually benefited from his willingness to hold court on any variety of subjects—often leading them into elaborate metaphors and tangents within the course of a single answer that pulled in references as disparate as astrophysics, Kurt Vonnegut, and Native American mythology—some of the older and more cynical hacks also wrote many cruel and contemptuous things about him. One disparagingly dubbed him "Spaceman," and the nickname stuck, with time and frequent use rounding into a more affectionate interpretation, and it still sticks to him today. Others liked to mock his off-field habits, like his use of ginseng and honey as an energy source before games, as if that were some kind of punkish rebuke to the old customary amphetamines. Despite all this routine abuse, Lee remained a consistently informative and engaging interview, who continued to cooperate with reporters even after they ripped him; in this way he was also one of the first contemporary athletes to understand that he was not just a performer but an entertainer, both on and off the field. He was also willing to make himself a lightning rod for critical bolts to take the heat off his teammates, as he had when, during a losing streak in the middle of the season, he publicly criticized Boston's reactionary response to the busing crisis. A firestorm of anger at Lee's political point of view ensued, but for the moment fans stopped ragging about the losing streak, and the team's fortunes on the field soon turned around. Lee often answered even the simplest questions in paragraphs, but also appreciated the art of brevity: When asked what he thought of the World Series so far, after the teams had split the first two games in Boston, he simply said: "Tied."

In most ways Bill Lee was much more representative of what had been going on within the fervid baby boomer culture than most of the blinkered athletes in professional baseball, who had been cloistered according to tradition in hermetic, tightly controlled conservative environments since signing their first contracts. That would soon change; only ten days before Game Six the boomer generation had planted one of its most prominent flags in the pop culture landscape when *Saturday Night* debuted on NBC with guest host comedian George Carlin. It's easy to forget now, after its multiple decades as a staple of weekly American programming, that the public had never seen any network show written, produced, and performed almost entirely by and for people under the age of thirty. Savagely satirical, casually hedonistic, a howl of protest and righteous irony

against the straightjacket Nixon-era Silent Majority, the show captured a moment in American time as concretely as Mount Rushmore.
By the time its second episode aired, hosted by singer-songwriter
Paul Simon on the night that Game Six had originally been scheduled to play, John Belushi, Dan Aykroyd, Chevy Chase, Gilda Rad-
ner, and the rest of the original Not Ready for Prime-Time Players
were already on their way to becoming household names. Bill Lee
had been raving about the show to his teammates since its debut.
He'd also been raving about a twenty-five-year-old singer-songwriter
from New Jersey named Bruce Springsteen, who since the release in
late August of his third album, *Born to Run*, had set the music world
on fire. With his gruff, tender, working-class poetry and serious
kick-ass chops, Springsteen and the E Street Band burst on the
American scene like a supernova, articulating the hopes and busted
dreams of the Silent Majority's children, braiding the disparate
strands of rock's varied influences into a singular, inspirational vision. In an unprecedented display of his impact, on the day Game
Six was played editions of both *Newsweek* and *Time* magazines—
America's top national arbiters of conventional mainstream
culture—hit the streets with Springsteen on the cover. Although
earnest, respectable dramas like *Dog Day Afternoon* and *Three Days
of the Condor* were topping the box office on movie screens that fall,
a phenomenon called *Jaws*—directed by twenty-eight-year-old Steven
Spielberg—had opened in July, become the first film in history to
gross over $100 million, and was still rewriting the record books;
in Hollywood's executive offices a new gold rush was already under
way, with producers desperate to cash in on this revealed appetite
for youthful summer blockbusters. Just ahead of that sea change,
operating under the radar in London, a low-budget sci-fi film called
Star Wars had been shooting since March. Like many others of his
age and temperament, Bill Lee and his generation were at this point
well on their way to finding, and raising, their voices.

For whatever reason—education, entitlement, or the arrogance of
youth produced by both—like many of his contemporaries, Lee did
not suffer fools or their authority gladly, and to his way of thinking

most of baseball, and the Red Sox in particular, had more than its share of both, starting with manager Darrell Johnson. Johnson's decision halfway through the weekend's rain delay to push back Lee's scheduled start in Game Six and throw Tiant instead had inspired a furious public tirade from the southpaw. Not unlike the way in which Jack Billingham had gone after Sparky, Lee called out Johnson in the press, calling the decision dumb and gutless, maintaining he should have been allowed to make his start in Game Six while giving Tiant an extra day of rest—which Lee, like few others, knew he needed—before hurling a decisive Game Seven. Missing from Lee's protest was, of course, any possibility that he might not win his Game Six start, but that was part and parcel of his confident makeup. He also knew that a cold, wet night in Boston was tailor-made for the baffling array of off-speed stuff with which, in a brilliant effort, he had held the Reds firmly in check through eight innings of Game Two, before the Red Sox bullpen let the game slip away in the top of the ninth. Darrell Johnson smoothed over Lee's anger to reporters—after unloading on him angrily in private—and stacked all the chips he had left on Luis Tiant as previously announced. Bill Lee was the only Red Sox pitcher Johnson did not dispatch to the bullpen for the start of Game Six, although he hadn't seen fit to use any of those other arms yet, a lack of action that by this point in the evening had driven Lee half-crazy; watching from the dugout, he knew that Luis hadn't had his best stuff since the fifth inning and was out there pitching on guts and guile alone. As the seventh inning stretch ended, Lee couldn't stomach any more and headed back up the tunnel to the clubhouse for some stretching and meditation, part of his usual between-starts regimen. If Game Six turned out to be another season-ending loss, it was all on manager Darrell Johnson as far as Bill Lee was concerned, unless the Red Sox could somehow dig down deeper now than they'd ever had to go and rally to even this Series.

Which, as the home team came to the plate in the bottom of the seventh, appeared less likely than at any other point in the evening; the team, for the moment, looked deflated and stale, stunned by the relentless way in which Cincinnati had caught and overtaken them, almost sleepwalking into the bottom of the seventh. The Reds recognized the symptoms, they'd seen it time and again; opponents absorbed so many body blows from the Big Red Machine by the late innings that they simply lost the will to fight back. That's when the finishers in Sparky's superb bullpen went to work nailing shut the coffin.

Pedro Borbon strode out for his second inning of work on the mound. John Kiley gamely initiated a traditional rallying cry on his Hammond, and the fans tried desperately to encourage them to fight, clapping rhythmically as second baseman Denny Doyle led off the inning. Pete Rose edged in at third, protecting against the possibility of a bunt.

Borbon, who was to put it mildly prone to bouts of overexcitement, had been so pumped up in his first inning that he overthrew a lot of his pitches. He missed here for the same reason with his first fastball, outside for ball one.

A snappy dresser off the field and on the road, Borbon liked to present himself as the model of an upscale businessman, in keeping with the Reds' conservative team philosophy. Whenever they traveled, he always carried an expensive designer leather attaché case in support of that image, a cultivated executive look and style.

Borbon came back with the fastball in on the hands and overpowered Doyle, who swung late, hit it on the handle, and popped up weakly to Dave Concepcion at short for the first out. As Carl Yastrzemski came to the plate, the crowd began to clap again in support of their captain. Borbon came inside with a sharp breaking ball that Yaz thought dropped out of the zone, but Satch Davidson called it a strike. Yaz stepped out of the box, letting Davidson know under his breath, without looking at him, what he thought of the call. Borbon's next pitch, fastball, came in low again. Yaz laid off, and this time Davidson agreed with him, evening the count at 1–1.

But according to his Reds teammates, the only things Borbon ever carried in that fancy briefcase of his were a brick to give it the appearance of heft, a steel comb for his immaculate Afro, and two razor-sharp spurs for the fighting cocks he raised and trained back in the Dominican.

Borbon's next pitch, a nasty breaking ball, fooled Yastrzemski, and he chopped it into the dirt, a weak grounder to Morgan at second, who had to run in to make the play, fumbled it slightly, and fired to Perez as Yaz hustled down the line, out by two steps. Two outs.

Borbon looked completely in control, but Sparky already had his bullpen humming again, getting his twin rookie closers ready, left-hander Will McEnaney and right-hander Rawly Eastwick, the best closing duo during the season in all of baseball.

Carlton Fisk came to the plate, and now the rhythmic clapping from the crowd was down to only a handful of people. Taking a deep breath, checking his bat, knowing this might be his last chance in the Series, Fisk watched the first pitch from Borbon miss outside for a ball. Working quickly, Borbon came right back with a challenging fastball that Fisk swung on and missed to even the count at 1–1.

Throw strikes: That was the mission, for Borbon or any member of Sparky's bullpen at this stage of the game. Don't walk anybody; make 'em put it in play and let that tremendous defense behind you go to work. Borbon came back with another slider thrown with the same sidearm motion as the last fastball, and just as Fisk swung, it dropped out of the zone and he chopped another weak grounder into the dirt, which Davey Concepcion scooped up on the second bounce and chucked to Perez at first.

No sound from the crowd. The seventh inning was over, only the second time in the game that they'd meekly gone out in order, and just like that the Red Sox were down to their last six outs.

Sometimes things go wrong, even when you're doing
your best. That just shows none of us are perfect. So I keep
trying with all my heart, and if that's not good enough,
I'm not going to hang my head.

LUIS TIANT

HE'D THROWN 110 PITCHES IN THE GAME NOW. HIS FAST-ball, landing consistently up in the strike zone, had visibly lost its sting, and the Reds had torched him for eight hits and five runs in the previous three innings. Darrell Johnson's devotion to his team's star pitcher and emotional leader now moved beyond reason as he sent Luis Tiant back out to the mound to start the top of the eighth. They trailed the best team baseball had seen in a generation by two runs, with only two innings left to rally or the Series would be lost. Johnson had a deep, rested, and ready bullpen to turn to in order to keep the game in reach. Watching now on television, each in his own separate clubhouse, pitchers Jack Billingham and Bill Lee—one long done for the night and into his third beer, the other trying to mentally and physically prepare for a tomorrow that might never come—simply couldn't believe their eyes when they saw Tiant emerge from the dugout.

A dread silence from the crowd as Reds center fielder Cesar Geronimo came up to open the inning.

First pitch, fastball, on the inside half of the plate, and Geronimo, greeted by exactly the pitch he was looking for, turned on it. High and deep, just inside the right field foul line. Way back in the seats. Gone. The Reds' eleventh hit off Tiant in the game and Geronimo's second home run of the Series.

Reds, 6; Red Sox, 3.

A cascade of boos echoed around Fenway, not directed at Tiant, but at manager Darrell Johnson as he finally left the dugout to do what everyone else in the park knew should have been done at least an inning earlier. Johnson signaled the bullpen, asked his pitcher for the ball, and as Luis Tiant made the long walk in, the crowd rose for one last standing ovation. Pitching coach and former teammate Stan Williams was the first to greet him, with a handshake and embrace, and the rest of the coaching staff and reserves soon followed. Stoic but clearly downcast, Luis gathered his warm-up jacket and took a seat on the bench. His night, his season, and his World Series were over.

With Reds pitcher Pedro Borbon due up—and for once, no pinch hitters in sight—Red Sox left-hander Rogelio "Roger" Moret rode in and accepted the ball from Darrell Johnson on the mound. The tall, rail-thin, twenty-six-year-old Moret—who uncannily resembled what a young Luis Tiant Sr. might have looked like in his prime—had turned in a brilliant 1975 campaign, his third full year with the team. A native of Puerto Rico, signed as a free agent out of high school, he had, like so many of his Red Sox teammates, found himself as a pitcher while playing for Darrell Johnson in the minor leagues. Moret had been astonishing during his first full season with the Red Sox in 1973, leading the American League in winning percentage with a 13–2 record, but then taken a step back in '74, finishing 9–10. Beginning the 1975 season in the bullpen, Moret reentered the rotation as the fifth starter in late June and down the stretch helped propel the team to the pennant, finishing the year at 14–3, topping the league in winning percentage for the second time in three years. With his record now at 41–18 during his tenure in Boston—and the recipient of a revised mid-season contract from a pleased and generous Tom Yawkey—Moret seemed poised to become a fixture in the Red Sox rotation for years to come.

But something had since gone terribly wrong between Roger Moret and the Red Sox. In the first week of August, at four-thirty in the morning before a night he was scheduled to start a crucial game against the Baltimore Orioles at Fenway, Moret totaled his new Audi

while driving back to Boston from Connecticut, was briefly hospi-
talized with lacerations to his head and scalp, and according to
eyewitness accounts was lucky to be alive. He said he had driven a
cousin who was staying with him home to Connecticut after the
previous night's game, then fallen asleep at the wheel while making
the return trip early that morning, ramming into the back of a logging truck in heavy fog. He was not fit enough in the opinion of the
team to pitch again; for nearly a week after the accident, for the Red
Sox, this turned out to be the final straw. A quiet, friendly man who
had done everything the team had asked him during his stint, Moret,
it now emerged, had all along been contending with a substance
abuse problem. Although neither drugs nor alcohol had apparently
played a part in the accident, serious concern about his emotional
and physical stability now influenced the team's attitude toward
their emerging star. Moret appeared to put the incident behind him
and continued to pitch well in the clutch down the stretch. After
being named to the postseason roster, he secured the team's crucial
win in Game Two of the League Championship Series with a strong
relief outing against Oakland. But Moret was clearly disappointed
when Johnson then passed him over for a starting assignment in
the World Series, and in his only appearance to date he'd given up
the winning hit to Joe Morgan in the tenth inning of Game Three,
when Cincinnati took their first lead in the Series, two games to one.
Johnson hadn't called on him since, and as he entered the game
now, Moret's future with the Red Sox seemed very much in doubt.

After his strong two innings and the heart of his bullpen still in
reserve, Sparky decided to let Pedro Borbon take his at bat against
Moret, and then continue pitching into the bottom of the eighth.
Sparky knew he held an almost unbeatable hand now; a three-run
lead and the ironclad insurance of two aces in the hole: His best
young relievers, with thirty-seven saves on the season between
them—left-hander Will McEnaney and right-hander Rawly
Eastwick—began to loosen in the Reds' bullpen.

Sparky wasn't the only person in Fenway who felt that way. During the commercial break, while Roger Moret finished his warm-up

tosses, NBC's veteran director Harry Coyle consulted with producer Chet Simmons in the command truck under the right field bleachers. It was time, they decided, to prepare for the end of the game and the Big Red Machine's postgame celebration of their first World Series victory. Coyle sent word up to the booth that Tony Kubek should quietly leave the broadcast at the end of the eighth inning and make his way down to the visitors' clubhouse to prepare for interviews with the new world champions. NBC had brought in some expensive state-of-the-art mobile video cameras for this Series—and had periodically used them for shots from unusual angles around Fenway throughout every broadcast—but the bulky, remote radio microphones that had been designed to go with them required extra setup time, and Kubek needed to leave early to get fitted for his rig.

Relief pitchers taking at bats for Captain Hook's Reds were a rare occurrence, but the right-handed Pedro Borbon was the best hitter among them, making it to the plate twenty-seven times in 1975 and batting a more than respectable .292. Dick Stockton, who'd watched Moret pitch throughout the season, made reference to his outstanding fastball and excellent changeup. Pedro Borbon was about to see both of them.

Borbon chopped awkwardly at Moret's first pitch, a changeup that he hammered foul into the dirt. He waved futilely at Moret's second offering—that live fastball Stockton had referred to—after it was already past him. Borbon did manage to just get his bat on the next pitch, another fastball, and squib it down to Cecil Cooper at first, who hustled to the bag and beat Borbon for the first out of the inning.

Pete Rose briskly followed Borbon to the plate. Rose had faced Moret once, during his brief stint in Game Three, drawing an intentional walk before Joe Morgan drove in the game-winning run with his clutch single. The Reds' book on Moret was simple: fastball pitcher with decent, but not great, control; swing hard and early in the count before he can set up his effective change.

Moret went right at Rose with a fastball, which he fouled back to the right side for strike one. Working quickly, Moret threw another fastball high, to even the count. Changing speed—but not his delivery—Moret now came in with his deceptive changeup to the same spot, high and out of the zone, but Rose thought it looked fat and offered on it, and knocked a harmless grounder back just to Moret's right, which he fielded smoothly and threw to Cooper at first for the second out.

Ken Griffey came up for his fifth at bat of the game, and for the third time swung and connected on the first pitch he saw, another Moret fastball, a low-arcing line drive that Fred Lynn loped in on to make an easy catch and end the inning.

The Red Sox trotted in, and the crowd tried to rally them with cheers that didn't carry much conviction. Dick Stockton, who'd seen every game at Fenway that year and often marveled at the fans' willingness to maintain their energy and keep the team emotionally charged, thought that they didn't seem to believe it could happen now; the wind had gone out of them ever since Fred Lynn had crashed into the center field wall in the fifth.

Pedro Borbon began his third inning of work, but McEnaney and Eastwick continued to loosen in the Cincinnati bullpen. The Red Sox had Fred Lynn coming to the plate to lead off in the bottom of the eighth. They hadn't scored a run now since his big homer in the first—they had managed only three hits off the Reds' hydra-headed bullpen—and their great rookie hadn't seemed the same since his collision.

Time was running out. This would be the Red Sox's last, best chance to respond.

FRED LYNN looked a little smoother taking his warm-up swings, starting to feel his legs under him again; after hurtling around American League outfields all season without consequence, this one-sided dispute with the center field concrete had left him physically and mentally shaken, but now the deceptively determined former football star felt back in form.

Starting off the inning, Lynn stepped to the plate in attack mode. He knew the Reds wouldn't be pitching around anybody at this point in the game; no waiting for your pitch now, it was time to hack. Although he had never faced him before, he knew Borbon was a sinker ball pitcher, and that was Lynn's bread and butter.

Johnny Bench called for a low fastball, Borbon delivered; Lynn saw the ball all the way in and drilled it straight back toward the box, where it kicked sharply off Borbon's right shin and caromed all the way to the third base foul line. Borbon chased the ball down and prepared to turn and throw, but Bench saw that Lynn was already too far down the line, so he planted himself between Borbon and first and waved both arms at him to hold on to the ball, trying to prevent an unnecessary throw and possible error that would compound the problem.

The crowd stirred to life. Lynn on first, nobody out, with the first hit they'd managed off Borbon in the game.

Rico Petrocelli came to the plate, and he couldn't wait to get there. They were getting too close to their final out now, and his team was going numb in the dugout, half-beaten, staring straight ahead. Lynn's seeing-eye single had given them a spark of life, but it wouldn't mean anything if he couldn't now follow it up. He also knew full well this might be the last at bat of his career.

Make it count, Rico.

Borbon made a couple of throws to determine if the line drive hitting his leg would affect his delivery. It didn't; at this point a gunshot wound wouldn't have driven the ferocious pitcher off the mound.

Bench set his outfield and called for the sinker. Petrocelli checked his swing and bounced Borbon's first pitch high off the plate; quick as a cat Bench had the mask off and pounced on it, but the ball landed just past the on-deck circle along third, in foul territory for strike one.

A chant began in the depths of the outfield at Fenway and slowly spread around the park: "Rico, Rico, Rico!"

Borbon came back with the sinker, low for ball one, evening the count. Bench wanted a ball on the ground, looking for the double play to kill this threat hard and fast, so he stayed with the call. Rico fouled Borbon's next sinker straight back, behind in the count 1–2.

Rico was down to his last strike.

Another sinker, this one low and away—"Good eye, Rico!"—and the count evened at 2–2. Full life from the crowd now, which rose even higher when Borbon missed again with the sinker.

Full count, 3–2. Sparky was up off the bench now, pacing, hands thrust in his pockets, feet kicking at the ground. He almost couldn't bring himself to watch.

Bench changed things up: called for the fastball high and in, and Borbon hit the target. Still looking for a ball low, Rico was hand-cuffed, but he managed to square around and fight it off, foul, and keep his at bat alive.

Another fastball, on the outside corner, another half-desperate swing from Rico, just nicking a fraction of the ball, fouling it down into the dirt and back.

The crowd seemed to know: This is the at bat. This is where it has to happen. This is where Rico has to come through for us, like he has so many times over the years. He'd always played the game with openhearted passion, that's what New England's fans loved about him, a big part of how and why he could deliver so often in situations like these . . .

And there it was: Borbon's sinker didn't sink—it looked as if he'd failed to firmly plant into his follow-through; maybe that line drive to his right leg was starting to bother him—and missed high for ball four.

Petrocelli trotted down to first with the walk—a tenacious, bat-tling at bat—and Lynn moved over to second. First and second, no-body out.

Right fielder Dwight Evans was due up next, all of a sudden rep-resenting the tying run for the Red Sox. Sparky had seen enough. He hopped up the steps and strode to the mound, signaling for his right-hander, Rawly Eastwick, who grabbed his jacket and slid it over his warm right arm, refused a ride from the waiting baseball golf cart, and jogged in toward the mound.

Rawlins Jackson Eastwick the Third, three days shy of his twenty-fifth birthday, had just completed a sensational rookie season, doing most of his work after the All-Star break, when he overtook teammate Will McEnaney and tied for the National League lead in saves with twenty-two. Eastwick had been in the Reds organization since 1969, an intelligent, aloof, upper-middle-class kid from suburban New Jersey who was an odd duck in the jockocracy of the Reds' blue-collar locker room. He liked to read, write, paint still lifes and landscapes, and instead of hitting the bars preferred antiquing when they were on the road, but he had delivered consistently between the lines down the stretch and saved his best stuff for last; Eastwick had recorded the win for the Reds in both Game Two and Game Three of the Series, pitched three scoreless innings that kept them in Game Four against Tiant until the final out, and nailed down Don Gullett's win in Game Five with a save. This would be his fifth appearance in the six games they'd played, and most of the writers and broadcasters in attendance felt that if he came in and put out the fire here to finish off the Red Sox, Rawly Eastwick was hands-down their choice for the World Series' Most Valuable Player. Few doubted that he would do just that. Up in the press box, sportswriter Dick Schaap had already started to collect the ballots; this thing, the game's senior scribes had decided, was all but over.

Dwight Evans would have something to say about that. He'd faced Eastwick three times in the Series, striking out swinging to end a late threat in Game Two, then tagging him for his dramatic two-run ninth-inning home run that sent Game Three into extra innings, and flying out to deep center in Game Four. Evans liked the matchup, felt he saw the ball well out of Eastwick's hand, and the success he'd had earlier against him filled him with confidence.

Sparky handed Eastwick the ball, left him to the moment, and the pitcher completed his warm-up tosses out of the stretch to Bench.

Lynn at second, Petrocelli at first; both had a feeling Dewey Evans was about to come through, and so did the rest of the Red Sox lined up along the top step of the dugout. The crowd shared that feeling, and most rose to their feet as Evans stepped into the box. The Reds and their coaches moved around restlessly, prowling the dugout; Pedro Borbon couldn't bring himself to abandon this confrontation for the clubhouse and stayed on the bench to watch. The game's unique pendulum swing of desultory lulls and tense, antici-patory highs had reached its zenith in Fenway Park.

Eastwick's first pitch betrayed a hint of butterflies, an incomplete delivery that sent his fastball flying high and tight. He was a classic power pitcher, threw a hard fastball with movement in the zone that tailed or even seemed to rise, and when he was on—as he had been for much of the last three months—Eastwick was as close as a pitcher can get to unhittable.

Eastwick challenged Evans with his second fastball, and Dewey swung from his heels, a home run cut that nearly knocked off his helmet, but he missed it low for strike one. Eastwick came back with the same pitch and same location—running in on Evans's hands—and he fouled it back to fall behind in the count, 1–2.

Eastwick had pleasantly surprised the Reds with his dominant second-half surge; most of Bob Howsam's brain trust had thought he was a season or two away from meaningful innings, but every so often "the light just goes on"—as Sparky put it—and a major leaguer suddenly arrives. Eastwick's confidence snowballed, and he ex-plained his surprising success this way: "I never have a negative thought. This radiates to the hitter. He can feel it when you know you're going to get him out."

Evans fouled Eastwick's next fastball back as well, a more defen-sive swing to stay alive against Eastwick's pure smoke. Eastwick really leaned into his next pitch, another fastball that missed just outside, and cracked into Bench's mitt with an audible thump: 2–2. Bench signaled he wanted the next one inside, and the runner snaked in on Evans's hands, and again he fought it off foul to stay even in the count.

Then Eastwick came back with a dart, his first low pitch of the at bat, a fastball that appeared to crease the zone right at Evans's knees, but Satch Davidson wasn't buying; Bench and Eastwick looked disappointed—Bench appeared ready to dispute Davidson's sanity, but bit his tongue—and the count went full to 3–2.

The whole stadium was on edge now. Eastwick reared and delivered a searing fastball toward the outside corner. Evans couldn't lay off it, swung hard, and missed.

Down on strikes, one out.

The burden now fell to Red Sox shortstop Rick Burleson, but the stakes changed; nowhere near the home run threat that Evans represented, he'd hit only six all season. The Rooster would have to go station to station, manufacture something, poke it past the infield, get Lynn around from second, score one run at a time.

In the home dugout, manager Darrell Johnson walked over to his reserve outfielders Bernie Carbo and Juan Beniquez and told them each to grab a bat. He ordered the left-handed-hitting Carbo out into the on-deck circle, to pinch hit for Roger Moret if Burleson avoided a double play and the right-hander Eastwick stayed in the game. If Sparky played the percentages, as Johnson expected him to, and brought in his own left-hander McEnaney to face Carbo, the right-handed Beniquez would be sent to the plate in his place. Carbo had been periodically swinging a weighted bat and stretching back in the clubhouse since the fifth inning; the routine of the dedicated pinch hitter. Although he'd only been to the plate two times in the Series against his former teammates, Carbo had already contributed: In the seventh inning of Game Three in Cincinnati, pinch-hitting for pitcher Reggie Cleveland, Carbo had homered off Reds right-hander Clay Carroll, bringing the Red Sox within two runs and setting the stage for Dwight Evans's game-tying home run two innings later. Surely Sparky wasn't going to make the same mistake twice; Carbo felt certain he was on the field primarily as a decoy to force Sparky's hand.

Eastwick came in low to Burleson—Bench was looking for that ground ball and double play again now—and missed for ball one.

Then, a flash of hope: fastball up in the zone, a hard swing from Burleson, and a line drive toward the Green Monster. But hope died quickly; he'd caught only half of the ball on the bat, and George Foster scarcely had to move to gather it in for the second out.

Two on, two out, bottom of the eighth, down three runs. Four outs left in the game and their World Series.

From the public address system booth, Sherm Feller announced "Pinch-hitting for Moret: Bernie Carbo." Fully expecting Sparky—whom he knew very well—to now emerge from the dugout and pull Eastwick for McEnaney, Carbo hesitated in the on-deck circle, anticipating the move from Sparky for so long that umpire Satch Davidson finally growled at him: "Come on, get in here, time to hit!" Looking across at the Cincinnati dugout, Carbo finally realized that Sparky wasn't coming out for his pitcher; he was unaware that Sparky, concerned that the right-handed pull hitter Beniquez might hit one to the wall on McEnaney, had made the decision to stay with Eastwick and take his chances with the erratic Carbo. Struggling to quickly gather himself, Carbo turned to his old friend Johnny Bench.

"Wow," said Carbo. "I'm gonna hit."

Only twenty-eight and already in the eleventh year of his professional career, Carbo had been such a highly regarded prospect coming out of high school in his native Detroit that the Cincinnati Reds had made him their number one pick, and sixteenth player taken overall, in the first amateur free agent draft in 1965—one round ahead of that superstar playing catcher for them now, Johnny Bench. Two years later, Bench had already established himself as the Reds' starting catcher, while Carbo was still languishing in the minors, where teammates on his first two teams had nicknamed him the "Idiot" and the "Clown." As those labels suggested, Bernie suffered from some educational shortcomings and concentration issues. He appeared to be a loose, fun-loving, and lovable working-class kid, but his baggage also included an ungovernable temper, an insidious substance abuse problem, and enough personal demons to populate a psych ward; Bernie had grown up with an abusive, alcoholic father and, by his own reckoning, had become an alcoholic himself by the age of sixteen. But baseball, in those days, had its own habit of looking the other way as long as players produced on the field; amphetamine use to fuel flagging energies through baseball's marathon seasons remained an established part of major-league locker room culture. Jars of amphetamine "greenies" stood readily available—often even a designated water cooler was juiced—at the trainer's table in every clubhouse. "Don't go out there alone" was the veterans' coded phrase for taking their boost. And if the boys needed or wanted to wind down afterward by spending their recreational hours drunk, high, or any combination thereof, nobody was going to say boo about it. In other words, Bernie fit right in.

And Carbo soon began to produce. He recorded his best season in the Reds' system in 1968, for Sparky Anderson's pennant-winning team in Triple-A Asheville. Sparky insisted on calling him "Bernardo," moved him from third base to the outfield, and for the first time in his life treated the boy like a man—Sparky came to regard Bernie almost as a son—while expecting him to act like one in return. He disciplined Bernie hard, drilled him on the fundamentals, sure of his natural talent, equally determined not to allow this screwup kid to let it go to waste. Although he initially rebelled under Sparky's tough love, Carbo credited Anderson with teaching him to grow up, how to approach and play the game like a professional; Sparky single-handedly turned the class stooge into a ballplayer. The first in a series of surrogate fathers Carbo desperately needed and would find in baseball, Sparky frequently invited Bernie into his home, where Sparky's wife Carol and their two young sons and daughter adopted him as well. One season later, after an exceptional year in Triple-A, Carbo made the big club during Sparky's first year at the helm in Cincinnati and more than fulfilled the organization's high expectations of him; he hit .310, with twenty-one home runs and sixty-three RBIs, played in his first World Series with the Reds, and the *Sporting News* named him the National League Rookie Player of the Year. A storybook beginning and a once wayward promise fulfilled, but it went nowhere but downhill from there.

Hoping to buy a house and make Cincinnati his home, Carbo was bitterly disappointed when after his outstanding rookie season the hard-line Reds front office refused to renegotiate his contract. Without the benefit of counsel a good agent would have afforded, Bernie ill-advisedly held out until near the end of spring training and slumped badly when he signed and reported, out of shape both physically and mentally. His drug and alcohol use accelerated, and both his performance and playing time plummeted; this was no ordinary sophomore slump. During another acrimonious contract negotiating session the following spring with GM Bob Howsam, Carbo lost control of his senses; he reached over, grabbed Howsam by the tie, dragged him across the desk, and began to beat and choke him. People rushed in to yank him off and hustle the still raging Carbo out of Howsam's office; at Howsam's insistence the incident was covered up and never publicly revealed, but a month into the 1972 season, the Reds unloaded Carbo in a dismissive trade to St. Louis. After two mediocre seasons with the Cardinals, Carbo was dealt again in the fall of 1973, going to the Red Sox along with starting pitcher Rick Wise. During his first visit to the Red Sox clubhouse at Fenway, Carbo saw an old man in a tattered raincoat shuffling around, handed over a twenty, and asked him to fetch him a cheeseburger and fries. The food arrived soon afterward, delivered by a locker room attendant who clued Carbo in that he had just placed his order with team owner Tom Yawkey.

As a fourth outfielder and left-handed designated hitter, Carbo became a steady contributor to the 1974 Red Sox, hitting twelve home runs and driving in sixty-one, finding much more common ground in the team's looser clubhouse than he had with the regimented Reds and Cardinals. Kindred free spirits Bill Lee, Rick Wise, and Jim Willoughby welcomed him into their playfully anarchic circle. Carbo found a comfort zone as the Red Sox's informal court jester, delighting the press with his goofy, offbeat pronouncements: "If baseball execs are Nixon," he once told them, "I'm Woodstock." Bernie soon took to traveling everywhere with a stuffed toy gorilla that he dressed in a Cardinals uniform and named "Mighty Joe Young," often deferring to the monkey in interviews. Hoping to now make a home in Boston, and with his wife pregnant with their second child, Carbo made a personal appeal after the 1974 season to

Tom Yawkey, who had subsequently befriended him after their awkward introduction, for a $10,000 raise. Team officials offered him $4,000—Yawkey always avoided turning players down himself—and Carbo became the first Red Sox player to file for the newly available option of independent salary arbitration. He lost the arbitration, but the next week found a check in his locker, from the personal account of Tom Yawkey, for $10,000. Bernie and his wife bought their house; he had found another father figure.

In 1975, Carbo retired the gorilla and replaced him with a statue of the Buddha, which he kept in his locker, another good luck talisman the team adopted. Carbo came out of spring training with a hot bat and helped carry the Red Sox during the first two months of the season when Carlton Fisk was injured, finishing the year with fifteen homers and fifty RBIs in 107 games. He played a solid outfield, and always had a strong, accurate throwing arm, but with the emergence of Rice, Lynn, and Evans he found it increasingly difficult to break into the everyday lineup. As his dependence on drugs and alcohol deepened, along with the severity of his hangovers, he also lacked the conditioning to go out there every day. By September, beset by a couple of nagging injuries, convinced he'd never get out of Darrell Johnson's doghouse, Bernie hardly got off the bench and his attention appeared to drift; on occasion, while on the road, other players sometimes wondered if Bernie even knew what ballpark they were in. Bill Lee speculated that, in Bernie's case, ignorance might actually be an asset; the less thinking he did at the plate, and the more pure reacting he could bring to bear on major-league fastballs with his lightning-quick wrists and Popeye forearms, the better.

In the Boston bullpen, Red Sox closer Dick Drago was warming up on the mound and had already been told by the dugout that he was going in to pitch the ninth. Absent the usual tension of a closer's close-game situation, Drago had been throwing a pitch, then turning to watch the game like any other spectator, hoping against hope they could find a way to get back in it. Back in the clubhouse, when Bill Lee saw on television that Bernie had actually made it to the plate in the bottom of the eighth of Game Six, against the fireballing Eastwick, with Lynn and Petrocelli on base, he hurried back to the Red Sox dugout to watch their confrontation.

BOSTON FANS had developed a genuine affection for Bernie Carbo, and they cheered him wildly as he dug in at the plate; Bernie didn't often feel in control of much at this stage of his life, but he came the closest when he had a bat in his hand.

Eastwick stared in at Bench. Fred Lynn watched closely as he took his lead off second. Eastwick surprised Bernie with a moving fastball that broke to the outside corner. Davidson called strike one.

The book on Bernie was to bust him with fastballs inside, then get him to chase low and away; his power was almost exclusively to the opposite field. Carbo had grown up as the only left-handed hitter in his neighborhood, where they were often short of kids to field complete teams; right field, as a result, was the first position vacated, which meant any ball hit in that direction became an automatic out. So Bernie grew up learning to hit the other way and muscle the ball to left—the home run he'd hit in Game Three at Riverfront had been a towering shot to left field—and since coming to Boston he'd made the Green Monster his best friend.

Now Eastwick came back inside and low for a ball, 1–1.

Joe Morgan turned, saw that his outfielders had crept in too far, and urgently waved them back; the only run that mattered now was the tying one, the man at the plate, and he wanted his defenders arrayed in the deepest parts of the park to take away extra bases if Carbo managed to hit one in the gap.

Eastwick delivered another smoking fastball inside and higher, just missing the corner; Bernie didn't appear to pick up the pitch out of Eastwick's hand and reacted late but laid off it, and Davidson called ball two.

Bernie Carbo had never exactly qualified as someone living the examined life, but the sight of his old teammates and manager when the World Series began in Fenway Park inspired some perspective-taking. During a workout on the field the day before Game One, Bernie sought out Sparky, asked if he could speak to him, just the two of them alone for a moment sitting on a grounds-keeper's bench in the outfield. In his typically endearing, fumbling way Bernie tried to apologize for the terrible behavior that ended his time with the Reds, and how he felt he had betrayed the fatherly care and affection Sparky had shown to him.

"You said to me then that someday I'd be playing for somebody else and that I'd see that you cared about me, that you cared about what happened to me then and later in my life. I was immature then, and didn't understand what you meant. Now I do."

Bernie had to pause for a moment to control his emotions. Sparky kept quiet for the same reason.

"And I just wanted to thank you," said Bernie finally. "For everything you did for me."

After two pitches inside, Bench called for the cutter on the outside corner, and Eastwick threw his purest pitch of the night. Bernie swung for the fences, late, missed by a foot, and looked terrible doing it. As he watched from first base, Rico Petrocelli's guts churned; no way Carbo was catching up to this guy's fastball tonight. Two balls, two strikes.

Sparky took his time responding to Carbo; he still didn't know the full extent of Bernie's substance problems, and would be shocked when he eventually did. Given the interest he'd taken in Bernardo, his shamed departure from the Reds had been one of the manager's greatest personal disappointments. But Sparky had been doing some perspective-taking of his own in the last few years. He'd always concealed his own feelings from the people he lived and worked with, just as his father had done; that's what men who'd grown up during the hard times of the Depression had done by necessity. You did what's right; you obeyed and enforced the rules as you'd learned them, whether your employees or kids liked it or not. Much of the anguish between fathers and sons during the tumultuous sixties and early seventies had resulted from this rigidity, and for Sparky it had come at a painfully personal cost; after he bullheadedly insisted that his teenage son, Lee, cut his long hair—and Lee just as stubbornly refused—an awful yearlong estrangement had resulted. Sparky loved his son dearly—it had truly broken his heart—and they had only just recently reconciled, after another blowup between them ended in a transcendent moment of insight and forgiveness: Sparky realized and admitted he'd been wrong.

"I was putting my image of what was right ahead of my love for my son. I was ashamed of myself. I was being the child, and Lee was being the man. I wasn't man enough to father my own child."

That moment changed Sparky for good; and he had vowed never to hide his feelings again. He was also living with the knowledge that one of his closest friends—Milt Blish, the LA car dealer who had given Anderson a life-saving job when his playing career ended and before his managerial career began—was dying of cancer, and facing his mortality with a grace and courage that had inspired Sparky to reevaluate many of his own hard-driving values. The human connections are what matter most in life, he'd come to realize, maybe they're *all* that matter; certainly more than anything to do with a *game.* He had already told Milt that he would dedicate whatever happened in this World Series to him, and for the first time in his own life, Sparky felt at peace with himself; in other words, it was a perfect moment for this conversation with Bernie Carbo to occur.

"Bernardo," he said. "I appreciate what you've told me, but let me tell you something. If you've grown up, I think I had some growing up to do too. We all have our faults. And as soon as we realize that, we become what is known in our society as a man."

They shook hands, neither of them entirely dry eyed, and wished each other luck.

Now Sparky stepped up onto the top step of the Cincinnati dugout, hands thrust deep in his pockets, to watch Carbo closely; Bernardo had always been a more dangerous hitter with two strikes. Some strong intuitive voice told Sparky to march out there, right now, yank Eastwick and bring in McEnaney. Sparky always listened to that voice, had learned to trust his instincts implicitly; that, finally, is all a manager has to rely on, what Stengel and Dedeaux had taught him from the beginning of his life in the game, the margin that separated the good from the great.

People won't even remember half the moves you make that work, but they'll never forget or forgive you for the ones you *didn't* make.

Sparky didn't move.

Eastwick delivered another fastball, low and outside, Carbo late on the swing again, just sending it foul into the stands past third.

Go out there now, said the voice again. *Make the change and McEnaney will strike him out.* But Sparky's eyes saw his pitcher dominating a hitter, completely on top of him, Bernardo barely able to get the bat around on the ball.

One more pitch, said Sparky to himself. *I'll give him one more.*

Bench set up back inside, and Eastwick uncorked a nasty moving cutter headed for the inside corner, running right at Carbo's hands. At the last possible instant Bernie chopped down at it awkwardly, the ball nearly past him already, and nicked it just as it was about to land in Bench's glove; the ball glanced sharply down off the plate and bounced away foul. The swing came so late that Satch Davidson had already begun to call out "Ball three," then changed midstream to "Foul ball!" Bench didn't hear him make the second call, and yelled at Davidson that Carbo had made contact; as they sorted that out, Bernie stepped out of the box and tried to breathe.

The crowd seemed to lose its breath also; the tension unbearable, their prospects too dim. At third base, Red Sox coach Don Zimmer had to look away; that was one of the worst swings he'd ever seen. Pete Rose caught the pained look on Zimmer's face and smiled; Carbo looked like a Little Leaguer against Eastwick's wicked stuff. At second and first, Lynn and Petrocelli felt their hearts sink; Bernie's swing had actually looked worse with each succeeding pitch. In the Red Sox dugout, Fisk and Yastrzemski glanced at each other and shook their heads: not tonight. On the top step of the Cincinnati dugout, Sparky stayed put; he couldn't pull Eastwick now, not after his best pitch of the night. As he settled back into his stance, Johnny

Bench had one thought about his old pal Bernie: *He's done.* In the press box, an entire row of America's best sportswriters winced, and immediately began chasing down metaphors to convey the sheer naked ugliness of Carbo's last swing. In the broadcast booth next door Tony Kubek expressed a wiser and more practical perspective: Bernie had protected the plate, fought off a hellacious pitch, and he was still alive.

I just took the worst swing in the history of baseball, thought Bernie, as he stepped out of the box to regroup.

Perhaps, but Bernie, for all his troubles—maybe because of them—still possessed any hitter's most valuable asset: He always stayed in the moment, when all that mattered was the next pitch. A pitcher usually didn't make more than one mistake to a hitter in an at bat, and it was the hitter's job to be ready for it whenever he did.

And Bernie knew beyond certainty that after that nasty unhittable inside slider, his old minor- and major-league teammate Johnny Bench would come back with the fastball away.

Bench said afterward that his pitchers had thrown only two bad pitches in the entire game. The first was Nolan's first-inning fastball to Fred Lynn.

Eastwick's next fastball was the second.

No movement, belt-high, a mediocre pitch over the heart of the plate. Bernie committed to the swing so early he fully extended his arms and actually *pulled it.* Bernie was so unused to seeing a ball he'd hit go anywhere near right center field that he had no idea where it would end up—it didn't *feel* as if he'd even hit it that hard—so he sprinted down the line, where the first thing he registered made him realize, maybe, could be, yes: Center fielder Cesar Geronimo was turning his back to watch. Stationed off second, Fred Lynn looked up, saw the ball soaring overhead, and just knew. Rico Petrocelli, headed cautiously toward second, wasn't sure until he nearly got to the base, and by then, every other living soul in Fenway had leapt to their feet in astonishment and joy, because Bernie Carbo had just deposited Eastwick's fat fastball over the wall ten rows into the seats of deepest right center for a three-run pinch-hit homer with two outs in the bottom of the eighth inning and tied the god damned game.

People claimed you could hear it a mile away: The loudest explosion of sound even Tom Yawkey had ever heard in his ballpark erupted from Fenway, surely the biggest sonic event in the open air of Boston since Francis Ouimet sank a putt at the nearby Country Club in Brookline in 1913 to win the U.S. Open. The deafening ovation never let up as Bernie flew around the bases in a trance. Hands on hips, Rawly Eastwick stared out at right center field in shock and disbelief. As he passed Pete Rose near third, Bernie shouted, almost incoherently: "Don't you wish you were this strong, Pete? Ain't this fun?"

Pete had to smile at the little fuckup: "Yeah, this is fun, Bernie."

Bernie shook hands with Red Sox coach Don Zimmer as he rounded third, then crossed home plate, chest thrown out with pride like a sprinter at the finish line, welcomed by Lynn and Petrocelli, and they gathered him up and ran him back to the Boston dugout, Bernie thrusting his fists in the air as the crowd continued to roar and his teammates grabbed him and carried him down the steps into their swarming arms. Bill Lee stepped up and pointed three times out toward where the ball had left the park, fixing the moment in memory, then immediately retreated to the clubhouse for treatment on his arm, convinced they would win it now, and that he'd be pitching Game Seven on Wednesday night. Carbo had not only tied the game, he'd also tied a record that had stood since 1959: two pinch-hit home runs in a single World Series. But in the history of baseball, no one had ever hit one quite like this.

Out in the bullpen, Red Sox closer Dick Drago, watching from the mound, where he was warming up to pitch what he thought would be a meaningless top of the ninth to close out a losing World Series, along with the rest of Boston's relief corps went berserk when they saw Carbo's ball land in the stands near them. "Then it hit me, the giant butterflies started," said Drago. "I'd be coming into a tie game in the ninth, instead of mop-up duty. That's what any closer wants, the game to be on the line; I pitched better. But I had some work to do now to get my game face on."

Darrell Johnson, the first man in a Red Sox uniform to get his head back in the game as the jubilation around him continued, calmly told Bernie to grab his glove; he was going in to play left field in the top of the ninth. Yaz would move to first base and the new Red Sox pitcher, Dick Drago, would hit in the next man's slot. The cheering had abated only slightly as Cecil Cooper stepped into the box—with an impossible act to follow—for his final at bat of Game Six.

Eastwick, cold and furious at himself, came right after him with high heat. Cooper fouled the pitch back. Working quickly, Eastwick went high fastball again, another late foul ball. Then came the slider, Cooper swung, missed badly, and that was that; three pitches, three strikes, and the third out, one man too late. Bench tossed the ball, now an object of contempt, back toward the mound. Young Eastwick looked stunned as he walked in; a negative thought, it appeared, had finally occurred to him.

In the improbably resuscitated, celebratory air of Fenway Park, only one man blamed himself: in the Cincinnati dugout, Sparky, nearly doubled over in pain and despair and disbelief that he hadn't listened to the voice. Why? Why? Why?

Here came the top of the ninth, and, for the second time that night, it was a whole new ball game.

No one goes anywhere in life without talent.
No one becomes a champion without confidence.

SPARKY ANDERSON

THREE WEEKS BEFORE GAME SIX THE ENTIRE SPORTING world had been enthralled by an extraordinary heavyweight championship fight, the third between reigning champ Muhammad Ali and his dogged nemesis Joe Frazier. This was the rubber match of their bitter rivalry, and the brutal showdown, contested in the hundred-degree heat and high humidity of the Philippines, ended when Frazier, his eyes swollen blind from a fearful beating, wasn't allowed by his loyal trainer, Eddie Futch, to answer the bell for the fifteenth and final round. Ali fainted in the ring when it was over, and both men ended up in the hospital that night; Ali claimed he'd never been so close to death. They had billed their fight as "The Thrilla in Manila," and it more than lived up to the hype, the last time a heavyweight match could be considered a global cultural event, and if there had been any doubt remaining, this victory cemented the legitimacy of Ali's repeated claims for himself as the "greatest of all time." His universal fame, and social influence in America, had reached its apex. Many of the same top sportswriters who'd covered that fight were in attendance for Game Six, and the dramatic ebb and flow of what was unfolding this night at Fenway began to remind more than a few of the battle they'd witnessed earlier in the month halfway across the world.

It was after eleven-thirty Eastern time now, but as phones rang off the hook across America relaying news of Bernie Carbo's unlikely heroics, the number of sets switched to NBC's coverage of

Game Six spiked to the highest level the network had ever recorded for a World Series game; more than 76 million people were now tuned in to watch, riveted as the Reds came to bat in the top of the ninth. Joe Garagiola announced that Johnny Carson and *The Tonight Show* would not be seen on NBC that night, as the game continued toward the witching hour.

Sparky still felt sick inside, physically anguished: *All my fault. All my fault.* He had *never* ignored the voice before, and look at the devastating result. He glanced over at his batting coach on the bench, Ted Kluszewski—Klu had been through all the team's recent disappointments as a coach—and for the briefest moment Sparky let his feelings show, convinced that he had just cost his team another World Series.

This is like being in an axe fight, and coming in second.

Sparky choked back his pain and remorse, clapped his hands, and tried gamely to rally his men as they clattered back into the dugout; they had the heart of their lineup due now, time to forget what just happened, as the Big Red Machine had been able to do time and again during its run, and go back to work.

The new Red Sox pitcher Dick Drago made his final warm-up tosses on the mound. Since being traded to the Red Sox from the Royals two years earlier, the thirty-year-old Drago had split his time between the starting rotation and the bullpen. After they'd selected him out of the Tigers system in the 1969 expansion draft, he'd spent five years as a starter for the fledgling Kansas City franchise. He'd become the lead sled dog on their staff, and pitched well—going 17–11 in his best year—but perpetually suffered from a lack of offensive support on a new team trying to build itself from scratch. So Drago had welcomed the move to the contending Red Sox, and Darrell Johnson put his strong arm to immediate good use. In this era before the extreme specialization of pitchers—which Sparky was just now instituting with the Reds as the wave of baseball's future—it was far more common to see pitchers move freely between the bullpen and the starter's role, but it often put them in an awkward limbo that made their contributions harder to value. Drago had pitched effectively as a starter for Johnson in 1974, but the numbers he posted and the kind of pitcher he was—a pure power fastball pitcher—suggested he might have more to offer in shorter stints closing out games; his ERA in relief that season was a dominating 1.37. When Rick Wise returned from injury as a key starter for Boston in '75, Drago made a full-time move to the bullpen, and by the time of the stretch drive he had established himself as one of the better relievers in the American League, finishing fifth with fifteen saves. He had gone on to pitch brilliantly in the Championship Series against Oakland, earning a save in the last two games of the Red Sox three-game sweep over the A's.

A fiery guy, with a big deep voice and personality to match, Drago wore his hair long and sported a piratical black mustache, so he also had the look of the era's dominant firemen down pat. Almost all favored elaborate facial hair; the nineteenth-century presidential whiskers of Goose Gossage, the lush Cossack foliage worn by Al "The Mad Hungarian" Hrabosky, and the famously fastidious handlebars of Rollie Fingers. Drago also possessed what has since been defined as the ideal psychological makeup for a closer: He thrived in pressure situations, and, limited to a smaller number of pitches per game by definition of his role, he enjoyed going after the game's best hitters with unadulterated heat.

One of the best in all of baseball came to the plate as Joe Morgan led off the inning. Drago threw him a fastball that ran just outside for a ball.

By his own admission, Morgan had been pressing at the plate during the Series games in Boston, but as the leadoff batter in a late-inning tie, his job was to get on base any way he could manage; Drago knew that one of the most disciplined hitters in baseball wouldn't be swinging at anything outside the zone. He went right after Morgan with a fastball on the inside corner that the second baseman took a big cut at and missed, 1–1.

With Luis Tiant winning his two complete games, Drago had made only one appearance in a save situation in the Series so far, nine days earlier, way back in Game Two, coming in to replace starter Bill Lee in the ninth inning with a one-run lead, nobody out, and Johnny Bench on second after a leadoff double.

Drago leaned into his next fastball and hit the low outside corner, a beautiful unhittable strike, to go ahead of Morgan 1–2.

Prior to his stint in Game Two Drago had warmed up and sat down twice before coming into the game—a frequent bullpen routine resulting from Darrell Johnson's chronic indecision; his relievers often lost their edge in the process—and after retiring Tony Perez and George Foster, Drago induced Reds' shortstop Dave Concepcion to hit a ground ball to second base.

Drago overthrew his next effort to Morgan, a fastball that soared high to even the count at 2–2.

But Red Sox second baseman Denny Doyle had been handcuffed by Concepcion's grounder—although the game's official scorer ruled the tough chance a single—and Johnny Bench scored the tying run for the Reds. After Concepcion quickly stole second, Ken Griffey doubled him in for the run that would win Game Two to even the Series at one apiece; Dick Drago was tagged with that uncomfortable loss, and the tough competitor had been itching to get another shot at the Reds ever since.

Drago's next fastball seemed to fool Morgan, and he just caught a piece of the ball, popping it up softly down the first base line, where Carl Yastrzemski—now wearing his infielder's mitt—drifted over to make the easy catch for the first out.

Johnny Bench came to the plate, the first time Drago had ever faced the best-hitting catcher in the game. This was the kind of confrontation both men thrived on: dead-red fastball against dead-red fastball hitter. The crowd stirred to life in anticipation.

But instead of straight heat, Fisk signaled for the slider, a perfect call and a great delivery that appeared to be headed for the outside corner then broke sharply away from the plate. Bench appeared to break his wrists at it before holding off, but when both Fisk and Satch Davidson deferred to first base umpire Art Frantz, he signaled that Bench had resisted: ball one. The crowd booed its disapproval.

Drago came back with the fastball now, inside, and Bench turned on it, driving the ball hard on the ground toward the hole at short. Guarding the line, Rico Petrocelli showed why he'd always been one of the best infielders in Boston club history, racing three steps to his left, scooping it deftly with the glove hand, and beating Bench to first by three steps with his strong arm. Two outs. The crowd jumped to its feet.

Tony Perez dug in, the last of three future Hall of Famers in a row to step to the plate. Dick Drago had been a four-pitch pitcher as a starter, but he predominantly used only two as a closer: fastball and hard slider. Drago started Perez with the fastball, which tailed inside for ball one.

Sparky continued to pace in the Cincinnati dugout. The bad feelings just wouldn't go away. His two best men quickly down, only the Big Dog left; with all the momentum on their side and the crowd back in the game, he dreaded what the Red Sox might do now in the bottom of the ninth.

Drago threw a slider low that just missed the zone for ball two, but Fisk didn't complain: *That's it, just keep the fastball away from the outside of the plate on this guy, don't let him extend his arms.* Drago came back inside with the fastball, running in on the handle, and Perez couldn't lay off it; he sliced a looping pop fly foul down the first base line and Yaz put it away for out number three.

Three up, three down. Dick Drago had retired the heart of the Big Red Machine, momentum had shifted with the force of gravity; the fired-up Red Sox now had a chance to steal Game Six in the bottom of the ninth.

BETWEEN INNINGS Tony Kubek had left the booth and made his way down toward the clubhouses on ground level. NBC executive Chet Simmons, producer Roy Hammerman, and broadcast director Harry Coyle wanted Kubek in place to conduct interviews immediately after the game was over, and both felt certain it was going to

end soon, probably now in Boston's favor. Coyle instructed Joe Garagiola that he should now use Dick Stockton as his color man for the
remainder of the game, without referencing Kubek's sudden absence
on the air.

Inside Fenway, as the clock neared midnight, the crowd was on its
feet, chanting in support as Red Sox second baseman Denny Doyle
came to the plate. Doyle took a couple of deep breaths to compose
himself before stepping in, but the Reds' pitcher Rawly Eastwick appeared to be the one in need of composure. Sparky paced the dugout
restlessly, his early, profligate use of his bullpen haunting him now.

Eastwick's first pitch to Doyle came in high for a ball.

Sparky hadn't wanted to send his young reliever back out there
after Carbo's crushing blow, but he was nearly out of options; left-
hander Will McEnaney was his last bona fide reliever in the bullpen, and his only left-hander, so he didn't want to bring him in until
it was absolutely necessary. Beyond that he had right-hander Pat
Darcy, a young, occasional starter who had made only one relief appearance in Game Three of the Series, and right-hander Clay Kirby,
who hadn't pitched at all in the postseason and was suffering from
arm trouble. Starter Don Gullett, being held in reserve in case of a
Game Seven, wasn't even in the bullpen.

Doyle fouled back Eastwick's next inside fastball to even the
count.

Doyle knew his job as the leadoff man here; get on base any way
he could manage. He was a contact hitter who didn't walk that
often—only fourteen times during his three months with the Sox—
but Darrell Johnson had told him to make the rattled Eastwick throw
strikes.

Eastwick missed high again with the fastball for ball two.

The tall, cool Eastwick looked the same on the mound, but Johnny
Bench saw a young pitcher suddenly struggling with his release
point, his lower body lagging, a confidence issue manifesting as a
mechanical fault. When Eastwick missed high again to fall behind
3–1 in the count, Bench shouted out to him—*Keep it down now!*

The crowd revved up. At third base, Red Sox coach Don Zimmer had to shout to get Doyle's attention, wagging the index finger of his left hand at him: the take sign.

Listening to his catcher, Eastwick used his legs more and brought the next pitch down a notch—Bench thought he'd thrown a strike—but there was no way Doyle was swinging now, and Satch Davidson remained unconvinced: ball four. The crowd erupted and, confused by the noise, Doyle thought for a moment that Davidson had called a strike; the ump, looking irritated, pointed him toward first. Eastwick had lost the least dangerous hitter in the Red Sox lineup on five pitches, and now he had to face their most dangerous one.

Fenway rose to its feet as Carl Yastrzemski came to the plate. His job in this situation under normal circumstances would have been to advance the runner to second and into scoring position, particularly with Fisk and Lynn coming up after him, but Yaz hadn't been asked to lay down a sacrifice bunt once all season. Sparky decided to play the percentages anyway; he relayed the sign through Alex Grammas, and Rose and Perez crept in on the corners, protecting against the bunt.

On Eastwick's first fastball—*I'll be damned*—Yaz squared to bunt; the ball was right over the plate, but he tipped it foul down third.

The crowd quieted and seemed puzzled: What was their manager thinking? Yaz bunting? Now? He could end this freakin' thing with one swing. Ever the good soldier, even Yaz seemed slightly perplexed, looking down to Zimmer to see if the sacrifice was still on.

Sparky quickly chewed it over: He had to keep Rose and Perez on the grass to get the sure out, but would Yaz be swinging away now? Or was this just a sucker play to draw his infield in?

That's exactly what it was: On Eastwick's next pitch Doyle broke for second, and Yaz, choking up on the bat, tried to chop the high fastball past Rose down the third base line, but it bounced foul wide of the line by about four feet.

Sparky popped another piece of gum. Two strikes on Yaz, so the bunt wouldn't be coming back; Rose and Perez returned to their normal depth, guarding the line against extra bases.

Yaz, at thirty-six, wasn't the same hitter he'd been in his absolute prime, but he still had more sheer guts and gritty work ethic than any man who'd ever played the game. He'd come to the majors as a kid with extraordinary talent, been tutored in the art of hitting by the man he replaced, the franchise's irascible genius Ted Williams, and even after becoming a star kept grinding relentlessly to refine his skills. Standing tall in the box, holding the bat straight up and high—one of the most imitated stances in the game; ask any kid in New England—he'd gradually lowered his hands to compensate for whatever fraction of reaction time he'd lost over the last few years, and could still lash out like a cobra at a pitcher's slightest mistake.

And Eastwick made one now. Another high fastball—the third in a row he'd thrown him—out of the zone but on the plate and fat. After a violent, churning swing, the ball screamed out to right field; Ken Griffey raced to his left to cut it off and nearly overran the ball, reaching back to nab it just before it snaked past him—if he'd been right-handed it surely would have run by and sent Doyle home to end the game. By the time Griffey fired it back in and Concepcion cut it off at second, Denny Doyle was standing on third with the winning run. First base coach Johnny Pesky slapped Yaz on the back repeatedly as the fans leapt to their feet and went wild; just as he'd been doing for the last fifteen seasons, Yaz had come through again when they needed him.

Bottom of the ninth, first and third, nobody out.

Sparky had seen, and lived with his error of judgment, enough. As Carlton Fisk moved to the plate, the Reds' manager, looking tired beyond his years, stepped over the line and took the long walk to the mound, signaling for the young left-hander McEnaney, his seventh pitcher of the night. This immediately clarified two issues: Carlton Fisk would be walked intentionally to load the bases with nobody out, and Sparky didn't want to see Rawly Eastwick throw another pitch, not even one that was out of the strike zone on purpose.

The crowd stayed on its feet. Johnny Bench and Sparky waited on the mound for McEnaney to arrive in the golf cart. Don Zimmer trotted into the Red Sox dugout to confer with Darrell Johnson. Sparky gave McEnaney his marching orders when he arrived: walk Fisk, pitch carefully to Lynn, try to get the ground ball for the force at home. Almost any fly ball now with nobody out surely meant the end of the game.

After four years in the Cincinnati system, twenty-three-year-old Will McEnaney had spent the last half of the 1974 season with the Reds, and in the first half of the 1975 season had emerged as their most effective stopper, leading the team—and the National League— in saves at the All-Star break. A free-spirited Ohio native, McEnaney had been drafted by the Reds on the day of his high school graduation, after being thrown off his high school's team earlier in the season for extracurricular carousing. Pitching effectively wherever he played, McEnaney also maintained his reputation as the class cutup. While playing for gruff, no-nonsense manager Vern Rapp at Triple-A, McEnaney patrolled the outfield during rain delays with a comic novelty stiff-but-empty "dog collar" so often that Rapp finally screamed at him to get off the field and "take that god damned dog with you." But McEnaney had enough talent to get away with pushing back at the Reds' regimented ways; he earned his way to the big leagues within four years and had been promised that the Reds would renegotiate his contract after he was named an All-Star in 1975; he was making $14,500 and asked for a bump to $22,000. The Reds countered: We'll give you $15,000 for the rest of this season, then two additional years at $22,000. Negotiating for himself without the counsel of an agent or lawyer, the headstrong McEnaney refused their offer. Even Sparky tried to convince him to sign, which McEnaney resented, causing him to further dig in his heels. None of which endeared him to Bob Howsam and the Reds' front office, and all of which contributed, along with the unexpected emergence of Rawly Eastwick, to McEnaney recording only five more saves for the rest of the 1975 season.

But if the Reds had given McEnaney the cold shoulder then, they desperately needed him now. His job was simple: After walking Fisk, all he had to do was strike out the man he had specifically been brought in to face, Rookie of the Year, and soon to be named as the American League's Most Valuable Player, Fred Lynn. This was

McEnaney's fourth appearance in the Series: four and two-thirds innings of work, allowing two runs, striking out five, without yet figuring in a decision. But the most important stat as far as Sparky Anderson was concerned: McEnaney had faced Fred Lynn twice, and struck him out both times.

"Here we go, Red Sox! Here we go, Red Sox!" the crowd chanted and clapped. And, once again, they predictably booed all four of the ensuing outside pitches to Carlton Fisk. Fisk tossed his bat to the bat boy and trotted down to first to load the bases.

Bases loaded, nobody out, bottom of the ninth.

Up came Fred Lynn. Sparky shifted his outfielders around; Geronimo and Griffey crept in to shallow center and right field. George Foster, playing a little deeper in left, edged closer to the left field foul line. All four of the Reds infielders moved in onto the edge of the grass; any ball on the ground, their play was at home to force Doyle. Anything deep and in the air, game over.

And with the fastest men on his team—outfielders Juan Beniquez and Rick Miller—in the dugout and available to pinch run for one of the slowest—Denny Doyle at third, representing the winning run— stone-faced Red Sox manager Darrell Johnson never moved from his perch in the dugout.

Bench called for a slider, McEnaney's out pitch, hoping that Lynn would chop something into the ground, but McEnaney, almost the only pitcher on the Reds staff who occasionally ignored the game's best signal caller, instead went right after Lynn with a fast-ball, high and tight. Lynn, looking first-ball fastball, something he could drive, swung hard and got under it, slicing it inside out.

The ball arced high over third down the left field line. George Foster drifted over, waiting for it just inside the foul line, only a few inches from the stands and less than two hundred feet from home plate. The crowd rose to its feet, all around Fenway, screaming and yelling.

Setting a foot against the edge of third base, Denny Doyle turned and glanced over his shoulder just long enough to see that Foster was settling into position to make the catch.

The Red Sox scouting report had said they could run on Foster, and had with success been doing so throughout the Series, but Don Zimmer, the Red Sox third base coach, didn't like the odds: way too risky on such a shallow ball, take the out here, hold the runner; with an out to spare they could still drive in the run they needed with another fly ball.

Zimmer watched the ball all the way into Foster's glove, then ran right to the bag and shouted at Denny Doyle: "Don't go, you can't go! No, no, no!"

Having difficulty hearing his coach over the wall of sound issuing from the stands, Doyle thought he heard Zimmer shout: "Go, go, go, go!"

Foster gripped the ball. Doyle took off for home. Zimmer's jaw dropped.

Foster, he of the strong but erratic arm, had made the catch just inside the foul line, and as he stepped back and wound up to throw, he had the benefit of sighting straight down the chalk that pointed toward home plate like a rifle scope. The ball bounced once, about twenty feet shy of home, just inside the base path, by which point it had already caught up to the scrambling, hurtling Doyle. The bounce kicked it high and to the right, and Bench reached out for it, standing directly in front of home plate in fair territory. Fifteen strides down the line, only ten feet from the plate, and victory, Doyle saw Bench stretch for the ball and took two awkward steps to evade him, coiling into a crouch, reaching out his left hand toward home as Bench swung his glove around. Two feet before he got there, with Doyle still not fully committed to a headfirst dive, Bench slammed the tag onto Doyle's left shoulder and knocked him clear off his feet, all the way over the plate, where Doyle rolled in the dirt. Bench ended up on his hands and knees, the ball firmly in his glove. Umpire Satch Davidson, who had positioned himself perfectly to observe the action from less than a yard away from the violent collision, raised his right arm and signaled out.

Double play. A strong throw from Foster, a textbook reaction at home by the best catcher in the business, who had just tagged his *fourth* runner out at the plate in the six games of this Series. As he got to his feet, Bench glanced down at his old friend Zimmer and shook his head: *What the hell were you thinking?*

Will McEnaney, backing up the play behind home, walked over to retrieve the ball from Bench. Bench instead escorted him back toward the mound, quietly chewing out his pitcher: He had called for the slider, and McEnaney had thrown a fastball. The only man on the Reds staff who could get away with ignoring Bench's signs was Pedro Borbon, and only because not even Johnny wanted to argue with him, and he wasn't sure Pedro completely understood the signs anyway. Bench knew that good relievers were as he put it, "rare and necessarily insane," but this wasn't the first time McEnaney had crossed him up, and Bench, who had long ago mastered the art of conducting a completely private conversation in front of forty thousand people, gave him a royal reaming.

"He called me everything but a white man," McEnaney recalled later.

"I mean, come on, what the hell, Will?" Bench said as they finally reached the mound. "I gave you the slider sign. You know the damn sequence."

"Yeah, okay, maybe I screwed up," admitted McEnaney. "But I guess it turned out all right, didn't it?"

Satch Davidson walked out after them to ask what was going on. Bench shook his head and started back to the plate. *Left-handers.*

"You wouldn't believe me if I told you," said Bench.

Just like that, two outs and almost dead silence: A dagger stuck in the heart of the crowd at Fenway. *Oh yes,* you could hear the reminders echoing through their minds, *I nearly forgot; these are the Red Sox.*

At third, Pete Rose turned to his flummoxed old buddy Don Zimmer. He had clearly heard Zimmer's exchange with Doyle—apparently better than Doyle had—and said to him now, not without sympathy: "How many times can you say 'no' to a guy?"

Sparky trotted out to have a little chat with his pitcher and infielders. Fisk at first, Yaz at third, let's everybody be clear about their assignments now: As often happened at their infield confabs, after Sparky spoke first, Joe Morgan did most of the rest of the talking.

The Red Sox's starkly diminished hopes rested now with Rico Petrocelli. The crowd tried to rally and urged him on as he dug in. McEnaney started him with a hard fastball that Rico barely got a bat on, sending it back foul, 0–1.

McEnaney, pitching from the stretch, looked off Fisk and came in with another fastball. Fisk broke for second on the pitch.

A nasty slider, breaking low and outside. Rico reached out and smashed it hard into the dirt wide of third; Rose dug to his left to snatch it cleanly and then made an extremely careful throw to get Petrocelli easily at first for the third out of the ninth inning.

Two weeks earlier, McEnaney's wife had given birth to their first child; watching at home in Cincinnati she hopped out of bed now and cheered loud enough to wake the baby. His sister Kathy, a navy nurse watching the game at a mess hall in Japan, where it was two o'clock Wednesday afternoon, stood up and screamed. Will McEnaney had pitched out of an impossible jam, calling it later the inning of his life, and the Reds had dodged certain death. Already down behind the Red Sox dugout, wired up with his wireless mic to interview the winners, Tony Kubek suddenly had no one to talk to.

The Reds poured into their dugout, clapping hands all around, new life.

Game Six was going to extra innings.

EIGHTEEN

My whole career has been a
struggle just to stay in the lineup.

BERNIE CARBO

R ED SOX FANS—CONNOISSEURS OF DESPAIR—HAD A NEW flavor to reckon with: *Usually they just break our hearts and get it over with; now they're torturing us.* Fenway Park felt like a hospital waiting room when you know you're there for bad news that's inevitable but refuses to arrive. Too many "what ifs" to even comprehend, but while we're on the subject, Why did Doyle run on that ball to Foster with nobody out? What in the name of all that's holy was he thinking? No one knew yet about the miscommunication at third between Doyle and Zimmer. And why oh why wasn't Beniquez or Rick Miller pinch-running for Ducky to begin with? Well, on the bright side, at least now they'd have plenty to bitch about in the bars of New England all winter.

Dick Drago hopped up out of the Boston dugout and walked back to the mound. Only moments before, inches from thinking he had a win in a World Series game, and Bench makes the tag for the double play.

"Now it's real simple," said Drago afterward. "We've still got business to do here. We can't lose this game. This is a team and it's your turn to go to work."

Tony Kubek remained stuck in limbo beneath the stands, awaiting word from director Harry Coyle. In the broadcast booth as the tenth began, after Chet Simmons and Coyle had decided that their two remaining men should now alternate play-by-play duties each inning, Joe Garagiola turned over the mic to young Dick Stockton.

And as so often seems to happen in baseball, the man making the key play in the inning just ended now came up first to the plate: George Foster.

As Drago prepared to throw, Foster immediately went into his familiar delaying tactics, stepping out of the box, asking for time. The crowd booed. Irritated, Drago retaliated when Foster stepped back in, staring in at Fisk's signs without moving, until Foster, uncomfortable, finally stepped out again; advantage Drago.

Finally, the first pitch, inside fastball, one hop smash toward Burleson at short, easy play, Foster's out at first by three strides. One out.

Dave Concepcion, hitless in four at bats, stepped in. Fastball, high, ball one. Fastball, inside, ball two.

The usually voluble Joe Garagiola, consigned to "color" commentary for the inning, had gone curiously silent, perhaps unhappy that he'd been asked to yield the mic to the rookie at such a crucial moment. Smooth and professional, relying on his exceptional preparation, Dick Stockton continued to carry and fill out the narrative of events on the field.

Fastball, high, ball three to Concepcion.

Rookie left-hander Jim Burton began throwing in the Boston bullpen, preparing, if they needed him later in this inning, to face Griffey and Morgan.

Taking all the way, Concepcion watched a strike down the middle run the count to 3–1. Fisk called for a slider in the same spot, and Concepcion smacked it into the dirt and out past second for a single, the Reds' twelfth hit, and his first of the game.

Center fielder Cesar Geronimo came to the plate, and Garagiola finally broke his silence, commenting that Concepcion might be running in this situation. Drago, conscious of the fleet shortstop's threat, threw three times to Yaz at first, driving Concepcion back to the bag, before coming in to Geronimo for a called strike on the outside corner.

Concepcion continued to take his lead, digging in to get a jump and leaning toward second, when Drago drove him back with another throw to first. Under Joe Morgan's aggressive tutelage, Concepcion had become an exceptional thief on the bases, stealing seventy-four over the past two seasons, successful on 86 percent of his attempts.

Drago's next pitch just missed outside to even the count at 1–1.

Another throw to first, his best yet, and Drago nearly picked Concepcion off; there'd been so much action at the bag that director Harry Coyle now called for a split-screen shot—Drago on the right, Concepcion on first on the left—and when Drago finally made a throw to the plate Concepcion lit out for second. Fisk handled the fastball well under Geronimo's missed defensive swing, but his throw sailed high and wide of the bag to the right, and Concepcion slid safely into second under Rick Burleson's tag with the stolen base.

One and two to Geronimo, with the go-ahead run now at second. The crowd, waking to the Reds' scoring threat, came to life and tried to urge on Drago. Geronimo fouled off the next two tough fastballs, staying alive. Looking and feeling out of place, Reds pitcher Will McEnaney swung a bat in the on-deck circle; almost out of reserves—and pitchers—Sparky had not yet committed to replacing him.

The crowd groaned as Drago's next pitch missed just outside, 2–2 now to Geronimo. They shouted their disapproval when the next one missed as well, low and inside, a full count to Geronimo.

Drago reached back for something and lasered a fastball at the low outside corner, the best pitch of his outing. Geronimo swung late, helplessly, ticked it ever so slightly, and Fisk hung on to the ball as it rattled around in his glove for Drago's first strikeout and the Reds' second out of the inning.

With two down, Sparky reluctantly called McEnaney back to the dugout, sending out the Reds' last left-handed bat in his place, infielder Dan Driessen. Darrell Johnson trotted out to have a word with Drago, raising speculation that he might lift him for southpaw Jim Burton. Knowing that if he did make the change, in all likelihood Sparky would respond by sending up a right-handed batter in his place, Johnson simply went over the book on Driessen with Fisk and Drago, then left them to their work.

This was Dan Driessen's first trip to the plate in the World Series. A favorite of GM Bob Howsam's, Driessen had been signed by the Reds at eighteen just out of high school and made the parent club four years later, hitting .301 in more than a hundred games, most of them played at third. A prototypical line-drive hitter, and decent defensive first baseman, Driessen was very much the same sort of player as Boston's Cecil Cooper. Although he hadn't developed a home run stroke yet, the Cincinnati brain trust had such high hopes for his abilities that ever since he'd arrived there had been talk about trading the aging Tony Perez to give Driessen a chance to play every day.

Drago looked in at Driessen, glanced back at Concepcion, and delivered a slider on the outside corner for a called strike.

That trade talk had grown louder and more persistent each season, to the point where the stable and self-assured Perez, after being subjected to constant impertinent questions about his imminent departure, had during 1975 grown irritated enough to stop answering them. Driessen, an amiable, laid-back South Carolina native whose team nickname was "Sleepy," continued to hit for a good average whenever given the chance and never complained about sitting on the bench, but had to date demonstrated none of the intangible personal qualities that made Tony Perez such a remarkable, and irreplaceable, teammate.

Drago's second pitch to Driessen missed high for a ball to even the count.

No knock on Driessen, but Tony Perez's superstar teammates expressed constant dismay whenever the trade talk about him periodically surfaced. Even the one waiting to hit on deck, ultimate company man Pete Rose, was on record that the Reds would have to be insane to trade the Big Dog. Johnny Bench had gone so far as to say that the day Tony Perez left Cincinnati would be the day the Big Red Machine ceased to exist. But each season the trade rumors continued to percolate.

Drago's next fastball overpowered Driessen, and he popped it up straight down the left field line—about thirty feet in front of where George Foster had caught Lynn's ball in the ninth—and Bernie Carbo raced over from left field just ahead of Petrocelli and Burleson for his first defensive chance of the World Series. He nearly overran the ball as the wind caught it, then he reached back at the last second, somehow directed his glove to it, and held on when it tried to pop out, to retire Driessen.

The Reds were gone in the top of the tenth, and Sparky would have to dig even deeper into his now dangerously thin bullpen.

AFTER THROWING 130 innings during the regular season, Pat Darcy had pitched only two innings in this World Series, in relief of Gary Nolan in Game Three back in Cincinnati, giving up a run, two hits, and a couple of walks, an uncertain performance that had given Sparky reason for concern. The twenty-five-year-old Arizona-raised Darcy had come over to the Reds only the year before in a trade with the Astros, put in an all-star season in Triple-A, and even won a key September call-up start for the parent club against the Braves. Tagged as a comer, Darcy then earned a spot on the Reds' 1975 roster with an exceptional spring training. His rookie season had been a major success; he compiled an 11–5 record in twenty-two starts, with a 3.58 ERA. But along with the rest of the rookies and role players on the Big Red Machine, once the regular season ended and the team's established veterans took the stage, Darcy turned understudy. Sparky had sound reasons for that policy. In the middle of his outing in Game Three, Darcy had looked up and realized: *Oh my God, I'm pitching to Carl Yastrzemski in the World Series.* He promptly walked him, then walked Carlton Fisk, and then threw a wild pitch to Fred Lynn, before giving up a sacrifice fly. He yielded one more single at the top of his next inning before Sparky took him out. After Boston tied them in the ninth, the Reds had rallied to win that game, and after Sparky pulled him, Darcy had stayed on the bench to watch it all happen. This was the Cincinnati way: Fold the young guys in slowly, protect them from situations they might not be ready to handle, let them learn how to breathe in this rarified air before you ask too much of them.

They were asking a whole lot more of him now; after appearing only five times in relief all season, he was literally the last man Sparky could send to the mound, his eighth pitcher of the night, a new World Series record for a single game. And the first man Pat Darcy would have to face in the bottom of the tenth had also singled sharply off him during their last confrontation: right fielder Dwight Evans.

Darcy's first pitch was a fastball running in on Evans's hands, and he fouled it back for a strike.

Darcy was a tall, good-looking kid with a heavy fastball, a hard sinker, and an effective changeup, in the opinion of backup and bullpen catcher Bill Plummer some of the best stuff on the staff. In their methodical, systematic way the Reds were grooming him to become one of their key starters, perhaps to replace the aging Jack Billingham—who had from the moment Darcy arrived generously taken him under his wing—but this was easily the toughest spot the young right-hander had ever been in with a baseball in his hand.

Darcy blew his best fastball right by a swinging Evans for strike two.

Johnny Bench, encouraged by his young pitcher's start, called for the fastball again. Darcy, betraying the first sign of nervousness, threw it over Bench's head all the way to the backstop for ball one. Then Darcy's next pitch missed low to even the count at 2–2.

Darcy had finished the second-to-last game of the regular season for the Reds but sat out the playoff series against the Pirates, so aside from his brief outing a week before in Cincinnati, he hadn't thrown in a game in three weeks. Less than an hour ago, he'd had no expectation of getting into this one.

Evans cracked Darcy's next offering, a low fastball, right back at him in the box. Darcy stabbed down and got his glove on it, knocked it a few feet to the left and took the sting off it, then raced after it, picked it up, and fired off-balance to Perez in time to beat Evans to first by a step. One out. Knowing exactly how tough this spot was, after they threw the ball around the infield, Joe Morgan trotted in to tell his young pitcher: "You just made a great play in the World Series." That meant the world to him; Darcy felt some of the butterflies start to settle.

Shortstop Rick Burleson came to the plate. Darcy started him with a fastball that missed low and outside. He came back with the fastball for a called strike, evening the count, then missed low again to Burleson, behind now 2–1. His next pitch was an overpowering fastball, up in the zone; Burleson swung late and popped it up to Davey Concepcion at short, easy play, two outs.

Darcy had been sitting out in the bullpen earlier watching their ace Rawly Eastwick pitching to Bernie Carbo in the bottom of the eighth, thinking how overmatched Carbo looked, thinking how amazing it was going to be when they wrapped this up in the ninth, winning a World Series in his rookie season. And with Will McEnaney still available, the last thing Pat Darcy was thinking at that point was: I still have to pitch tonight.

And then seconds later in the bottom of the eighth, with one swing Carbo had changed everything, and the call had immediately come from Larry Shepard in the dugout to Bill Plummer, and Plummer signaled to Darcy: *Time to get ready.* As he got up to throw, the whole stadium was still shaking from the noise.

And it was again now, as Bernie Carbo came up for his second at bat of the game, to a thunderous standing ovation.

Johnny Bench went out to talk to Darcy about their approach to Carbo, in particular how to avoid the mistake that Eastwick had made, which they weren't going to repeat now. As he returned and settled back in behind the plate, Bench shook his head at Bernie again.

"I don't believe it," he said. "I just don't believe it."

"John," said Bernie, grinning, "I don't believe it either."

Darcy came at him with the fastball, moving toward the outside corner. Bernie's feet had barely touched the ground since his home run, but with two outs and a fastball pitcher facing him, he had no reason to hold back; dreaming of even greater glory, he swung from his heels and missed, strike one.

Bench, a step ahead of him, now called for Darcy's changeup, and Bernie—swinging for the seats again—missed badly, behind in the count 0–2. Darcy missed low for a ball, trying to induce Bernie to chase one out of the zone, and then missed again in the same spot, another pitch Carbo resisted, evening the count at 2–2.

Red Sox pitcher Dick Drago waited in the on-deck circle, kneeling with his jacket on, not bothering even to swing a bat, knowing he wouldn't be going to the plate if Bernie somehow got on base. Veteran starter Rick Wise was already getting loose in the Boston bullpen. Drago knew Bench would call for the fastball now—it's what he would have thrown in the same situation—and Bernie would be looking for it.

Bench did exactly that, but Darcy's best fastballs had movement on them, and this one tailed away from the left-hander, and Bernie swung hard again and missed again, strike three, and the Red Sox were done in the bottom of the tenth. For the moment, Pat Darcy had answered Sparky's prayers.

So transported had Bernie Carbo been by the ecstasy of his eighth-inning pinch-hit home run that for decades afterward, until he turned sixty, he wouldn't remember that he'd even batted a second time in Game Six.

NINETEEN

A good catch means just as
much to me as getting a base hit.

DWIGHT EVANS

AFTER MIDNIGHT NOW, THE BRIGHT FULL MOON HUNG in a cool clear sky over Fenway. The wind had faltered some, the air felt electrically charged. A momentary lull in the lurching swings of momentum left the crowd quieter than they'd been since the ninth inning, worn out by surges and screeching halts of adrenaline. Sparky began to allow himself to think that his Reds might have just weathered the storm, maybe they could steal this one back now to take the Series; in support of that hope he had the top of his lineup coming to the plate as the eleventh inning began.

For the last two weeks Pete Rose had never seen the ball better: *It looked like a beach ball,* he said. He'd hit everything Boston had thrown at him on the screws since Game One. And through all the whipsaw charges, retreats, and reversals of fortune on this night, being the competitor he was, he'd never enjoyed himself more. He turned to Carlton Fisk as he dug into the batter's box to open the inning and said: "This is some kind of game, isn't it?"

At least three other members of the Red Sox and an umpire remember Pete saying to them, at one point or another in the long eventful evening: *How much fun is this? What a great game. Can you believe this?* In all sincerity. This wasn't just about winning, it was the lure of the arena, the juice, being in the action; a night like Game Six was what Pete Rose, with all his contradictions and complexities, had lived for and hoped to experience his entire life.

Dick Drago began his third inning of work with a slider that popped off of Fisk's glove outside for ball one. It wasn't nearly as much fun for Drago at this moment. Twenty-seven pitches in now—one of his longest stints of the season—he would have to rely on the stamina and guts he'd developed during his years as a starter to get through this inning, surely his last; he was due up to lead off the bottom of the inning.

Drago came back with a low heater, and Rose, seeing it all the way, fouled it back for strike one.

Rose had gone 2–5 on the evening, and now led all hitters on either team for both hits and average; he'd do anything to get on base now, anything to ignite the stacked lineup behind him and get his Reds that last, elusive win.

Another low fastball—Drago still had his good stuff—and another foul, as Rose tried to take it to left field, behind in the count 1–2. Fisk dropped one finger to signal fastball and set up inside for the strikeout.

Anything, anything to get on base now, by any means possible.

Drago came inside with his fastball, high, toward the right elbow, and Rose spun around to his left to avoid it, but umpire Satch Davidson immediately and floridly gestured: *It hit him, it hit him!* Rose flipped his bat toward the dugout and sprinted for first; the ball hadn't even grazed him, but he wasn't about to argue a gift. Fisk yanked his mask and got up into Davidson's face again, veins popping in outrage; the crowd booed, and Darrell Johnson came running out from the dugout to join in.

Nowhere near him! shouted Fisk. *That's a horrendous call!* Johnson laid into him as well, and as umpires have been doing since the dawn of time, Davidson stood his ground and ignored them both.

Rose stood on first base, grinning, and tried out his line about what a great game this was to Carl Yastrzemski. Yaz wasn't buying.

Sparky began pacing in the Reds dugout again, clapping his hands. *Here we go, here we go.*

Davidson claimed later that he'd seen the ball tick the sleeve of Rose's shirt. NBC's slow-motion replay revealed no obvious intimate or incidental contact between ball and any part of Peter Edward Rose or his uniform. Below the stands, feeling the momentum swing again, Tony Kubek moved over to the Cincinnati clubhouse and started down the tunnel toward the visitors' dugout.

Dick Drago barked at Satch Davidson, too, but had to eat it, knowing it was a lousy call, and that Rose had sealed the deal with the way he ran to first; he did everything but ask for a tourniquet. *That's baseball; you have to take the bitter with the bad.* Back to work.

Right fielder Ken Griffey came to the plate. The Red Sox expected him to sacrifice the runner to second; Yaz and Rico crept in at the corners as Rose took his lead. Drago spun around out of his stretch for a pickoff, realized Yaz wasn't on the bag, then had to soften and alter his throw. Yaz reached back for it, and Drago just avoided what would have been a disastrous balk.

Drago came to the plate with a fastball, outside for a ball, and Griffey showed bunt. Rico and Yaz remained drawn in; the percentage play, that was Sparky's MO: He would give up this out to advance that runner to second for his RBI men, Morgan and Bench. Griffey confirmed the sign with coach Alex Grammas at third.

Another high fastball, outside, Drago giving him nothing offspeed he could kill into the dirt, and another show of bunt by Griffey, ahead in the count now, 2–0. Anxiety for the infield: Would Sparky take the sacrifice off and let Griffey swing away, try to punch something past the drawn-in corners? The Red Sox stood pat.

Drago came back with the fastball again on the outside corner, and Griffey laid it down, almost too softly into that brick red New England clay; the ball died just inside the third base line, and with mask already flying, Fisk pounced out from behind the plate like a cougar, gathered it up barehanded, and fired to Burleson rushing over to cover second . . . and Rose, flying in with that reckless trademark headfirst slide, was forced out by the slightest measurable fraction.

Brilliant play by Fisk, the crowd whipped to life again. The sacrifice had failed. Sparky's stomach turned over.

Griffey on first. One out. Joe Morgan came to the plate. The sacrifice bunt was off the table now, but the steal or hit-and-run might be in play. A throw to first from Drago checked Griffey back to the bag, then another. Harry Coyle punched up the split screen again for NBC, detailing the action at home and first.

Drago missed outside with heat for ball one. Morgan glanced down at Grammas again for the sign, made sure Griffey wasn't running. This was his second look at Drago in the game now; he'd been watching closely from the bench and thought Drago was losing velocity. Morgan wanted that fastball again, and he wanted it inside, knowing he could turn on it.

Drago came back with the fastball, but outside, on the corner, popping into Fisk's glove for a called strike, 1–1. No loss of velocity there.

Drago gathered himself, deep breaths. How many more of those heaters did he have in him?

Morgan saw something he couldn't quite decipher in the signs from Grammas and left the box, walked down toward third to clarify with his coach; both covered their mouths: *Is he going? No, Joe, look for your pitch.* Morgan turned back to the box.

Denny Doyle saw Fisk flash the sign to Drago for the cutter and shifted to his left, and he signaled back to Dwight Evans so he knew that the hard breaking ball was coming inside. Behind him in right field, Dwight Evans took two steps to his left.

And through Evans's mind's eye flashed an isolated, fleeting vision he'd had in a dream some days earlier: making a catch of a Joe Morgan drive that prevented a home run from reaching the seats.

Drago went into his stretch and unleashed his cutter, a two-seam fastball that ran in on a left-hander's hands and often sawed off the bat at the handle, and the moment he let it go Drago knew he'd made a mistake; the ball was headed inside toward Fisk's glove but not far enough, and instead of breaking toward Morgan it was running back to the right.

Morgan turned on it.

Dwight Evans saw the flash of Little Joe's bat in the bright lights and immediately picked up the track of the ball. He'd played right field in Fenway now for three years, and this one looked like trouble from the jump, if not a home run then at least a line shot off the short right field fence. Normally whenever a left-hander hit an inside pitch this hard toward him, it turned over toward the line, hooking like an errant golf ball, and that's where Evans headed on instinct.

Where's he think he's going? thought Morgan. *He'll never get to that ball.*

Griffey took off for second at the crack of the bat. Drago's heart sank as he spun around to watch the ball rocket toward right; he was reduced for a dreadful heartbeat to just another spectator.

But as Evans sprinted toward where his heightened senses had told him this ball was going to land, his chest facing the foul line, he was already on the warning track when he realized it wasn't breaking toward the line at all, it was headed straight for him; he'd taken the wrong path, and in another split second the ball would be behind him, over his head, right where the Reds' bullpen ended, three hundred and eighty feet from home plate, where the fence dropped down to little more than a yard high. This ball was about to end up in the seats.

Fred Lynn raced over from center field to back up the play, toward the section of the field he and Yaz called "Death Valley" because the ball just didn't seem to carry there, but this one had looked gone from the moment it left Morgan's bat.

Griffey rounded second, motoring for third.

And somehow, at full speed, even losing sight of the ball for a split second, Dwight Evans adjusted in a single step back toward center, threw his glove hand up behind his head, leapt into the air, and came down somehow in balance, with his left knee and hip bumping up against the lowered wall, and, to his infinite surprise and delight, the baseball stuck firmly in the webbing of his glove.

The front row of fans and ushers in the right field bleachers jumped to their feet screaming, the first and so far only ones in Fenway to realize he'd pulled off the impossible grab, and Reds pitcher Clay Kirby—the lone man now in their bullpen, less than ten feet from the play—flung his arms down in disgust.

The moment he landed, Evans was already working on regaining his composure—knowing they had Griffey dead, he didn't want to wheel around to his left, which would delay the throw back in by a beat—so he pushed back off the top of the wall with both hands, turned to his right, and unsheathed his rifle arm, firing the ball back toward the infield twenty feet wide of first in foul territory, where Yaz slid over to pick it up on one hop and tossed to Rick Burleson, alertly backing up the play and covering first base all the way from short . . . and Ken Griffey, who had slammed on the brakes after the catch but only just now made it back around second base, might as well have been out by a mile on the double play that had just abruptly terminated the Reds' eleventh inning.

Yeah, that's right, thought Dick Drago, as he walked to the dugout, his work done for the night, the most relieved man in North America. *Another routine double play.*

Oh my God in heaven, thought Sparky.

Jubilation in Fenway Park.

"Nice *throw*, Dewey," said Fisk, needling him as they made it back to the dugout.

By answering George Foster's double play in the ninth, he had saved a certain run, if not two, and if Dwight Evans had not just made the greatest catch in the history of the World Series—as Sparky was the first to say afterward—no man had before or ever since made a better one at a more important moment.

TWENTY

That was the greatest catch I've ever seen.

SPARKY ANDERSON

To LEAD OFF THE BOTTOM OF THE ELEVENTH, RED SOX manager Darrell Johnson sent reserve outfielder Rick Miller to pinch-hit in pitcher Dick Drago's spot. A light-hitting left-handed defensive specialist, the twenty-seven-year-old Miller had seen action in only one World Series game, four innings of work in Game Four, replacing Juan Beniquez in left field to successfully help protect Luis Tiant's lead. He had grounded out then to Joe Morgan in his only at bat.

As Miller stood in, the crowd, whipped into a frenzy by Evans's extraordinary catch, clapped and cheered in rhythm, trying to will their Red Sox to get this thing over with *now.* Pat Darcy, beginning his second inning of work, missed outside with a fastball, and then another in the same spot, falling behind to Miller, 2–0.

Miller had attended Michigan State on a scholarship as a pitcher, but after converting to the outfield, he won the Big Ten batting title in his junior year, was named an all-American, and signed with the Red Sox after they made him their number two draft pick in 1969.

Darcy came back with the fastball, and Miller fouled it back, 2–1.

Working his way up through the Red Sox organization at Pittsfield and Pawtucket, Miller became good friends with minor-league teammate Carlton Fisk, and was introduced to Fisk's younger sister Janet Marie. They began dating, and married three years later, the first full season that Miller joined his now famous brother-in-law on the Boston roster. He believed he was about to earn a spot in the everyday lineup in 1975, but the stunning arrival of Rice and Lynn had rendered Miller the forgotten man in the Red Sox outfield; dispirited by a lack of playing time, he had nonetheless made valuable contributions through the team's stretch drive, with key hits and sound defense.

Miller fouled another Darcy fastball down the left field line to even the count at 2–2, then another in the same spot to stay alive.

Joe Garagiola, back in charge of calling play-by-play since the top of the inning, finally made reference to Tony Kubek's absence—calls had been coming into the NBC switchboard from viewers, concerned about his sudden disappearance—explaining that he was shuttling back and forth between clubhouses, waiting to interview the winners. Down below the stands, Vinnie Orlando—Fenway's longtime visiting team locker room attendant—opened the door for Kubek and, bending the rules a little for one of his favorite guys in baseball, waved him on in.

Darcy's fastball appeared to be losing some steam; Miller got good wood on his next outside pitch, spraying it to left field, but right at George Foster, who barely had to move to make the catch for the inning's first out. After they'd tossed it around, Pete Rose walked the ball back to Darcy, pumping him up with chatter: "Keep it up, kid, you're doing great. What a game, huh? I'd pay to see this one."

Red Sox second baseman Denny Doyle followed Miller to the plate, and Darcy started him with a fastball, high for ball one. The crowd had grown quiet again; they needed a rest, or another spark to jump-start them.

Tony Kubek and his NBC soundman Aaron Traeger—lugging the heavy equipment required by Kubek's cumbersome radio frequency microphone—now crept along the dank, low, ancient tunnel that cut down from the visitors' clubhouse through the fens toward the Cincinnati dugout.

Darcy followed his first-pitch fastball with a second one, on the outside corner for a called strike. Bench asked for another in the same spot, and Doyle fouled it back for strike two.

As Kubek approached the dugout, he was surprised to find Sparky, standing back down in the shade of the tunnel, watching the game and sneaking a smoke out of sight of NBC's roving cameras. Sparky never wanted kids to see him with a cigarette, but a man with this much tension and nervous energy to discharge could only chew so much damn gum.

Bench went right back to the outside fastball, and Doyle pounded it into the dirt right to Davey Concepcion, who hoovered it and threw to Perez at first for the second out. It was Yaz's turn at the plate, and the Fenway crowd stood and cheered him yet again. Three for five on the night, Yaz watched Darcy's first fastball catch the inside corner for a strike.

Sparky sensed someone behind him in the tunnel, turned, saw that it was Kubek, then smiled and waved him forward. Kubek, always reluctant to intrude on players or managers while they were on the job, cautiously advanced until he could just catch sight of the field.

Joe Morgan retreated all the way onto the edge of the outfield grass, playing Yaz to pull it hard to right. The veteran took a fearsome cut at Darcy's next fastball, fouling it straight back and falling quickly behind 0–2.

Sparky dropped his cigarette, ground it out underfoot, took off his cap, and ran his fingers through his silver shock of hair. In the dim light of the tunnel, he looked weary and drained, two decades older than his forty-one years.

Darcy's next pitch missed low in the dirt, 1–2 now to Yaz.

Sparky looked back at Kubek—he knew Tony understood—and just shook his head. *Boy oh boy.* A stolen moment alone in the tunnel, wrestling with the game's damnable, obdurate gods. Sparky waved Tony closer, encouraged him to stay, then popped up the three steps to the dugout and went back to work, clapping his hands, prowling up and down the bench. Kubek mounted the steps to where he could see home plate but still remain out of sight from cameras and the crowd.

Yaz drilled Darcy's next pitch on the ground right toward Concepcion, a carbon copy of the ball he'd just handled from Doyle, the kind of play he could make in his sleep.

Three up, three down for the Red Sox in the home half of the eleventh. Kubek began to wonder: Did either team have the energy left to win this thing?

RICK WISE walked in from the Boston bullpen to pitch the top of the twelfth inning for the Red Sox. This would be his first appearance in relief all year, but they couldn't have found a more solid or dependable man to turn to at such a point in this game, World Series, or season. The son of a talented collegiate pitcher, Wise had early on found his footing on the path of life; he'd been a baseball prodigy, leading his team to the Little League World Series at the age of twelve, and his high school team to the Oregon state championship. When he graduated, the Phillies drafted him at seventeen, and he made their club the very next year. A big, strong, durable power pitcher with excellent control, during the next nine seasons he won 129 games in the National League, 86 of them complete games, an astonishing figure by today's standard. He swung a mean bat, too, cracking fifteen career home runs. On one amazing day at Riverfront Stadium in 1971 Wise tossed a no-hitter against the Big Red Machine and hit two home runs in the bargain, a performance unmatched in baseball history. After seven years anchoring a perpetually mediocre Phillies staff, and in the midst of a difficult contract negotiation, Wise was traded straight up to the Cardinals for starter and future Hall of Famer Steve Carlton. All Wise did over the next two years was lead St. Louis in victories, and notch a win as the starting pitcher in the 1973 All-Star Game, before he was traded again at the end of that season, to the Red Sox, along with teammate and friend Bernie Carbo. A torn shoulder muscle derailed his first year in Boston—an injury he attributed to being overworked in cold weather during the first weeks of the season by his new manager, Darrell Johnson—but Wise had bounced back as strong as ever in 1975, leading the Red Sox with nineteen wins and winning the third game of their sweep over the A's in the League Championship Series. He had given Boston exactly what they'd hoped for when they acquired him; a bellwether arm for their starting rotation and plow-horse durability, one of the most dependable, strong-minded men in all of baseball.

Because he had faced the Reds before—often and successfully—Wise had been held back by Darrell Johnson until Game Three in Cincinnati, where he'd no-hit them four years earlier. Although a long time in coming, the Reds that night exacted their revenge on Rick Wise: He gave up five runs, and three home runs, in only four and a third innings, before Johnson sent him to the showers. This was the infamous Armbrister game, when the Red Sox fought back bravely to tie it in the ninth before coming undone after the fateful collision in front of home plate in the tenth. No one had been more disappointed in his performance in that game than Wise himself, but Johnson hadn't called on him again, and he had been itching to get a redemptive shot at the Reds ever since. The mortal blow during Wise's stint in Game Three had been a two-run shot struck by catcher Johnny Bench, who was the first man he would now have to confront in the top of the twelfth inning of Game Six.

Although he was never one to complain, and his numbers had been as good as or better than his lofty career averages, 1975 had been one of Johnny Bench's most difficult seasons. From that early car accident in his first year with the Reds organization, Bench had ever since been regularly beset by a series of injuries and odd misfortunes. Most of them were attributable to the wear and tear of the game's most demanding physical position and the take-no-prisoners way in which he played it. But in the last month of the 1972 season Bench's doctor had noticed a spot on his lung during a routine X-ray. Extensive tests failed to determine its nature—although he had never been a smoker, cancer was the obvious concern—and while the Reds were losing their agonizing World Series that fall to the Oakland A's, Bench was staring down an appointment with the knife once the season ended. Although contemporary diagnostic techniques would have obviated the need for such drastic measures, doctors had to open his chest and split his ribs to get at the lesion, which turned out to be a rare, but completely benign, fungal infection called San Joaquin Valley Fever. Bench recovered from the postoperative trauma to play 152 games the following year, but posted some of his lowest numbers of the decade.

After another excellent campaign in 1974, Bench had come into 1975 in his best shape in years, but a home plate collision in late April with Giants outfielder Gary Matthews changed all that; the blow shredded the cartilage along the top of his left shoulder. Enduring cortisone shots injected three inches into the joint every few days to dull the severe pain, Bench could barely lift his left arm and needed help just taking off his shirt. The frayed tissue constantly scraped an underlying nerve, making it difficult for him to sleep whenever the medication wore off, but he kept playing with the injury throughout the long march of the '75 season, missing only twenty games, making the All-Star team yet again, hitting .280 with 28 home runs while driving in 110, leading the club in both categories. For his troubles, he was treated to repeated speculation by hometown sportswriters that the great Johnny Bench was washed up and his extraordinary talent had hit the downhill side. Nor could he find much relief from this bruising treatment at home, privately suffering through the messy public unraveling of his first marriage. Instead of giving in to despair, Bench treated all these slings and arrows with the same wry, privately amused, slightly removed perspective that had always sustained him, and simply went out every day and did his job.

The fourth Red Sox pitcher of the night, and the twelfth to appear in Game Six—a new World Series record—the tall, solid, bespectacled Wise consulted briefly with his catcher, Carlton Fisk, as Johnny Bench dug into the box. Wise started him with a hard fastball, outside for ball one.

Bench had slugged a fastball from Wise out of the park in Cincinnati, a pitch Wise had let stray over the plate without its usual effective movement; as a power pitcher, Wise knew that home runs were a frequent consequence of his worst mistakes, his Achilles' heel. He was not going to make that same mistake tonight; his next fastball headed for the high outside corner and Bench swung late, skying it foul all the way above the grandstand directly behind home plate. Fisk hurled his mask aside and raced back to the screen in front of the first row, retreating two steps when the ball spun back away from the screen on the way down, then making the difficult catch as he tumbled back onto his rear. Fisk had retired Bench—the man writers had invariably compared him with since the moment he'd arrived—and Wise had won their rematch.

Tony Perez stepped in, 1–5 on the night. Wise started him with a good-moving fastball that just missed low for ball one.

Perez had gone 0–1 but drawn a walk off Wise in Game Three, and then startled him, with Bench at the plate, by stealing second, something he'd done only once all season; but the Reds' scouting report had said anyone could run on the deliberate Wise. Perez confirmed it, and Bench had then promptly hit his home run, giving the Reds their early lead.

Having waited patiently for his pitch, Perez watched another hard fastball catch the outside corner to even the count.

Tony Perez had done every last thing the Reds had asked of him ever since they'd signed him as a raw teenager out of Cuba—switching positions, driving in more than ninety runs for nine consecutive years, all the while providing the emotional stability that had cemented this remarkable group of athletes together—and still he had to face the harsh reality that these World Series games might be the last he ever played in a Cincinnati uniform.

Wise's next fastball cut across the lower half of the zone—the pitch Perez was looking for—but he caught only a fraction of it, fouling it back hard, flush into Carlton Fisk's mask, 1–2.

Tony Perez was thirty-three now, an age when many good players, so history tells us, begin their inevitable decline. Although he was a year younger than Pete Rose, the Cincinnati front office still considered him the older, more expendable player—but then everyone seemed older than the hyperactive Charlie Hustle, particularly their wise and patient first baseman.

Perez watched another fastball miss just low, evening the count again at 2–2.

No matter that the Big Dog had not yet exhibited a single symptom of decline, an old baseball axiom held that it was far better to rid oneself of a player a year too soon, when he still had marketable value, than a year too late, when the bell had already tolled. Born of the unfettered arrogance granted to baseball's owners by their age-old, iron-clad reserve clause, such mechanical thinking often led, as it would in Cincinnati before too much longer, to downfall and ruin.

When Rick Wise had his good fastball—as he did tonight—almost no one could get around quickly enough to pull the ball on him, but Perez did here. After measuring the repeated low pitches he'd seen, he looked for another and swatted the one Wise then threw him sharply past a diving Rick Burleson for a single to center field; the Reds had the potential go-ahead run on base.

George Foster stepped in, deliberate hitter versus deliberate pitcher, but perhaps conscious of the late hour, both men worked at faster than their normal pace; Wise fired a perfect pitch on the low outside corner for a strike.

Wise looked Tony Perez back to first as he went into his stretch; he wasn't about to let Perez surprise him with another steal, but he also knew that with the powerful Foster at the plate there was no chance Sparky would risk sending him.

Wise made his second straight good pitch to Foster, low and outside, looking for the ground ball to end the inning; Foster chopped it foul to fall behind 0–2. Looking for the strikeout now, Wise threw his first curve of the inning, breaking low and away; Foster almost bit but laid off it and Davidson called it a ball, 1–2.

Fisk set up inside, aiming to bust one in on Foster's hands. Wise's fastball ran in on him, and the prodigiously strong Foster muscled it into the air, floating gently out to left field, where it fell in for a bloop single in front of Bernie Carbo for the Reds' fourteenth hit of the game. Perez advanced to second. Rick Wise hadn't thrown a single bad pitch in the inning, but the Reds were in business, with two men on and only one out in the inning.

From his perch on the tunnel stairs behind the Cincinnati dugout, Tony Kubek saw renewed purpose in Sparky and the Reds; this was character, this was who they were. Never give up, impose your will on the opponent, always keep fighting. Another hit now and they'd retake the lead, and if they did, it didn't seem possible that the Red Sox could find a way to come back yet again at this late hour.

Davey Concepcion came to the plate, looking for anything he could poke or prod past the infield. Wise fired a fastball on the black of the outside corner for a called strike. The moment seemed made for Concepcion; if he could drive in Perez from second, and the Reds could hold on to win this game and the Series, that might just do it—elevate him to the level of the team's Four Horsemen, from the very good to one of the greats.

Wise missed high with a fastball, evening the count at 1–1.

With almost dead silence in the park, Wise went back to the outside fastball, and Concepcion sliced it into right field, with the runners advancing halfway. Dwight Evans retreated a few steps to his left, pulled it in for the second out, and Perez retreated quickly to second as Evans fired the ball back to the cutoff man, Doyle.

Sparky thrust his hands in his back pockets and paced again. Darrell Johnson ran out to talk to Wise and Fisk on the mound about their book on the next batter, Cesar Geronimo. *Low and away, low and away.* That's where Wise started him, but the fastball just missed outside, 1–0.

No one was throwing in Boston's bullpen—Wise would have to get this done himself—but next door in the Reds' pen the last man left got up to throw with Bill Plummer; Clay Kirby, suffering from arm trouble, hadn't thrown a single pitch in the postseason, but he was all Sparky had now, and his current pitcher, Pat Darcy, was crouched out in the on-deck circle if Geronimo somehow got on. He was running out of pinch hitters as well; down to outfielder Merv Rettenmund—who began to swing a bat—reserve infielder Doug Flynn, and catcher Bill Plummer, still stationed out in the bullpen.

Geronimo fouled Wise's next fastball back to the screen to even the count. He came back to paint the low outside corner with his next fastball, just missing, 2–1. Then fastball again, hard and moving to the right, and Geronimo swung and missed, evening the count. They had him set up now; Fisk dropped the sign, slid to his right, and Wise fired the first inside pitch that Geronimo had seen, pure gas, smack dead on the high and inside corner of the zone. Still looking for something outside, Geronimo was handcuffed; Davidson rang him up and the inning was over.

The Fenway crowd stood and cheered as his teammates sprinted in off the field to bat in the bottom of the twelfth, while Rick Wise slowly and deliberately walked toward the Red Sox dugout.

TWENTY-ONE

Other than being the father of two children,
this was the greatest thrill of my life.

CARLTON FISK

I T WAS 12:34 ON WEDNESDAY MORNING, OCTOBER 22, NOW, 241 minutes into Game Six, already the second longest game in World Series history, and only minutes away from becoming the longest.

Back in the Boston clubhouse, where he had finally retreated in the last inning, worn out, Luis Tiant settled into the whirlpool, watching the game on the training room television, an ice pack taped to his right shoulder, his long Cuban *Presidente* freshly lit.

Due up first, Carlton Fisk swung a bat around violently as Pat Darcy completed warm-up tosses for his third inning of work. Fisk watched Darcy throw, then turned to Fred Lynn, also loosening, who would follow him to the plate.

"I'm gonna try and hit one off the wall," said Fisk. "You drive me in. Let's get this over with."

"Okay, Pudge," said Lynn.

Lynn liked to cheat forward and to the left from the on-deck circle, so he could get a better view of home plate and a pitcher's locations. He'd never faced Pat Darcy before and wanted to see what kind of stuff he had, so as Fisk stepped in, he leaned over to take a look.

Bench didn't like his pitcher's warm-ups, they weren't popping; Darcy had lost measurable velocity, this looked like batting practice stuff. Bench glanced over at the bench, caught Sparky's eye, and gave him the slightest shake of the head.

On the steps behind the Reds' dugout, eyes on the field, Tony Kubek overheard Sparky Anderson then turn to his pitching coach, Larry Shepard, who was keeping their chart of the game.

"How many pitches has he thrown?" asked Sparky, looking out at Darcy on the mound.

Shep scanned the chart. "Twenty-nine."

Sparky felt a sudden chill from the cooling night air. "Damn. He ain't thrown that many in weeks."

Ever since that moment in the eighth, thought Sparky, *I could feel the devil getting ready to poke his pitchfork.*

As he settled behind the plate, Bench shot a glance down toward third at Don Zimmer, his old coach in the Puerto Rican winter league, one of his closest friends in baseball; they'd been woofing at each other all Series, and now Zimmer was clapping his hands with a ferocious look in his eye.

He can feel it, too, thought Bench.

Fisk stepped into the box, snapping his arms back to stretch, shaking his head like a man fighting off sleep, trying to sharpen himself to full alertness. The crowd had come to life again with him, a low rumbling washed over the field. Umpire Satch Davidson leaned in low behind Bench for the pitch, his right hand resting on his shoulder.

Darcy's thirtieth pitch of the game missed high for ball one, overheated, his stride a bit off mechanically. He hadn't thrown a mistake that hurt him yet, and had retired six Red Sox in a row, but judging by his diminished velocity Bench knew that if they were going to survive, he'd have to coax Darcy through this inning by moving the ball around the plate. Bench signaled for the sinker, inside, and Darcy delivered. It didn't have his usual hard kick, cutting low and inside, and probably would have finished out of the zone, a pitch most hitters couldn't do much with, but Pudge Fisk, unusual for such a tall right-handed man, was a notorious inside/low-ball pull hitter, and that, finally, was Darcy's one and only mistake.

Fisk saw it, liked it, reached down, and crushed it.

In the broadcast truck, director Harry Coyle tried to hail his left field cameraman, Lou Gerard, stationed inside the Green Monster scoreboard, on his headset. Fisk's ball was headed straight down the left field line, a high towering shot, exactly the kind of flight path they'd planted a camera in there to pan up and capture. Gerard, at that moment, stood frozen in terror at his post, staring down at the biggest rat he'd ever seen in his life—*the size of a frickin' housecat*—that had just crawled across his foot. Half-paralyzed with fright, he couldn't swing his camera around; he held the close-up he'd established on Fisk.

Fred Lynn jumped up from the on-deck circle to align himself with the left field foul line, the first person in the park to realize this was going to turn out well; he jumped straight into the air. As the ball reached the apex of its flight, it began to hook to the left, toward the yellow foul pole and screen. With his great bat speed, and the way he jumped on inside pitches, Fisk hit dozens of foul "home runs" a year, and this might be another one; and in any other ball-park in baseball, absent the short left field wall, it undoubtedly would have been.

The crowd rose to its feet.

Carlton Fisk didn't run. He turned sideways and took three ab-breviated hops down the first base line, wildly waving his arms at the ball like a kid in a Little League game, urging, willing, begging it to stay fair.

Pete Rose turned and sprinted down the left field line, following the flight of the ball toward the pole, willing it to turn foul, and never saw Fisk's dance toward first.

Tony Kubek stepped forward right into the Reds dugout, along-side Sparky and everyone else in the club, all of them craning their necks forward to keep the ball in sight.

Eyes fixed on the training room television, Luis Tiant sat up in the whirlpool. Hearing the deep rumbling about to crescendo in Fenway all the way down in the depths of the old building, Bill Lee jumped off the training table nearby and started shouting.

In the owner's box, Tom Yawkey and Duffy Lewis stood up, their hands reaching out for each other.

In the broadcast booth, Dick Stockton, taking his turn back on play-by-play, his voice hoarse with emotion as he narrated: "There it goes, a long drive, if it stays fair . . ."

Thirty-five thousand people locked in a suspended passage of time—less than four seconds by the clock—and then, yes, the ball crashed off the screen near the very top of the left field foul pole.

". . . home run!" finished Stockton, then wisely realized that the best thing now was to sit back and let the magic of the moment speak for itself.

Fisk rounded first by the time the ball kicked sharply back down into the glove of a motionless George Foster. Without breaking stride Pete Rose pivoted and ran back toward the dugout. Joe Morgan stayed close to second and watched Fisk carefully, making sure he touched all the bases. Fans broke out of the stands past the red-coated ushers and police security, rushed onto the tops of both dugouts, and then poured onto the field as the rest of the Reds hurried out of the way. Pat Darcy lowered his head and walked off the mound, lost in despair.

"Well, shit," said Jack Billingham, watching the Reds' clubhouse television.

Luis Tiant catapulted himself out of the whirlpool and sprinted for the tunnel to the dugout, whooping and hollering, Bill Lee a step ahead of him.

Sparky and the men in the dugout immediately headed for the tunnel to their clubhouse. Tony Kubek signaled his soundman, Aaron Traeger, and they rushed past the retreating Reds toward the melee on the field.

Next to the press box, organist John Kiley turned up the volume and broke into the thundering opening chords of Handel's "Hallelujah Chorus."

By the time Fisk reached third, the fans on the field had started to reach him; he high-fived the first two that came toward him, then nearly straight-armed a third who stupidly stood in the base path, and by the time he jumped up and landed on home plate with both feet, the entire Red Sox team was there waiting for him, flinging their hats in the air. Satch Davidson waited to make sure Fisk touched home and then quickly moved out of the way, as fans and photographers mobbed in around them, trying to capture a piece of the moment.

Luis Tiant made it all the way down the tunnel to the back of the dugout before realizing he was wearing nothing but his jockstrap, then quickly stepped back and wrapped himself in a towel before the cameras found him.

Dick Stockton came back on the air as Fisk disappeared into the sea of people surrounding the Red Sox dugout. "Carlton Fisk becomes the first man in this Series to hit one over the Wall . . . the Red Sox win it in the twelfth!"

In the broadcast truck under the right field stands, NBC executive Chet Simmons, marveling at the events unfolding before him on their multiple screens, spotted the footage from Lou Gerard's camera inside the Monster on one of their replay monitors: a close-up of Fisk as he bounced down the first base line waving at the ball, his face a kaleidoscope of emotion.

"What the hell is that?" he shouted. "Look at this. Put that up, Harry!"

As Fisk dropped into the dugout, director Harry Coyle had already punched up their first replay, from a camera in the left field seats, but it captured only the end of Fisk's dance, focused on his back as he began to run and rounded first, and then Coyle went for the shot from a roving camera in the grandstand behind home that zoomed in to catch the moment of the ball ricocheting off the foul pole screen down into Foster's glove.

Joe Garagiola, prodded back to business by Coyle on the headset, quickly announced the broadcasting particulars for what would now, in less than nineteen hours, be that night's deciding Game Seven of the 1975 World Series, and then finally Coyle replayed the almost forgotten angle that Chet Simmons had seen from their left field camera, of Carlton Fisk's home run swing and his hesitant, urging, ecstatic dance down the first base line, an instant classic that soon became one of the most enduring and iconic images in the history of televised sports.

In the press box, as a hundred others around him scrambled for superlatives against the sudden pressures of their impending deadlines, Peter Gammons of the *Boston Globe,* his senses whirling with wonder and amazement, cranked a fresh sheet of paper into his Underwood and prepared to quickly compose in a single pass one of the most lyrical, inspired, and impressionistic columns ever written about a baseball game. But first he had to ask a colleague to remind him what the final score had been.

Tony Kubek and his wireless microphone reached Carlton Fisk first, when he reemerged onto the field moments later, and for NBC's cameras secured the first breathless interview with Boston's freshly minted local hero. Cheeks flushed, eager and articulate, Fisk embraced and embodied the wonder he'd just inspired, a tall and handsome all-American Galahad, and at that moment, at quarter to one in the morning, in the steeple of his church in Fisk's native Charleston, New Hampshire, bells rang out to commemorate the birth of a legend.

The crowd simply refused to leave, and when John Kiley played "For He's a Jolly Good Fellow" when he saw Fisk come back onto the field, they clapped and sang along, the buoyant mood irresistible. After he finished his interview with Tony Kubek, and as NBC's broadcast abruptly went off the air, Fisk trotted all the way around the warning track, waving and shaking hands with the faithful. As John Kiley played his entire upbeat repertoire—from "Give Me Some Men Who Are Stout-Hearted Men" to "The Beer Barrel Polka"—the transported crowd lingered in Fenway Park for another half an hour. Umpire Larry Barnett quickly changed and left the park with his armed FBI escort, and for the first time since the Armbrister incident, no one in Boston gave him a second look.

After they'd gone off the air, Dick Stockton made his way down to NBC's hospitality tent and met up with Tony Kubek and the Reds' Marty Brennaman, who'd just finished the network's radio broadcast with Curt Gowdy. Everyone floated on the high of the moment, and even though the team that signed his paychecks had just lost the game, Brennaman said, "There was so much magic in the air, you just couldn't seem to mind." Chet Simmons came by to congratulate Dick on his outstanding work during the game; all three of them already knew it and commented on it, right then, before any ratings numbers had been tallied or rapturous columns printed, that this one game was going to bring baseball back from the dead.

"And to think," said Stockton, "that yesterday people were saying let's just get this thing over with."

Press, photographers, and friends jammed around the players in the Red Sox locker room; quotes on every indelible moment were dutifully dispensed and recorded, the ineffable quickly reduced down to phrases, impressions, and snatches of narrative, most of them wholly inadequate to capture the fullness of feeling, the spiritual satisfaction derived from participating in an event that had packed so many unforgettable moments into a single night.

Darrell Johnson sat placidly at the desk in his small office, talking to the press as if his team had just won an afternoon game in April. Although he'd taken part in that mad scramble on the field after Fisk's home run, the Red Sox manager was already back to business and appeared, oddly but characteristically, to take little pleasure in what they'd just accomplished.

Bill Lee stood calmly in the center of the maelstrom, patiently answering questions for nearly an hour after Game Six ended. Yes, of course he would be ready for tonight's game. Yes, he thought the Red Sox could and should win this Series now.

Fred Lynn followed up a session with trainer Charlie Moss with a dip in the whirlpool; as the adrenaline wore off, his whole body felt stiff and aching from his collision with the wall, as if he'd been in a car wreck. But yes, he would be more than ready to play in Game Seven.

The resolutely modest Dwight Evans, finally stating when pushed that his game-saving catch in the eleventh had been "okay, I guess," tried to direct reporters to give more credit to Bernie Carbo, who in the rush to celebrate Fisk's immortal moment seemed at risk of being reduced to a sidebar. Bernie, deep into the beer and his own tangled, turbulent interior, didn't seem to mind or even notice that thanks to Fisk's home run he was on his way to becoming an unsung hero, pouring out a flood of flavorful prose to every reporter in the room, a lifetime's thwarted dreams at last uncorked; manager Darrell Johnson took Bernie aside before he left that night and told him that he'd be in the starting lineup for Game Seven.

After waiting patiently for the older sportswriters to finish their work, young reporter David Israel finally found himself alone with Carlton Fisk in the locker room; still in his uniform after most of the players had showered and left, Fisk had had a little time now to reflect on everything this game and that moment had meant to him, as a New England native and a lifelong Red Sox fan. Israel had found the big story he'd sensed was out on the field that night. Staying up till dawn, he would write one of the most insightful pieces about Game Six and its intelligent, thoughtful, and most obvious hero; Israel's future as a sportswriter was assured.

Luis Tiant walked out near one-fifteen to find his father, wearing a broad, weary grin, waiting for him outside the clubhouse—his mother and wife had left at the end of the game to get the kids home to bed on a school night—and they embraced.

"I am so proud of you," his father whispered in his ear.

Forty years in pro baseball between them, from Havana to the Negro Leagues, Mexico, the minors, and the bigs, through disappointment, poverty, pain, loneliness, despair, and resurrection, to this pinnacle. Accepting the grateful thanks of the many fans who still lingered there, they made their way to the players' parking lot under the right field stands, arms around each other, and lit up a couple of fresh cigars for the drive back home to Milton. Whatever happened in the final game later that day, he had now done all he could do, given every last measure of himself; Luis Tiant's work in this World Series was over. He had his family together with him in America—there was no way his parents were going back to Castro's

Cuba after this—and that was what mattered most; dreams, on the larger scorecard, sometimes do come true.

The magic spread with them from Fenway Park as the crowd finally dispersed, filtering out into Kenmore Square and then all around Boston, horns honking, strangers embracing, tossing streamers into the trees. The Red Sox had finally shaken off their star-crossed legacy, stared down the mighty Reds and their own long, woeful history in the big games that mattered; clinching the Series now seemed a mere formality and miles away, tomorrow's problem—that job was all but done. Dick Stockton strolled back alone to his hotel through the enlivened street scenes, soaking it all in, a whole city walking on air at one-thirty on a Wednesday October morning. When he made his way into the bar at the Lenox Hotel, Stockton was surprised to find Game Six's winning pitcher, Rick Wise, and his wife—with his family still in St. Louis, Wise had spent most of the season living at the Lenox as well—and they shared a drink and the once-in-a-lifetime feeling that required no words whatsoever.

Rico Petrocelli drove himself home from the park, twenty miles to the North Shore, his wife, their four kids, his mother and father and brother all caravanning together in a happy two-car tumble. Rico hardly slept a wink that night—"on cloud nine"—his mind already racing ahead to Game Seven.

He was going to play in at least one more ball game.

IT WAS ALL matter-of-fact in the Cincinnati clubhouse. Downcast, sure, for a few difficult moments, but you lose a ball game, big fucking deal, there's another one tomorrow, right? That was the Reds' way: *It's just one game.* Indulging in remorse or self-pity was for losers. And the first thing they always did as a team was take care of their own. Jack Billingham, who'd watched the end of it on the clubhouse television, made a point of finding his young charge, Pat Darcy, shaking his hand, and looking him straight in the eye.

"You did great out there," said Billingham. "Shit happens. Don't let it bother you."

Joe Morgan came by Darcy's locker, and then Rose. Sparky patted Darcy on the rear as he passed. "You stay ready. We might need you tomorrow."

Sparky called them all together, ran his hands through his hair, made the short speech he was obliged to give before the press was admitted. "Great game, guys. Nothing to worry about. And we'll do business tomorrow."

Sparky went off to change, then Rose and Perez and Morgan and Bench jumped in and picked their team up, keeping the chatter going, any whiff of morbidity or self-doubt banished from the room. Joe Morgan dressed and showered quickly, following his disciplined routine, then gave his own speech, the last word after the reporters cleared out:

"We know what we have to do. We're the better team, we've got Don Gullett going tomorrow, and we're exactly where we want to be. Everybody get your rest, get back here, and we'll get it done."

They'd been "here" twice before, '70 and '72, and lost the World Series both times. That it could happen now again was in the back of everybody's mind, but no one dared give a voice to it. Every man on the Machine was back on task by the time they filed out in their coats and ties and loaded into the bus for the ride back to the hotel.

Everyone but Sparky.

"All I could think about inside was that I'd cost my team another World Series," he said. "And who knew now if we'd ever have another chance."

As he walked out alone to the bus, Sparky felt a pair of iron hands slam down and grip him by the shoulders. Pete, grinning, without a care in the world: *Good God, what is wrong with this man?*

"That was the best game I ever played in," said Rose, finally locating the last man in Boston he hadn't said that to yet.

"Are you fucking nuts?" said Sparky, then more quietly, just this once giving words to his torment. "I just lost us the World Series and all you can say is it's the best game you ever played?"

Pete Rose, calm and confident as a certified lunatic, looked his manager dead in the eye. "You and I were part of history tonight; that was the greatest World Series game ever. First time I've ever been happy about a game I lost. What the hell are you so worried about? We're gonna win this thing tomorrow, Skip."

Sparky remained unconvinced. Rose moved on, happy as a pup, looking for someone else to convert.

Johnny Bench huddled down in his seat on the bus, shivering, miserable, and feverish, sucking on lozenges to relieve his burning sore throat. Damn New England weather—he felt worse now than he had when the Series began. He saw the Red Sox fans still going crazy, exulting on the streets outside. *How in the world are we going to find a way to beat these guys tonight?*

When he got back to his room at the Statler Hilton, Sparky called his wife back home in Southern California with the kids. Carol, his gal since junior high, who always gave it to him straight, listened and commiserated, and then realized there was only one way to puncture her husband's melancholy.

"I hate to break it to you, George," she said, "but everybody here was pulling for Bernie Carbo."

That finally brought him out of it; he found the punch line of the cosmic joke. After the call, his old friend Ray Shore, the Reds' super-scout, came up to the room and sat with him, chewing it all over, until Sparky finally drifted off to sleep at four o' clock on Wednesday morning.

GAME SEVEN

Except for spitting and telling a lie, there ain't
nothing easier to do than quit. Quitting is for losers.

SPARKY ANDERSON

THE AFTERGLOW OF GAME SIX CAST A SPELL OVER NEW England that lasted all through the following day. Wednesday, October 22, felt like a holiday in Boston's downtown business district. Bleary-eyed from their shared late night celebration, workers and bosses basked in the bliss, schoolkids snoozed or skipped altogether, productivity plummeted, and almost nobody cared. Even the weather cooperated, bright sun and a hint of Indian summer warming the air. Photos of Carlton Fisk made the front page of every newspaper in America: Game Six had put baseball, for this day at least, back on top of the country's consciousness. NBC's preliminary overnight figures on Wednesday morning revealed that more people had watched Game Six than any other sporting event in television history. Halfway across the country, Cincinnati's fans marked a quietly anxious day; their team, which all the numbers insisted had been the best in baseball for the last five years, once again was on the brink of losing a World Series to what they had believed, and been told by the media time and again, was an inferior team.

Red Sox owner Tom Yawkey, looking weary and fragile after a largely sleepless night, but with spirits still riding high after last night's miracle finish, arrived at his Fenway office shortly after midday and puttered through a low-key, solitary afternoon, knowing his last, best chance for the elusive championship he'd chased for forty-three years was at hand. As evening approached in Boston, thousands flowed back toward Fenway Park and scalpers had a field day, topping the previous day's record haul. Among those unable to afford after-market prices, many tried to claim early spots on the overhanging billboards nearby that offered glimpses of the field; two fell, one fractured an ankle. Police cleared them all away by game time.

Two left-handers took their turns on the mound at Fenway beginning at eight-thirty Wednesday night, offering another stark study in contrasts: quiet, shy, conservative, twenty-four-year-old Kentucky country boy Don Gullett, a Cincinnati Red since the day he left high school, purveyor of the nastiest fastball in the National League; and Bill Lee, the twenty-six-year-old Southern California college graduate, the motormouth rock-and-roll philosophizer, an artist at heart who disdained the whole fastball-strikeout phenomenon as "fascist." Lee took great pride in being a pitcher, not a "thrower," and particular pleasure in outthinking the kind of home run/fastball hitting sluggers that filled the Reds lineup. Don Gullett didn't do much of anything outside of what Sparky told him to, or give it much thought before, during, or after that he was willing to talk about; his remarkable record, 75–39 over the previous five years, spoke for itself. Gullett had been outdueled by Luis Tiant at Fenway in Game One, but then rebounded with the Series' most dominating win back home in Cincinnati in Game Five; that was the pitcher Sparky desperately needed to show up for Game Seven.

"After this game tonight," said Sparky at his pregame press conference, trying to light a fire, "Don Gullett's going to the Hall of Fame."

"After this game tonight," said Lee on hearing that comment, referencing his favorite nearby neighborhood watering hole, "I'm going to the Elliot Lounge."

Rotating broadcasters as it had done all Series, NBC tapped its number one on-air team to call Game Seven, Curt Gowdy, alongside his former partner during Gowdy's years in Boston—still the venerated radio voice of the Red Sox—Ned Martin; and the stalwart Tony Kubek. When NBC executive Chet Simmons arrived at the production truck at Fenway Wednesday morning, director Harry Coyle was cutting together the highlight package from Game Six for use on the network's weekly baseball show. Joe Garagiola, who would work Game Seven on radio with the Reds' Marty Brennaman, was there that morning as well, in the process of lobbying Coyle that he should be allowed to revoice the winning Fisk home run call for the highlight reel, replacing the young and relatively unknown Dick Stockton. Simmons, to his credit, stepped in and diplomatically told Garagiola that Stockton had made the original call, and they were sticking with it.

A few hours before the game, Sparky was working in his cramped little office in the visitors' clubhouse agonizing over his lineup card again when the phone rang; it was Red Sox owner Tom Yawkey, calling to tell him that, no matter what happened in Game Seven that night, Yawkey wanted to thank him for everything Sparky and his team had done to make this such an extraordinary World Series, and for everything Sparky himself had done for baseball.

"I won't be able to come down and congratulate you if you win tonight," said Yawkey. "So, if you do, I'm congratulating you in advance."

The crowd cheered wildly as the happy, loose Red Sox starters lined up between first and home during pregame introductions. The eight Reds starters and Sparky lined up along the third base line, silent, grim, and purposeful.

If it hadn't followed so immediately on the heels of Game Six, what followed in Game Seven would be better remembered as a classic in its own right. Bill Lee, tuned up to pitch the biggest game of his life, set down the Reds in order in the top of the first, striking out Joe Morgan—Sparky, reversing course on instinct again, had inserted Joe back into the second spot of his order, dropping Griffey down to seventh—for the first time in the Series. Red Sox manager Darrell Johnson had not only penciled last night's hero Bernie Carbo into his starting lineup, he had him batting leadoff, only the second time he'd started against a left-hander all year. Although he discovered that the bat he'd used to hit his historic home run had been stolen overnight, Bernie's impressive streak continued. Carbo crushed

Don Gullett's fourth pitch of the game and sent a towering double off the very top of the Green Monster in left center; only the wind, which had shifted and was blowing in tonight, kept Bernie from notching his third home run of the Series. But when Denny Doyle followed by flying out to right, Carbo failed to advance to third when Ken Griffey's off-line throw skittered away from cutoff man Davey Concepcion. Carbo would have scored from third when Carl Yastrzemski then grounded out to second; few seemed to notice or care at the time about this early missed scoring opportunity, but Bernie had hardly slept after Game Six, which his lack of an alert response on the bases here seemed to indicate. Fisk—who hadn't even gotten home until four that morning, couldn't get to sleep himself until seven, and then only for three hours—followed Yastrzemski and was greeted with a tremendous ovation, but struck out on a Gullett fastball to end the inning.

Bill Lee could never have gotten away with all his off-field irreverence and verbal bravado if he wasn't able to back it up during a game; on the mound, where he mattered, he was every inch as tough a competitor as Luis Tiant. Facing Tony Perez to lead off the second, Lee tossed him a 60 mph curve that dropped in like a slow-pitch moonball for a called strike and drew cheers from the crowd. First made famous by a Pittsburgh Pirate pitcher in the 1950s named Rip Sewell, the "Eephus pitch"—a nonsensical piece of slang attached to it by one of Sewell's teammates—had since become a treasured knickknack of baseball mythology. In a long career Sewell gave up only one home run off his tantalizing Eephus, to Ted Williams in the 1946 All-Star Game, but only after throwing him one that Williams swung on and missed, and then announcing he was going to throw him another. A mere handful of pitchers had both the skill and showmanship to employ the Eephus in the years since Sewell; Bill Lee, not surprisingly, was its most devoted current practitioner, to the point where he'd named his variation on Sewell's theme the "Leephus pitch." So Tony Perez took a good long look at his "Leephus" as the ball softly descended into Fisk's mitt, taking the time to consider and then decline Lee's invitation to foolishly hack at it, but you could see its pace and trajectory lodge into Big Doggie's for-midable sense memory. He then grounded the next pitch sharply to third, where a superb defensive play by Rico Petrocelli saved a base hit. George Foster followed by belting Lee's next pitch off the middle of the Monster, but after playing the carom perfectly, Bernie Carbo cut down Foster at second as he tried to stretch it to a double with a powerful sidearmed peg to Denny Doyle. Yaz ended the inning with a third strong defensive effort, tagging Davey Concepcion out before he reached the bag at first, after grabbing an errant throw from Rick Burleson.

While Lee blithely cruised during his first trip through the Reds lineup, Gullett struggled with his control, ringing up strikeouts but frequently overthrowing and missing the zone with his formidable heater. He walked Carbo after striking out Lee to open the bottom of the third, then gave up a right field single to Doyle, the first and only man on either team to have now hit safely in all seven games of the Series. Carbo advanced on the play to third, and Ken Griffey missed his cutoff man, Concepcion, for the second time in the game while trying to throw Carbo out. Yaz then came through in the biggest at bat of the game with another sharp single to right, driving in Carbo for the first run of the game, and when Griffey missed Concepcion with his third straight throw, as Doyle ran to third, Yaz alertly advanced to second behind Doyle, removing the possibility of an inning-ending double play. That exceptional piece of base running forced Sparky to signal Gullett that he should now intentionally walk Carlton Fisk to load the bases, to better match his southpaw against left-hander Fred Lynn. Gullett responded by striking out Lynn for the second out of the inning, but then his release point mysteriously deserted him; he walked the ever-patient Petrocelli on a full count to force in Doyle and reload the bases, and then surrendered his fourth walk of the inning on four straight pitches to Dwight Evans to force in Yastrzemski. Gullett finally recovered, striking out Rick Burleson to end the threat, but for the second time in consecutive nights and games, the Red Sox had seized an early 3–0 lead. Captain Hook reluctantly cranked up his bullpen—Pedro

Borbon and Jack Billingham got up to work—while the Fenway crowd rejoiced, beginning to believe that the glorious promise of Game Six was about to be fulfilled.

After setting down the Reds without incident in the top of the fourth, Bill Lee, who prided himself on his hitting, pulled a single to right off Gullett to lead off the bottom of the inning, advanced to second on a wild pitch, and reached third with one out when Bernie Carbo did his job by grounding to Morgan at second. But for the second time in the early going the Red Sox squandered a prime scoring opportunity, when Doyle and Yaz failed to hit the ball out of the infield; the first uneasy hint of past misfortune insinuated itself into some of the Boston faithful.

The Reds finally appeared to have something going when Concepcion led off the top of the fifth by legging out an infield single. Denny Doyle was then unable to handle a bad-hop ground ball from Griffey; Doyle was charged with an error, and Concepcion advanced to third: first and third with nobody out. Bill Lee, who never seemed to mind giving up hits or pitching into a jam—he considered it more "democratic" to let hitters put the ball into play and allow his defenders to participate in the game—then struck out Cesar Geronimo with a perfect rainbow curve. With runs he desperately needed on base, Sparky had no choice but to then send up pinch hitter Merv Rettenmund in Gullett's spot. Displaying his best stuff of the night in the most critical at bat of the game so far for the Reds, Lee induced Rettenmund into an inning-ending double-play grounder, Boston's second of the game.

Bill Lee and the Red Sox were now only twelve outs away from winning the World Series.

Sparky called on Cactus Jack Billingham to face Boston in the bottom of the fifth; after watching Lee record out after out on ground balls, he wanted a sinker-ball pitcher of his own out there on the mound at Fenway. Concerned that Pedro Borbon, the man he would usually go to at this point in a game, had thrown three tough innings the night before, Sparky also wanted to reward the veteran Billingham for his steadying performance in Game Six. After striking out Carlton Fisk on a sinker, Billingham walked Fred Lynn and gave up a single—his eighth hit of the Series—to a determined Rico Petrocelli. Lynn advanced to third when Dwight Evans drove the first pitch he saw to deep center field. The night before, with the wind blowing out, Evans's ball might well have ended up in the seats, but Cesar Geronimo chased it down for a long, loud out at the base of the wall. Rick Burleson then toughed out a walk to once again load the bases, and the Fenway crowd gave Bill Lee a standing ovation as he walked to the plate for the biggest at bat of his life. Lee gamely tagged a Billingham fastball to almost exactly the same spot in center field, but the wind again held it up, and Geronimo raced back to make his second outstanding catch in a row and end the inning. Another opportunity to distance themselves from the Reds had been squandered; longtime Red Sox fans began to squirm in their seats.

As the Reds prepared to hit in the top of the sixth, Tony Perez, due up fourth, pulled out his lumber from the bat rack and caught sight of Sparky around the corner, just finishing a smoke, pacing and fretting in the tunnel.

"What the hell's wrong with you, Sparky?" said Perez.

"God damn it, Doggie," said Sparky, running his hands through his hair, "we're down three to nothing!"

"Don't worry about it, Skip," said an unearthly calm Perez. "We get somebody on, I'm gonna hit one; I'm gonna hit a *bomb*."

Something about Doggie's manner got through to Sparky; he walked right into the dugout and, completely out of character, said this to his team: "Look, fellas, we've got some outs left here, I don't want anybody to panic. Don't go up there thinking home run—somebody get on base and Bench or Perez will hit one out and we'll be back in it."

Following those orders, to lead off the top of the sixth Pete Rose singled sharply to right off Bill Lee for his ninth hit of the Series, but Joe Morgan flied out softly to Evans, and then Johnny Bench hit a routine ground ball to short that looked like it would end the inning. Rick Burleson flipped to Doyle at second to force Rose for the second out, but when Doyle turned to complete the easy double play at first he saw the combative Rose barreling down on him like an enraged linebacker about to take out his legs.

"There are some things you just can't allow to happen," said Rose. "And a double play at that point was one of them."

The little second baseman leapt to avoid Rose, and his throw sailed wild and high over Yastrzemski's glove, into the Red Sox dugout, where it landed in Don Zimmer's lap, Doyle's second error in the last two innings. A rumor started afterward that Bench had hit the ball so hard he'd knocked the cover half off and that precipitated the bad throw, a story that Doyle later refuted. He also claimed that Rose's slide hadn't caused his bad toss either, that his timing to the bag with Burleson had simply been off, but whatever the reason for it, Bench advanced down to second on the error, and instead of being out of the inning, the Reds now had a runner in scoring position with Tony Perez coming to the plate. When he returned to the dugout, Pete Rose slapped hands, pounded teammates on the back, then restlessly prowled up and down in front of the bench, snorting and clapping, shouting at the field, urging them forward. Johnny Bench stood on second, looking in at the Big Dog as he dug in at the plate.

Please, oh please, thought Bench, *give him something off-speed again.*

Bill Lee fumed on the mound, visibly upset by Doyle's gaffe, but no one wearing a Red Sox uniform—a fellow infielder, his manager or pitching coach, or his catcher—picked up on the cues and walked out or over to take Lee's temperature and calm their passionate pitcher down. If he matched Luis Tiant's competitive fire, Lee at this point in his life didn't quite have his older teammate's ability to quickly recover his emotional equilibrium after a setback, and it was about to lead him into misfortune.

Lee started Perez with a fastball, outside, and then, ill-advisedly, came back at him with his third "Leephus" pitch of the game. Perez, who had clocked a slight hitch in Lee's windup when he tossed him that melon in the second inning, spotted the same hesitation now, again, knew it was coming, watched it, timed it perfectly, and this time absolutely nuked the ball, powering it way up over the Green Monster, over the netting above it, over everything, a majestic mortar shot that landed all the way on Lansdowne Street outside the ballpark. Bench slowed down to greet Tony at home plate, having crossed just ahead of him, then bear-hugged Perez on the way back to the dugout.

Red Sox 3, Reds 2. The Big Dog had called his shot, and his teammates swarmed him as he and Bench came down the steps; Perez winked at Sparky. As he'd been doing steadily for more than a decade, whenever they needed it most, Tony Perez had just applied jumper cables to the Big Red Machine.

Reds' GM and team president Bob Howsam, seated just to the right of the Cincinnati dugout beside Commissioner Bowie Kuhn in the first row, knew it right then as he settled comfortably back into his seat: "We're going to win this one now."

The Boston bullpen went to work for the first time in the game, with southpaw Roger Moret and right-hander Jim Willoughby up and throwing. Bill Lee watched the next batter, George Foster, step back out of the box and ask for time twice after Lee had already started his windup, trying to deliberately upset his timing. Lee, visibly angry, overthrew two fastballs off the plate to fall behind 2–0. Foster tried to step out yet again during his next delivery, but home umpire Art Frantz, equally tired of Foster's antics, called a strike on the fastball Lee fired down the middle. When the count reached 3–1, Lee finally retired Foster on an easy fly ball to right to end the inning.

Jack Billingham, working quickly and steadily, set the top of the Red Sox lineup down in order in the bottom of the sixth. Just as they had during Cincinnati's comeback in the middle innings of Game Six, the Red Sox offense turned suddenly toothless, and as the Reds' confidence grew, the mood in Fenway darkened.

Bill Lee marched back out to start the seventh, and recorded an easy first out when Dave Concepcion grounded to short. But as he then walked Ken Griffey on four straight pitches—the first free pass he'd given up in the game—Lee noticed that a blister that had quickly risen on the thumb of his throwing hand had just broken. Lee gestured Fisk out to the mound, and manager Darrell Johnson quickly joined them. Lee showed Johnson the bleeding wound, and when asked if he thought he could still go, Lee had to admit that he could no longer grip the ball; Johnson's unwillingness to use Lee for the weeks before the Series had allowed the customary calluses built up by regular throwing to recede. Johnson immediately signaled to the bullpen, calling for the left-hander Moret, and a dejected Bill Lee walked off the field at Fenway to another standing ovation. For the second time in the Series, the gallant Lee had pitched into the closing innings and departed while holding the lead; his ERA would be the lowest for any pitcher on either team who'd started more than one game in this World Series.

Roger Moret had pitched so effectively in Game Six that he was not only out of Darrell Johnson's doghouse, but a second such performance might give him a chance to redeem himself with the entire organization. Moret faced Cesar Geronimo with Griffey on first, and jammed him with a heavy fastball that Geronimo popped up to Burleson at short for the second out of the inning. Sparky then sent up pinch hitter Ed Armbrister to bat for Billingham, and the appearance of the bit player who had stirred such controversy in this Series—most in Boston believed a Game Seven wouldn't and shouldn't have been necessary, had it not been for his notorious interference in Game Three—carried at such a perilous moment something like a foreshadowing of doom. The crowd booed Armbrister; umpire Larry Barnett, stationed at second base tonight, pulled down his cap and tried to disappear. When Moret fell behind 2–1 to Armbrister, Griffey lit out for second and reached easily ahead of Carlton Fisk's off-line throw, the ninth straight base the Reds had stolen on Fisk and the Red Sox pitching staff. Looking rattled, Moret then walked Armbrister with his next two pitches, and up came the switch-hitting Pete Rose. Johnson, with his entire bullpen available, decided to stay with Moret.

As much as he professed his joy during the wonders of Game Six, this was the moment Pete Rose had waited all his life for; with the World Series on the line, Rose belted Moret's second pitch into center field and scored Griffey from second base ahead of Fred Lynn's throw to tie the game at three runs apiece. Armbrister raced over to third, and when no Red Sox infielder moved to the mound to cut off Lynn's throw, Pete Rose advanced to second. Moret then walked Joe Morgan on six careful pitches, bringing up Johnny Bench with the bases loaded. Darrell Johnson came out to take the ball; Roger Moret didn't know it yet, but he had just thrown his last pitch as a member of the Boston Red Sox.

Johnson called in right-handed sidewinder Jim Willoughby, a twenty-six-year-old mid-season acquisition from the Cardinals. Willoughby, another unconventional California native and an exceptional chess player, had reinvigorated the Red Sox bullpen down the stretch of the pennant drive, saving eight games. He had pitched three strong innings in Game Three but was on the mound for the Armbrister incident, and ended up taking the loss without giving up an earned run. After another strong two-inning stint in Game Five, this was his third appearance in the Series, and Willoughby came through for Boston again, getting Bench to pop up behind the plate, where Fisk leaned deep into the stands to make the final out of the seventh.

Reds 3, Boston 3. But almost nowhere, not in shell-shocked Fenway Park or throughout fatalistic New England—and certainly not to the revived fans back home in Cincinnati—did Game Seven any longer feel like a contest set on equal footing.

Sparky now turned to his oldest warhorse, Clay "Hawk" Carroll, to pitch the bottom of the seventh, and he promptly retired the Red Sox in order for the second inning in a row. Jim Willoughby continued his strong work in the top of the eighth, quickly setting down Perez, Foster, and Concepcion. When Dwight Evans worked Carroll for a hard-earned walk to open the home half of the eighth, reviving hopes in Fenway, Don Zimmer signaled Rick Burleson to sacrifice him to second; after two failed attempts, Burleson grounded to Pete Rose, a tailor-made, morale-busting third-to-second-to-first double play. Now, with two outs and nobody on, Johnson went for broke; he decided to send up Cecil Cooper to bat for the effective Willoughby, a pretty fair hitter in his own right. On the first pitch, Cooper popped out meekly to third, ending his unfortunate World Series at 1–19.

Red Sox closer Dick Drago was in the Boston bullpen, pumped and ready to pitch the top of the ninth, but Darrell Johnson, whose brief managerial career had been clouded by head-scratching decisions, now made perhaps his most baffling move of all; with left-handers Ken Griffey and Cesar Geronimo due up to lead off the inning, Johnson played percentages instead of common sense and sent his last remaining left-hander, rookie Jim Burton, to the mound. A former collegiate star at Michigan State, Burton had faced only two batters in the World Series, more than a week before in Game Three back in Cincinnati, walking one and giving up a run-scoring sacrifice fly to the other. Since joining the Red Sox in mid-season, he had appeared in only twenty-nine games, the full extent of his major-league résumé, and nothing about his performance to date suggested that he was up to the task Johnson now sent him in to face. Young Burton was shocked numb even to find himself in this situation, and had been so nervous in the bullpen just thinking about what lay in store on the mound that he'd been unable to get loose. He later admitted he was scared to death, so there's little surprise that he had trouble locating the strike zone against the first man he faced, when he walked Ken Griffey on five pitches.

What then followed played out with a stubborn air of inevitability. Sparky asked for the textbook sacrifice and Cesar Geronimo laid down a beautiful bunt just inside the third base line, moving Griffey to second; Rico Petrocelli charged in, slipped on a wet patch of grass, and made a tremendous throw from the seat of his pants to retire the swift Geronimo at first. Reds reserve infielder Doug Flynn had gone out to the on-deck circle to pinch-hit for Clay Carroll—this was as close as Flynn would come to making an appearance in this World Series; he recalled that the experience of standing just off stage at such a critical moment seemed to suck all the oxygen out of the open air in Fenway—but Sparky then called him back to the dugout and sent up the left-handed Dan Driessen in his place. Driessen, showing not much more comfort than Flynn had just been feeling, flailed at Burton's first pitch and grounded out weakly to Denny Doyle at second, but Griffey moved over to third on the play.

Darrell Johnson went out with Fisk to talk to their young pitcher, who now had to face the indomitable, switch-hitting Pete Rose for the first time in his life, reminding him that the team's book on Pete was to feed him a steady diet of breaking balls. Burton did his best to follow their advice, taking the count full while Rose never took the bat off his shoulder, making the rookie work; Burton then lost him on a wild curve, and Rose trotted down to first with the walk.

First and third, two outs, tied in Game Seven in the top of the ninth, and in stepped the National League's Most Valuable Player, Joe Morgan. He'd already won Game Three of this World Series in the final inning, and probably would have won Game Six as well if not for Dwight Evans's miraculous catch. There would be no show of nerves or panicked thoughts now for Morgan; just like his running mate Pete Rose, he'd been preparing for this moment his entire life: He *wanted* to be the guy at bat with the Series on the line.

But Jim Burton had burned through his initial nervousness by now; no longer thinking about who was up to bat anymore, he was ready. His first pitch missed just outside for a ball, and then Morgan fouled a good hard slider back for strike one.

In the Cincinnati bullpen, left-hander Will McEnaney—who'd dug the Reds out of certain death with the bases loaded and nobody out in the ninth the night before—had just been told he was coming in to pitch the bottom of the inning. He watched anxiously from right field as Morgan slashed Burton's next pitch foul down the left field line, behind in the count now 1–2. Morgan fouled the next pitch, too, a good slow curve from Burton, down the right side wide of first, staying alive.

Morgan stepped out, took a deep breath, dug back in, twitched his elbow four times, and Burton fired his best pitch of the game— he later called it the best pitch of his life—a slider that tailed toward the low outside corner. Morgan saw it moving, adjusted while the pitch was in the air, kept his weight back, whipped his bat inside out, felt a dull impact as he caught it on the end of the wood, and gently lofted a soft liner toward left center field. Playing Morgan deep with two outs, Fred Lynn raced desperately forward but could only reach the ball after the first hop. Ken Griffey watched the ball touch grass and then made it home with the go-ahead run for the Reds. Rose soared headfirst safely into third, just ahead of Lynn's throw to Petrocelli, while Morgan alertly advanced to second.

Reds 4, Red Sox 3.

Dead silence in Fenway Park. Darrell Johnson trudged out to remove the devastated Burton, calling in right-handed starter Reggie Cleveland to face Johnny Bench. Giving him nothing to hit, the Canadian-born Cleveland pitched the count full before walking Bench to load the bases. Tony Perez followed, flying out to Dwight Evans to end the inning, but the damage had been done. Trailing for the first time in Game Seven, the Red Sox were down to their final three outs.

Thrusting a player with as little experience as Jim Burton into a moment as fraught with peril as this would never have occurred to Sparky Anderson. Twenty-three-year-old Will McEnaney might have been the youngest player on either roster, but he was no rookie, and because he'd showed he had the brass to rescue them in the ninth the night before, Sparky felt no hesitation in calling on him to now close out Game Seven. The Red Sox also had three left-handers due up to start the inning, making Sparky's decision even easier.

McEnaney came briefly into the dugout before taking the mound, and Sparky went over to say something to him. McEnaney held up a hand: "It's okay, Skip, I know what I'm doing." McEnaney trotted out onto the field, and Sparky retreated into the tunnel for another cigarette.

But the first batter of the Red Sox's last stand wouldn't be Bernie Carbo, who might have been able to reach down for another miracle with a single swing; Johnson had replaced Carbo in left field two innings earlier, when Boston still held a one-run lead, with defensive specialist Rick Miller, another decision that now came back to haunt him. Now, in place of the left-handed Miller, Johnson played percentages again, hoping he might elicit a pitching change from Sparky—perhaps to Rawly Eastwick, whose confidence had suffered such a blow the night before—and sent to the plate his last outfielder, right-handed Juan Beniquez, who had played sparingly in the last month and gone only 1–7 in the Series. Sparky, who only played percentages until his trusted gut told him otherwise, didn't take the bait, and elected to stay with his tough left-hander McEnaney.

Looking calm and collected, and this time paying rapt attention to Johnny Bench's signs, McEnaney worked Beniquez to fly weakly to Griffey in right on the third pitch he threw him, for the first out. Now events in the Red Sox dugout turned chaotic: Red Sox second baseman Denny Doyle, the only man on either team to hit safely in all seven games of the Series, had been the reliable sparkplug for their offense since the moment he'd arrived in mid-season. After the Reds took the lead in the top of the inning, Darrell Johnson had taken aside his right-handed backup second baseman Doug Griffin, who'd had one at bat in the entire Series, and told him that he'd be hitting for Doyle in the ninth. But Johnson never told Doyle, who was just now leaving the on-deck circle for the batter's box, and who was shocked and not a little angry to hear his manager call him back to the dugout. But a moment later so was Doug Griffin, because as he walked onto the field to take Doyle's spot, without telling him, Darrell Johnson now sent up yet *another* right-handed pinch hitter in his place: backup catcher Bob Montgomery, who had hit .226 with only two home runs on the year, the slowest man on the team, now being asked to make his first appearance in the entire postseason. Griffin returned to the dugout, fuming and humiliated.

Percentages be damned, this was a sequence of events far beyond baffling; in the Cincinnati dugout, Sparky could scarcely believe his eyes. The Reds' coaches had to quickly consult their scouting book on how to position their fielders for Montgomery. A curious footnote: Montgomery was the last man in the major leagues who still went to the plate without a batting helmet; although a rule mandating their use had been instituted four years earlier, it allowed players who had preferred not to use them prior to 1971 to continue the practice.

None of which mattered: Montgomery swung at McEnaney's first-pitch fastball and hit a routine grounder to Dave Concepcion.

Two gone in the ninth.

Down one run, and down to his last out in the World Series, Johnson had no more moves to make, because the Red Sox couldn't have asked for a better man who'd ever worn their uniform to enter the arena.

Carl Yastrzemski.

The crowd rose to its feet one last time, trying to will their aging captain to one last marvel. Yaz stood in, thinking home run; McEnaney knew it, and so did everyone else in Fenway Park. Yaz had been one of McEnaney's baseball gods ever since he was a kid, and his mouth went dry as he watched him dig in; he suddenly couldn't swallow. Will knew he couldn't give Yaz anything to hit, but he couldn't afford to pitch around him either, not with Fisk and Lynn to follow. McEnaney and Yastrzemski had faced each other twice before in the Series to date so there were no secrets or tricks to fall back on; it would be strength against strength.

Bench called for the slider; McEnaney missed with it outside for a ball. Bench asked for it again, and he missed low, behind in the count 2–0.

Now Yaz looked for the fastball, and Bench called for one inside, and it was perfect, on the black; Yaz laid off it and Art Frantz called strike.

Bench signaled fastball again, and again Yaz looked for it, but this time McEnaney let it get away from him, up in the zone and out over the plate, a dangerous pitch, and Yaz took a powerful rip. A high fly ball soared out toward left center field, and Yaz's first thought was that he'd caught most of it, certainly enough to knock it off the wall, if not over.

But the wind held it up. Swinging for the fences, he realized then that he'd dropped his hands the smallest fraction and gotten just under the ball. He looked on helplessly as Cesar Geronimo glided backward, ten feet in front of the warning track. The clock on the Green Monster behind him read 11:35 on Wednesday night.

Final score: Cincinnati 4, Boston 3.

Will McEnaney watched the ball land in Geronimo's glove. Johnny Bench ran out toward him on the mound, tearing off his mask, his eyes wide with wonder, overwhelmed by the realization it was over.

"What do we do?" asked Johnny.

McEnaney answered by jumping into his arms and thrusting his fists in the air; a *Sports Illustrated* photographer immortalized the moment. The rest of the Reds piled out of the dugout toward the mound, as their teammates out in the field and the bullpen sprinted in to join them in a mass embrace.

But Sparky turned the other way, walking quickly up the tunnel toward the clubhouse, and he sat himself down on the ancient steps below Fenway, where it had suddenly gone as silent as a church, alone for a moment to offer up his private gratitude and prayers for this gift, preferring not to let all his young victors see the tears that flowed freely from him now.

Johnny Bench caught Don Zimmer's eye—instantly seeing his heartbreak—and ran over to shake his old friend's hand, before they were separated by an unruly pack from the crowd who jumped onto the field and began scavenging for souvenirs. A few tried to tear gloves or warm-up jackets out of the Reds' hands, so forming a phalanx, the winning team quickly retreated past the line of police that had assembled along the dugout steps and ran up the tunnel. After gathering himself in privacy, Sparky now greeted his men one by one as they came in, handshakes and hugs, and led them into the sanctuary of their clubhouse to celebrate.

Some of the Red Sox lingered for a while in their dugout, staring blankly out at the diamond. Tactical police, wearing riot helmets, escorted the last of their pitchers in from the Boston bullpen through the unruly remnants. Luis Tiant, his hat off, looking out at the mound from the steps of the dugout, was the last man to quit the field.

On this night, less than twenty-four hours after the dizzying crescendo of Game Six, the rest of a silent, depressed, and orderly crowd cleared out of Fenway Park in less than ten minutes. Four hundred policemen had been stationed between the ballpark and Kenmore Square, prepared for either trouble or even greater celebration, and they scarcely needed to move. Only eighteen minor injuries were reported on the night, most of those from people falling in the bleachers.

Tony Kubek, who'd made his way from the booth to the Cincinnati clubhouse during the bottom of the ninth, on this night without having to change direction, jumped up on some tables they'd thrust together and prepped for interviews alongside the Reds' young broadcaster Marty Brennaman in front of NBC's cameras.

Eight hundred and sixty-two miles away, car horns blared and firecrackers crackled through the night as thousands of fans celebrated in Cincinnati's downtown Fountain Square: The Reds had won their first World Championship in thirty-five years.

Pete Rose and Joe Morgan hung on to each other in their locker room; their strong, unbreakable bond—perhaps the closest friendship in baseball history between a white and black player—had at last captured a championship for the Big Red Machine. If Tony Perez represented the soul of this team, and Bench its sturdy backbone, these two unlikely superstars remained its beating heart.

Tony Kubek brought a red-eyed Sparky Anderson up on the tables for the first interview. "This one's for my friend Milt Blish, and my family who's not here, and for all my friends and everybody I love." Then, overcome with emotion once again, Sparky couldn't say another word, turned away from the cameras, and down into the embraces of his coaches and players.

A beaming Joe Morgan gave all credit to Pete Rose and their hitting coach Ted Kluszewski, whom he credited with teaching him how to handle tough outside pitches, and then went out of his way to compliment losing Red Sox pitcher Jim Burton, saying he'd thrown him an almost perfect final pitch and that he'd been fortunate just to get a piece of it to drive in the winning run. Morgan had collected only seven hits in the World Series, but two of them had won exactly half the games they needed for the title.

Tony Kubek informed Pete Rose, who'd hit .370 and driven in Game Seven's tying run, that he'd just been named the Series' Most Valuable Player; the writers also couldn't help but notice that Pete had reached base on eleven of his last fifteen plate appearances, remarkable by any standard. As Morgan poured champagne over his mop-top haircut, Rose barely appeared to hear what Kubek told him. His vocal cords shredded from shouting at his teammates, Pete gave all the credit to Tony Perez for getting them back in it with his home run in the sixth—"That was the turning point"—and to Joe Morgan for coming through in the ninth just as he had ever since he'd become the final piece of the Big Red Machine. The power, the defense, the bullpen, and timely hits and speed and hustle—in the end this flesh-and-blood wonder that Bob Howsam and Ray Shore and Sparky Anderson envisioned, designed, and assembled had at last come together.

"This is the happiest moment of my life," said Rose. "Let's do it again; I'm ready to start spring training tomorrow."

An elated, articulate, exhausted Johnny Bench echoed that sentiment, his voice cracking with emotion, and also gave worlds of credit to the Red Sox, who had fought them longer and harder and tougher than they or anyone else had ever imagined they would be able to do. Reds team president Bob Howsam shook hands with Commissioner Bowie Kuhn, accepting his congratulations for the cameras. Both men agreed that they had just witnessed the end of the greatest World Series in baseball history.

Three of the team's second-stringers jumped up on a table and mocked the Fenway crowd's chant of "Loo-ee, Loo-ee!" Joe Morgan, annoyed, told them to knock it off and show some respect.

"Luis Tiant can pitch on any team in any league and be a winner," he said.

After Johnny Bench was done talking to the press, utterly spent, he sat and watched Tony and Pete and Joe and Gary and the others letting loose, the pressure finally off them all, and then his gaze settled on Sparky, his eyes dazzling now, moving through the room,

29. Jack Billingham

30. Pedro Borbon

32. George Foster

31. Ken Griffey Sr.

33. Senator George McGovern and Fidel Castro, discussing the Tiant case, Havana, 1975

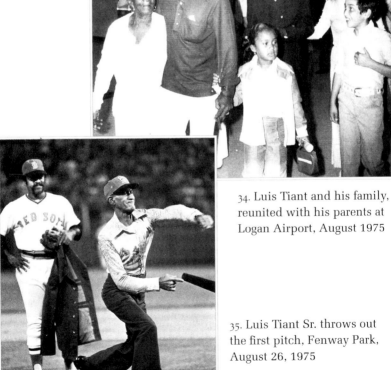

34. Luis Tiant and his family, reunited with his parents at Logan Airport, August 1975

35. Luis Tiant Sr. throws out the first pitch, Fenway Park, August 26, 1975

36. Fred Lynn, after the fifth inning collision

37. Rawlins "Rawly" Eastwick, III

38. Bernie Carbo

39. Rawly Eastwick, Bernie Carbo, eighth inning, Game Six; "It's a whole new ball game."

40. Roger Moret

41. Dick Drago

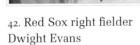

42. Red Sox right fielder
Dwight Evans

43. Red Sox right fielder
Dwight Evans; the catch,
eleventh inning, Game Six

45.
. . . going,
going . . .

46.
. . . gone

44. Pat Darcy, the last pitch

47. Fisk, the winning run, Game Six

48. Rick Wise

49. Red Sox pitcher
Bill "Spaceman" Lee

50. The umpires,
before Game Seven
(L TO R: George Maloney,
Dick Stello,
Larry Barnett,
Satch Davidson,
Nick Colosi,
and Art Frantz)

51. Bill Lee, Tony
Perez; "the Leephus
Pitch," sixth inning,
Game Seven

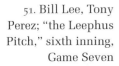

52. The Great Eight,
before Game Seven

53. Will
McEnaney,
the end of
Game Seven

54. Sparky Anderson
and Johnny Bench,
Fenway Park
Visitors' Clubhouse,
after Game Seven

55. Johnny Bench, Fenway Park Visitors' Clubhouse, after Game Seven

stopping to savor and share the triumph with each and every one of his players, and Bench felt happier for him at that moment than for anyone else there. The lively little man who'd chased the dream for a decade but never found success as a player himself, who with hard work, persistence, and bedrock strength of character had made himself into the best manager in the game, showing more insight, fairness, and compassion for the men in his charge than anyone Bench had ever known. Sparky had always tried to tell them that what they'd all been striving for wasn't about money or fame or trophies; it was about the *feeling,* what getting there together would give their hearts and souls that no one could then ever take away.

And this was it, right here and now—*this moment, this feeling*—after all their years of striving and winning and falling short, they had finally made it to the top, and with that peculiar, distant second sight of his, Johnny knew right then that it would live on in all of them forever.

THE RED SOX stayed in their clubhouse while the Reds celebrated long into the night. The mood in the home locker room remained solemn, and they spoke dutifully to reporters, but no one seemed to have the energy for anger. Subdued and wrung out, all struggled for words to adequately express their disappointment; the contrast from the extraordinary high they'd experienced less than twenty-four hours earlier was almost too great to comprehend.

Only an agitated Bill Lee couldn't let it go, already sick and tired of talking about the lollipop pitch he'd thrown to Perez, wondering why nobody asked him about the pitch he'd thrown to Bench just before that should have resulted in an inning-ending double play if Doyle had made the throw to first.

"Dynasty, my ass," Lee said bitterly, when asked if he thought the Reds were now confirmed as the best team in baseball.

"I know we made believers out of a lot of people," said a red-eyed Don Zimmer. "Especially the Cincinnati Reds. They know they were in a dogfight."

Denny Doyle didn't come out of the showers until the last of the reporters had drifted away. Cecil Cooper sat banging a bat into his duffel bag after he'd packed up his belongings. Rick Burleson just stared into his locker.

As Rico Petrocelli sat in front of his locker, contemplating his uncertain future—his doctors would now have to decide whether he should keep playing—Bernie Carbo came by to quietly shake his hand: "I really hope you come back, Rico."

"What do I do now? How do I take this? I just feel dried out, mentally," said Dick Drago. "I mean, it's been a lot of fun, but . . ."

"We should have won five of the seven games," said Jim Willoughby. "We lose on a bleeder. We lose the World Series on a chip shot to center field."

"We had nothing to be ashamed of," said Dwight Evans. "We gave it all we had."

"Yes, I'm drained," admitted Carlton Fisk. "I think we all were tonight after last night's game, and that's probably why we couldn't take advantage of the opportunities we had early in the game."

"I think this brought us closer as a team," said Carbo. "We know what we can do now. With all this talent, we'll be back in this thing again. But I know, right now, I couldn't play another game tomorrow."

When asked if this defeat felt more disappointing than the last World Series the Red Sox had lost, in 1967, their grim but resolute captain Carl Yastrzemski shook his head, trying to correct and set the tone. "This is tough, but we'll put this one behind us. We have a good, young team. Let's start thinking about next year."

But he also thought back to a conversation he'd had with Tom Yawkey years earlier, when in a brutal on-field collision he'd suffered two broken ribs and a lacerated kidney during the 1965 season. Yawkey had come to visit him every day during his nine days in the hospital after surgery; that was when Yaz felt he'd really gotten to know his employer, and they'd been extremely close ever since. Yawkey was never comfortable talking much about himself—he kept the focus on his young ballplayer and how he was progressing—but one day he opened up to him. "Yaz, you have no idea what it would mean to me to win it all. Just once."

Slumped on a bench in the corner of the locker room, Coach Johnny Pesky, who'd spent more years in a Red Sox uniform than anyone else in the room, had tears in his eyes: "I just feel so badly for Mr. Yawkey that we couldn't win that seventh game for him again."

TOM YAWKEY, who'd remained in his private rooftop box until most of the crowd had filed out of Fenway Park, walked out haltingly, ashen but with his head held high. A single reporter stood outside in respectful silence, waiting for him to speak first.

"Three times for the World Series Championship, three times into the seventh game . . . three times a loser." His voice trailed away, and then he tried to rally. "But I'm proud of my players. They gave it everything they possibly could."

His wife Jean gripped his arm and helped her ailing husband slowly toward the stairs.

"I guess it just wasn't meant to be," he said quietly.

AFTERWARD

We didn't win this World Series. Baseball did.

Sparky Anderson

I want to own the Red Sox until the day I die;
then I'll decide what to do with them.

Tom Yawkey

T HAT THESE TWO TEAMS HAD JUST PLAYED THE MOST competitive World Series in baseball history remains beyond dispute; five one-run games, five come-from-behind wins—including all four won by the Reds—and two extra-inning affairs, including the unprecedented drama and spectacle of Game Six. The Red Sox had outscored the Reds in the Series by a single run, 30–29, while logging sixty hits to the Reds' fifty-nine. The Red Sox pitching staff had recorded an ERA of 3.86, to the Reds' 3.88. Both teams had played extraordinary defense; of those fifty-nine runs scored, only three in the entire Series were unearned. The numbers confirm that never had two teams in a championship been more evenly matched, but there had been much more than routine excellence on display; stars had delivered under pressure, unknowns had turned into heroes, and millions of fans with no rooting interest in either team had been brought back to baseball by the extraordinary drama the two teams had created. As a result, more people had watched the 1975 World Series on television than any ever played—NBC banked record revenues for their good fortune—and the excitement it generated, if only temporarily, lifted the spirits of a country in dire need of distraction from hard and troubled times. Professional baseball benefited more directly: The 1975 World Series ignited a major revival in both ratings and live attendance for the sport that would last throughout the decade. And due to its exposure during the broadcasts, Fenway Park began its transformation from a battered old local landmark to a beloved national baseball mecca.

Based on the strength, guts, and experience of their rosters, both teams now seemed poised to dominate their respective leagues for years to come, but the fairy tale ending promised by Game Six for the long-suffering Red Sox and their fans died hard and fast. The World Champion Reds returned to Cincinnati in triumph, and while that city turned out in force to celebrate their ascension with a daylight parade that lifted civic pride to levels unseen in two generations, Boston was about to endure a long, cold winter of discontent, dominated by headlines of racial strife in its forcibly integrated schools and furious political protest on its streets. Politicians in Washington grudgingly admitted that the nation's economy was mired in its second year of the most serious recession since the Great Depression—resulting in a combination of runaway inflation and economic stagnation that the press dubbed "stagflation"—while all Western democracies confronted not only the continued tensions of the Cold War but a new threat posed by a cartel of hostile oil-producing nations called OPEC; a darker global reality had dawned. On the heels of the disastrous Watergate disgrace, and only six months after the last American military forces had withdrawn in defeat from Vietnam, America's image and standing in the world appeared suddenly and shockingly diminished. Gerald Ford, the nation's unelected president, his own image indelibly tarnished by his controversial pardon of Richard Nixon, faced a serious challenge within his own party for the coming bicentennial-year election from a retired movie star, California's former governor Ronald Reagan, a man long considered too radically conservative and outside the mainstream of political discourse for national office. Late that fall, almost unnoticed, an obscure one-term governor of Georgia and peanut farmer named Jimmy Carter declared that he would seek the Democratic nomination for President in 1976.

Red Sox owner Tom Yawkey's health seriously deteriorated after the World Series, and the news that he was undergoing chemotherapy for leukemia slowly filtered out of the organization and into the community. Although fans and many writers preferred to believe that their team's youth and precocious success had just sounded the overture to a certain future dynasty, this most recent defeat had delivered a mortal blow to Yawkey's endurance and will to survive. He would spend the coming months in and out of the hospital, while his capacities to provide direction and leadership for his team steadily declined, at a moment when it turned out they were needed the most.

Because the rules of baseball, as the game had always been played *off* the field, were about to change forever.

On December 23, 1975, in the office of MLB's official arbiter, the nearly century-long reign of baseball's reserve clause came to a shocking and sudden end. Since its inception in the late nineteenth century, the reserve clause had stipulated that every player currently under contract to any team—traditionally one-year deals—remained under legal obligation for an option year beyond the life of that contract, during which they were compelled to negotiate and sign their *next* contract exclusively with that same team. If the team failed to come to terms with players before a season began, they possessed the unilateral right to then renew their contracts for an additional year, which triggered yet another "option" year. As the owners' logic had evolved over the intervening decades, baseball teams therefore "reserved" the right to maintain a legal vise grip on their players, as long as any signed contract existed, in perpetuity. There had been many challenges by players over the years to this brief, stubborn legal provision, one that owners argued was the key to their ability to operate as a business, but all had been turned aside by the American judicial establishment, up to and including the Supreme Court in the case of Cardinals outfielder Curt Flood in 1969. A three-time All-Star, Flood sacrificed his career while trying to free himself from the reserve clause; when his attempt failed, he was out of baseball in less than two years. Many others had tried to buck the system before and since, but no one on the players' side of the argument had ever before stopped to consider: What would happen if the reserve clause was challenged by a player *without* a signed contract?

With the encouragement and support of Marvin Miller, the former labor lawyer and then director of the Major League Baseball Players Association, starting pitchers Andy Messersmith and Dave McNally—of the Dodgers and Montreal Expos, respectively—had for different reasons refused to sign contracts with their teams prior to the 1975 season. Both teams then exercised what the reserve clause maintained was their legal right and unilaterally renewed their contracts, offering small raises, for the 1975 season. Both men showed up to work in 1975—Messersmith would win nineteen games for the Dodgers that year; McNally ended up retiring before the season ended—and both were paid according to the terms of their "option year" contracts, but neither man ever put pen to paper *agreeing* to those terms in a *new* contract. At the conclusion of the 1975 season, Messersmith and then McNally—who had no plans to play again, but participated on principle alone—then filed with Major League Baseball legal grievances claiming that because they had played out their option year *without* signed contracts, they were no longer bound or obliged by the stated terms of the reserve clause to negotiate exclusively with their current teams for the coming 1976 season. The next move in this high-stakes chess match was dictated by a concession Miller had won from baseball's owners in 1970's Basic Agreement: that instead of being decided internally by the owners themselves, this troublesome case would now be submitted to professional arbitration. And that meant their arguments would be heard by the arbitrator retained by baseball for exactly this purpose, seventy-year-old New York attorney Peter M. Seitz.

The heart of the players' brief was simplicity itself: The language of the reserve clause concretely stated that the rights of teams to renew a player's contract extended "for a period of one year" beyond the life of the current signed contract. That period, in both men's cases, had now clearly expired, and therefore they claimed the reserve clause no longer exerted any limits or authority over their ability to seek employment elsewhere within the sport of professional baseball. And on December 23, 1975, Major League Baseball's salaried legal arbiter, Peter Seitz, handed down his ruling—known forever after as the "Seitz Decision"—that he agreed with the players' interpretation of the language in the reserve clause. He founded his decision on a central tenet of American contract law, that whenever a clause is ambiguous, the ambiguity should be interpreted in a manner *least* beneficial to the party who had placed that clause in the contract to begin with. That party was Major League Baseball, and if team owners had truly wanted an eternal iron-clad grip on their players—according to Seitz—they should have spelled it out in more concrete terms. Seitz didn't find that the reserve clause was in any way illegal, he simply agreed with the players that the clause, as written, should only be legally binding for one year.

It should not surprise anyone to learn that the first person to lose his job as a result of this ruling was Peter Seitz. Major League Baseball immediately filed an appeal with what they thought would be a sympathetic district court in Western Missouri, but on February 4, 1976, Judge John Oliver upheld the Seitz Decision. When the Eighth Circuit Court of Appeals followed suit shortly thereafter, Major League Baseball ran out of legal options; the Seitz Decision now stood affirmed as the law of the land. Paralyzed since Seitz's initial ruling, the owners responded by locking players out of spring training, and players answered by saying they wouldn't show up anyway without a new Basic Agreement that incorporated the seismic ramifications of the Seitz Decision; the 1976 season, and the future of baseball itself, appeared to be in jeopardy. After the players rejected what the owners threatened would be their final offer, Commissioner Bowie Kuhn ordered both sides to shut up, sit down, and figure it out—and show up for work in the meantime until they did. Both sides—thanks to the credibility and influence of a more or less "independent" commissioner—complied. The lockout ended and the games began again, as the brutal negotiations between management and labor to craft a new Basic Agreement that incorporated these radically altered legal dimensions into baseball dragged on until after America celebrated its two hundredth birthday in July. But in the interim, this new reality remained beyond dispute: Any player under contract in 1975 who now played through the 1976 season—the so-called "option year"—*without* a new signed contract would at the end of the season immediately become a "free agent"—a freshly minted term that now dominated the lexicon of baseball—and would possess the right to then offer his services and negotiate freely with any team for any price he could get for the 1977 season. Teams tried to circumvent the issue by scrambling to sign their best players to multi-year contracts, but before the Basic Agreement could be hammered out, nearly sixty players—all now represented or advised, many for the first time, by professional agents—announced that they intended to take advantage of the Seitz Decision and enter the 1976 season unsigned. As far as baseball's twenty-four owners were concerned, this was a doomsday scenario: Their employees had been granted the right to a level playing field. The inability, or stubborn unwillingness, of many of them to accept the game's new social and economic paradigm would soon consign many of its franchises to disaster.

None more notably than the Boston Red Sox and the Cincinnati Reds.

FIVE DAYS AFTER America celebrated its bicentennial with the most lavish and elaborate nationwide party in its history, Tom Yawkey passed away in his sleep at New England Baptist Hospital, early in the morning of July 9, 1976. The flag flew at half-mast in Fenway Park that night, John Kiley refrained from playing his usual version of "Take Me Out to the Ballgame" when the Red Sox took the field, and the home crowd observed a reverent moment of silence before the game. The eulogies in Boston's papers elaborately detailed Yawkey's four decades of devotion to the city's beloved team. Much was made of his legendary kindness to players, past and present, and tributes poured in to honor his accomplishments as a philanthropist, conservationist—he designated that most of his vast South

Carolina estate should become a natural game reserve—and "gentle-man sportsman," an archaic term that with Yawkey's passing had lost one of its last connections to the current age. Tom Yawkey had been nearly the last of a vanishing breed in professional baseball, the individual owner who wrote all the checks because he loved the game more as a pastime than a business. If his team lost money through the lean years, and there were many, so be it, Yawkey's fortune could well afford red ink, and the good years, the pennant runs, the three World Series they'd fought their hearts out for in his accounting more than balanced the ledger. The two stars with whom he'd been the closest—Ted Williams and Carl Yastrzemski; he always called them his "two sons"—were both moved to tears as they recollected the years they'd spent in Yawkey's company and employ. Yaz recalled the particular kindness that Yawkey had shown his mother, Hattie, during her own battle with cancer the previous year, when he had seen to it she was treated by the best doctors available, even giving up his seat in the owner's box in Cincinnati for Game Five so Hattie could be closer to the field.

Tom Yawkey took his leave from life and the game he loved at a moment when baseball was about to become unrecognizable to him. He had moved far beyond the restless rich dilettante who'd bought the team as a shiny new toy in the depths of the Depression, the silver spoon tycoon who had so desperately craved the company and friendship of the working-class athletes on his payroll. He had been raised in strange and splendid isolation, a multimillionaire many times over since his teenage years, and had only grown steadily richer, through no visible effort of his own; nothing had ever been denied him but a parent's love, and perhaps that's the Rosebud at the heart of America's sporting Citizen Kane, a soft, shy puzzle of a man with no apparent gift for intimacy, or interest in a family life, who'd received or expressed most of the affection he'd known with people on his payroll. After carefully selling off over half of his diverse holdings in the months before he died, and distributing their worth to his heirs in order to avoid estate taxes, Yawkey still bequeathed a fortune in excess of $50 million to his widow Jean. The ownership of Fenway Park and the Red Sox he also passed, through the instrument of a complicated trust, to the control of Jean Yawkey. Tom Yawkey's only daughter, Julia, from his first marriage, received $10,000.

Based on the last few negative statements he issued about the game's dawning age that he was about to miss—the gold rush frontier of free agency—Tom Yawkey never grasped the irony that he had, in many ways, set the table for this new era with his own spendthrift pursuit of superstars during his first decades with the Red Sox. George Steinbrenner was about to seize center stage in baseball as the newly installed, bellicose, free-spending monarch of the New York Yankees—buying them back into championship form through free agency with the flowing coffers of his cable television revenues—and Steinbrenner's brash, buccaneer attitude toward his fellow owners resembled no one so much as young Tom Yawkey tossing his wallet on the table in 1933 and daring his colleagues to sell him their best players. He couldn't legitimately complain now about other teams' players fighting for whatever wage the market would bear when he'd been coddling and overpaying his own men since day one, a grudge that his sport's fellow owners had perpetually held against him. The awkward truth about Tom Yawkey's record-setting tenure at the helm of a single sports franchise—not only the longest in baseball history, but the longest in any American sport spent without capturing a championship—was that he'd never been particularly good at building or sustaining a team. He'd constantly packed his front office with big-talking, egotistical former stars who he'd once admired as players, most of whom clearly had no executive discipline or eye for talent. The Red Sox teams they assembled had coalesced into a pennant winner just three times in forty-three years, but each time almost accidentally—in spite of the owner and his cronies—and each time, just as quickly but for different reasons, the team had settled back into its familiar pattern of colorful but consistent mediocrity.

Let it also be noted that the grief of Ted Williams, and Carl Yastrzemski, and countless others who had been the beneficiaries of his many acts of kindness was as genuine as Tom Yawkey's generosity. If he seemed unable to verbalize his deep feelings for the people around him, he clearly emanated those feelings in a way that they understood and appreciated. Ask Carlton Fisk, with Yawkey's hand on his shoulder at the end of a heartbreaking pennant race, or Bernie Carbo, when the personal check that allowed him to buy a house for his family landed in his locker. Perhaps what Yawkey had learned by life's end—we'll never know for certain—was that in his final reckoning those moments of personal connections were more valuable to the unloved boy he'd been than a room full of championship trophies. Add that to the boundless affection he'd received from those grateful fans in Boston as he roamed the stands and city during his final seasons, and perhaps he'd found some measure of what he'd always needed, if not the actual prize he thought he'd been seeking from the start.

The last baseball decision that Tom Yawkey took an interest in, a few weeks before his death, epitomized the new freewheeling, school's-out-forever atmosphere of the game, and presaged the dismantling to come. After their glorious fall of 1975, the Red Sox struggled out of spring training during the tumultuous early months of the 1976 season, despite some strong front-office moves during the winter to bolster what was already a roster laden with talent. They had acquired All-Star starting pitcher—and future Hall of Famer—Ferguson Jenkins from the Texas Rangers for the little-used Juan Beniquez, some prospects, and cash, to further strengthen their solid starting rotation. Just before spring training, closer Dick Drago, the first man from the '75 roster to move on, had been traded to the California Angels; his place in the bullpen would be taken by Jim Willoughby and a left-hander they then acquired from Atlanta—for the unfortunate, inconvenient Roger Moret—named Tom House. Most importantly, Boston had a healthy Jim Rice back in their everyday lineup, alongside Lynn and Evans, Fisk and Yaz, and a revived Cecil Cooper, a wrecking crew to rival even the mighty Cincinnati Reds. On paper, no other team in the American League matched up.

But trouble resulting from the game's new rules would lay waste to these best-laid plans. During the off-season Fred Lynn and Rick Burleson had joined Carlton Fisk—who'd hired the same man two years earlier—as clients of Jerry Kapstein, one of the first and most aggressive baseball agents, and as the regular season approached, all three of Boston's brightest young stars remained unsigned. Kapstein had spurned all of the Red Sox offers, counseling his players to wait and see what riches this strange new marketplace might offer for his potential "free agents," or at the very least until a new Basic Agreement was reached defining the contractual parameters of the game from that point forward. Kapstein also made it clear to Boston's front office that this was a package deal; there had to be satisfaction for all three of his players or not one of them would sign, a sharp negotiating ploy and as blunt an instrument as anyone had ever wielded against the famously player-friendly Red Sox. And so all that a shocked and weakened Tom Yawkey could perceive from his hospital bed was insubordination and disloyalty in these surrogate sons: Hadn't he always taken special care of his "boys," gone above and beyond to make them feel like part of the family? Yawkey took their strictly business decision as a personal affront, raging in Lear-like isolation at their betrayal, a blow to his heart and soul that some around him claimed hastened his decline. But Red Sox fans around New England shared Yawkey's dismay. Unimaginable only eight months earlier when these players had been cheered as demigods in Fenway, all three of the team's holdouts were booed in the early weeks of the '76 season, and trade winds bearing their names—probably at Yawkey's request—began to blow.

Expectations still soared in Boston as the season began, but amid all this high backstage melodrama the Red Sox stumbled out of the gate, losing their opener to the Orioles on a Jim Palmer shutout. By late May the team was laboring at 13–16, already six games behind George Steinbrenner's first-place Yankees. Red Sox fans' historical hatred of the Yankees, dating back to the Babe Ruth debacle and the pinstripers' four subsequent decades of dominance, had lain dormant during the Yankees' mediocre last decade, but with the revival of the Bronx Bombers under the ruthless management of Billy Martin, a genuine ill-will between the two franchises resurfaced. Bill Lee, the Red Sox union representative who had spent an eventful spring engaged in the ongoing MLB negotiations, had yet to win a game when he started the opener of their first series of the season against the Yankees, on May 20. The Sox trailed by a run in the sixth, when a nasty collision between Yankee outfielder Lou Pinella and Fisk at home plate erupted into a bench-clearing brawl. After trading punches with him, Lee was tossed to the ground by New York's third baseman Graig Nettles; the impact tore a ligament in his left shoulder and afterward Lee angrily branded the Yankees "Steinbrenner's brown shirts." The fight seemed to finally wake up the Red Sox, who after falling behind in the game, came back to win on two Yaz home runs, but Lee, their only effective left-handed starter, would be lost for two months. The Red Sox ended up splitting the four-game series with the Yanks, gaining no ground.

Two weeks later the next wheel fell off: Fall Classic hero Bernie Carbo, who had been largely confined to the bench with the return of Rice and the resurgence of Cecil Cooper, was traded to Milwaukee for reliever Tom Murphy and outfielder Bobby Darwin. When he heard the news after a night game, Carbo went ballistic, careening his car recklessly out of the players' parking lot and straight into a hot dog vendor's stand before speeding away, fortunate that no one was injured or worse in the incident. The fragile, despondent Carbo couldn't bring himself to report to the Brewers for a week. As the June 15 trading deadline approached, rumors abounded that Lynn, Fisk, and Burleson—still playing without contracts—would now be moved as well. Yawkey, desperately ill and entirely removed from the public eye, remained silent. On the morning of the 15th, while on the road for a series in Oakland, Red Sox general manager Dick O'Connell instead announced that an astonishing deal had been reached with the A's cantankerous owner Charlie Finley. A notorious cheapskate, Finley despised the impending idea of free agency with every fiber of his excitable being. His players, almost to a man, loathed Finley in return, and although the A's began play in 1976 with the same roster that had recently won three straight World Championships largely intact, the majority of his stars had decided to enter this pivotal season without signing their contracts. Finley had already traded away slugger Reggie Jackson and left-handed ace Ken Holtzman, both unsigned, to the Orioles, and had no intention of stopping there: Finley had determined he would rid himself of every unsigned player on his team before they walked away without giving him any value in return.

The deal was this: The Red Sox would acquire All-Star outfielder Joe Rudi, and the league's best relief pitcher, Rollie Fingers, for two disposable utility players and $2 million in cash. Finley also announced the same morning that he was sending his best starting pitcher, Vida Blue, to the Yankees for a million and a half. A flurry of other similarly motivated trades involving potential free agents throughout both leagues—although none as patently suspect as Finley's—crowded the transaction wire that day; entire teams that had remained intact for years exploded in minutes. But, for their part, Boston fans and writers rejoiced at the deal, unwilling to look this gift horse in the mouth, certain that the stunning move guaranteed another pennant. The Red Sox immediately initiated negotiations to sign both Rudi and Fingers with their agent, who just happened to be the ubiquitous Jerry Kapstein. Before the game that evening in Oakland, both Rudi and Fingers moved their gear over to the Boston locker room, dressed in their new uniforms, and joined their new teammates in the dugout, but Red Sox manager Darrell Johnson—who later claimed both men had asked him for a rest, worn out by their emotional ordeal, a version of events that both players later denied—used neither of them in that night's game. If they had actually taken the field as Red Sox, it's easier to imagine that what happened next might never have occurred, but Johnson, as had so often been the case during his tenure in Boston, felt more comfortable doing nothing.

"It's all beyond my comprehension," said Johnson after the game, summing up the day's manic events better than anyone in baseball.

The bubble burst early the next morning, when Commissioner Bowie Kuhn—who had been determined to act like the only grown-up in the room since the Seitz Decision—declared that Finley's latest fire-sale deals were null and void because they violated the best interests of baseball. A meeting of all the principals except Yawkey followed in Kuhn's New York office, but the commissioner refused to yield. Two days later, when the Red Sox left Oakland for a series in Anaheim, neither Joe Rudi nor Rollie Fingers were on the flight. Along with Vida Blue, they ended up staying in Oakland and playing out the season as A's, and as they had threatened to do from the start, Rudi and Fingers moved on a few months later as part of the first wave of free agents. An outraged Charles Finley brought a $10 million vanity lawsuit against his own commissioner; nothing came of it but billable hours. Tom Yawkey, worn down and disgusted by the entire affair, took no action at all.

Veteran Red Sox third baseman Rico Petrocelli, who had decided on his doctor's advice to come back for one last campaign with his Boston teammates, watched all of this chaos unfold with dismay. "The whole game has gone completely crazy," he told the *Globe*'s Peter Gammons.

Three days after Tom Yawkey died, on the day before the All-Star Game was to be played in Philadelphia, Major League Baseball announced that terms of a new Basic Agreement had been reached with the Players' Association, which included these first codified definitions of free agency: Any player who had spent six years on a major-league roster could declare for free agency. Any free agent could then be drafted by up to twelve teams, in reverse order of their finish in the just concluded season to try and skew the benefit to less successful franchises; all teams were restricted to signing a maximum of two free agents, or as many as they themselves had lost. The new Basic Agreement would take effect on August 9, and any players signed before that date would still have an option year tacked onto the end of their contracts; any that signed afterward would not.

Darrell Johnson managed the American League All-Star team the next day—Fisk, Lynn, Yaz, and Tiant had made the squad—with the Red Sox stuck at .500, in third place, while rumors that Johnson was about to lose his job ran rampant. On the other side of the field, Sparky Anderson led the National League team onto the field. Four of his Cincinnati regulars had been named to the Senior Circuit's starting lineup—Bench, Morgan, Rose, and George Foster, who was having his first monster year—and Sparky would name three others to the team as reserves, Tony Perez, Davey Concepcion, and Ken Griffey, off to the best start of his young career. President Gerald Ford attended the game, and the National League won the meaningless exhibition easily, 7–1, with Sparky's own Reds providing most of the muscle—seven hits, four runs, and four RBIs among them, including a massive two-run shot by George Foster. Fred Lynn produced the American League's only run, with a solo homer.

From their virtual dead heat atop the sport only nine months before, the two teams from Boston and Cincinnati were now headed in opposite directions. The world champion Reds were already well on their way to another runaway win of the National League's West Division, and in the second half of the season would only play better. It was clear to all observers and participants in Boston that Darrell Johnson had irrevocably lost the confidence of his players and control of his clubhouse; even his former protégé Carlton Fisk had a serious falling-out with him and now openly questioned Johnson in print. When the team lost five of their first six games after the All-Star break, on July 19, less than a year after being named baseball's Major League Manager of the Year, Darrell Johnson was fired as the field manager of the Red Sox and replaced by his third base coach, Don Zimmer, who vowed to restore order and discipline in the Boston locker room.

Now that the new rules were established, within three weeks—all before August 9, when the new Basic Agreement would take effect—the team signed Carlton Fisk, Fred Lynn, and Rick Burleson to expensive, but not crushing, five-year contracts; the plague of free agency had been avoided, for the time being, by the Red Sox after all.

. . .

"THE BIG RED MACHINE" wasn't just the centerpiece of a clever marketing campaign, nor did it simply describe the juggernaut team that had dominated the National League during the 1970s; it was an apt description of the entire organization that team president Bob Howsam had so carefully assembled in Cincinnati since his arrival in 1967. The Reds had had only nine hundred season ticket holders on the books when Howsam was hired by the consortium of local businessmen who owned the team. Only six years later, in 1973, the Reds drew more than 2 million fans at home, the first of eight straight seasons they would pass that benchmark, a remarkable record for a team playing in the second smallest market in major-league baseball. By turning the Reds into a *regional* franchise—thanks to the game's first truly modern marketing department, headed by Dick Wagner—while fielding one of the strongest lineups in baseball history, in 1976 Cincinnati led both leagues in attendance by drawing nearly 2.7 million paying customers. And that year the squad of players that Howsam and Anderson and scout Ray Shore had constructed with such extraordinary care and precision reached its zenith.

The Reds won 102 games in 1976, and captured the National League's West Division by ten games, for their fifth divisional title in seven years. Joe Morgan won his second consecutive Most Valuable Player Award, the fifth awarded to a Red in seven years—teammate George Foster finished second—and Little Joe led the league in both on-base *and* slugging percentage, while stealing sixty bases. Tony Perez drove in more than ninety runs for the tenth consecutive season. Pete Rose led the league in both hits and runs scored, with 130, finishing fourth in the MVP voting. Ken Griffey turned in the league's second highest batting average at .336. Five of the Great Eight hit over .300, and their only starter who *didn't* make the All-Star team—center fielder Cesar Geronimo—hit .307 and won his third Gold Glove in a row. Three other Reds were awarded their customary Gold Gloves—Bench, Morgan, and Concepcion—and the team led all of baseball in fielding percentage, while committing the fewest errors. Whenever his regulars needed a rest, Sparky's disciplined and ready bench players picked up the slack with no visible drop-off. Following Captain Hook's now established formula of relying on his entire pitching staff, the 1976 Reds featured seven ten-game winners—a National League record—and once again led the league in saves.

That fall, for the second year in a row, the Reds swept their first playoff opponent—this time the Philadelphia Phillies, who had won 101 games in the regular season—in the National League Championship Series 3–0. Their opponent in the 1976 World Series would be the New York Yankees; under manager Billy Martin they had withstood a late charge by the Red Sox—who had come to life belatedly once Don Zimmer took over, but ended up finishing third behind the Yanks and Orioles—coasting to the East Division title by ten and a half games, and then squeaked by the Kansas City Royals in five games to capture their first American League pennant since 1964.

Ray Shore's extensive scouting reports told Sparky that the Reds had little to worry about from the Yankees, and once again Shore was on target. Stronger in every measurable category—and even more so in the less tangible ones, like mastery of fundamentals and cast-iron confidence—the Reds hit .313 as a team and swept the Yankees 4–0 to win their second consecutive World Championship, the first time any team from the National League had turned that trick since the New York Giants in 1922. Johnny Bench slugged a three-run home run in Yankee Stadium in the top of the ninth in Game Four to clinch their final victory—he hit .533 in the Series, with six RBIs and two home runs—and was named the Series' Most Valuable Player. After the Reds marched undefeated through their 1976 postseason, the national press combed through all of baseball history for comparisons, found precious few, and delivered a consensus opinion that the Cincinnati Reds of the seventies under Sparky Anderson had earned the right to be considered—along with the Yankees of the twenties and sixties, the Brooklyn Dodgers of the fifties, and the recent Oakland A's—as one of the greatest dynasties that had ever played the game. The same writers predicted that the Reds also had to be considered the odds-on favorite to win their third straight championship in 1977.

But inside Cincinnati's front office, even as the Big Red Machine on the field reached its highest level of perfection, a seed of destruction took root. President Bob Howsam had long been one of baseball's most hardline, conservative critics of the game's deepening labor crises, claiming that America's pastime could not survive without the age-old protections of its reserve clause. After the players won the right to free agency when the Seitz Decision was upheld in federal court, Howsam predicted that its future consequences would one day ruin baseball, driving up payrolls to unimagined levels and forcing teams to price tickets out of the average fan's reach. Large media market franchises with deep pockets would now dominate the sport, he claimed, destroying any illusion of parity and driving smaller city clubs into inevitable decline. Players moving with impunity from team to team in search of bigger paychecks would also ruin any semblance of roster continuity and alienate the blue-collar fans whose forged loyalties to established squads of identifiable players had always supplied baseball's financial and emotional backbone.

So instead of trying to adapt to the rapidly changing times, Howsam determined that his Reds would simply ignore baseball's stark new reality. They quickly signed Rose and Morgan to single-year contracts for 1976 at roughly the same figure—around $200,000, negotiated by their lawyers, not agents—and took the unprecedented step of inking the younger Johnny Bench to a two-year deal for nearly the same money. But when their fourth superstar, Tony Perez, held out for a comparable figure, the team initially wouldn't give it to him. Uber-agent Jerry Kapstein had by then signed six of the Reds as clients, almost all of them pitchers, including their young ace Don Gullett, and at first the Reds' chief negotiator, Dick Wagner, simply refused to deal with him. The owners' lockout postponed the opening of spring training and jeopardized the regular season, but when it ended at Bowie Kuhn's insistence, the team finally signed Tony Perez, grudgingly, to a single-year deal close to what they'd given their other three superstars. Jerry Kapstein's clients were among the last Reds to sign; one, veteran reliever Clay Carroll—

winner of last fall's Game Seven—held out and was promptly traded in late 1975 to the White Sox. Don Gullett, after being told that he didn't deserve a multiyear contract, refused to sign at all, and became the only Cincinnati Red who would declare free agency when the 1976 season ended. The Reds then went about their business as if nothing else had changed, and stormed through the season to the National League pennant and the World Series.

At which point a much less significant rule change in the game that year helped seal the fate of the Big Red Machine: Major League Baseball had decided that the use of a designated hitter should be available to both teams for every game of the 1976 World Series. Sparky penciled in his best left-handed bench player at DH, backup first baseman Dan Driessen, against the Yankees, and Driessen responded by hitting .357 while coming through repeatedly in the clutch. His performance convinced Howsam and Wagner that the twenty-five-year-old Driessen, in their minds long the heir apparent at his position, was at last ready to supplant Tony Perez—who by his high standards had played a subpar postseason, hitting .269, with six RBIs and no home runs—as the Reds' everyday first baseman.

On November 2, 1976, American voters elected Jimmy Carter as the thirty-ninth President of the United States, definitively turning the page on Gerald Ford and his lingering association with Richard Nixon and the Watergate era. Two days later, only two weeks after the Reds had secured a place in the game's pantheon with their second consecutive World Series win, the game's twenty-four owners gathered at the Plaza Hotel in New York for baseball's first free agent draft. Slugger Reggie Jackson generated the noisiest headlines when he was drafted and then signed a few weeks later by George Steinbrenner's Yankees for five years and the staggering sum of nearly $3 million. The Yankees had earlier filled their free agent quota when Reds' ace Don Gullett signed with them for a multiyear, million-dollar deal.

The Boston Red Sox made an equally big splash in the pool later that night by becoming the first team to actually finalize a contract with a free agent they had selected: a relatively unknown right-handed reliever named Bill Campbell, from penny-pinching Calvin Griffith's small-market Minnesota Twins, who had paid Campbell all of $22,000 in 1975 and then refused to give him a $5,000 raise. Campbell had responded by turning in the most spectacular season of his career during his option year, 1976, winning seventeen games and saving twenty, and the Red Sox signed him away for four years and just over a million dollars.

When the Cincinnati Reds' turn to draft a player came that day—they were scheduled, according to the rules, as world champions, to pick last—team president Bob Howsam instead read a prepared statement for the press and the record: "In fairness to the players who have won the World Championship for us two years in a row, and considering the way our organization is structured, we do not think it would be right for the Cincinnati club to get into bidding contests that must come out of this draft." Many, even most, of baseball's owners and management had until recently felt exactly the same way, but when the game's new rules became reality, only the Cincinnati Reds refused to participate.

Twenty-four players in all were selected and eventually signed that day in the first free agent draft, for what turned out to be an average salary of just over $200,000, nearly a 400 percent increase from what had been a major-league player's average working wage in 1976. The future of baseball, as far as its long-suffering players were concerned, had arrived. The owners, even the more free-spending ones, remained wary; they would now wait to see results on the field before opening their wallets any wider.

Neither the Reds nor the Red Sox were finished with their off-season moves. A few weeks later, in early December, Boston traded the gifted Cecil Cooper—who hit .282 with fifteen home runs in 1976, and still hadn't won the confidence of the front office—to the Milwaukee Brewers for two former, problematic Red Sox: first baseman and more traditional slugger George Scott—who suffered from both weight and IQ issues—and prodigal son Bernie Carbo.

On December 16, the Cincinnati Reds finalized a trade of another Kapstein client, reliever Will McEnaney, never mind that he had now saved the final game of two straight World Series, and first baseman Tony Perez to the Montreal Expos for two journeyman pitchers, Woodie Fryman and Dale Murray. Bob Howsam had offered Perez a chance to stay with the Reds in 1977, but only if he would platoon at first with Dan Driessen and accept a pay cut; Perez declined, as was his right, and Howsam knew that if kept Tony on the squad as a part-time player and let him play out his option year, he would then lose him to free agency without compensation. Only his teammates seemed to understand at the time—although both Howsam and Anderson later admitted their mistake—that the unique, intangible qualities of leadership that Tony Perez took with him could never be replaced.

"I never knew until he left that Tony Perez was our number one leader," said Sparky later. "I should have stood up for him, but I didn't. That's how stupid I was."

Perez's attorney, Reuven Katz, organized a press conference in his office, for Perez to give his reaction to the trade before it was officially announced. He also called in his other client, Johnny Bench, Tony's teammate and close friend for ten years, to let him know about it before the news broke. When Bench arrived, he saw the look on Tony's face and neither of them needed to say a word. They hugged, and held on to each other for a long time, in silence. Regaining his composure, Perez remained characteristically professional and dignified in his final Cincinnati press conference and, after fifteen years with the organization, refused to criticize the Reds, saying only that he would always be grateful for the chance they'd given him to come to America from Cuba and make a better life for himself and his family. Bench was too upset to answer questions, but in their hearts both men knew they had come to the end.

And just like that, the glory years of the Big Red Machine were over.

THE BICENTENNIAL YEAR of 1976, which celebrated so many of Boston's contributions to American history, would only be remembered as an ugly season in Fenway Park. The Red Sox faithful fell out of love with the team's three stubborn holdouts—Fisk, Lynn, and Burleson—savaging them that summer for daring to put their own futures ahead of their sacred franchise. Under this unkind scrutiny, only the Rooster improved his performance on the field, while Pudge and Freddy suffered through what fans and writers decided, judged against their own previous Olympian standards, were subpar seasons. Carlton Fisk, the most articulate, proud, and passionate Red Sox player in a generation, never recovered his idealist's love for the purity of the game; that might in most other walks of life simply be called learning the way of the world, but the sensitive Fisk took the very public process of his disillusionment particularly hard. The ageless, always dependable Yaz posted another solid year, and Jim Rice came on strong in the second half after Don Zimmer took over the team; the Red Sox even finished by winning fifteen of their last eighteen games, but they still ended the 1976 season in third place, only four games above five hundred. Bill Lee returned late in the year from his injured shoulder, but won only five games. Ferguson Jenkins, the team's centerpiece off-season acquisition, won only twelve, and lost eleven. The new two-headed bullpen committee of Jim Willoughby and Tom House saved only fourteen games between them.

The most consistent man on the team's troubled pitching staff remained the remarkable Luis Tiant, who at the age of thirty-five went 21–12, with a 3.06 ERA, and finished fifth in the voting for the Cy Young Award, on a team that hadn't spent a single day in first place all season. Luis had treated all of the season's insanity with his customary calm, and simply gone out every fifth game and done his job. In light of the monstrous distractions swirling around him, Tiant's stellar performance in 1976 has to be considered as perhaps his most remarkable achievement. His parents, Luis Senior and Isabel, were there to watch it all unfold. They never did return to their native Cuba when their visas expired; Luis wouldn't allow it, knowing how negligible the chances of ever seeing them again would have been, and the family had spent an idyllic year at their home in

Milton, three generations under one roof, when for the first time in his adult life Luis spent many hours talking about the art and craft of pitching with his father. Then, not long after the 1976 season ended, after suffering through a few weeks of poor health, Luis Senior was diagnosed with an advanced, aggressive and inoperable form of cancer; there was nothing they could do, doctors told Luis, but try to make his father's final weeks as comfortable as possible. With his family around him, very much at peace, Luis Senior left this life on December 9 at Carney Hospital in Boston.

"When my father passed away," said Tiant a while later, "I had a feeling something would happen to my mother. She felt it, too, but she didn't want to make me feel sad."

Three days later, the day before the funeral, during a small gathering with friends and family at their home in Milton, Isabel excused herself and went upstairs to her bedroom, saying she wanted to sit in her favorite chair by the window and spend some time alone with her thoughts. They found her there a short while later; although she had been in good health, Isabel had died quietly of a heart attack or, perhaps more accurately after thirty-six inseparable years with her husband, a broken heart. The end, because they all must end, of a beautiful love story.

So their only son, Luis Tiant, buried his beloved parents together two days later, in twin bronze coffins, side by side at Milton Cemetery. Luis's teammates Carlton Fisk, and his wife and oldest daughter, and Rick Burleson and his wife, were there, along with hundreds of others to share and mourn his loss. In his eulogy for them, Monsignor John Day said that during their fifteen months in America the Tiants had done "more for international peace and goodwill than all the diplomats put together." The cheers thundering around Fenway Park on the night that Luis Senior threw out the first ball after their reunion had been offered as "a sign of love and respect for this man and his family—for their devotion and love of family, which had prevailed against all obstacles." The monsignor closed the service by offering a prayer for the Tiant family, asking that they be given the strength to bear this terrible double blow. Most people, even close friends and teammates, didn't know or realize what a deeply religious man Luis Tiant was; it sustained him now.

"I just thank God for answering my prayers," he said afterward. "To bring them here, and share my best hours, and not be away from them at the end. I have my faith. I accept God's will."

ON THE STRENGTH of free agency, the average major-league salary took another quantum leap forward in 1977, from $52,000 to $74,000, but as the Red Sox had already started to do, now the Reds began to trend downward. In the wake of the Tony Perez trade, what goodwill remained between Reds players and management from the championship years in Cincinnati evaporated like summer rain; the new economic realities had almost instantly reduced the team game of baseball to every man for himself. With only Johnny Bench signed through the coming season, every negotiation became fraught with tension generated by the rising financial tide; Bob Howsam managed to work out three-year deals with Morgan, Foster, and Griffey, and a five-year, $1 million contract for Davey Concepcion, the only Jerry Kapstein client now left on the Reds' roster. But thirty-five-year-old Cincinnati native Pete Rose, the public face of his franchise now for more than a decade, held out for a better deal all through spring training, trading barbed insults with team officials in the press. Not until the night before Opening Day—which baseball traditionally observed with an afternoon game in Cincinnati, home of the first professional team—did Rose and the Reds reach agreement on a two-year deal. With Rose back on board, the Big Red Machine's vaunted offense, they had every reason to believe, would continue to roll.

And so it did, but scoring runs remained only half of the game's complex equation; Cincinnati's underappreciated pitching staff had suffered crippling losses. With ace Don Gullett gone, none of their aging veterans or new acquisitions stepped in to fill the void, and as the season began, both Gary Nolan and Rawly Eastwick—fed up with team management for different reasons—announced that 1977 would be their last season with the Reds. Ineffective early in the season, Woodie Fryman, the veteran starter obtained in the Perez trade, walked away from his guaranteed contract rather than accept a demotion to the bullpen. With the rising Los Angeles Dodgers off to a blazing start under their new manager, Tommy Lasorda—an old Dodger farmhand friend of Sparky's—the Reds found themselves already nine and a half games out of first place by the end of May. Despite being desperate for pitching help, the team sent Gary Nolan packing to the Angels before the June 15 trade deadline for a minor leaguer who never panned out. Their closer, Rawly Eastwick, followed him out the door to the Cardinals, for an untested youngster named Doug Capilla, who returned nothing close to equal value. Both trades attracted far less attention on deadline day because in a trade with the Mets Bob Howsam also managed to bring over Tom Seaver, the first legitimate superstar pitcher that Sparky Anderson had ever managed. The intelligent, disciplined Seaver came through for the Reds as advertised, going 14–3 over the remainder of the season, but he couldn't carry an otherwise woeful pitching staff alone; gutted by the team's disposal of all Jerry Kapstein's clients, the arsenal of reliable bullpen arms Captain Hook needed to succeed was empty. Despite banner years by George Foster—who tied Willie Mays's National League record with 52 home runs, drove in a Reds' record 149 runs, and won the MVP trophy—and Johnny Bench, a mid-season swoon coupled with the Dodgers' continued hot play effectively ended the pennant race by the end of July. Cincinnati finished the 1977 season in second place, ten games behind Los Angeles. By the end of the year—the rockiest behind the closed doors of their clubhouse that the Reds had suffered since Sparky's arrival—even Bob Howsam acknowledged that the absence of the stalwart, stabilizing Tony Perez had wrecked his team's once perfectly balanced chemistry. The other superstar egos that Big Doggie had always helped deflate and keep in check clashed repeatedly, while the younger players coming up felt continually disrespected by both management and teammates. Meanwhile, for his new team in Montreal, all Tony Perez did was bring the same solid leadership qualities to their locker room, and drive in ninety-plus runs for the eleventh straight year.

The Red Sox faced startlingly similar problems in 1977. Their offensive prowess as a team hit an all-time peak, as they launched 213 home runs while scoring 859 runs, both franchise records. Carlton Fisk turned in the finest campaign of his long and distinguished career: 26 home runs and 102 RBIs while hitting .315. Second-year player Butch Hobson wrested the third base job from Rico Petrocelli, who announced his retirement during spring training, and knocked 30 homers with 112 RBIs. George Scott banged 33 round trippers, and Bernie Carbo, back home and comfortable in Fenway again, returned to form with 15 home runs off the bench, while hitting .289. Jim Rice's remarkable talent came to full fruition and he simply dominated the league, 39/114/.320. The wondrous Yaz (who turned thirty-eight during the season) hit 28 homers, with 102 RBIs, and averaged .296. In New York, the arrival of the Yankees' egocentric free agent Reggie Jackson (prefaced by his infamous "I'm the straw that stirs the drink" comment) led to inevitable clashes with their unstable, alcoholic manager Billy Martin, which climaxed in a nationally televised near fistfight between them in the dugout. Boston had built a six-game lead over New York by midsummer, but ineffective pitching and manager Don Zimmer's erratic handling of his staff proved their undoing. Following a spring holdout for a long-term contract—which, citing his age, the team's front office refused to give him—Luis Tiant ended up going only 12–8 on the season, but he still led the team's starters in wins; Rick Wise won eleven, Ferguson Jenkins only ten, Bill Lee only nine. Due to Zimmer's incessant tweaking of his rotation, every starter but Tiant and Jenkins ended up spending time in the bullpen. The Red Sox's expensive free agent reliever Bill Campbell justified his pricey contract by winning thirteen and leading the league in saves with thirty-one, but Zimmer burned out his arm with shortsighted overuse; Campbell would never produce another comparable season.

A festering culture clash also came to a head during the summer of '77 between the straightlaced, old school Zimmer and a group of free-spirited souls—empowered now, it seemed, by the mere existence of free agency, to challenge all authority in their way—led by Lee, Wise, Jenkins, and Carbo. The group called themselves the "Buffalo Heads," after their disparaging nickname for Zimmer, and although their brash irreverence provided great copy for the town's hipper young sportswriters, the long-term effect on team chemistry would have graver consequences. Boston lost its lead in the East Division by the end of August, and in mid-September, when the hated Yankees, who had momentarily risen above their own raucous personality disputes, took two from the Red Sox in a three-game series, the issue was settled; the Red Sox and Orioles ended the 1977 season tied for second in the division, two and a half games behind New York. The Yankees and Dodgers went on to meet in a memorable World Series that the Bronx Bombers won four games to two, led by Reggie Jackson's five home runs, including three in the clinching game. Former Red Don Gullett, who had gone 14–4 in his first season for the Yankees and won Game Five of the Series, collected his third straight World Series ring. Reggie Jackson, standing up to ungodly pressures in the toxic crosshairs of the New York media, had transformed himself into one of the sports world's rare single-name icons. Despite Bob Howsam's dire predictions about the advent of free agency, attendance and television ratings trended higher throughout both leagues, and given the sudden, startling success of Steinbrenner's mercenary Yankees, the future of free agency as the shortest path to baseball championships had been affirmed.

Eighty-nine players entered 1977's free agent draft that fall, and once again as a matter of principle only the Cincinnati Reds refused to play. In Boston, Jean Yawkey fired Dick O'Connell, the one competent general manager her late husband had ever hired, turning the team over to Haywood Sullivan, a onetime minor leaguer and former director of player personnel. That winter, Oakland A's owner Charles Finley tried yet again to sell his left-handed ace Vida Blue before losing him to free agency, this time to Cincinnati for $1.75 million and a minor leaguer; and once again Commissioner Bowie

Kuhn voided the deal, in the interest of maintaining baseball's "competitive balance." At which point the Reds' sixty-year-old president, Bob Howsam, chief architect of the Big Red Machine, had seen, and had, enough of the game's new through-the-looking-glass rules. He announced his retirement to a boardroom position before the 1978 season, turning over day-to-day operations of the franchise to his marketing guru and longtime hatchet man Dick Wagner. The abrasive Wagner's first move was to give away Jack Billingham, the Reds' winningest pitcher for the last six years, to the Tigers for two middling prospects.

Both Sparky Anderson in Cincinnati and Don Zimmer in Boston announced that they planned to return to a more disciplined managerial style in the upcoming 1978 season. While Cincinnati largely stood pat, Boston made aggressive trades for the Angels' speedy middle infielder Jerry Remy—again replacing Denny Doyle, the man whose job he'd won three seasons earlier in Anaheim—and the Indians' dashing young starter Dennis Eckersley, and they reacquired the fiery Dick Drago to shore up their bullpen. All those moves paid off. Tiant and Lee returned to form, Jim Rice got white-hot early, carrying the Red Sox offense—he would win the American League MVP award that year—and by the All-Star break Boston had built a nine-game lead in the East Division. In Cincinnati, thirty-seven-year-old Pete Rose, playing out his final contract year, collected his three thousandth hit and then dominated every sports headline in America with a riveting forty-four-game hitting streak that tied an eighty-one-year-old National League record, during which the Reds kept pace with both the Dodgers and Giants in a tight, three-way West Division race. With his team fourteen games behind Boston, the Yankees' Billy Martin self-destructed after an escalating string of conflicts, calling out both his star Reggie Jackson and employer George Steinbrenner in the press. ("One's a born liar, and the other's convicted.") Steinbrenner demanded Martin's resignation and replaced him with the team's placid former pitching coach Bob Lemon. At this point, a World Series rematch that fall between the Reds and Red Sox seemed increasingly likely.

But as the season wore on, hidden flaws in both teams' rosters surfaced. Uncertain of his reserves—which once again no longer included the erratic Bernie Carbo, banished to Cleveland in mid-season—Zimmer drove his regulars hard, trying to increase Boston's lead and secure his own uncertain future as manager, but only succeeded in wearing them out. Despite Sparky's efficient use of a thin pitching staff, Cincinnati's lack of solid starters behind Seaver eventually came back to hurt them, and for the first time cracks appeared in their dependable offense: Joe Morgan and Johnny Bench broke down physically, Ken Griffey retreated from the promise of his early seasons, and while George Foster continued to produce, Cesar Geronimo suddenly lost his way at the plate and Dan Driessen proved conclusively that he was no Tony Perez. Without the same depth he'd always had on his bench to paper over those flaws, and despite one last desperate September winning streak, Sparky and the Reds won ninety-two games and finished second, two and a half games behind the Dodgers. Most longtime observers of the team agreed that in light of the problems with which he'd had to contend, 1978 might well have been Sparky Anderson's finest season as Cincinnati's manager.

Meanwhile, in Boston, the old familiar aura of pending disaster returned to Fenway with bad intent. Although they had squandered most of their commanding lead over the previous eight weeks, the Red Sox still led the Yankees—who had charged back from the dead under Bob Lemon—by four games at the start of September, when the Yankees came into Boston for a crucial four-game series. The Red Sox lost the first three games without putting up any visible fight. Tony Kubek, broadcasting one of those games for NBC, remarked in wonder: "This is the first time I've ever seen a first-place team chasing a second-place team." Don Zimmer had both Bill Lee—whom he had banished to the bullpen because of their intractable personality clash—and Luis Tiant available to start the final game of the series, both confirmed Yankee-killers, but he stubbornly refused, sending instead an untested rookie fresh from Pawtucket named Bobby Sprowl to the mound. The Yankees predictably destroyed Sprowl—who in his career would never win a *single* major-league game—completed their sweep and moved into a tie for the lead in the East Division; in New York, sportswriters gleefully dubbed their march through New England the "Boston Massacre." The deflated Red Sox tumbled three and a half games behind the Yankees but then, on the verge of elimination in mid-September, gamely battled back in a manner not seen since the glorious summer of the "Impossible Dream"; Boston won twelve of their last fourteen games, including the last eight in a row, to catch the Hated Ones at the finish line and force a one-game playoff at Fenway for the Eastern Division Championship.

Which only succeeded in adding, then, to the list of Boston's tragic messengers of doom ("Pesky, Gibson, Armbrister . . .") the name of Yankees shortstop Bucky "Fucking" Dent. When the light-hitting shortstop's long pop fly to left field in the seventh inning caught a suddenly refreshed outgoing breeze and just cleared the Monster for a three-run home run, Boston lost their 2–0 lead, the playoff game, the Division Championship, and, many believed, their will to live. And for the third time in three elimination games in the last eleven years, Carl Yastrzemski—a man who deserved so much better—recorded the Red Sox's final out.

Boston's new front office team kept Don Zimmer in their dugout but at his insistence dispatched the last of the bedeviling Buffalo Heads: For a warm body named Stan Papi, Bill Lee—seventy-five wins in six seasons—was traded to Montreal, where he would flourish and become a favorite new teammate of Tony Perez. To thirty-eight-year-old Luis Tiant, who had just completed his eighth straight outstanding season for Boston, and most recently pitched a brilliant two-hit shutout against the Blue Jays in the do-or-die final game of 1978 that moved them into the playoff against the Yankees, the Red Sox now offered only a lowball single-year contract. Buddy Leroux, the former Red Sox trainer who had wormed his way into Jean Yawkey's favor as a partner in the team's new ownership group, told Tiant bluntly that he was now too old to justify a longer or larger investment. His fierce pride cut to the bone, *El Tiante* turned his back on Boston and signed a two-year deal with the Yankees for $840,000. Since the day he arrived, Luis Tiant had not only been the most important presence in the Boston clubhouse, he was the greatest money pitcher in the history of the franchise—31–12 lifetime in September and October—and the Red Sox had just shown him the door without so much as a pat on the back.

Carl Yastrzemski wept when he heard the news.

"They've torn out our heart and soul," he said.

In Cincinnati, at around the same time, new hard-line president Dick Wagner let the almost thirty-eight-year-old Pete Rose know that if he wanted to remain a Red he would have to accept a pay cut for the coming 1979 season. Rose made it clear he would have been willing to take a smaller raise than what he could land on the open market to stay with the Reds, but this insult was too much to bear. Privately, the Reds had also begun to hear unsettling reports about Pete's off-field problems with bookies and gambling losses, the first shadows of the coming scandals that would bulldoze Rose's last decade in baseball, and decided it was more prudent to cut their ties to him. Embracing his freedom with the enthusiasm of a born hustler, Rose broke off negotiations, made a public relations show of shopping his services around all of baseball, and a few weeks later signed with the Philadelphia Phillies for more than twice what the Reds had just refused to pay him: $810,000 a year for four years.

Then, on November 27, a week after their negotiations with Rose collapsed, and the team had just returned from an exhibition tour of Japan, Dick Wagner flew out to Los Angeles and asked Sparky Anderson to drive down and meet him for breakfast at the LAX Marriott. Sparky assumed that, with Bob Howsam gone, they were finally going to discuss the possibility of signing some free agents during the off-season to fill the team's widening roster gaps. After a quick meal, Wagner asked Sparky to come up to his room, where Sparky took a seat and Wagner went into the bathroom for a moment. When he came out, Wagner dropped a bombshell.

"I'm not bringing you back," said Wagner.

Too stunned to speak, Sparky didn't even ask why, and Wagner offered no explanation. He hugged Sparky when they parted, with tears in his eyes. Sparky drove home to Thousand Oaks in a daze.

Baseball managers have always known they live on a razor's edge—in the pro game's three centuries only four managers have lasted with a single franchise for as long as twenty years—but Sparky had just set the Reds' franchise record for career wins. In nine seasons he had captured five division titles, taken the team to four World Series and won two of them, half of Cincinnati's total in a hundred years. There was talk that Sparky had lost his once firm grip on his men, or that he was going to quit rather than yield to a front office demand that he make changes on his coaching staff, but none of those issues ever even came up in meaningful discussion. Instead, just like that, nearly tripping over Pete Rose as he made his own way out the door after sixteen seasons in red, Sparky Anderson was gone.

MANAGER DON ZIMMER LOST his job after the 1979 season. A year later, by late 1980, the triumvirate of Carlton Fisk, Rick Burleson, and Fred Lynn would all be gone from Boston. The Red Sox, flailing under their incompetent, feuding new management, would not seriously compete for or win another American League pennant until 1986. As Peter Gammons then summed it up, the expected dynasty of the great team that the Red Sox had assembled in the mid-seventies lasted exactly one night, from the end of Game Six to the end of Game Seven. Jim Rice and Dewey Evans were the last remaining members of the '75 squad to participate in 1986's memorable World Series, which ended in yet another tragic fall for New England's fans after a less fondly remembered Game Six carved the name "Buckner" into their wall of infamy. Around this time a fanciful, long-suffering Boston sportswriter decided that the Red Sox's multiple twentieth-century disappointments could only be the product of a Stephen King–like "curse" that sprung from the sale of Babe Ruth—

King himself, fittingly, is a passionate, lifelong Red Sox rooter—and a colorful, half-baked urban legend crept into popular culture. Perhaps the fable provided some irrational comfort for New England's perpetually bereaved, but it was never more than poppycock; the harder truth behind the Red Sox failures lay in Tom Yawkey's often willfully obstructionist tendencies as the team's lord and master— his blind loyalty to front-office sycophants, his early distrust of a "farm" system, his insupportable holding of the color line a decade after Robinson—and the comic-opera mess that his widow and her proxies quickly made of the best roster the team had ever assembled. Most of that sorry legacy was overlooked in favor of his longevity and service to the game when, in 1980, five years after his death, Tom Yawkey became the first man involved with Game Six to be inducted into baseball's Hall of Fame.

The Cincinnati Reds, baseball's dominant franchise of the 1970s— without question one of the greatest teams of all time—would not make it back to the World Series until 1990, when that endearing underdog edition unexpectedly won a fifth championship title, drawing even with Boston's all-time mark. But the Reds haven't been back to the Series since, a small-market team struggling in a deep-pockets game, a victim of the unbalanced business environment that Bob Howsam had so accurately predicted for baseball.

Joe Morgan followed Pete Rose and Sparky out of Cincinnati at the end of his two-year contract, after the 1979 season. He would play his last five seasons in baseball for four different franchises, a proud, aging star with declining skills, reuniting briefly in 1983 with both Pete Rose and Tony Perez on a mercenary Phillies team that lost the World Series to the Orioles. Carl Yastrzemski ended his career in Boston that same fall with striking dignity and an unsurpassed outpouring of emotion both for and from this singular, taciturn man, at the age of forty-four, after twenty-three seasons in a Red Sox uniform, the longest tenure spent by any one player with only one team in all of baseball history. Yastrzemski, the last of his breed, a self-made blue-collar superstar with the work ethic of an immigrant blacksmith, embraced that last great public good-bye and then disappeared into the private life he'd always craved, and from which he has since only seldom emerged. Of Cincinnati's four great Hall of Fame–caliber stars, only Johnny Bench would end his career as a Red, after seventeen years. He said good-bye at the end of 1983 as well; although limited by age and injury to first and third base for his last few seasons, Bench played his last game behind the plate at home, where to this day he represents the standard by which all others must be judged for baseball's most demanding position. Of all his contemporaries, Johnny moved the most seamlessly into life without a uniform: broadcasting, business, public speaking—all unqualified successes. His keen mind and street smarts had led him to figure out how the world worked very early on during his eventful journey out of Binger, Oklahoma; with at last a solid marriage and late fatherhood recently coming his way, it's a pleasure to report that Johnny Bench now lives a happy, satisfied, and well-examined life. Davey Concepcion followed Bench into retirement in 1988, after nineteen seasons as a Cincinnati Red, amassing numbers that in any other era, for his position, might have secured a ticket to the Hall of Fame. But in the era he played into and that immediately followed him, when shortstops began mysteriously hitting like center fielders—for a variety of reasons, some of which will continue to haunt and shame baseball for another generation—Davey Concepcion's exemplary career has as a result been mistakenly overlooked. Although he remains something like a god in his native Venezuela, where he now lives, an inspirational figure to kids and countrymen, Concepcion remains somewhat in the shadow of his four former teammates in America. Resigned to this fate, he said it best near the end of days for the Big Red Machine: "They are superstars: I am a Concepcion."

In his wanderings through the wilderness of free agency, Tony Perez made a three-year stop in Boston for the struggling Red Sox before moving on to the Phillies and his brief reunion with Morgan and Rose. All three men were released after the Phillies lost that World Series, and their diaspora continued: Morgan back home to Oakland for his final year, Rose for a single season to Montreal—where he finally passed four thousand hits—and Perez back to Cincinnati. Big Doggie finally hung 'em up there in 1986 after his last three seasons, playing part-time while functioning as an unofficial coach toward the end, for the native son who had likewise returned home and taken over as the player-manager of the Reds in 1985, Pete Rose. So Doggie was on the bench to see his old friend finally break Ty Cobb's all-time hit record on September 11, 1985, the number that the now-forty-four-year-old Rose had been obsessively chasing for years after his skills had begun to seriously erode. Once their Captain Ahab finally killed his whale, the Cincinnati front office kept Rose on as manager, but the Reds quietly dropped him from their forty-man roster after the end of the 1986 season; by then Pete Rose had posted 4,256 hits, putting the most cherished of his many records almost unquestionably out of reach. But unlike all of his celebrated contemporaries, Rose never said good-bye, never officially retired as a player—the aging process being the least of so many truths he refused to face about himself—always keeping that door cracked open for a return that never happened. Then, in 1989, baseball's commissioners—the outgoing Peter Ueberroth and his successor, the erudite former president of Yale University, Bart Giamatti—began their extensive investigation into allegations that Pete Rose had placed bets on baseball games. The rest of Pete Rose's sorrowful, stuttering fall from grace has been extensively documented elsewhere. Since his release from federal prison in 1991 after serving five months for income tax evasion, Charlie Hustle has been forbidden to wear any major-league baseball uniform—although the Cincinnati Reds, in a private gesture of both respect and protest, have since refused to issue his unofficially retired number 14 to any of their players at any level—and to this day Pete Rose remains on the Hall of Fame's "permanently ineligible" list. While doing little over the years in either print or public behavior to help his forlorn cause, Pete Rose lives in perpetual hope that his name will someday be removed from that list and added to the longer one those walls were built to contain and honor.

Rose's downfall was just beginning when, fittingly, Johnny Bench and Carl Yastrzemski entered the Hall of Fame together in 1989, their first year of eligibility. In his first eligible year Joe Morgan joined them there in 1990, unquestionably the greatest second baseman in baseball history, and by this time well launched in his second career as a broadcaster for ESPN. Somehow—someone please explain this—Bench received only 96 percent of all votes cast, Yastrzemski 95 percent, and Morgan only 82 percent. Foolishness in this boy's game, we learn, is hardly confined to the field or front office. Two latecomers to the Reds and Red Sox stories soon followed them into the Hall in 1991: Ferguson Jenkins—whose candidacy was delayed by but survived a 1980 suspension for drug possession; the habits of his "Buffalo Head" days died hard—and in 1992 the splendid Tom Seaver, who tallied nearly 99 percent of the votes, which is more like it. Eight more years would pass before more members of their company from that night at Fenway Park would join them in Cooperstown, along with a couple of the men who worked Game Six behind a microphone.

DICK STOCKTON, whose call of Fisk's home run offered such perfect accompaniment to a classic moment, thrived in the aftermath of Game Six. The attention that came his way as a result of his outstanding work in the 1975 Series not only soon resulted in a long-term national contract with CBS Sports, he also got the girl: Stockton and *Boston Globe* reporter Lesley Visser had their first dinner date in Boston a week after Game Six. He took her to the romantic, Hungarian-themed Café Budapest at a downtown hotel. One of Lesley's girlfriends pointed out to her that this would be the *third* time in less than a week that the dapper Stockton had squired a date to that particular restaurant; when Lesley brought that up to Dick over dinner, he responded with a twinkling candor that helped his cause: "What can I say? I like the chicken *paprikash*." Dick and Lesley married a few years later, and remain married, happily so, to this day. After establishing her own career as a sportswriter, Lesley became a pioneering figure among female sportscasters for CBS, the first woman beat reporter ever to cover the National Football League, Major League Baseball, and the National Basketball Association, while serving on the broadcast team for every major event in American sports. In 2006, she became the first woman ever honored by the Pro Football Hall of Fame, for her contributions to their game as a broadcaster. Dick Stockton's long and distinguished career has touched just as many bases, as the lead play-by-play man for the NBA during the 1980s, and during two decades covering pro football and Major League Baseball for Fox and basketball for TNT, where he continues to appear. In 2001, Stockton was given the Curt Gowdy Award by the Basketball Hall of Fame for his outstanding contributions to the sport. His smooth, informed style and thorough professionalism has never wavered, and remains an asset to any contest he covers.

Curt Gowdy, who covered Game Six on radio for NBC, left the network's baseball broadcast team shortly after the 1975 World Series ended, when lead sponsor Chrysler expressed a preference that Joe Garagiola—already on their payroll as a corporate spokesman—become baseball's number one voice. Gowdy stayed on to cover football for NBC until 1978, then split his time between CBS and ABC, working for his close friend Roone Arledge, with whom years earlier he had co-created the groundbreaking series *Wide World of Sports.* Gowdy continued to cover countless other sporting events—in a prodigious career that included, to name just a few highlights, thirteen World Series, nine Super Bowls, and eight Olympic Games—and produced and hosted the show closest to his heart and Wyoming roots, *The American Sportsman.* In 1984, Gowdy became the first broadcaster associated with Game Six to be given baseball's Ford C. Frick Award, bestowed annually since 1978 to a broadcaster who has made major contributions to the game of baseball. Gowdy announced his retirement in 1985, but continued to periodically appear on football and baseball broadcasts all the way up until 2003, when he called a Red Sox–Yankees game for ESPN as part of their "Living Legends" series. One of the most reliable and admired sportscasters of all time, Curt Gowdy died on February 20, 2006, at the age of eighty-six.

Joe Garagiola followed Gowdy as the principal play-by-play voice of baseball at NBC, teaming with Tony Kubek until 1982, when Vin Scully joined the network as their lead announcer. Garagiola continued on as Scully's color commentary partner until 1988, when after a contract dispute he finally resigned from NBC after nearly thirty years. After a short stay as part of the broadcast team for the California Angels, Garagiola moved to the Phoenix area, where he lives and continues to work to this day, a more mellow grandfatherly presence both off screen and on than during his network days. Among many other jobs he's done in television since—including his popular offbeat stints doing "play-by-play" for the Westminster Kennel Club's annual Dog Show—Garagiola provides his patented folksy color commentary on television for the Arizona Diamondbacks, an expansion franchise that joined the National League in 1998; Garagiola's oldest son, Joe Junior, served as the Diamondbacks' first general manager, and now works as senior vice president of baseball operations for Major League Baseball. (One of Garagiola's broadcast partners for the Diamondbacks from 1998 through 2006 was the team's lead play-by-play man Thom Brennaman, son of the Reds' longtime voice Marty Brennaman.) In 1991, Joe Garagiola followed Curt Gowdy as a recipient of the Ford C. Frick Award.

Marty Brennaman has manned the microphone for the Cincinnati Reds ever since the 1975 World Series, and since 2007 he has worked in the booth along with his son Thom, one of the most unique broadcasting partnerships in baseball history. Their spirited, opinionated on-air debates about the game are like listening to an elevated version of the dinner table/front porch conversations that take place within every baseball-loving family in America. When he was deservedly given the Ford C. Frick Award, Marty Brennaman joined Curt Gowdy and Joe Garagiola in the Hall of Fame in 2000.

Not only did the 1975 World Series return record revenue for NBC, their coverage of the event also won an Emmy for outstanding sports broadcast of the year. Executive Chet Simmons left the network a few years after the '75 series to become the first president and CEO of a new cable TV network—revolutionary at the time but often dismissed as an unworkable business model—called ESPN. After launching that network, Simmons went on to work as commissioner of the short-lived United States Football League, a competitor to the NFL that, as it happened, was an unworkable business model. Simmons is now comfortably retired and lives in Savannah, Georgia.

After winning election to a second term in 1976, baseball commissioner Bowie Kuhn remained at his post until the end of the 1984 season, when he was replaced by Peter Ueberroth. Often controversial during his time in office—one of the most tumultuous periods in the game's history—Kuhn is now rightly considered to have been one of the most effective and evenhanded stewards baseball has ever known. The former lawyer retired back into private practice, then into retirement in Florida, and died in 2007, at the age of eighty. Kuhn was inducted into the Baseball Hall of Fame the following year.

THE PLAYERS IN GAME SIX who had never been stars, and even some who were but whose careers were already in their twilight by 1975, never got a taste of the Monopoly money that free agency subsequently stacked on the table. Reserve infielder Doug Flynn went to the Mets in the Tom Seaver trade, and enjoyed productive years there and in Montreal as a starter before retiring after eleven seasons and entering the business world back in his native Kentucky. Back-up Reds catcher Bill Plummer, who played nearly his entire ten-year pro career behind Johnny Bench, now works in the minor leagues for the Arizona Diamondbacks organization.

Jack Billingham, who in his thirteen-year playing career, which ended in 1980, won 145 major-league games—talent that would have been worth multiple millions in today's marketplace—has remained in baseball ever since as a minor-league pitching coach, mostly in the Houston Astros organization, a respectable but modest living for a great competitor and all-time stand-up guy. The Red Sox's Rick Wise—eighteen years, 188 wins, through 1982—recently retired as the pitching coach for a nonaffiliated minor-league team, the Lancaster Barnstormers. Both Wise and Billingham were lifers, intelligent talents still in love with the game that entranced them as kids, having never known another profession, who missed easy street by a decade. At the other end of the scale, Boston left-hander Jim Burton, who surrendered the Series-winning hit to Joe Morgan in Game Seven, pitched only one more game in the major leagues and ever since his early retirement has owned a successful printing business in North Carolina.

When his dreadful arm troubles persisted, Gary Nolan finally called it quits in 1977—110–70 in his outstanding career—and has since prospered in a second career outside of baseball, working for Steve Wynn in the hotel and gaming industry. The classy, understated Nolan joined many of his former teammates in the Cincinnati Reds Hall of Fame in 1983. Scrappy starter Fred Norman stayed with the Reds until 1980, finishing his career a game over .500, at 104–103. Clay "Hawk" Carroll retired after fifteen years of pro ball in 1978 to a quiet life on his farm in Kentucky; he made it to the Reds Hall of Fame in 1980. It took Cesar Geronimo a while longer to join Nolan and Carroll there—he was finally inducted in 2008—after his fifteen-year professional career ended in Kansas City in 1983; active in many social and charitable programs, he's lived ever since back in his native Dominican Republic. His fellow countryman and Reds teammate Pedro Borbon, who retired after twelve years in the majors in 1980, now splits his time between the island and Houston. Reds' reserve infielder Ed Armbrister's pro career lasted only five years, until 1977, and he soon returned to his home in the Bahamas—still one of only five Bahamians ever to play Major League baseball—and for a while served as his country's director of sports, but his name lives on in New England: "Armbris-ter" remains graven in the memories of Red Sox fans of a certain age like a jailhouse tattoo.

Another stand-up guy whose time in baseball was all too short, pitcher Pat Darcy—forever known as the man who surrendered the home run in Game Six to Carlton Fisk—played only one more sea-son in the major leagues before a torn labrum in his pitching shoul-der curtailed his career. After struggling to get healthy during three years of minor-league ball, Darcy moved into life after baseball in 1981. He went back to college and finished his business degree, mar-ried and started a family in Tucson, Arizona, and has worked ever since in commercial real estate and banking. He stays in touch with many of his former Reds teammates, and unlike some players who've given up famous home runs in their pasts, he has never shied away from talking about his fateful encounter with Carlton Fisk in Game Six. Darcy's only gripe with his place in baseball history, and it's a small, good-natured one, has to do with the depiction of their shared moment that appeared in the Oscar-winning 1997 film *Good Will Hunting*. In order to draw out the suspense of Fisk's climactic at bat, just before the home run pitch is thrown, director Gus Van Sant cuts to a shot of Darcy kicking dirt around on the mound, looking con-cerned, as if he's trying to delay confronting Fisk. That little piece of landscaping actually occurred at the *beginning* of the inning, after Darcy had completed his warm-up tosses but before Fisk stepped into the box. Shocking, isn't it, Hollywood rearranging reality to suit its narrative requirements—and apparently there's gambling in Casablanca as well. (Speaking of Ben Affleck and Matt Damon's es-teemed screenplay, Dick Stockton and Lesley Visser couldn't help but notice when they saw the movie together that Robin Williams's psychiatrist character recounts to Damon's Will Hunting that he also met his future wife on the night of Game Six, at a bar just out-side of Fenway.) Anyway, Pat Darcy would like you to know that he didn't hesitate before throwing his last pitch to Fisk, acknowledging manfully that this does nothing to change the fact that Fisk still walloped it into the night. And you can still hear Dick Stockton's original call of that moment in the movie, permission for which the filmmakers graciously thanked him in the final credits.

Arm trouble bedeviled other members of the Reds' pitching staff. After his first championship free-agent season with the Yankees in 1977, pitcher Don Gullett was limited by injury to only eight starts the following year and wasn't on their active roster when New York won its second straight World Series, over the Dodgers, in 1978. The serious rotator cuff problems that then continued to plague him ended Gullett's baseball career when the Yankees released him in 1980, after only nine seasons and a remarkable record of 109–50. In 1993 he rejoined the Cincinnati Reds as their pitching coach, a post he held until 2005. Don Gullett entered the Reds' Hall of Fame in 2002.

On the heels of his MVP season in 1977, George Foster signed a healthy long-term deal with the Reds that kept him in Cincinnati as a frequent All-Star and consistently productive player—his numbers to this point earned him frequent mention as a potential future Hall of Famer—through the end of 1981. The five-year $10 million free agent contract he then signed with the Mets—the richest the game had then ever seen—brought him into the radioactive bull's-eye of the New York spotlight. The quiet, shy, and devout Foster—so dangerous for years as a central player of the Reds' Midwestern ensemble—did not prosper as a leading man on Broadway. He stumbled badly during his first season, never came close to matching his once lofty numbers, and the shocking way in which his productivity quickly trailed off—he was released outright by the Mets in August of 1986 during the final year of his contract—became a cautionary tale for the perils of long-term contracts in the era of free agency. George Foster's baseball career ended as suddenly as if he'd hit a wall, at the age of thirty-seven. He suffered through some serious financial difficulties after retirement, and it was rumored he'd been compelled to sell the famous Fisk home run ball that he'd caught off the foul pole in left field at the end of Game Six. Foster has since worked as a motivational speaker for various Christian organizations and causes, and as a committed supporter of youth baseball programs.

His fellow outfielder Ken Griffey Sr. left Cincinnati for the greener fields of New York as well after the 1981 season, signing as a free agent with the Yankees. If he never quite matched the lofty expectations that his first few seasons with the Reds had raised, Griffey remained an outstanding professional ballplayer for a career that lasted nineteen seasons, into the early 1990s, when after a brief sentimental return to the Reds he made major-league history by playing alongside his oldest son, Ken Junior, just then beginning his soon-to-be Hall of Fame career with the Seattle Mariners. (In one memorable game they even hit back-to-back home runs.) Ken Griffey Sr. collected more than 2,100 hits, drove in 859 runs, and averaged .296 in his two decades in uniform, and he retired comfortably to Winter Garden, Florida, when his playing days were done, one of the first beneficiaries—because he'd always been smart with his money—of the free agent era.

As recounted earlier, the Reds' two outstanding young relievers in 1975 both went their separate ways when the Machine broke down three years later—Will McEnaney with Tony Perez to the Expos, and Rawly Eastwick to the Cardinals—and less than four years after that both were out of baseball. The lively, personable McEnaney encountered serious arm trouble, retired in 1979, and has since lived and worked in Florida in various construction- and contracting-related businesses. After he was traded, Eastwick played out the 1978 season in St. Louis and then, courtesy of his agent Jerry Kapstein, signed as an expensive and much-ballyhooed free agent with the Yankees. He never recorded a save for the notoriously demanding George Steinbrenner and was traded away to Philadelphia before his first season in New York ended. He spent a year and a half with the Phillies, then a season each with the Royals and the Cubs, before retiring in 1981 at the age of thirty. After tallying fifty saves during his first two brilliant seasons, Rawly Eastwick ended his eight-year pro career with only sixty-eight.

. . .

FORMER RED SOX skipper Darrell Johnson, itinerant baseball man, landed another head job less than a year after Boston let him go. He became the first manager of the expansion Seattle Mariners, who entered the American League in 1977, with former movie star Danny Kaye as one of their principal owners, and their seriocomic origins perfectly capture the upside era of baseball in the late 1970s. The Mariners are the only team in baseball who owe their existence to the settlement of a legal dispute. The Seattle Pilots had begun life as the Pacific Northwest's first major-league baseball team in the expansion of 1969, played a woeful first season without a proper stadium, attracted few fans, and promptly went bankrupt. They were then purchased for two verses and a chorus and immediately relocated to Milwaukee—where they became the Brewers—by their new owner, baseball's future commissioner, Allan "Bud" Selig. Abandoned at the altar of commerce, the jilted city of Seattle, King County, and the state of Washington sued Major League Baseball for breach of contract. Six years later, in exchange for making their persistent, legitimate, and expensive suit go away, the American League awarded Seattle the Mariners franchise in their next expansion, which also included the Toronto Blue Jays.

Only confirming the adage that every manager is hired to be fired, leading Seattle's reborn franchise proved to be a thankless exercise; the Mariners spent most of the three seasons Darrell Johnson completed with them in the West Division's cellar before he was let go during the 1980 season in favor of former Dodgers great Maury Wills. The Mariners would burn through Wills and then six more managers before finally recording their first winning season in 1991, and remain one of only three major-league franchises that have never played in a World Series. Darrell Johnson landed his last big-league managerial gig for another of those luckless teams—the Texas Rangers—leading them for half a season on an interim basis in 1982, after old friend Don Zimmer, who'd brought him in as a coach, was himself let go by the Rangers after less than two years on the job. Johnson spent most of the next

two decades as a scout, coach, and administrative assistant for the
New York Mets; as a result, he was in the clubhouse when the Mets
celebrated their second World Championship title in 1986, over the
Boston Red Sox. After the 1999 season, and forty years in organized baseball, Johnson finally retired from the game at the age of
sixty-two, and five years later died of leukemia at his home in
California.

Don Zimmer, another old-school baseball lifer, went back to
coaching for most of the 1980s after the Rangers fired him, until the
Chicago Cubs hired him as their manager in 1989. He led them to a
rare division title and was named Manager of the Year; that was
Zimmer's high-water mark at the helm. The Cubs fired him two years
later, and he went back to work as a coach for the expansion Colorado Rockies. In 1996, Joe Torre brought him over to the Yankees as a
bench coach for their championship years during the second half of
that decade, and although this was his only stint with baseball's
most famous team, it remains the organization he is mostly closely
identified with by the modern fan. Zimmer made sympathetic headlines during the 2003 League Championship Series, when an ugly
brawl erupted between the Yankees and the Red Sox, and pitcher
Pedro Martinez violently tossed the then seventy-two-year-old Zimmer to the ground. After leaving the Yankees in 2004, Zimmer hired
on as a senior advisor for the Tampa Bay Rays, and at seventy-eight—
the last onetime Brooklyn Dodger player still active in the game—he
has still to this day, proudly, never drawn a paycheck outside of professional baseball.

Second baseman Denny Doyle, forever tied to Zimmer by their
misunderstanding at third base in the ninth inning of Game Six,
lasted only two more seasons in Boston. His eight-year major-league
career came to an end when he was thirty-three, after having the
odd distinction of being replaced at second base for the second time,
on different teams and opposite coasts, by the same player; the Red
Sox acquired the man who'd originally unseated him in Anaheim
in 1975—Massachusetts native Jerry Remy—from the Angels by

trade before the 1978 season, and when Denny was unable to hook up with another team that spring he called it a career. That same season he founded the Doyle Baseball Academy in Winter Haven, Florida, with his younger brothers Blake and Brian, twins who also both played infield in pro ball, Brian in the majors with the Yankees. The Doyle Academy is still thriving today—they have coached nearly a million young players over the years—one of the most highly regarded baseball training programs in the country, and Denny, a grandfather many times over now, still loves working with kids.

First baseman Cecil Cooper became a bona fide star after the Red Sox traded him to the Milwaukee Brewers in the George Scott deal. While Scott quickly fizzled in Boston, Cooper made five All-Star teams in the next seven years and never hit below .300, while the home run and RBI production that the Red Sox had impatiently given up waiting for arrived in a big way. The always personable, well-regarded "Coop" also led the Brewers to a memorable World Series in 1982, which they lost to the Cardinals in seven games, before retiring in 1987 at the age of thirty-seven, and he still holds many Milwaukee franchise records, including most hits and RBIs in a season. He then worked in numerous capacities on the field and off for the Brewers' front office, before moving back to his native Texas to coach for the Houston Astros in 2005. In 2007, Cecil Cooper became the first African-American field manager in the history of the Astros, the same team, you will recall, that employed in that capacity during Joe Morgan's early years the racist Harry "The Hat" Walker.

Pitcher Roger Moret, who was given away by the Red Sox shortly after the 1975 World Series, suffered the strangest and saddest fate of any participant in Game Six. After a single unproductive season in Atlanta's bullpen, the Braves traded Moret to the Texas Rangers, where his 1977 season was curtailed by surgery to his pitching arm. In 1978, after behaving strangely before a home game in April against the Tigers—he started burying practice balls in the outfield before teammates chased him off the field—Moret froze in front of his locker with a shower shoe in his hand for ninety minutes, unable to speak, in an impenetrable catatonic state. After giving him a sedative, team doctors drove Moret to a psychiatric hospital, where he was confined for nearly a month. Although he recovered sufficiently to throw a few more innings for the Rangers that season, Moret had now been stamped with the stigmatic and fearful scarlet letter of mental illness; although he was invited to two more spring training camps, Moret never pitched in another major-league game. He scratched out a living in various minor leagues throughout the Caribbean for the next few years, until he could collect his small major-league pension, and he lives now, in poverty, battling his various ailments and demons, in rural Puerto Rico.

Outfielder Bernie Carbo, once a Red and two times a Red Sox, nearly followed Roger Moret into personal disaster. Bernie's longtime drug and alcohol dependencies finally wore him down shortly after Boston traded him for the second time, to Cleveland, halfway through the 1978 season. He signed as a free agent with the Cardinals in 1979, but appeared in only fifty-two games, was traded to Pittsburgh, and then released by the Pirates at the end of the 1980 season; his twelve-year major-league baseball career was over. Bernie returned home to Detroit and opened a hair salon, but his troubles followed him, and by the end of the 1980s, when that business went under, he was, by his own admission, not only still using drugs extensively, he was also dealing them. His marriage ended shortly thereafter, and his downward spiral hit bottom in 1993, when his poor mother took her own life in a particularly gruesome way and his estranged father died a month later. After a failed attempt at rehab, not his first, Bernie found himself in the emergency room of a local hospital one dark night shortly thereafter, broke, panicked, his body wrecked, out of hope, contemplating his own suicide. A chance encounter with a serene old man in the next bed delivered him into a sudden, startling moment of religious grace. After this profound conversion experience, Bernie began the long walk home. His former Red Sox teammates Bill Lee and Ferguson Jenkins, who had never given up on him, found Carbo the practical help he needed from the Baseball Assistance Team, a charitable organization begun in 1986 by former players to help those of their own who are in need. Bernie Carbo made it all the way back. He's happily remarried now, the father of four—and a grandfather—and once he got himself straight Bernie fell back in love with the game that first brought him to the world's attention, dedicating his life to an organization he founded and still runs today called the Diamond Club Ministry. Bernie is sixty-two now, in good shape again, and he lives in Alabama but travels all around the country, conducting baseball workshops for kids while preaching the virtues of a life lived according to scripture and warning against the dangers of substance abuse. He begins every workshop with a short video that tells the story of his baseball career, shows the many greats he played alongside, and features his time-stopping home run in the bottom of the eighth inning in Game Six.

"I never knew God had a plan for me—and much of my life was hellish—but now I do, and I can see that it was there all along. Because I hit that one home run, and it allows me today to go any place and teach kids about baseball, and tell them about Jesus. God bless Tom Yawkey for the chance he gave me."

And to echo a sentiment shared by all of his former teammates, and managers, on both the Reds and the Red Sox, God bless Bernie Carbo.

GUTSY RELIEVER Dick "The Dragon" Drago, who returned to the Red Sox by trade in 1978, pitched effectively in another fateful game at Fenway, recording the last out against the Yankees in the top of the ninth in what has forever since been known as the "Bucky Dent" game. Drago threw hard and well for the Sox until 1981, when the new management team traded him again, this time to the Seattle Mariners, where he played his final season. Drago retired to Florida and opened a couple of successful small businesses, but he has always stayed involved with the game of baseball, playing in a senior league and at one point barnstorming across Canada with a merry band of former players led by his old friend and teammate Bill Lee. Also a grandfather now, and in good health after undergoing triple bypass surgery in 2004, Drago remains involved with Red Sox fantasy camps and cruises, a successful outreach program begun by Boston's principal current owners, John Henry and Tom Werner, that has brought many members of the once-estranged 1975 squad back into the fold.

Rick Burleson, who by 1980 had firmly established his credentials as the toughest and most valuable shortstop in Boston Red Sox history, was traded away to the California Angels when his original five-year deal expired after the 1980 season. Burleson proceeded to sign the biggest contract for a shortstop in baseball history: four years for $4.65 million. He also delivered, as he always had, on the field, making the All-Star team and being named the Angels' Most Valuable Player in 1981. Burleson suffered a devastating rotator cuff injury to his throwing arm the following spring, however, and missed almost all of the next three seasons as he struggled to recover. He put together his last good, healthy season in 1986, earning the American League's Comeback Player of the Year award. After one year as a free agent with the Orioles in 1987, Rick Burleson ended his playing career after thirteen years in the major leagues. After working as a coach, scout, and batting instructor for the Oakland A's, Burleson returned to the Red Sox as a coach for then manager, and his former Boston teammate, Butch Hobson. In 2002, Burleson joined many of his old Red Sox friends in the team's Hall of Fame. He has since embarked on a successful minor-league managing career and is currently the hitting coach for the Arizona Diamondbacks' Triple-A Reno Aces.

Third baseman Rico Petrocelli was one of the many teammates who preceded Burleson into Boston's Hall of Fame, when he was enshrined there in 1997. Rico and his family kept their home in the Boston area after he retired in 1977, and he spent time covering the team for the *Boston Herald,* on his own sports talk radio program— one of the first in the country—and then for a season as the color man for the team's radio broadcasts. He eventually spent three years managing in the White Sox organization, then returned to the Red Sox in 1992 to manage their Triple-A franchise in Pawtucket. After six years as a roving instructor for the team, Rico started his own marketing company in New Hampshire, a grandfather now and pater familias to his large and happy clan. He remains a welcome and familiar figure in Boston and a popular participant at the team's many alumni activities.

After being cast aside by the Red Sox in 1978, Bill Lee spent three seasons pitching for the Montreal Expos, basking in that city's sophisticated bonhomie, before his committed antiestablishment ways brought him once again into conflict with hard-line baseball management. In early 1982, when Lee protested the team's release of his friend and teammate Rodney Scott with a one-game walkout, the Expos front office responded starkly by cutting him adrift. Thirty-five at the time, Lee never played another inning in the major leagues, and not without reason suspected that collusion and conspiracy among the game's executives were involved—although in the interest of fairness, conspiracy is not an unusual theory for Lee, on any number of subjects. At which point, in many ways, the even more compelling chapters of Bill Lee's life as a wandering minstrel of baseball began. He has published four books, including two memoirs of his playing days, which are nothing less than the funniest and most literate, readable insider accounts of the professional game since Jim Bouton's seminal *Ball Four*. He played semi-pro ball for many years, and still takes the mound today, devotedly, at the age of sixty-two; if you've got a bat, a ball, a field, and seventeen other like-minded souls, he's there. Lee has barnstormed with countless teams he's assembled for just that purpose all around the world, including China, Cuba, and some remote places where few had ever seen a baseball before. He once ran for President as head of the Canadian Rhinoceros Party; he didn't garner enough support to make it onto any state's ballot, but "party" remained the operative word. At one time a polarizing figure during the divisive era in which he played, as time has passed, and those once hardened generational lines in American sports have softened, Bill Lee has come to be more often appreciated for what he has always been: one of the greatest living advocates for, and acolytes of, the pure and simple beauty of the game of baseball. He has always worked, tirelessly, for many charitable causes. He remains the most friendly and approachable former sports star you could ever hope to randomly encounter, and one of the most engaging conversationalists you'll ever find about a vast variety of subjects. He lives to this day on his farm in Northern Vermont, and has recently enjoyed an overdue reassessment of his best years in Boston, recognized now as one of the greatest left-handed pitchers in their team's storied history. The Red Sox's new owners have also wisely brought Lee back into the fold as part of their many alumni activities, and finally acknowledged his valued contributions to the team's rich culture by adding him to the Red Sox Hall of Fame in 2008.

Jim Edward Rice, who missed the 1975 World Series because of his broken wrist—thereby setting up one of the greatest "what ifs" in all of baseball history—inherited the left field position in Fenway from Carl Yastrzemski when he returned the next spring, and upheld the extraordinary standards established by the only two men who'd preceded him there over the previous four decades: Yaz and Ted Williams. One of the strongest men ever to play the sport, Rice dominated American League pitching for the decade that followed, at one point joining Ty Cobb as the only player to lead the league in total bases three years in a row. He also worked hard to turn himself into an excellent defensive outfielder—mastering the fine points of baseball's most eccentric corner—made eight All-Star teams, and finally led the Red Sox back to the World Series they lost in 1986 and the American League Championship Series they lost two years later. When he finally retired after the 1989 season, only six men had played more games as a left fielder in American League history. Continuing his post-retirement career in a Red Sox uniform, Rice served as the team's hitting coach for six years in the 1990s and is now part of their hugely successful NESN television network coverage team. His prodigious power numbers finally earned Jim Rice a ticket to baseball's Hall of Fame in 2009 in his last year of eligibility for inclusion by baseball's writers, the third and most recent Red Sox teammate who was on hand for Game Six that night to get there. His number 14 has since been retired by the Red Sox.

Dwight Evans, the second member of that great young Red Sox outfield, spent nineteen seasons in Fenway Park, and you could easily argue that Evans fulfilled Sparky Anderson's prediction that he would become the best player of that remarkable trio. Dewey led the American League in home runs during the 1980s—he hit 385 in his career, 79 more than Lynn and 3 more than Rice—and drove in nearly 1,400 runs, only 67 less than Rice. He also won eight Gold Gloves in that time—only five outfielders in history have ever won more, and only two of them played right field—and to the end of his career he remained the same modest, selfless, dedicated team man he had always been. Only Carl Yastrzemski has ever played more games in a Red Sox uniform, and if Evans has any regrets about baseball, they concern the one last year he spent playing for Baltimore; like his role model, Yaz, he wishes now he had ended his career where it began, in Fenway Park. After his playing days, Dewey spent a few years working for the White Sox and the Rockies, before Boston's new owners restored sanity to their front office and brought Evans back where he belongs. He has been an important member of the Red Sox organization ever since, as an instructor, hitting coach, goodwill ambassador, and living example of how a good, talented, decent man with solid values and a properly balanced ego should conduct himself in public life. Those responsible for voting veteran players into the Hall of Fame, please take note.

The third member of the Red Sox outfield triumvirate, Rice's fellow rookie "Gold Dust Twin" Fred Lynn, had set the bar so high with his amazing first season that the two that followed—after he finally signed his initial long-term deal—disappointed Boston's impossibly demanding fans; he suffered some nagging injuries, and although his astonishing defense never faltered, Lynn's power numbers declined. After undergoing off-season weight training, Freddy bounced back in 1978–79 with monster years that first equaled and then surpassed what he'd done in 1975. In 1980, his last year under contract to the Red Sox—while making his sixth straight All-Star team, and winning his fourth Gold Glove—Lynn's season ended in August, when a foul tip fractured his toe. Then Boston's Keystone Kops management team went to work driving off bridges. Under the terms of Lynn's expiring deal, Boston was still entitled to an option year, but, worried that they couldn't afford what he would undoubtedly be asking for, they tried to deal him to a number of different clubs. Those efforts failed. After some protracted legal wrangling about arcane clauses that had found their way into both Lynn's and Fisk's 1976 contracts, Major League Baseball officials ruled that both men were not in fact bound by an additional option year, and both were entitled to arbitration for the upcoming 1981 season as long as they received their contracts in the mail by December 20. Boston's front office did mail out the contracts, but because of numerous missteps and miscommunications, not until December 22. Afraid of losing him now without any compensation, due to their bungling, the Red Sox finally traded Fred Lynn to the Angels a month later, for nothing close to fair value. Playing ten minutes from where he'd grown up in Southern California, Lynn spent four typically productive years with the Angels, before moving on to the Orioles and the Tigers, and then ended his career after one last season with the Padres in 1989, the same year his old teammate Jim Rice retired. So Fred Lynn practiced his craft for sixteen more seasons in the major leagues after his stunning debut, a number of them sadly shortened or diminished by injury, and if voters have decided that he falls somewhat short of the cherished formula that would justify a plaque in Cooperstown, few men have ever played the game with such consistent grace on the field, or exhibited more intelligence and personal integrity off it. He has since done work as a television analyst for ESPN, CBS, and FOX, still lives in Southern California, and in 2002, Fred Lynn joined the Red Sox Hall of Fame.

As far as the Red Sox were concerned, Carlton Fisk's second contract dispute went even worse than Fred Lynn's, if that's possible, when arbiters ruled in early 1981 that the best catcher in Boston's history—a celebrated local hero who should have been the face of that franchise for decades—was now an unencumbered free agent, and their bruising legal wrangling had left him completely alienated from the team's fractious, incompetent front office. The Red Sox then offered Fisk a $2 million deal; the Chicago White Sox offered him $3.5 million. After watching teammates Rick Burleson, Fred Lynn, and Butch Hobson get dealt away, the thirty-three-year-old Fisk made the most difficult decision of his life and left New England for the Midwest. If he never looked quite right in the strange retro White Sox uniform of that era, Fisk worked just as hard for his new team and was also determined to eliminate the nagging injuries that had often marred his career to that point. Following a ferociously disciplined workout regime, Fisk ended up playing thirteen years in Chicago—twenty-four major-league seasons in all—while establishing every career record for his position worth tracking in baseball history. Fisk was forty-five years old when he finally hung 'em up, and if he eventually surpassed Johnny Bench's numbers with the sheer mass of his accomplishments, which man was the greater catcher in his prime remains one of the liveliest debates in baseball. Whomever you favor, if you believe such questions require answers, what's not in doubt is that between them they occupy the top two spots in that argument—Mike Piazza's hitting prowess notwithstanding; as a *catcher* he's not part of the same conversation—and that seeing them both at their best during the 1975 World Series remains one of its deepest pleasures.

Carlton Fisk wisely reached back out to his native New England after he retired, mending fences with the diligence of a Down East stonemason, and when he was elected to the Hall of Fame in his first eligible year—2000, when he received just less than 80 percent of the votes—Fisk announced that he would enter its hallowed corridors wearing a Red Sox cap. By then he was working as a special assistant to Boston's new general manager, Dan Duquette, who in turn announced that the team would now permanently honor and retire Fisk's old number 27. As part of their ongoing reconciliation, Fisk had earlier joined the Red Sox Hall of Fame in 1997, and in 2005 he was further enshrined in Fenway Park, when they decided to officially name that towering yellow left-field foul standard the Fisk Pole. (The fragment of the original pole that Fisk hit with his Game Six home run, which had been replaced during one of the park's recent renovations, was reclaimed from the scrap heap and now hangs on display inside Fenway's Hall of Fame.) As proud, principled, and dedicated to the things that matter as he has always been, Fisk retains his New Hampshire selectman's aversion to nonsense, fuss, outsiders, and phonies of any stripe. If he learned the hard way during his career that in the professional precincts of sports the once-cherished American concept of "team" no longer occupies the same high place as "family, state, and country," the remaining three ideals, in his mind at least, have not suffered the slightest diminishment at all.

WHEN AFTER twenty-three seasons his playing career finally ended in 1986, Tony Perez stayed on with the Reds organization as a coach under both Pete Rose and his successor Lou Pinella. He briefly managed the Reds in 1993, and when they let him go after only forty-four games, Perez joined the staff of the National League's newest expansion team, the Florida Marlins. Moving his family to Miami, Perez has worked with the Marlins in various field and front office capacities ever since, helping guide them to two World Series wins, in 1997 and 2003.

After two up and down seasons with the New York Yankees, Luis Tiant was released, and he pitched in the major leagues for parts of two more years. Having spent the first half of 1981 with the old minor-league team in Portland that he'd starred for nearly twenty years earlier, he spent the end of the season with the Pittsburgh Pirates and the following year joined the Angels. He won his last game for them in 1982, against the Boston Red Sox, and then finally faced the music at the age of forty-one. Luis wandered for a while, working as a scout for the Yankees in Mexico, and then as a minor-league coach for the Dodgers and the White Sox. He also spent four years coaching a college team in Savannah, Georgia, but all this time he kept Maria and their three children at home in Boston. The Red Sox elected Luis to their Hall of Fame in 1997, and when the team passed to its new ownership team in 2001, Luis Tiant was one of the first old soldiers they reached out to, bringing him back as a minor-league pitching coach and as part of their Spanish-speaking radio broadcast team. In addition to his continuing and varied work with the Red Sox, Luis today runs a successful cigar business with his oldest son, and a number of other smaller businesses, including El Tiante's sandwich shop just outside Fenway Park. Luis Tiant is a fixture in the Boston area again, recognized and revered wherever he goes, friendly and funny and genuinely approachable as he has always been. At least once a week he still visits the nearby graves of his parents, and recently made his first trip back to his native Cuba, an emotionally wrenching experience that did nothing to make him regret the decision he'd made as a young man to seek his fortune in America.

Despite the measurable fact that his record favorably compares with many pitchers who are already enshrined, during Luis Tiant's first fifteen years of eligibility for the Hall of Fame, the baseball writers of America never saw fit to grant him more than 31 percent of the ballots cast, when 75 percent remains the threshold for admission. His only route there now will be through the Veterans Committee, who should have a better appreciation of his true worth as a player and teammate, but to date nothing has come of it.

In 2000, his ninth year of eligibility, the baseball writers finally did see fit to elect Tony Perez to the Hall of Fame, with 77 percent of the vote. So Big Doggie sat up on the dais that late July afternoon in Cooperstown alongside fellow inductee Carlton Fisk—his teammate in Boston for one season in 1980—and the Cincinnati Reds' longtime voice Marty Brennaman, who that year was honored with the Ford C. Frick Award.

And one other man who'd been with them that night in Fenway Park.

WHEN THE REDS fired the most successful manager in their history—and in all of baseball during the previous decade—George Anderson, that kid whose driven work ethic like that of so many of his generation had been shaped by the Great Depression, just naturally assumed he'd never work again. After spending a few weeks back home with his wife and kids in Thousand Oaks, and watching amazed as the world beat a path to his door, he began to realize that "Sparky"—that gregarious character he played in public and on TV—had become not just a celebrity but an American household name. Offers of every variety poured in, and he accepted a few to pay the bills, but he took his time about getting back into uniform. When it appeared that he was on his way to sign as the new manager of the Chicago Cubs in 1979, the owner of the Detroit Tigers—pizza impresario Tom Monaghan—swooped in and made him an offer he couldn't refuse.

Sparky spent the next eighteen seasons as the manager of the Tigers. To this day he remains the most successful manager in Detroit's history as well, and in 1984, after six years at the helm, he guided them to their first World Series Championship since 1968. He did it employing exactly the same principles that he'd established and followed with the Reds, relying on power and speed and his team's defensive strength up the middle, utilizing a strong pitching staff built from top to bottom, and assembling a seasoned, versatile bench. Along the way Sparky became just as beloved and familiar a figure to his players and fans in Michigan as he had been in Ohio. Older now and wiser—finally growing into that famous shock of white hair—as his later career progressed, he grew to resemble no one so much as the beloved baseball sage from whom he'd first learned the game, the "Ol' Perfessor" Casey Stengel. George and Carol still live in the same simple unadorned suburban house they bought in 1967. He remains as authentic and charming and vivid an American character as Will Rogers, and no one else in the world today can talk baseball and life, philosophically intertwined and dispensed in the most original and delightfully singular syntax, like Sparky Anderson.

During Sparky's time in Detroit, the Pandora's box opened by the dawn of free agency changed the game of baseball almost beyond recognition. As salaries and revenues continued their meteoric rise, ugly labor disputes threatened or curtailed seasons each time the Basic Agreement between owners and players came up for renewal. A mid-season strike in 1981 wiped out nearly 40 percent of that year's schedule and cost the sport more than $150 million in lost revenue; when the games resumed in August, all the recent gains in attendance and ratings initiated by the 1975 World Series had been lost, and a flawed split-season compromise, which erased the games played before the strikes, deprived teams with better overall records of a postseason. A two-day work stoppage marred the 1985 season, and an owners' lockout of players in 1990 wiped out spring training. Shortly afterward, when an arbitrator ruled that owners had repeatedly colluded against players to avoid raising the price of free agent contracts in violation of the Basic Agreement, Major League Baseball had to pay the Players Association $280 million in lost wages. This permanently poisoned relations between them, caused both sides to dig in their heels, and precipitated a disaster for all concerned four years later; unable to forge a new basic agreement with owners, players again walked away from their teams in mid-season on August 12, 1994. The rest of that season, and all of the postseason, including the World Series—the first break in its history since 1904—disappeared; this time an estimated $580 million in revenue and $230 million in player salaries washed away with it. Many attributed the impasse to the absence of a strong, independent commissioner; since the owners had forced out their last one, Fay Vincent, in 1992—still angry that in salvaging the 1990 season he had unilaterally ordered owners to end their lockout—the post had been filled, supposedly on an interim basis while they looked for a replacement, by one of their own, Milwaukee Brewers owner Bud Selig, who had been a principal figure in the collusion scandal. Despite the attempted intervention of everyone from Congress to President Bill Clinton, no one could break baseball's most bitter deadlock, and by a vote of 26–2 owners approved plans to go through spring training and begin the 1995 season with what they referred to as "replacement players."

As the date for spring training approached, in Detroit, alone among all of baseball's managers, Sparky Anderson notified his employers that he would not agree to manage any baseball team that used replacement players. The day before spring training began, the Tigers suspended Sparky for his courageous stance and put him on an unpaid leave of absence. Although many at the time mistakenly believed that Sparky was taking a stance in support of the players, his point of view was simpler and purer than either side's position. According to his hard-earned principles, to knowingly put anything less on the field than the best players in the world and charge admission and call it baseball was an unforgivable affront to the game itself. So Sparky walked away and went home to California, while all around Florida and Arizona "replacement players" filled spring training camps and played games in largely empty parks. A few days before the season was scheduled to begin, when Bud Selig finally called and asked Sparky what he would do to end the disastrous impasse, he said: "Put locks on all the doors and hide the keys until the thing is settled."

They settled the thing on April 2, the day before the season was scheduled to begin; at 232 days, still the longest work stoppage in the history of American sports. Sparky and his Tigers and every other team went back to work, and the 1995 season began, but this time the fans stayed away. Perceiving their long-running conflict as a selfish argument between billionaire owners and millionaire players—the average major-league salary had by now nearly reached $700,000 a year—much of America turned its back on baseball; attendance and ratings plummeted throughout the 1995 season, and in the years that followed.

His protest cost Sparky Anderson about $150,000 of his salary that year, which he never recovered, and at the end of the 1995 season the Detroit Tigers fired him. He was sixty-one years old at the time, in perfect health, had won more baseball games in his managing career than all but two men who'd held that job in history, and at that point remained the only manager ever to win a World Series in both leagues. Aside from a few of his players, just about the only other person in the rest of the sport who stood up for Sparky publicly was broadcaster Tony Kubek. Since leaving NBC in 1989, Tony had been calling games for the Yankees' cable TV baseball network, and few men have seen more baseball games in their lives; fewer still care more about the integrity of the game. When the strike ended the 1994 season, Tony Kubek wrote acting commissioner Bud Selig a sixteen-page letter detailing the many ways in which he believed the sport had lost its way, and offered solutions for how he thought those critical problems could be addressed. Selig never answered him.

Kubek resigned from the Yankees that winter and never called another baseball game; he's never even watched one since, so distraught is he at what has happened to the game he loved, a disaster for which he holds players and owners equally accountable. In an honor long overdue for one of the finest, most honorable men in baseball history, Tony Kubek was finally given the Ford C. Frick Award in 2009.

Sparky Anderson never managed another baseball game, but that was not a choice in which, it turned out, he had any say. Although he refuses to even consider the idea that he's been blackballed, there's little doubt that Sparky's principled position cost him his place in the game he'd served so faithfully for forty-three years. No matter; he still calls his decision to refuse any part of that 1994 fiasco the proudest moment of his life.

"The game is bigger than all of us," he says.

The principal recipients of Sparky's forced retirement have been his many friends and family, including his fourteen grandchildren, who have since had him more to themselves. And when he stood up to give his speech beside Carlton Fisk and Tony Perez and Marty Brennaman as he was honored with them at baseball's Hall of Fame in late July of 2000, here's what else Sparky Anderson said, when he turned back and pointed emphatically to those two players:

"I want you to take a look at the people behind me and put it in your brain when you look at 'em; the people that came before them, and these people, and the people that will come after them. That is *baseball*. All the other stuff you've heard about baseball is just makeup. Those people made this game and they will protect this game, and I hope every manager that follows me will listen very carefully: Players earn this, by their skills. Managers come here, as I did, on their backs, for what they did for me. My father never got past the third grade, but there ain't a guy that ever went to Harvard as smart as my daddy. My daddy said this: 'I'm gonna give you a gift. It's the greatest gift to take all the way through your life. And if you live with this gift, everything will work out perfect, and it'll never cost you a dime, and that gift is this: If every day of your life, with every person you meet, you will just be nice to that person, and treat that person like they are someone.' "

Johnny Bench and Joe Morgan, already in the Hall, were there that day, and so was Yaz, and forty-two other Hall of Famers, the largest alumni turnout to that point, and most were in tears by the time Sparky finished. Tony Perez followed him to the podium; he was introduced by Commissioner Bud Selig. When Pudge Fisk followed Perez to make his own speech, he had this to say:

"I'd like to congratulate Sparky and his family. I played against you in the '75 World Series, just for a few games; you might remember . . . seems a lot of the guys I played against from '75 are here for some reason. I'm not quite sure, but I played against Tony in '75, and then he came to the Red Sox and I found out why they call him the Big Dog . . . Doggie for short . . . They shouldn't have called him just Big Dog, because he was the *lead* dog . . .

"I played with Rico, and Yaz, and Dewey, and Freddie, and Spaceman, and Jim Ed and Rooster, but the guy I had the most fun playing with, catching for? Luis Tiant. The best and most colorful pitcher I've ever caught, and the best and most colorful ever, I think, in a Red Sox uniform."

Fisk and Johnny Bench had joked with each other for years that because of the remarkable way Game Six had ended, the Red Sox and their fans still thought that "their team had won the 1975 World Series three games to four," and Fisk referenced that now when he turned to Marty Brennaman.

"And as you called it, Marty, we won that Series three games to four, you know that."

Marty Brennaman's speech that day narrowly averted controversy when some older hard-line Hall of Famers caught wind of a rumor he was going to press the case that Pete Rose should be there with all of his old teammates in Cooperstown, and let it be known that they'd get up and walk out on him if he did. Johnny Bench heard about it and let Marty know shortly before the ceremony, but Brennaman stuck to his guns. While thanking all of those who were there that day from the Big Red Machine, he also mentioned "those who *should* be here—Bob Howsam, Dave Concepcion, and yes, by God, Peter Edward Rose."

He left it at that. No one walked out.

"I wouldn't have walked out," said Joe Morgan afterward. "This day should not be about Pete Rose, and it would have been disrespectful to Tony and Sparky and Pudge if we had walked out. This is their day, and they earned it."

And the whole time during their induction ceremony, less than a mile away at a memorabilia store in Cooperstown unaffiliated with the Hall of Fame, Pete Rose was signing autographs and selling merchandise for a paycheck.

AFTER GAME SIX and the Seitz Decision, this confusing new world became the reality of baseball for all its players; untethered, cast loose, without lasting allegiance. There was suddenly too much money to be made on the open market, and after nearly a hundred years of indentured servitude, who could blame these boys and men for trying to make the most of their brief productive years? So in the aftermath of Seitz, baseball's liberated players scattered like *ronin* set adrift by their shogun, free to chase real or imagined fortunes during the short half-lifes of their professional careers. Fans to this day continue to rage about the sport's astronomical salaries—the average as of this writing is now more than $3 million a year—but most also fail to consider that the average American worker spends forty years in the job market; the average major-league career is four years long, and if the "average" salary in these public arenas still seems wildly out of line with the working-class standards to which professional sports used to adhere, the time spent earning that wage is an equally important factor in the equation. In a culture so single-mindedly devoted to entertainment and return on the dollar, stars in any high-profile profession—actors, rock stars, corporate CEOs—by any rational measurement are now "overpaid"; they also represent less than a fraction of 1 percent of the people working in their field. Begrudge these players their fortunes, then, if you will, but they are to a real extent only possible because of you, as long as you pay the rising ticket prices, buy the cable or satellite packages, purchase the merchandise, obsess over the radio talk show chatter. The value of both the Cincinnati and Boston franchises in 1975—stadiums included—lay between $11 and $12 million, which translates to about $47 million in contemporary money. That's less than a certain third baseman in New York will make over the next two seasons. The estimated worth of the Red Sox today is more than three quarters of a billion dollars. Gross revenue throughout baseball in 2008 reached almost $6.1 billion. Money, we can say without fear of contradiction, changes everything, and nothing's ever gained, but something else is lost.

Baseball did come back a few years after hitting bottom in 1994, gloriously it seemed at the time, on the brute strength of Mark McGwire and Sammy Sosa and Barry Bonds and their thrilling pursuit of ancient home run records. The extent to which we now know that revival was predicated on biological manipulation, deception, and dishonor has since dug the game into an even darker hole with no end in sight. But regardless, incredibly, the money keeps pouring in. His fellow baseball owners recently voted Bud Selig, no longer "interim" and under whose leadership they have all become wealthy beyond measure, as the greatest "commissioner" in baseball history.

Old-timers used to say that baseball games played at night actually began at 1:30 in the afternoon, when players would first gather in the clubhouse and the locker room chemistry that formed that elusive thing called "team" began to work its alchemical magic. What happened back then on the bus rides and plane flights was as important to the sum total as the games themselves. Most players today show up an hour or two before game time, plug in their iPods, deal with agents and marketing deals and off-field business, isolated in their solipsistic bubbles, turning their collective focus to the game at hand only shortly before the first pitch. Each team is a consortium of wealthy, independent contractors who happen to, temporarily, wear the same uniform. Baseball never needed names on jerseys before 1976; fans knew their local lineups by their numbers. Names are a necessity now.

They're in late middle age now, all the players who strode the stage of Game Six. The youthful, big-league dreams they all shared had come to pass, lifted them up, making possible a large American life during and after their careers that for most would have otherwise remained hopelessly out of reach. To a man they all still love the game that gave them their measure of glory, and if baseball has more than its share of the intractable dilemmas informing so much of modern life, it also still has the game itself, in all its sweet formal simplicity and complex interior reality; that remains its richest, most valuable asset. The idea of finding meaning in a game, no matter how elevated the level of play or its artificially inflated significance in a culture that all too often celebrates size over substance, is easy to write off against the weight of the world's concerns or the pressing limits of finite life spans. But such condescending assessments miss the essential nature of the nourishment these contests provide; because it is the human qualities embodied and displayed by the players in these arenas that we drink in and from which we derive soulful benefit: grace, stalwart strength, determination and inner fire, standing up under pressure, persistence and faith in something larger than the self, taking joy in victory, yielding with dignity in defeat. These things matter and they are, as much as any identifiable part of the human experience, eternal.

The world these teams electrified in the fall of 1975 is a vastly different place now, but if it's a better one, well, that depends on who you talk to. Faster, certainly, we're as connected and jacked up as a juggler's nervous system; sadder, absolutely, maybe even wiser, or—one hopes after this new century's sobering first decade—at the least wised up. The past recedes more rapidly from sight than it once did, abandoned for the next big thing without a backward glance, particularly by the young; they'll learn otherwise, most likely, once they taste the melancholy of mortality. Headlines tell us that greed hasn't lost its death grip on the human spirit, but they also suggest that some poisonous age-old racial hatreds have genuinely softened; to its everlasting credit baseball has had more than a little to do with that. Even "entertainment" itself ain't what it used to be— forms are breaking down all over, through repetition, overuse, or the evergreen lust for money; music, movies, novels, newspapers, network television, and even professional sports, now irreversibly razed and rebuilt into a multibillion-dollar wing of the "entertainment industry." So few things remain constant, but not everything changes for the worse; the Boss and the E Street Band are still rocking the world like their lives depend on it, standing up to time, sure as every spring men break out the bats and balls and gloves, and every once in a while on the way to the financial planner's office a blade of grass busts through the concrete, a miracle "team" falls together and lifts our hearts: the Twins of '87 and '91; Kirk Gibson, Orel Hershiser, and the Dodgers in '88; the redemptive Series between the Diamondbacks and Yankees in the shadow of 9/11. It even happened for that battered old franchise in Boston in '04 and again in '07, finally burying all that nonsense about a "curse." And somewhere, someday, maybe this year if we're lucky, it will happen again.

"Baseball don't belong to the owners, with all their power and money, and it don't belong to the players who make a million bucks a month, and walk around like they're doing folks a favor just by showing up," says Sparky. "The game belongs to the fans. Fans are the real owners, and someday they could pull the plug if they ever get fed up with all the nonsense. And we owe it to the game and those fans to make it the best sport in America again. We've got to solve all these problems together, and here's a place to start:

"A man takes care of his family, that's what my daddy taught me. He knows how to treat people right; the way *he* wants to be treated. He never steals, he never cheats, and he gives something back. He does his profession proud, and he represents it with class instead of just filling his pockets. That was the most important thing about our team in 1975, and that Boston team, the thing that made them both great, the thing that put so many of 'em in the Hall of Fame.

"They were all *men*."

Luis Tiant Jr. greets his father, Luis Tiant Sr.,
Logan Airport, Boston, August 1975

You come here with two pockets.
One is the winning pocket and the other
is the losing pocket, and you have to
carry them both with dignity.

LUIS TIANT

Appendix

1975 WORLD SERIES GAME 6

Fenway Park, Boston, Massachusetts

Tuesday, October 21, 1975
Attendance: 35,205
Time of Game: 4:01

	1	2	3	4	5	6	7	8	9	10	11	12	R	H	E
Reds	0	0	0	0	3	0	2	1	0	0	0	0	**6**	**14**	**0**
Red Sox	3	0	0	0	0	0	0	3	0	0	0	1	**7**	**10**	**1**

Boston Red Sox 7
Manager: Darrell Johnson

Cincinnati Reds 6
Manager: Sparky Anderson

W: R Wise (1-0), **L:** P Darcy (0-1)
Winning run scored with 0 outs

BATTING

CINCINNATI REDS

	AB	R	H	RBI	BB	SO	BA	OPS	Pit	PO	A	Details
P Rose 3B	5	1	2	0	0	0	.348	.942	18	0	2	HBP
K Griffey RF	5	2	2	2	1	0	.250	.766	17	0	0	3B
J Morgan 2B	6	1	1	0	0	0	.217	.582	25	4	4	
J Bench C	6	0	1	1	0	2	.240	.709	14	8	0	
T Perez 1B	6	0	2	0	0	2	.174	.704	26	11	2	
G Foster LF	6	0	2	2	0	0	.280	.628	14	4	1	2B
D Concepcion SS	6	0	1	0	0	0	.167	.525	24	3	4	SB
C Geronimo CF	6	1	2	1	0	3	.318	1.082	20	2	0	HR
G Nolan P	0	0	0	0	0	0	.000	.000		1	0	
D Chaney PH	1	0	0	0	0	0	.000	.000	1	0	0	
F Norman P	0	0	0	0	0	0	.000	.000		0	0	
J Billingham P	0	0	0	0	0	0	.000	.000		0	0	
E Armbrister PH	0	1	0	0	1	0	.000	.500	5	0	0	
C Carroll P	0	0	0	0	0	0				0	0	
T Crowley PH	1	0	1	0	0	0	.500	1.000	4	0	0	
P Borbon P	1	0	0	0	0	0	.000	.000	3	0	0	
R Eastwick P	0	0	0	0	0	0	.000	.000		0	0	
W McEnaney P	0	0	0	0	0	0	1.000	2.000		0	0	
D Driessen PH	1	0	0	0	0	0	.000	.000	3	0	0	
P Darcy P	0	0	0	0	0	0	.000	.000		0	1	
Totals	**50**	**6**	**14**	**6**	**2**	**7**			**174**	**33**	**14**	

BATTING

2B: G Foster (1, off L Tiant).

3B: K Griffey (1, off L Tiant).

HR: C Geronimo (2, off L Tiant; 8th inn, 0 on, 0 outs to Deep RF).

HBP: P Rose (1, by D Drago).

TB: C Geronimo 5; K Griffey 4; G Foster 3; T Perez 2; P Rose 2; J Morgan; T Crowley; D Concepcion; J Bench.

RBI: K Griffey 2 (4); G Foster 2 (2); C Geronimo (3); J Bench (4).

2-out RBI: G Foster 2; J Bench.

Team LOB: 11

With RISP: 3 for 13.

FIELDING

DP: 1. G Foster-J Bench.

BASERUNNING

SB: D Concepcion (3, 2nd base off D Drago/C Fisk).

BATTING

BOSTON RED SOX

	AB	R	H	RBI	BB	SO	BA	OPS	Pit	PO	A	Details
C Cooper 1B	5	0	0	0	0	1	.056	.164	17	8	0	
D Drago P	0	0	0	0	0	0				0	0	
R Miller PH	1	0	0	0	0	0	.000	.000	5	0	0	
R Wise P	0	0	0	0	0	0	.000	.000		0	0	
D Doyle 2B	5	0	1	0	1	0	.269	.706	22	1	2	2B
C Yastrzemski LF-1B	6	1	3	0	0	0	.333	.747	24	7	1	
C Fisk C	4	2	2	1	2	0	.273	.974	18	9	1	HR, 2·IW
F Lynn CF	4	2	2	3	1	0	.304	.798	11	2	0	HR
R Petrocelli 3B	4	1	0	0	1	1	.304	.708	17	1	1	
D Evans RF	5	0	1	0	0	2	.318	.966	25	5	1	2B
R Burleson SS	3	0	0	0	2	0	.333	.798	19	2	2	
L Tiant P	2	0	0	0	0	2	.250	.650	9	0	2	SH
R Moret P	0	0	0	0	0	0				0	1	
B Carbo PH-LF	2	1	1	3	0	1	.500	2.500	10	1	0	HR
Totals	**41**	**7**	**10**	**7**	**7**	**7**			177	**36**	**11**	

BATTING

2B: D Doyle (1, off F Norman); D Evans (1, off J Billingham).

HR: F Lynn (1, off G Nolan; 1st inn, 2 on, 2 outs to Deep CF-RF); B Carbo (2, off R Eastwick; 8th inn, 2 on, 2 outs to Deep CF). C Fisk (2, off P Darcy; 12th inn, 0 on, 0 outs to Deep LF Line);

SH: L Tiant (1, off J Billingham).

IBB: C Fisk 2 (2, by W McEnaney, by F Norman).

TB: C Fisk 5; F Lynn 5; B Carbo 4; C Yastrzemski 3; D Doyle 2; D Evans 2.

RBI: F Lynn 3 (5); B Carbo 3 (4); C Fisk (4).

2-out RBI: F Lynn 3; B Carbo 3.

Team LOB: 9.

With RISP: 2 for 10.

FIELDING

DP: 1. D Evans-C Yastrzemski-D Doyle.

E: R Burleson (1).

PITCHING

CINCINNATI REDS

	IP	H	R	ER	BB	SO	HR	ERA	Pit-Str
G Nolan	2	3	3	3	0	2	1	6.00	31–20
F Norman	0.2	1	0	0	2	0	0	9.00	22–9
J Billingham	1.1	1	0	0	1	1	0	1.29	21–11
C Carroll	1	1	0	0	0	0	0	4.91	10–7
P Borbon	2	1	2	2	2	1	0	6.00	33–17
R Eastwick, BS (2)	1	2	1	1	1	2	1	2.25	24–14
W McEnaney	1	0	0	0	1	0	0	3.18	7–3
P Darcy, L (0–1)	2	1	1	1	0	1	1	4.50	29–18
Totals	**11**	**10**	**7**	**7**	**7**	**7**	**3**		**177–99**

BOSTON RED SOX

	IP	H	R	ER	BB	SO	HR	ERA	Pit-Str
L Tiant	7	11	6	6	2	5	1	3.60	113–72
R Moret	1	0	0	0	0	0	0	0.00	7–6
D Drago	3	1	0	0	0	1	0	2.25	35–18
R Wise, W (1–0)	1	2	0	0	0	1	0	8.44	19–12
Totals	**12**	**14**	**6**	**6**	**2**	**7**	**1**		**174–108**

P Borbon faced 2 batters in the 8th inning.
R Eastwick faced 2 batters in the 9th inning.
L Tiant faced 1 batter in the 8th inning.

Balks: None.
WP: None.
IBB: W McEnaney (1; C Fisk); F Norman (1; C Fisk).
HBP: D Drago (1; P Rose).

OTHER
Umpires: HP–Bob Davidson
1B–Art Frantz
2B–Nick Colosi
3B–Larry Barnett
Time of Game: 4:01.
Attendance: 35,205.
Field Condition: Unknown.
Weather: Unknown.

1975 World Series (4–3): Cincinnati Reds (108–54) over Boston Red Sox (95–65)

SERIES GAMES

GAME 1 / BOX SCORE AND PLAY-BY-PLAY

October 11, 1975, at Fenway Park (Boston Red Sox)

	1	2	3	4	5	6	7	8	9	R	H	E
Cincinnati Reds	0	0	0	0	0	0	0	0	0	0	5	0
Boston Red Sox	0	0	0	0	0	0	6	0	x	6	12	0

HOME RUNS: CIN–none; BOS–none
ATTENDANCE: 35,205

PITCHERS:

CIN–Gullett, Carroll (7), McEnaney (7)

BOS–Tiant

WP–Luis Tiant
LP–Don Gullett
SAVE–none

GAME 2 / BOX SCORE AND PLAY-BY-PLAY

October 12, 1975, at Fenway Park (Boston Red Sox)

	1	2	3	4	5	6	7	8	9	R	H	E
Cincinnati Reds	0	0	0	1	0	0	0	0	2	3	7	1
Boston Red Sox	1	0	0	0	0	1	0	0	0	2	7	0

HOME RUNS: CIN–none; BOS–none
ATTENDANCE: 35,205

PITCHERS:

CIN–Billingham, Borbon (6), McEnaney (7), Eastwick (8)

BOS–Lee, Drago (9)

WP–Rawly Eastwick
LP–Dick Drago
SAVE–none

GAME 3 / BOX SCORE AND PLAY-BY-PLAY

October 14, 1975, at Riverfront Stadium (Cincinnati Reds)

	1	2	3	4	5	6	7	8	9	10	R	H	E
Boston Red Sox	0	1	0	0	0	1	1	0	2	0	5	10	2
Cincinnati Reds	0	0	0	2	3	0	0	0	0	1	6	7	0

PITCHERS:

BOS–Wise, Burton (5), Cleveland (5), Willoughby (7), Moret (10)

CIN–Nolan, Darcy (5), Carroll (7), McEnaney (7), Eastwick (9)

WP–Rawly Eastwick

LP–Jim Willoughby

SAVE–none

HOME RUNS: BOS–Carbo, Evans, Fisk; CIN–Bench, Concepcion, Geronimo

ATTENDANCE: 55,392

GAME 4 / BOX SCORE AND PLAY-BY-PLAY

October 15, 1975, at Riverfront Stadium (Cincinnati Reds)

	1	2	3	4	5	6	7	8	9	R	H	E
Boston Red Sox	0	0	0	5	0	0	0	0	0	5	11	1
Cincinnati Reds	2	0	0	2	0	0	0	0	0	4	9	1

PITCHERS:

BOS–Tiant

CIN–Norman, Borbon (4), Carroll (5), Eastwick (7)

WP–Luis Tiant

LP–Fred Norman

SAVE - none

HOME RUNS: BOS–none; CIN–none

ATTENDANCE: 55,667

GAME 5 / BOX SCORE AND PLAY-BY-PLAY

October 16, 1975, at Riverfront Stadium (Cincinnati Reds)

	1	2	3	4	5	6	7	8	9	R	H	E
Boston Red Sox	1	0	0	0	0	0	0	0	1	2	5	0
Cincinnati Reds	0	0	0	1	1	3	0	1	x	6	8	0

HOME RUNS: BOS–none; CIN–Perez (2)

ATTENDANCE: 56,393

PITCHERS:

BOS–Cleveland, Willoughby (6), Pole (8), Segui (8)

CIN–Gullett, Eastwick (9)

WP–Don Gullett

LP–Reggie Cleveland

SAVE–Rawly Eastwick

GAME 7 / BOX SCORE AND PLAY-BY-PLAY

October 22, 1975, at Fenway Park (Boston Red Sox)

	1	2	3	4	5	6	7	8	9	R	H	E
Cincinnati Reds	0	0	0	0	0	2	1	0	1	4	9	0
Boston Red Sox	0	0	3	0	0	0	0	0	0	3	5	2

HOME RUNS: CIN–Perez; BOS–none

ATTENDANCE: 35,205

PITCHERS:

CIN–Gullett, Billingham (5), Carroll (7), McEnaney (9)

BOS–Lee, Moret (7), Willoughby (7), Burton (9), Cleveland (9)

WP–Clay Carroll

LP–Jim Burton

SAVE–Will McEnaney

SERIES MVP

Pete Rose

SERIES BATTING STATS

CINCINNATI REDS

	SERIES STATS														REGULAR SEASON					
Player	G	AB	R	H	2B	3B	HR	RBI	BB	SO	BA	OBP	SLG	SB	AB	H	HR	BA	OBP	SB
Ed Armbrister	4	1	1	0	0	0	0	0	2	0	.000	.667	.000	0	65	12	0	.185	.254	3
Johnny Bench	7	29	5	6	2	0	1	4	2	4	.207	.258	.379	0	530	150	28	.283	.359	11
Jack Billingham	3	2	0	0	0	0	0	0	0	0	.000	.000	.000	0	65	7	0	.108	.205	0
Pedro Borbon	3	1	0	0	0	0	0	0	0	0	.000	.000	.000	0	24	7	0	.292	.292	0
Clay Carroll	5	0	0	0	0	0	0	0	0	0				0	19	0	0	.000	.000	0
#Darrel Chaney	2	2	0	0	0	0	0	0	0	1	.000	.000	.000	0	160	35	2	.219	.280	3
Dave Concepcion	7	28	3	5	1	0	1	4	0	1	.179	.200	.321	3	507	139	5	.274	.326	33
*Terry Crowley	2	2	0	1	0	0	0	0	0	1	.500	.500	.500	0	71	19	1	.268	.333	0
*Pat Darcy	2	1	0	0	0	0	0	0	0	1	.000	.500	.500	0	47	4	0	.085	.085	0
*Dan Driessen	2	2	0	0	0	0	0	0	0	1	.000	.000	.000	0	210	59	7	.281	.386	10
Rawly Eastwick	5	1	0	0	0	0	0	0	0	0	.000	.000	.00	0	15	1	0	.067	.067	0
George Foster	7	29	1	8	1	0	0	2	1	1	.276	.300	.310	1	463	139	23	.300	.356	2
*Cesar Geronimo	7	25	3	7	0	1	2	3	3	5	.280	.357	.600	0	501	129	6	.257	.327	13
*Ken Griffey	7	26	4	7	3	1	1	4	4	2	.269	.367	.462	2	463	141	4	.305	.391	16
Don Gullett	3	7	1	2	0	0	0	0	0	2	.286	.286	.286	0	62	14	0	.226	.246	0
*Will McEnaney	5	1	0	1	0	0	0	0	0	0	1.000	1.000	1.000	0	14	0	0	.000	.000	0
*Joe Morgan	7	27	4	7	1	0	0	3	5	1	.259	.364	.296	2	498	163	17	.327	.466	67
Gary Nolan	2	1	0	0	0	0	0	0	0	0	.000	.000	.000	0	68	12	0	.176	.253	0
#Fred Norman	2	1	0	0	0	0	0	0	0	0	.000	.000	.000	0	60	7	0	.117	.159	0
Tony Perez	7	28	4	5	0	0	3	7	3	9	.179	.258	.500	1	511	144	20	.282	.350	1
Merv Rettenmund	3	3	0	0	0	0	0	0	0	1	.000	.000	.000	0	188	45	2	.239	.356	5
#Pete Rose	7	27	3	10	1	1	0	2	5	1	.370	.485	.481	0	662	210	7	.317	.406	0
Total	7	244	29	59	9	3	7	29	25	30	.242	.315	.389	9			124	.271	.353	168

* bats left-handed; # switch hits

SERIES BATTING STATS

BOSTON RED SOX

Player	SERIES STATS G	AB	R	H	2B	3B	HR	RBI	BB	SO	BA	OBP	SLG	SB	REGULAR SEASON AB	H	HR	BA	OBP	SB
Juan Beniquez	3	8	0	1	0	0	0	1	1	1	.125	.222	.125	0	254	74	2	.291	.358	7
Rick Burleson	7	24	1	7	1	0	0	2	4	2	.292	.393	.333	0	580	146	6	.252	.305	8
Jim Burton	2	0	0	0	0	0	0	0	0	0				0	0	0	0			0
*Bernie Carbo	4	7	3	3	1	0	2	4	1	1	.429	.500	1.429	0	319	82	15	.257	.409	2
Reggie Cleveland	3	2	0	0	0	0	0	0	0	2	.000	.000	.000	0	0	0	0	.000	.000	0
*Cecil Cooper	5	19	0	1	1	0	0	1	0	3	.053	.050	.105	0	305	95	14	.311	.355	1
*Denny Doyle	7	30	3	8	1	1	0	0	2	1	.267	.313	.367	0	+325	97	4	.298	.339	5
Dick Drago	2	0	0	0	0	0	0	0	0	0				0	0	0	0			0
Dwight Evans	7	24	3	7	1	1	1	5	3	4	.292	.393	.542	0	412	113	13	.274	.353	3
Carlton Fisk	7	25	5	6	0	0	2	4	7	7	.240	.406	.480	0	263	87	10	.331	.395	4
Doug Griffin	1	1	0	0	0	0	0	0	0	0	.000	.000	.000	0	287	69	1	.240	.288	2
*Bill Lee	2	6	0	1	0	0	0	0	0	3	.167	.167	.167	0	0	0	0			0
*Fred Lynn	7	25	3	7	1	0	1	5	3	5	.280	.345	.440	0	528	175	21	.331	.401	10
*Rick Miller	3	2	0	0	0	0	0	0	0	0	.000	.000	.000	0	108	21	0	.194	.326	3
Bob Montgomery	1	1	0	0	0	0	0	0	0	0	.000	.000	.000	0	195	44	2	.226	.241	1
#Roger Moret	3	0	0	0	0	0	0	0	0	0				0	0	0	0			0
Rico Petrocelli	7	26	3	8	1	0	0	4	3	6	.308	.379	.346	0	402	96	7	.239	.310	0
Dick Pole	1	0	0	0	0	0	0	0	0	0				0	0	0	0			0
Diego Segui	1	0	0	0	0	0	0	0	0	0				0	0	0	0			0
Luis Tiant	3	8	2	2	0	0	0	0	2	4	.250	.400	.250	0	1	0	0	.000	.000	0
Jim Willoughby	3	0	0	0	0	0	0	0	0	0				0	0	0	0			0
Rick Wise	2	2	0	0	0	0	0	0	0	0	.000	.000	.000	0	0	0	0			0
*Carl Yastrzemski	7	29	7	9	0	0	0	4	4	1	.310	.382	.310	0	543	146	14	.269	.371	8
Total	7	239	30	60	7	2	6	30	30	40	.251	.333	.372	0			134	.275	.344	66

* bats left-handed; # switch hits; + before season totals indicates the player was with multiple teams this year

SERIES PITCHING STATS

CINCINNATI REDS

Player		SERIES STATS									REGULAR SEASON					
	G	ERA	W-L	SV	CG	IP	H	ER	BB	SO	W-L	IP	ERA	WHIP	SO	SV
*Don Gullett	3	4.34	1–1	0	0	18.7	19	9	10	15	15–4	160	2.42	1.15	98	
Jack Billingham	3	1.00	0–0	0	0	9.0	8	1	5	7	15–10	208	4.11	1.43	79	
Rawly Eastwick	5	2.25	2–0	1	0	8.0	6	2	3	4	5–3	90	2.60	1.13	61	22
*Will McEnaney	5	2.70	0–0	1	0	6.7	3	2	2	5	5–2	91	2.47	1.26	48	15
Gary Nolan	2	6.00	0–0	0	0	6.0	6	4	1	2	15–9	211	3.16	1.10	74	
Clay Carroll	5	3.18	1–0	0	0	5.7	4	2	2	3	7–5	96	2.62	1.30	44	7
Pat Darcy	2	4.50	0–1	0	0	4.0	3	2	2	1	11–5	131	3.58	1.48	46	1
*Fred Norman	2	9.00	0–1	0	0	4.0	8	4	3	2	12–4	188	3.73	1.31	119	
Pedro Borbon	3	6.00	0–0	0	0	3.0	3	2	2	1	9–5	125	2.95	1.33	29	5
Total		**3.88**	**4–3**	**2**	**0**	**65.0**	**60**	**28**	**30**	**40**			**3.37**	**1.310**		

BOSTON RED SOX

Player		SERIES STATS									REGULAR SEASON					
	G	ERA	W-L	SV	CG	IP	H	ER	BB	SO	W-L	IP	ERA	WHIP	SO	SV
Luis Tiant	3	3.60	2–0	0	2	25.0	25	10	8	12	18–14	260	4.02	1.28	142	
*Bill Lee	2	3.14	0–0	0	0	14.3	12	5	3	7	17–9	260	3.95	1.32	78	
Reggie Cleveland	3	6.75	0–1	0	0	6.7	7	5	3	5	13–9	171	4.43	1.32	78	
Jim Willoughby	3	0.00	0–1	0	0	6.3	3	0	0	2	5–2	48	3.54	1.28	29	8
Rick Wise	2	8.44	1–0	0	0	5.3	6	5	2	2	19–12	255	3.95	1.31	141	
Dick Drago	2	2.25	0–1	0	0	4.0	3	1	1	1	2–2	73	3.84	1.38	43	15
*Roger Moret	3	0.00	0–0	0	0	1.7	2	0	3	1	14–3	145	3.60	1.43	80	1
Diego Segui	1	0.00	0–0	0	0	1.0	0	0	0	0	2–5	71	4.82	1.61	45	6
*Jim Burton	2	9.00	0–1	0	0	1.0	1	1	3	0	1–2	53	2.89	1.45	39	1
Dick Pole	1	inf	0–0	0	0	0.0	0	1	2	0	4–6	90	4.42	1.49	42	
Total		**3.86**	**3–4**	**0**	**2**	**65.3**	**59**	**28**	**25**	**30**			**3.98**	**1.360**		

* throws left-handed

Acknowledgments

MANY PEOPLE TO THANK: none more than Marty Brennaman, the first person I spoke to about the book and without whom so much of this work would not have been possible. Special thanks to Chet Simmons, Tony Kubek, Thom Brennaman, Dick Stockton, and Lesley Visser; Michael Weisman and David Israel; Carolyn Sullivan and Dick Williams with the Reds; John Blake, Pam Ganley, and Dick Bresciani with the Red Sox; and Bill Francis at the Baseball Hall of Fame, for his tireless research and diligent fact-checking. Special thanks to my researchers, Jim Farmer in Cincinnati and Alex and Meghan Law in Boston, couldn't have done it without you. Thanks in Boston as well to Stan Abrams, Bob Donovan, Dick Connolly, Ryan Connolly, Ed Carpenter, Curt Flight, Bruce Hauck, Dan Meyer, and Justin Ansel. In Los Angeles, Billy Crystal, John Marin, and Al Michaels.

To the players, without whom this book would be neither possible nor necessary, live long and prosper: Johnny Bench, Jack Billingham, Bernie Carbo, Dave Concepcion, Pat Darcy, Denny Doyle, Dick Drago, Dwight Evans, Doug Flynn, George Foster, Ken Griffey Sr., Bill Lee, Fred Lynn, Will McEnaney, Joe Morgan, Gary Nolan, Tony Perez, Rico Petrocelli, Bill Plummer, Jim Rice, Luis Tiant, Rick Wise. To Yaz: get well soon, everyone involved sends their best wishes.

Many thanks as always to my friend and agent Ed Victor, and to Bob Miller and Will Schwalbe. At Hyperion, my publishers Ellen Archer and Will Balliett and my wonderful longtime editor Gretchen Young. Many thanks also to my photo editor, David Plotkin.

Finally, special thanks to two extraordinary gentlemen who, despite the sport's many self-inflicted wounds, have always made it easy to love the game of baseball: Vin Scully and Sparky Anderson.

Photo Credits

Photo on page iii courtesy of Getty Images.
Photo on page 379 courtesy of Associated Press.

For the two photo sections:
National Baseball Hall of Fame and Museum, Inc.:
Photos 1, 2, 3, 7, 8, 26, 27, 30, 31, 32, 34, 38, 41, 48
Getty Images: Photos 4, 5, 6, 12, 13, 16, 18, 19, 22, 23,
25, 28, 29, 36, 44, 47, 50, 52, 55
Associated Press: Photos 9, 11, 15, 21, 35, 37, 40, 43, 45,
46, 51, 53, 54
Corbis: Photos 10, 17, 20, 24, 33, 39, 42, 49
Photo 14 courtesy of Dick Stockton

Index

Aaron, Hank, 39, 199
ABC sports, 17, 19, 20
Ali, Muhammad, 244
American Association, 92
American League:
　designated hitters in, 20, 60, 74–75,
　　117, 195
　early years of, 93, 95–97, 127–28
　Eastern Division title, 21
　"Junior Circuit" of, 93
　pitching in, 60
American Sportsman, The (TV), 349
Anderson, George Lee "Sparky," 90,
　　113–14, 168, 244, 378
　and balk, 69–71
　and Carbo, 238–40
　discipline of, 42–43, 47–48, 216, 234,
　　279, 292, 328
　early years of, 1–5, 42, 46, 49
　and fatherhood, 238–39
　fired by Cincinnati, 343–44
　and Game Seven, 293, 294, 305–6,
　　308, 309
　and Game Six, 11, 41–44, 46, 56, 86,
　　136, 166, 267, 272–73, 282, 290–91
　in Hall of Fame, 373–74
　instinct of, 51, 239–40, 243, 245, 248,
　　294, 306
　and lineup, 43–44, 50–51, 66, 74, 103,
　　294
　as manager, 46–48, 49, 104, 106, 140,
　　201, 311, 340, 344, 369, 372
　as mentor, 234, 238
　nicknames of, 5, 42, 49
　and 1970 season, 47–48
　and 1975 season, 42, 44
　and 1976 season, 327, 329
　and 1978 season, 340, 341
　personal traits of, 49, 238
　and pitchers, 41–43, 78–79, 85, 111,
　　114, 123, 124, 125, 130, 131–32,
　　138–42, 164, 165, 188, 229, 232, 233,

　　239–40, 249, 251, 255, 261–62, 282,
　　305–6, 329
　principles of, 371, 372–74
　public image of, 48–49, 369
　and team building, 104, 121, 122, 152,
　　156, 290, 310, 311, 328, 333, 369
　and Tigers, 369–70, 371, 372
　and World Series (1975), 49, 79, 103,
　　204, 271, 310–11, 314
Anderson, Leroy, 2
Angell, Roger, 53
Aparicio, Luis, 84, 107, 143
Arizona Diamondbacks, 350, 351, 377
Arledge, Roone, 349
Armbrister, Edison Rosanda, 192, 342
　career of, 173, 352–53
　in Game Seven, 301, 302
　in Game Six, 172–76, 182–84
　in Game Three, 173–75, 176, 177, 275,
　　301, 302, 353
Associated Press, All-Star voting, 13
Atlanta Braves, 93, 188
Autry, Gene, 47
Avila, Bobby, 8, 9

Baltimore Orioles:
　early years of, 128
　and 1973 season, 84
　and 1975 season, 55
　and 1976 season, 323, 329
　and 1977 season, 339
　World Series lost by, 21
　World Series won by, 48, 156, 345
Barnett, Larry, 174–78, 193, 286, 301
baseball:
　aging audiences, 20
　aging players, 278
　antitrust exemption of, 19, 94
　audiences dwindling for, 18, 19
　audiences returning to, 314–15
　baby boomer generation in, 216, 218
　balk in, 69–71

baseball (*continued*)
barnstorming teams, 91, 360–61, 362
Basic Agreements (1970s), 317,
318–19, 323, 326, 327, 370
batting helmets in, 145, 306–7
belonging to the fans, 378
blue-collar fans of, 330
changes in the game, 19–20, 33–34,
316, 320, 323, 331–32, 336, 345, 370,
377
color bar in, 7, 8, 34, 98, 151, 345
computer stats in, 73–74
dead ball era, 213
designated hitters, 20, 60, 331
dishonor in, 375–76
early years of, 90–97
as entertainment, 65, 218, 375, 377
farm system, 33
finding meaning in, 376–77
free agency, 19, 319, 323, 324–27, 330,
331–32, 336, 339–40, 346, 351, 354,
370, 374–75
instant replay, 176
intentional walks, 136–37
large media market franchises, 330
Latin players in, 62, 67, 98, 102, 119,
171–72
leagues divided in, 19–20
living the moment in, 289, 311
managers in, 344
and money, 32, 91, 371, 375–76
multi-use stadiums, 37
as "National Pastime," 91
night games, 17, 33, 56, 376
owners vs. players, 19, 93–94, 312–19,
370, 371
pitcher specialization, 245
pitching charts, 192
pitching mound, 129
postseason games, 20
reserve clause, 18–19, 94, 95, 316–19,
330–31
as "rounders," 90
rules of, 90
salary arbitration in, 236
scouting, 33
seventh-inning stretch, 215
skills needed in, 133
substance abuse in, 233–34, 375
syndicates in, 94
team spirit in, 53, 376
television ratings, 18, 339
ticket prices in, 330, 375
umpires, 177–78, 193
women's league in, 216

Baseball Assistance Team, 360
Batista, Fulgencio, 99
Bench, Johnny Lee, 11, 48, 101, 260
at bat, Game Six, 72, 153–56, 185–86,
208–9, 210, 247–48, 275–77
as catcher, 43, 81, 83, 86, 114, 132,
136, 138, 153, 198, 228, 240, 254–55,
263, 281–82, 366
early years of, 81, 153–54
in Game One, 70, 71
and Game Seven, 291, 298–300, 302,
305, 307, 308
in Game Three, 277
in Game Two, 247
Gold Gloves to, 45, 328
in Hall of Fame, 348, 373
injuries to, 155, 275, 276
in lineup, 45, 103, 105, 122
and 1975 season, 74, 216, 275, 276
and 1976 season, 330
and 1977 season, 336, 337
and 1978 season, 341
and pitchers, 130, 241, 249, 255
retirement of, 346
skills of, 153, 154, 156, 185
as superstar, 25, 42, 107, 157
and teammates, 290, 333
and World Series (1972), 137
and World Series (1975), 310–11
and World Series (1976), 329
Beniquez, Juan, 74, 75, 232, 233, 253,
271, 306, 322
Berra, Yogi, 23, 185
Bicentennial Year (1976), 333–34
Billingham, Jack, 75, 189, 220, 340
as "Cactus Jack," 142
career of, 78, 139, 167
and Darcy, 289–90
early years of, 139
and Game Seven, 297–98, 300, 301
and Game Six, 78, 79, 86, 111, 133,
139–42, 144–46, 164–67, 223
and Game Two, 78, 131–32, 141, 145
in later years, 351–52
and 1975 season, 130, 132
and World Series (1972), 137
Blackwell, Tim, 85, 163
Blish, Milt, 239, 309
Blue, Vida, 325, 326, 339
Bonds, Barry, 375
Borbon, Pedro Rodriguez, 196–98,
255
at bat, Game Six, 225, 226
early years of, 196
and Game Seven, 296–97

in Game Six, 196–97, 198, 203,
    221–22, 227–29
retirement of, 352
Boston:
    baseball culture in, 93, 96, 214, 289,
        291, 292
    racial tensions in, 168–71, 218, 315
    "Rooters" in, 96, 111, 126–27
    sportswriters of, 13–15, 33, 201,
        217–18, 241, 244, 286, 339
Boston Americans, 95–96, 109–11,
    126–27, 204
Boston Braves, 39, 92–93
Boston Globe, 13–15, 33, 204, 286
Boston Herald, 361
Boston Nationals, 205
Boston Red Sox:
    and AL Championship (1975), 14, 39,
        55, 80, 88, 144, 201, 246
    the Babe as player for, 27, 213–14
    "Buffalo Heads" in, 339, 342, 348
    and "curse of the Bambino," 344–45,
        377
    downward trend of, 336, 344–45
    faithful fans of, 37, 171, 214, 227, 229,
        242, 248, 249, 257, 292–93, 297, 353,
        374
    and fans' elusive dreams, 14, 208, 211,
        212, 215, 227, 257, 315, 344, 364
    fantasy camps and cruises, 361
    farm system of, 35, 345
    franchise value, 375
    and free agency, 331–32, 339
    Hall of Fame, 361, 363, 365, 368
    history and culture of, 213–15
    and "Impossible Dream," 36, 37, 38,
        89, 143, 168, 342
    lineup of, 73, 74, 75
    management ineptitude of, 345, 365,
        366
    name change to, 205–6
    and 1912 season, 213
    and 1967 season, 35–36
    and 1973 season, 84
    and 1974 season, 54, 55
    and 1975 season, 39, 54–55, 200–201
    and 1976 season, 322–26, 329, 334
    and 1977 season, 338–39
    and 1978 season, 340–43
    and 2004 and 2007 seasons, 377
    "Picket Line" of (1912–1918), 27
    undisciplined players in, 216, 235,
        338–39
    unhappy endings amassed by, 14, 214,
        255, 257, 315, 334, 341, 342, 344

and World Series (1975), 46, 311–13,
    314, 315, 381–90; *see also specific
    games*
World Series lost by, 34, 36–37, 116,
    308, 311–13, 344, 357
World Series won by, 27, 213, 214
Yankee rivalry with, 323–24, 341–42,
    357
see also specific players
Boston Red Stockings, 92–93, 205
Bouton, Jim, *Ball Four,* 362
Brennaman, Marty:
    career summary of, 350
    and Game Seven, 294, 309
    and Game Six, 22, 23, 45, 174, 216,
        286–87
    in Hall of Fame, 350, 368, 373, 374
Brennaman, Thom, 350
Brooke, Edward W., 147, 148–49, 160–61
Brooklyn Dodgers, 46, 47, 92, 152, 329
Brush, John, 128
Bryant, Don "Bear," 200, 212
Burleson, Rick, 52, 173, 200, 323, 327,
    335, 344, 366
    at bat, Game Six, 114–17, 165, 198,
        232–33, 263
    early years of, 114–15
    fielding in Game Six, 158, 159,
        193–94, 195, 196, 210, 211, 212, 258,
        267, 270, 278
    in Game Seven, 296, 298, 301, 302,
        309
    in later years, 361
    and 1976 season, 334
    in Red Sox Hall of Fame, 361
    as "Rooster," 116
    in World Series (1975), 116–17, 312
Burton, Jim, 186, 193, 258, 259, 303–5,
    352
Busch, August, family of, 151

California Angels, 162, 163, 337, 340,
    361
Campbell, Bill, 332, 338
Capilla, Doug, 337
Caray, Harry, 215
Carbo, Bernie, 154
    and Anderson, 238–40
    at bat, Game Six, 232, 233–43, 244,
        263–64, 360
    career of, 233, 234, 237, 257
    fielding in Game Six, 243, 261
    in Game Seven, 294–95, 296, 297
    in later years, 359–60
    and 1974 season, 235

Carbo, Bernie (*continued*)
  and 1975 season, 236
  and 1977 season, 338, 339
  substance abuse problem of, 233–34,
    235, 236, 238, 359
  and teammates, 312, 359
  traded back and forth, 274, 324, 332,
    338, 341
  and World Series (1975), 74, 232,
    237–38, 287–88
  and Yawkey, 37, 235, 236, 322, 360
Carlton, Steve, 274
Carroll, Clay, 158, 164, 166, 330–31
  career of, 188–89, 197
  early years of, 190
  in Game Seven, 302–3, 331
  in Game Six, 188–91
  in Game Three, 232
  as "Hawk," 188, 189
  and 1975 season, 189
  retirement of, 352
Carson, Johnny, 245
Carter, Jimmy, 315, 331
Castro, Fidel, 99, 119–21, 149–50,
  160–61
CBS Sports, 348, 349
Cepeda, Orlando, 84
Chaney, Darrel, 106, 123–24, 125,
  129
Chapman, Ray, 134
Chicago Cubs, 357
Chicago White Sox, 98, 366
Cincinnati Reds:
  Big Red Machine of, 14, 41, 44, 45, 48,
    76, 93, 102, 105, 157, 216, 221, 310,
    328
  and designated hitters, 331
  discipline of, 215–16, 279, 328–29
  early years of, 92–93
  farm system of, 98, 100
  franchise value, 375
  and free agency, 332–33, 339–40
  glory days ended, 333, 336
  Hall of Fame players, 41, 352, 354
  and 1970 season, 47–48
  and 1975 season, 44, 46, 49, 69, 166,
    216
  and 1976 season, 327, 328–31
  and 1977 season, 336–37
  and 1978 season, 341
  pitchers in, 41–43, 49, 221, 226,
    261–62, 336–37
  and reserve clause, 330–31
  superstars in, 25, 42, 107, 152, 157,
    216, 310

  team building, 104, 121, 122, 123, 152,
    156, 289, 310, 328
  values of, 77, 152, 215–16
  and World Series (1919), 49
  and World Series (1961), 49, 199
  and World Series (1970), 76, 290
  and World Series (1972), 137, 290
  and World Series (1975), 46, 50,
    214–15, 230, 275, 308, 309–11, 314,
    315, 381–90; *see also specific games*
  and World Series (1976), 329, 331
  and World Series (1990), 345
  World Series lost by, 49, 76, 156, 290
  see also specific players
Cincinnati Red Stockings, 91–93, 205
Civil Rights Movement, 168
Cleveland, Reggie, 232, 305
Cleveland Buckeyes, 7
Cleveland Indians, 98, 101–2
Cleveland Spiders, 96
Clinton, Bill, 371
Cloninger, Tony, 188
Cobb, Ty, 30–31, 347, 363
Colbert, Nate, 197
Collins, Bud, 14
Colorado Rockies, 357
Colosi, Nick, 70
Concepcion, Dave, 104, 122, 123, 374
  at bat, Game Six, 106–8, 158–59, 193,
    212, 258, 279
  baserunning in Game Six, 258–59
  as "Bozo," 107
  fielding in Game Six, 85, 131, 191,
    221, 222, 251, 263, 273
  in Game Four, 106
  in Game Seven, 295, 296, 297, 300, 307
  in Game Two, 247
  Gold Gloves to, 45, 106, 328
  and 1975 season, 106–7
  and 1977 season, 336
  retirement of, 346
Conigliaro, Tony, 36, 145
Connell, Scotty, 24
Cooper, Cecil, 70, 260, 332
  at bat, Game Six, 75–79, 130–31,
    166–67, 203, 243
  fielding in Game Six, 106, 159, 193,
    212, 226
  and Game Seven, 302–3, 312
  in later years, 358
  and 1976 season, 322, 324
  retirement of, 358
Coyle, Harry, and Game Six, 24, 56, 226,
    248–49, 257, 259, 268, 282, 285,
    293–94

Criger, Lou, 126, 128
Cronin, Joe, 32
Crowley, Terry, 122, 123, 158, 172, 194–95
Cuba:
    baseball in, 5, 8, 97, 98, 119–20
    diplomatic visits to, 148–50
    socialism-communism in, 99, 120–21, 148, 149
Culberson, Leon, 115–16
Cy Young Award, 129, 334

Darcy, Pat, 249, 279, 289–90
    in Game Six, 261–64, 271–73, 281–82, 284, 353–54, 381
    in later years, 353
Darwin, Bobby, 324
Davidson, Satch, 57, 101, 114, 138, 157, 194, 197, 202, 209, 231, 233, 240, 247, 250, 254, 266–67, 282, 285
Dedeaux, Rod (Raoul Martial):
    and Anderson, 2–4, 49, 50, 240
    career of, 2–4
    as mentor, 4, 13, 216
    NCAA championships of, 3, 13, 86
    and Stengel, 2, 4
Dent, Bucky, 115, 342, 360
Detroit Tigers, 204, 369–70, 371, 372
Diamond Club Ministry, 360
DiMaggio, Joe, 87–88
Dowd, Maureen, 12
Doyle, Denny, 70, 340
    acquired by Red Sox, 79–80, 85, 145
    at bat, Game Six, 79–80, 131–33, 167, 221, 249–50, 272–73
    baserunning in Game Six, 253–55, 257, 357
    as "Ducky," 80
    early years of, 79
    fielding in Game Six, 124, 152, 157, 158, 182, 193, 195, 210, 268, 279
    in Game Seven, 295, 296, 297, 298–99, 304, 306
    in later years, 357–58
    in World Series (1975), 80, 312
Doyle Baseball Academy, 358
Drago, Dick, 207, 209, 212, 236, 303, 312, 322, 340
    career of, 245–46
    in Game Six, 242–43, 245–48, 257–61, 266–69, 270
    in Game Two, 246–47
    in later years, 360–61
Dressen, Charlie, 46
Driessen, Dan, 259–61, 303, 331, 333, 341

Duffy, Frank, 104
Dunn, Jack, 213–14
Duquette, Dan, 366

Eastwick, Rawly, 173, 189, 222, 225, 252, 306
    early years of, 230
    in Game Six, 229, 230–33, 237, 238, 239–43, 249–51
    in later years, 355
    and 1975 season, 229–30
    and 1977 season, 336, 337
    retirement of, 355
Eckersley, Dennis, 340
Eisenhower, Dwight D., 99, 119
ESPN, 350, 351
Evans, Dwight "Dewey," 200, 265, 322
    at bat, Game Six, 111–14, 164, 197–98, 229–32, 262
    career of, 112, 113, 164, 364
    fielding in Game Six, 157, 172, 184, 193, 210, 268–70, 271, 279, 287, 304
    in Game Four, 230
    in Game Seven, 296, 298
    in Game Three, 173, 230, 232
    in Game Two, 230
    Gold Gloves to, 364
    in later years, 364
    and World Series (1975), 113, 312
    and World Series (1986), 344

Feller, Sherm, 38, 57, 233
Fenway Park:
    built on fens, 16, 206
    construction of, 206, 213
    "Death Valley" in, 269
    and "Duffy's Cliff," 28, 31
    Fisk Pole in, 367
    left field wall of, see Green Monster
    original land rights of, 28
    Pesky's Pole in, 115, 164
    preparations for Game Six, 15–16
    quirkiness of, 37, 113, 133, 186, 194, 363
    renovations of, 31–32
    right field of, 113, 115
    scalpers at, 292
    Yawkey as owner of, 28
Fenway Realty Company, 206
Field of Dreams (film), 4
Fingers, Rollie, 137, 144, 246, 325, 326
Finley, Charles, 18, 19, 44, 324–26, 339
Fisk, Carlton, 200, 312, 322, 323, 335, 344
    at bat, Game Six, 81–85, 136–37, 190, 222, 251, 252, 253, 281, 282–86, 367

Fisk, Carlton (*continued*)
  career of, 74, 82, 366
  catching in Game Six, 39, 57, 72, 159, 183, 210, 247, 248, 259, 266, 267, 277, 280
  disillusionment of, 334, 365–66, 367
  early years of, 81–83
  in Game Five, 59
  in Game Seven, 295, 296, 301, 302
  in Game Three, 77, 173–77, 261
  in Hall of Fame, 366, 367, 368, 373–74
  later years of, 365–67
  in lineup, 74
  and 1972 season, 83
  and 1973 season, 83–85
  and 1976 season, 322, 324, 327, 334
  and 1977 season, 338
  personal traits of, 82, 83–84
  as "Pudge," 82
  retirement of, 366–67
  and teammates, 80, 85
  and winning run, 285–87, 288, 292, 294, 367
Fitzgerald, John "Honey Fitz," 204
Fitzgerald, Ray, 14
Flood, Curt, 316
Florida Marlins, 367
Flynn, Doug, 279, 303, 351
Ford, Gerald, 179–80, 182, 315, 327, 331
Ford, Michael, 179
Ford, Whitey, 62, 102, 199
Ford C. Frick Award, 349, 350, 368, 372
Fosse, Roy, 59
Foster, George, 45, 328, 341
  at bat, Game Six, 103–6, 157–58, 192–93, 210–11, 258, 278
  career of, 354–55
  early years of, 104–5
  fielding in Game Six, 190, 232, 253–54, 270, 272, 284
  in Game Seven, 296, 300
  and 1975 season, 105
  and 1977 season, 336, 337
  retirement of, 354–55
Foxx, Jimmie, 33
Frantz, Art, 247, 300, 307
Frazee, Harry, 214
Frazier, Joe, 244
Fryman, Woodie, 333, 337
Futch, Eddie, 244

Game Five:
  Cincinnati victory in, 103, 230, 293
  Rose's slide to home in, 59

  stats, 387
  viewing audience for, 17, 39–40
Game Four:
  broadcast of, 22, 23, 39
  pitching in, 12, 59–60
  Red Sox victory in, 12, 51, 133, 182, 192, 202
  stats, 386
Game One:
  balk called, 70–71
  broadcast of, 22
  Red Sox victory in, 71, 163
  stats, 385
  Tiant pitching in, 57, 59, 70–71, 102, 163, 293
Game Seven:
  Cincinnati victory in, 308, 309–11
  looking forward to, 21, 220, 242, 249, 285, 289
  opening rituals of, 294
  play-by-play, 294–308
  Red Sox loss in, 308–9
  stats, 387
Game Six:
  attendance, 25–26, 39
  broadcast of, *see* NBC
  Cincinnati's loss in, 289–91
  early morning of, 10–15
  in extra innings, 256, 281, 314
  opening rituals of, 38–40
  rain delay of, 11, 12, 13, 14, 17, 24, 51, 78, 88
  Red Sox victory in, 285–89, 292
  stats, 381–84
Game Three:
  Armbrister's interference in, 173–75, 176, 177, 275, 301, 302, 353
  broadcast of, 23, 39
  Cincinnati victory in, 176, 225, 226, 230, 275, 277
  stats, 386
Game Two:
  Cincinnati victory in, 50, 78, 132, 220, 230, 247
  stats, 385
Game of the Week (TV), 23, 44, 65
Gammons, Peter, 14, 15, 52, 286, 344
Garagiola, Joe:
  baseball career of, 22
  broadcast personality of, 23, 349, 350
  and Game Seven, 294
  and Game Six broadcast, 22, 56, 136, 158, 188, 195, 245, 249, 257, 258, 272, 285

in Hall of Fame, 350
in later years, 350
Garagiola, Joe Junior, 350
Garrity, Arthur, 169, 170
Gerard, Lou, 24, 283, 285
Geronimo, Cesar, 341, 352
    at bat, Game Six, 121–23, 172, 193–94,
    223, 258–59, 279–80
    baserunning in Game Six, 194, 195,
    196
    early years of, 121–22
    fielding in Game Six, 79, 89, 241,
    253
    in Game Four, 191, 192
    in Game Seven, 297, 298, 301, 302,
    307–8
    in Game Three, 173–76, 177
    Gold Gloves to, 122, 328
Giamatti, Bart, 347
Gibson, Bob, 36, 342
Gibson, Kirk, 377
Good Will Hunting (film), 353–54
Gossage, Goose, 246
Gowdy, Curt, 22, 349–50
    death of, 350
    and Game Seven, 293
    and Game Six, 174, 175, 287
    in Hall of Fame, 350
Grammas, Alex, 157, 159, 207, 208, 209,
    210, 250, 267, 268
Green, Elijah "Pumpsie," 34
Green Monster:
    defensive challenges of, 113, 132, 300,
    342, 363
    and "Duffy's Cliff," 28, 31
    evolution of, 28, 31–32
    hole in scoreboard of, 24
    reason for existence of, 27–28
Griffey, Ken, 45, 50, 328, 336, 341
    at bat, Game Six, 66–68, 124, 182–84,
    206–7, 227, 267
    baserunning in Game Six, 186, 208,
    209–10, 211, 268–70
    career of, 355
    early years of, 66–67
    fielding in Game Six, 164, 251, 253
    in Game Four, 182, 192
    in Game Seven, 294, 295, 296, 297,
    300, 301, 302, 303, 304, 305, 306
    in Game Two, 182, 247
    and 1975 season, 67, 71
Griffey, Ken Junior, 355
Griffin, Doug, 79, 80, 114–15, 145, 306
Griffith, Calvin, 61, 332
Grove, Lefty, 32

Gullett, Don, 75, 79, 131, 230, 249, 290,
    336
    career of, 77, 293
    and free agency, 330, 331
    in Game Seven, 78, 293, 295–97
    in Reds' Hall of Fame, 354
    and World Series (1977), 339

Hammerman, Roy, 24, 248
Harper, Tommy, 53, 74
Harrelson, Bud, 59, 197
Harrelson, Ken "The Hawk," 21
Havlicek, John "Hondo," 56
Hearst, Patricia, 180–81, 182
Henry, John, 361
Herman, Billy, 142
Hershiser, Orel, 377
Hertzel, Bob, 141
Hicks, Louise Day, 169
Hobson, Butch, 338, 361, 366
Holtzman, Ken, 325
Hooper, Harry, 27, 112, 213
Hornsby, Rogers, 207
House, Tom, 322, 334
Houston Astrodome, 122
Houston Astros, 68, 139, 150–51, 156,
    352, 358
Houston Colt .45s, 68
Howsam, Bob, 130, 231, 260, 374
    and Anderson, 47, 152
    and free agency, 252, 339
    and Game Seven, 300, 310
    and 1977 season, 336
    and reserve clause, 330–31
    retirement of, 340
    and team building, 47, 121, 152, 310,
    328
    and trades, 104, 151, 152, 156, 188,
    194, 196, 333, 337
Hrabosky, Al "The Mad Hungarian,"
    246
Hubbell, Carl, 6
Hunter, Jim "Catfish," 19

Israel, David, 11–12, 56, 288

Jackson, Reggie, 325, 331, 338, 339,
    340
James, Bill, 73
Jazz Age, 30–31
Jenkins, Ferguson, 322, 334, 338, 339,
    348, 359
Jobe, Frank, 76
Johnson, Byron Bancroft "Ban," 93,
    94–96, 109, 126, 127, 128, 205, 206

Johnson, Darrell, 10, 188
    career of, 199–202
    death of, 357
    fired, 327
    and Game Four, 191–92
    and Game One, 70
    and Game Seven, 288, 302
    and Game Six batters, 81, 89, 102
    and Game Six infield, 185
    and Game Six victory, 287
    and Game Three, 174–76
    indecision of, 247, 325
    judgment questioned, 206, 209, 220,
        223–24, 302–3, 305–7, 327
    in later years, 356–57
    and lineup, 74, 75
    as manager, 84, 200–202, 216
    as mentor, 83, 84, 112, 200
    and 1975 season, 74, 199, 200–201
    and 1976 All-Star team, 326–27
    personal traits of, 200, 201–2
    and pitchers, 78, 186, 193, 211–12,
        220, 247, 259–60, 301, 302–4, 305
    retirement of, 357
    and Tiant, 63, 186, 191, 193, 199, 202,
        206–7, 209, 210, 211–12, 220,
        223–24
Johnson, Walter, 60
Josephson, Duane, 83

Kapstein, Jerry, 323, 325, 330, 332, 336,
    337, 355
Kasko, Eddie, 84, 200
Katz, Reuven, 333
Kaye, Danny, 356
Keane, Cliff, 14, 201
Kennedy, John F., 120, 204
Kiley, John, 38, 215, 221, 284, 319
Killilea, Henry, 109
King, Stephen, 344–45
Kirby, Clay, 249, 269, 279
Kluszewski, Ted, 66, 67, 106, 122, 124,
    245, 309
Kroc, Ray, 130
Kubek, Tony, 341, 350, 372
    baseball career of, 25
    and Game One, 22
    and Game Seven, 293, 309
    and Game Six, 52, 67, 78, 103, 136,
        158, 191, 193, 241, 279, 283, 284
    and Game Three, 174, 175
    and postgame interviews, 286, 309
    and postgame preparations, 226,
        248–49, 256, 257, 272
    and World Series (1962), 24–25

Kuhn, Bowie, 178, 300, 310
    death of, 351
    and free agency, 326, 339–40
    and Game Six, 10–11, 15–16, 17, 39
    in Hall of Fame, 351
    in later years, 351
    and reserve clause, 318, 330

Lasorda, Tommy, 337
A League of Their Own (film), 4
Lee, Annabelle, 216
Lee, Bill, 78, 84, 176, 188, 200, 213,
    216–20
    barnstorming, 361, 362
    and baseball as entertainment, 218,
        363
    career of, 216
    and "Eephus pitch," 295, 299
    and Game Seven, 287, 293, 294–301,
        311
    and Game Six, 220, 223, 242, 283
    in later years, 362–63
    and 1976 season, 324, 334
    and 1977 season, 338, 339
    and 1978 season, 340, 341
    as pitcher vs. thrower, 293
    and Red Sox Hall of Fame, 363
    as "Spaceman," 218
    and teammates, 217–18, 235, 236, 359
    traded to Montreal, 342, 362
Lee, Leron, 84
Lemon, Bob, 340, 341
Leroux, Buddy, 342
Lewis, George Edward "Duffy," 27–28,
    38–39, 112, 213, 283
Lindeman, Carl, 17
Lipon, Johnny, 101, 102
Lolich, Mickey, 55
Los Angeles Dodgers, 44, 317, 337, 341,
    354, 377
Lynn, Fred, 114, 283, 323, 344, 366
    acquired by Red Sox, 74, 87, 112
    at bat, Game Six, 86–89, 111, 136,
        137–38, 167, 190–91, 227–28, 241,
        253–54
    early years of, 13, 86
    emergence as star, 86–88
    fielding in Game Six, 108, 183–85,
        193, 211, 227, 269
    in Game Four, 182, 183, 192
    in Game Seven, 287, 296, 298, 302, 305
    in Game Three, 174, 176, 261
    Gold Gloves to, 365
    hitting the wall, 183–85, 189, 190,
        191, 211, 227, 287

in later years, 364–65
in lineup, 74, 164, 271, 322
and 1975 season, 75, 86, 88, 252
and 1976 season, 327, 334
in Red Sox Hall of Fame, 365
retirement of, 365
Lynn, Hattie, 189

Major League Baseball, see baseball
Mantle, Mickey, 87, 142, 153
Marichal, Juan, 67, 84
Martin, Billy, 117, 324, 329, 338, 340
Martin, Ned, 200, 293
Martinez, Pedro, 357
Mathewson, Christy, 128, 140, 167
Matthews, Gary, 276
May, Lee, 156
Mays, Willie, 34, 87, 104, 142, 337
McCarver, Tim, 85
McDonough, Will, 14
McDowell, "Sudden" Sam, 100, 101, 102
McEnaney, Will, 132, 189, 222, 225, 230,
    233, 249
    career of, 252
    in Game Seven, 304, 306–8
    in Game Six, 251–53, 255–56, 304
    retirement of, 355
    and salary dispute, 252
    traded by Reds, 332–33, 355
    and World Series (1975), 253, 259
McGovern, George, 148–50, 160–61
McGraw, John, 128
McGreevey, Michael T., "Nuf Ced," 111,
    126, 127
McGuire, Jim "Deacon," 205
McGwire, Mark, 375
McKay, John, 13
McNally, Dave, 317
Messersmith, Andy, 317
Mexico City Tigers, 9, 119, 120
Michael, Gene, 84
Michaels, Al, 22
Miller, Janet Marie Fisk, 271
Miller, Marvin, 19, 317
Miller, Rick, 253, 271–72, 306
Milwaukee Braves, 93, 199
Milwaukee Brewers, 39, 324, 332, 356,
    358
Minnesota Twins, 61, 171, 332, 377
Minoso, Minnie, 97–99
Monaghan, Tom, 369
Monday Night Football (TV), 13, 16,
    17, 19
Montgomery, Bob, 85, 306–7
Montreal Expos, 317, 337, 355, 362

Montville, Leigh, 14
Mooney, Joe, 15–16
Moore, Sarah Jane, 180, 181
Moret, Rogelio "Roger," 175, 212, 300,
    322
    early years of, 224
    in Game Seven, 301–2
    in Game Six, 224, 226–27, 232, 301
    in later years, 358–59
    and 1975 season, 224, 225
Morgan, Joe, 73, 122, 263, 330, 336, 341,
    345, 346–47
    acquired by Reds, 43–44, 121, 139,
        152, 156
    at bat, Game Six, 68, 71–72, 150–52,
        185, 207–8, 246–47, 267–70, 304
    baserunning in Game Six, 209–11
    career of, 207
    early years of, 68
    fielding in Game Six, 85, 136, 165,
        166, 167, 198, 203, 222, 273, 284
    in Game One, 70
    in Game Seven, 294, 297, 298, 302,
        304–5, 309–10, 352
    in Game Three, 175, 225, 226, 304
    Gold Gloves to, 45, 328
    in Hall of Fame, 348, 373, 374
    and Houston Astros, 150–51, 358
    in lineup, 43, 44, 45, 50–51, 294
    as mentor, 259, 290, 310
    MVP awards to, 43, 68, 207–8, 328
    and 1975 season, 71, 207
    as superstar, 25, 42, 107, 157
    and World Series (1975), 309–10
Moss, Charlie, 184–85, 287
Munson, Thurman, 84
Murphy, Tom, 324
Murray, Dale, 333
Murray, Jim, 53

Namath, Joe, 127
National Association, 92
National Football League, 19, 20, 349
National League:
    early years of, 92–97, 127–28
    owners' pact in, 94
    pitching in, 60
    "Senior Circuit" of, 92, 127
NBC:
    broadcasting teams for, 21–22, 188
    Emmy award to, 351
    and Game Seven broadcast, 293–94
    and Game Six broadcast, 16–17, 56,
        184, 244–45, 266, 268, 285, 292
    and Game Six highlight package, 294

NBC (*continued*)
  postgame preparations of, 226,
    248–49, 257, 272
  pregame meeting, 23–24
  television ratings, 18, 339
  World Series covered by, 11, 16, 17,
    18, 20, 22, 314
Negro League, 6–7, 98, 119
Nettles, Graig, 324
New England:
  baseball fever in, 37, 292
  fatalism in, 54, 302, 345
  respect for Yawkey in, 38
  Yankee temperament in, 169
  see also Boston
New York Cubans, 6–7
New York Giants (baseball), 127–28,
    204, 329
New York Giants (football), 13
New York Highlanders, 128
New York Knickerbockers, 90
New York Mets, 21, 44, 59, 357
New York Yankees:
  decline of, 18
  dynasties of 20s and 60s, 329
  and free agents, 19, 331, 339
  name change from Highlanders to, 128
  and 1977 season, 338, 339
  and 1978 season, 341–42
  Red Sox rivalry with, 323–24, 341–42,
    357
  Ruth sold to, 214
  salaries paid to, 321, 331
  and World Series (1957), 199
  and World Series (1961), 49, 199
  and World Series (1962), 25
  and World Series (1976), 329, 331
  and World Series (1977), 339
  and World Series (1978), 354
  and World Series (2001), 377
Nixon, Richard M., 58, 59, 149, 179, 315,
    331
Nolan, Gary, 106, 336, 337
  career of, 76, 77, 81, 155
  in Game Six, 76, 78–79, 80–82, 88–89,
    111, 112, 116, 118, 123, 140, 241
  in Game Three, 75, 77, 131, 261
  retirement of, 352
Norman, Freddie, 86, 111, 114
  early years of, 129–30
  in Game Six, 129, 130–34, 136, 137–39
  and 1975 season, 130
  retirement of, 352
  and World Series (1975), 75, 131, 132,
    133

Norworth, Jack, 215
NSN TV network, 363

Oakland A's, 216, 329
  and AL Championship games (1975),
    14, 39, 55, 80, 88, 144, 201, 246
  and free agents, 19, 324–26, 339
  World Series victories of, 18, 44, 76,
    137, 275
Oakland Trojans, 3
O'Connell, Dick, 35, 63, 79, 148, 324,
    339
Oliver, John, 318
Orlando, Vinnie, 37, 272
Ott, Mel, 6
Ouimet, Francis, 205, 242

Pacheco, Tony, 98
Palmer, Jim, 55, 119, 144, 323
Papi, Stan, 342
Parnell, Mel, 115
Paul, Gabe, 101
Pepitone, Joe, 143
Perez, Tony, 45, 105, 345, 346
  at bat, Game Six, 97–103, 156–57,
    186–87, 209–10, 248, 277–78
  career of, 156, 277, 347
  as "Doggie" or "Big Dog," 101, 373
  early years of, 98–100
  fielding in Game Six, 80, 117, 132,
    165–66, 167, 203, 262
  in Game One, 71, 102
  in Game Seven, 295–96, 298,
    299–300, 305, 310
  in Game Three, 277
  in Hall of Fame, 368, 373
  in later years, 367
  and 1976 season, 328, 330, 331
  and 1977 season, 337–38
  personal traits of, 100, 260
  as superstar, 42, 107, 157
  and teammates, 107, 290, 309, 333, 337
  and trade talk, 260, 277–78, 331, 333,
    336, 337, 355
  in World Series (1975), 102–3, 247, 310
Pesky, Johnny, 115–16, 251, 313, 342
Petrocelli, Rico, 36, 80, 113
  at bat, Game Six, 89, 139, 142–46, 191,
    228–29, 256
  early years of, 142–43
  fielding in Game Six, 185, 193, 248
  in Game Seven, 289, 296, 298, 303
  injuries to, 89, 143–45
  in later years, 361–62
  and 1975 season, 89, 144

and 1976 season, 326
retirement of, 338, 362
and World Series (1975), 144, 238, 289, 312
Philadelphia Athletics, 128
Philadelphia Phillies, 46, 329, 343, 345, 346
Phillippe, Deacon, 110
Phillips, Harold "Lefty," 4
Piazza, Mike, 366
Pinella, Lou, 324, 367
Pittsburgh Pirates, 151
and 1909 season, 44
and 1975 season, 46, 102, 131
and first World Series (1903), 96–97, 109–11, 126–27
players:
contract negotiations of, 19, 318
free agents, 19, 319, 323, 324–27, 330, 331–32, 336, 339–40, 346, 351, 354, 370, 374–75
names on jerseys, 376
owners vs., 19, 93–94, 312–19, 330, 370, 371
personal qualities of, 377, 378
professional agents hired by, 319, 323
replacement, 371
and reserve clause, 18–19, 94, 95, 316–19, 330–31
salaries of, 18, 93–94, 95, 96, 236, 332, 336, 370, 371, 375
strikes and walkouts, 370, 371
players union, 18–19, 94, 317, 370
Plimpton, George, 41
Plummer, Bill, 86, 133, 262, 263, 279, 351

Rapp, Vern, 252
Ratkowski, Father Joe, 135
Reagan, Ronald, 315
Remy, Jerry, 79, 340, 357
Rettenmund, Merv, 175, 279, 297
Rice, Jim, 112, 200, 344
in Hall of Fame, 363–64
injury to, 55, 75, 86, 215, 363
in later years, 363–64
in lineup, 74, 164, 271, 322, 324
and 1976 season, 334
and 1977 season, 338
and 1978 season, 340
retirement of, 363, 365
Rickey, Branch, 33, 151, 152
Riverfront Stadium, Cincinnati, 45, 66–67

Robinson, Jackie, 7, 8, 34, 98, 151, 208, 345
Rose, Pete, 41, 240, 242, 336
at bat, Game Six, 57–60, 64, 65–66, 124, 177–82, 195–96, 226–27, 265–67
baserunning in Game Six, 183–84, 267
being in the action, 265, 272, 290–91, 310
breaking Ty Cobb's record, 347
as "Charlie Hustle," 58
comparisons to, 83, 84, 113, 114
early years of, 45, 58
eligibility for Hall of Fame, 347–48, 374
fielding in Game Six, 132, 165, 167, 190, 256, 283
in Game Seven, 298–99, 301–2, 304, 305
in Game Three, 175, 226
in lineup, 43, 45, 50
move to Phillies, 343, 345, 346
and 1973 postseason, 197
and 1975 season, 46, 74
and 1976 season, 328, 330
and 1978 season, 340
off-field behavior, 59, 343, 347–48
as player-manager, 347, 367
as Series MVP, 310, 387
as superstar, 25, 42, 107, 157, 310
and teammates, 152, 260, 290
at third base, 44–46, 67, 85, 105, 255
trash talker, 45, 58, 60, 64
in World Series (1975), 265, 266, 290–91, 309–10
"rounders," 90
Rudi, Joe, 201, 325, 326
Russell, Bill, 56
Ruth, Babe (George Herman), 2, 6, 27, 39, 213–14, 323, 344–45
Ryan, Bob, 14
Ryan, Nolan, 145

SABR (Society for American Baseball Research), 73
St. Louis Cardinals, 33, 34, 36, 96, 115, 143, 358
San Diego Padres, 130
San Francisco Giants, 24, 25
Schaap, Dick, 12, 230
Scherger, George, 45, 193
Schreiber, Robert "Buddy," 147, 148, 161
Scott, George, 332, 338, 358
Scott, Jay, 175

Scott, Rodney, 362
Scully, Vin, 350
Seattle Mariners, 356
Seattle Pilots, 356
Seaver, Tom, 155, 337, 341, 348, 351
Seitz, Peter M., 19, 317–18
Seitz Ruling (Seitz Decision), 19, 318,
   326, 330, 374–75
Selig, Allan "Bud," 356, 371, 372, 373,
   376
Sewell, Rip, 295
Shapiro, Doc, 12
Shepard, Larry, 41, 43, 46, 78, 85, 124,
   140, 141, 158, 282
Shore, Ray, 104, 113, 121, 188, 196, 291,
   310, 328, 329
Simmons, Chet, 23–24, 293
   and ESPN, 351
   and Game Six, 11, 20–21, 285, 287
   and NBC's game coverage, 16–17, 226,
      248, 257, 285
   retirement of, 351
Simpson, O. J., 13
Slaton, Jim, 143
Slaughter, Enos, 115–16
Smith, Red, 56
Snider, Duke, 142
Sosa, Sammy, 375
Sparrow, Elise, 30
Speaker, Tris, 27, 112, 213
Sprowl, Bobby, 341–42
Stahl, Chick, 204–5
Steinbrenner, George, 117, 321, 323, 331,
   339, 340, 355
Stello, Dick, 174, 175, 193
Stengel, Casey, 2, 4, 199
   and Anderson, 3, 49, 50, 240, 369
Stockton, Dick, 289, 348–49, 353
   and Game Six broadcast, 56, 88, 136,
      181, 188, 226, 227, 249, 257, 258,
      284, 285, 286–87, 294, 354
   preparing for Game Six, 21–25, 52
   and Visser, 52, 53, 348–49, 353
Sullivan, Haywood, 63–64, 339
Super Bowl, 19, 127
Swann, Lynn, 13

"Take Me Out to the Ball Game," 213,
   215
Taylor, Charles, 204, 206
Taylor, John, 204–5, 206, 213
"Tessie," 127
Texas Rangers, 356
Tiant, Isabel, 5, 7–8, 147, 148, 160, 162,
   334–36

Tiant, Luis Clemente:
   and balk, 69–71
   at bat, Game Six, 117–18, 165–66,
      198–99, 202–3
   bringing parents to U.S., 147–50,
      160–63, 171, 288
   career achievements of, 54, 55, 60–61,
      117, 288, 310
   career comeback of, 53, 54, 63–64,
      102, 168, 202
   comparisons to, 76, 77, 100, 101, 295,
      299
   and Cuban revolution, 99, 119–21
   early years of, 5–9, 60–62, 100–102
   eligibility for Hall of Fame, 368, 374
   fielding in Game Six, 192–93
   in Game Four, 12, 103, 113, 118, 133,
      182, 191–92, 194, 202, 230
   in Game One, 57, 59, 69–71, 102, 117,
      293
   and his father, 5, 8, 9, 62, 120–21,
      161–63, 171, 172, 288–89, 334–36,
      379
   injuries to, 61, 77
   in later years, 367–68
   and 1975 season, 54, 55, 65
   and 1976 season, 334
   and 1977 season, 338
   and 1978 season, 340, 341, 342–43
   personal traits of, 53, 65, 171, 202,
      223, 379
   pitching arsenal of, 64–65, 67, 68–69,
      101, 103
   pitching in Game Six, 51, 53, 55,
      57–60, 66, 67–68, 78, 97–103, 105–6,
      107, 122–25, 150, 151–59, 177, 178,
      179, 180, 181, 182–83, 185–87,
      191–92, 193–96, 206–12, 220,
      223–24
   public image of, 54, 65, 119, 368
   in Red Sox Hall of Fame, 368
   Red Sox poor treatment of, 342–43
   Twins' poor treatment of, 61, 171
   and World Series (1975), 55, 57, 60, 72,
      117, 192, 246, 283, 285
   and Yastrzemski, 53–54, 64–65, 343
Tiant, Luis Eleuterio "Lefty" (father):
   career of, 6–7, 97, 119, 147, 172
   death of, 334–35
   and his son, 5, 8, 9, 62, 120–21, 161–63,
      171, 172, 288–89, 334–36, 379
   move to U.S., 147–50, 160–63, 171
   as role model, 97, 172
Tiant, Maria del Refugio Navarro, 119,
   120, 147, 161, 162

Tolan, Bobby, 121
Toronto Blue Jays, 356
Torre, Joe, 357
Traeger, Aaron, 272, 284

Ueberroth, Peter, 347, 351
umpires, 177–78, 193

Van Sant, Gus, 353
Vecsey, George, 12
Veeck, Bill, 215
Vincent, Fay, 370
Visser, Lesley, 14–15, 52–53, 348–49, 353
Von Tilzer, Albert, 215

Wagner, Dick, 328, 330, 340, 343–44
Walker, Harry "The Hat," 150–51, 358
Watergate, 59, 149, 315, 331
Weaver, Earl, 48, 55
Werner, Tom, 361
Western League, 94–95
Wide World of Sports (TV), 349
Williams, Dick, 35–36, 137, 143
Williams, Robin, 353
Williams, Stan, 62, 73, 155–56, 184, 224
Williams, Ted, 34, 35, 36, 115, 251, 295, 363
and Yawkey, 27, 38, 320, 321–22
Willoughby, Jim, 175, 186, 193, 235, 300, 302, 312, 322, 334
Wills, Maury, 356
Winship, Tom, 14
Wise, Rick, 235, 264, 289
early years of, 274
in Game Six, 274, 276–80, 381
and 1971 season, 274
and 1975 season, 246, 274–75
and 1977 season, 338, 339
retirement of, 352
Wooden, John, 4
World Series:
advertisers for, 17, 20
first, 97, 109–11
NBC coverage of, 11, 16, 17, 18, 20, 22, 314
night games in, 17
profitability of, 17, 350
umpires for, 178, 193
viewing audience of, 17, 19
World Series (1903), 96–97, 109–11, 126–27, 129
World Series (1905), 128
World Series (1907), 29
World Series (1915), 214

World Series (1919), 49
World Series (1922), 329
World Series (1946), 34, 115–16
World Series (1953), 117
World Series (1957), 199
World Series (1961), 49, 199
World Series (1962), 24–25
World Series (1967), 36, 143
World Series (1968), 55
World Series (1969), 21
World Series (1970), 47, 76, 152, 156, 290
World Series (1971), 44
World Series (1972), 76, 106, 137, 216, 275, 290
World Series (1975):
commercial success of, 350
Emmy award to, 351
as most entertaining series in years, 20–21, 310, 314–15
MVP award in, 230, 310, 387
stats, 381–90
see also specific games
World Series (1976), 329, 331
World Series (1977), 339
World Series (1978), 354
World Series (1979), 345
World Series (1982), 358
World Series (1984), 369
World Series (1986), 344, 363
World Series (1990), 345
World Series (1997), 367
World Series (2001), 377
World Series (2003), 367
World War I, 27, 30, 213
World War II, women's league in, 216
Wright, George, 205
Wright, Harry, 91–93, 205
Wright & Ditson Sporting Goods, 205
Wynn, Steve, 352

Yastrzemski, Carl, 10, 322, 364
at bat, Game Six, 80–81, 133–36, 189–90, 221–22, 250–51, 273–74
early years of, 134, 135–36
fielding in Game Six, 65, 124, 184, 186, 208, 209, 247, 248, 270
at first base, 75, 243, 247, 258, 266, 267
in Game Seven, 295, 296, 307–8
in Game Three, 81, 261
in Hall of Fame, 348, 373
injuries to, 312–13
and 1967 season, 36
and 1976 season, 334
and 1977 season, 338
and 1978 season, 342

Yastrzemski, Carl (*continued*)
  personal traits of, 53–54, 134, 251
  and Petrocelli, 142–43
  retirement of, 345–46, 363
  and teammates, 53–54, 80, 217
  and Tiant, 53–54, 64–65, 343
  and World Series (1975), 178, 312
  and Yawkey, 36, 38, 312–13, 320,
    321–22
Yastrzemski, Carl Sr., 134, 135–36
Yastrzemski, Hattie, 320
Yawkey, Augusta, 29
Yawkey, Bill, 29–30, 31, 33
Yawkey, Jean Hiller, 34, 40, 320–21, 339,
  342, 345
Yawkey, Julia, 321
Yawkey, Tom:
  and American League, 38
  and Carbo, 37, 235, 236, 322, 360
  and changes in baseball, 33–34, 321,
    326
  "checkbook" baseball introduced by,
    32, 321
  and color bar, 34
  death of, 319–21, 326
  estate of, 320–31
  family background of, 29–30
  and Fisk, 83
  and Game Six, 11, 39–40, 283
  in Hall of Fame, 345
  health problems of, 39, 40, 316, 324
  lifestyle of, 30–31, 33, 34

  and managers, 32–33, 35–36
  and players, 32, 33, 36–37, 224,
    321–22, 323
  as Red Sox owner, 27, 28, 31–35, 37,
    208, 314, 320, 321, 345
  and Tiant, 55, 148, 162
  and Ty Cobb, 30–31
  wealth of, 28–29, 30, 31, 37
  and Williams, 27, 38, 320, 321–22
  and World Series (1975), 39–40, 294,
    313
  World Series win sought by, 31, 34,
    37, 38, 39, 292, 313
  and Yastrzemski, 36, 38, 312–13, 320,
    321–22
Yawkey, William Clyman, 29
Young, Cy, 95–96, 110, 111, 126, 127,
  128–29, 206
Young, Dick, 52

Zimmer, Don, 311, 344, 356–57
  and Bench, 282, 308
  and Burleson, 116, 165
  and Carbo, 240, 242
  and Doyle, 254–55, 257, 357
  as field manager, 327, 329, 334,
    338–39, 340, 341, 342
  and Rose, 132, 255
  and signs to batters, 81, 113, 165, 202,
    250, 302
  as third base coach, 81, 132, 250,
    254